Waging War

Waging War

Alliances, Coalitions, and Institutions of

Interstate Violence

Patricia A. Weitsman

Stanford Security Studies, An Imprint of Stanford University Press
Stanford, California

Stanford University Press
Stanford, California

Library of Congress Cataloging-in-Publication Data

Weitsman, Patricia A., author.
   Waging war : alliances, coalitions, and institutions of interstate violence / Patricia A. Weitsman.
      pages cm
   Includes bibliographical references and index.
   ISBN 978-0-8047-8799-4 (cloth bound : alk. paper) — ISBN 978-0-8047-8897-7 (pbk. : alk. paper)
      1. United States—Military relations—Foreign countries.   2. United States—History, Military—20th century.   3. United States—History, Military—21st century.   4. Combined operations (Military science).   5. Alliances.   I. Title.
   UA23.W3698 2014
   355′.0310973—dc23
                                                                                2013017358

ISBN 978-0-8047-8894-6 (electronic)

Typeset by Newgen in 10/14 Minion

For Sarah and Jonah
Hoffmann-Weitsman

Contents

Illustrations

Figures

Maps

Tables

Acronyms

ABC	American, British, Canadian
ACE	Allied Command Europe
ACLANT	Allied Command Atlantic
AFCENT	Air Force Central Command
AFRICOM	U.S. Africa Command
AMN	Afghanistan Mission Network
ANSF	Afghan National Security Forces
ANZUS	Australia, New Zealand, United States Security Treaty
AOG	Area Operations Group
ARCENT	Army Forces Central Command
ATOs	Air-tasking orders
AWACS	Airborne warning and control system
BFT	Blue Force Tracking System
C3IC	Coalition, Coordination, Communication and Integration Center
C4I	Command, Control, Communications, Computer, and Intelligence
CAOC	Combined Air Operation Center
CDR	Commander
CENTAF	U.S. Air Force Central Command (also AFCENT)
CENTCOM	U.S. Central Command
CFACC	Combined forces air component commander

CFC	Combined forces commander
CFC-A	Combined forces commander–Afghanistan
CFLCC	Coalition forces land component commander
CFMCC	Combined forces maritime component commander
CFSOCC	Combined Forces Special Operations Component Command
CINC	Composite Index of National Capability
CINCCENT	CENTCOM commander in chief
CJO	Chief of Joint Operations
CJSOTF	Combined Joint Special Operations Task Force
CJTF	Combined Joint Task Force
C-NARC	Counter Narcotics
COCOM	Combatant Command
COMIJC	Commander ISAF Joint Command
COMISAF	Commander International Security Assistance Force
CSF	Coalition Solidarity Fund
CSTC-A	Combined Security Transition Command–Afghanistan
DOS	U.S. Department of State
EC	European Commission
EUCOM	U.S. European Command
FDOs	Foreign Disclosure Officers
FRY	Federal Republic of Yugoslavia
FSCL	Fire-support coordination line
GCC	Gulf Cooperation Council
GWOT	Global war on terror
IAEA	International Atomic Energy Agency
IED	Improvised explosive device
IFF	Identification friend or foe
IJC	ISAF Joint Command
I-MEF	First Marine Expeditionary Force
IMS	International Military Staff
IRST	Iron and steel production
ISAF	International Security Assistance Force
ISR	Intelligence, surveillance, and reconnaissance
JDOP	Joint Directorate of Planning
JDT	Joint Deployable Team
JECC	Joint Enabling Capabilities Command

JFACC	Joint force air component commander
JFC	Joint forces commander
JFLCC	Joint force land component commander
JOPP	Joint Operation Planning Process
JTF	Joint Task Force
JTF-HOA	Joint Task Force-Horn of Africa
KFOR	Kosovo force
KLA	Kosovo Liberation Army
MARCENT	Marine Forces Central Command
MC	Military Committee
MIC	Multinational Interoperability Council
MID	Militarized Interstate Disputes
MILEX	Military Expenditures
MILPER	Military Personnel
MIP	Multilateral Interoperability Program
MNC-I	Multinational Corps–Iraq
MND	Multinational Division
MNF-A	Multinational Force–Afghanistan
MNF-I	Multinational Force–Iraq
MSTC-I	Multinational Security Transition Command–Iraq
NAC	North Atlantic Council
NATO	North Atlantic Treaty Organization
NAVCENT	Naval Forces Central Command
NCC	National Contingent Command
NCTS	Naval Computer and Telecommunications Station
NTM-A	NATO Training Mission in Afghanistan
NTM-I	NATO Training Mission in Iraq
OAF	Operation Allied Force
OEF	Operation Enduring Freedom
OIC	Organization of the Islamic Conference
OIF	Operation Iraqi Freedom
OMB	U.S. Office of Management and Budget
OMLTs	Operational mentoring and liaison teams
OOD	Operation Odyssey Dawn
OPCOM	Operational Command
OSCE	Organization for Security and Cooperation in Europe
OUP	Operation Unified Protector

PACOM	U.S. Pacific Command
PRTs	Provincial reconstruction teams
QDR	Quadrennial Defense Review
R2P	Responsibility to protect
RAF	Royal Air Force (United Kingdom)
RDJTF	Rapid Deployment Joint Task Force
SACEUR	Supreme Allied Commander Europe
SACLANT	Supreme Allied Command Atlantic
SEATO	Southeast Asia Treaty Organization
SECDEF	Secretary of Defense
SHAPE	Supreme Headquarters Allied Powers Europe
SOCCENT	Special operations component commander
SOCOM	Special Operations Command
SOE	Special Operations Element
SOFs	Special Operations Forces
SOUTHCOM	Southern Command
TACOM	Tactical Command
TPOP	Total Population
UAV	Unmanned aerial vehicle
UN	United Nations
UNMOVIC	UN Monitoring, Verification, and Inspections Commission
UNSC	UN Security Council
UPOP	Urban population
USCINCCENT	U.S. Central Command commander in chief
USFOR-A	U.S. forces in Afghanistan

Acknowledgments

IN WRITING THIS BOOK, I discovered something that a lifetime of doing research on military alliances could never teach me, especially as someone who has written extensively on the strategic liability of allies in war. I learned that alliances, especially in wartime, are an indispensable component of survival. Without the best of allies, I would not have been alive to finish this book. In the middle of working on it, I was diagnosed with a terminal illness—myelodysplastic syndrome (MDS), a bone marrow failure disorder that is a precursor to acute myeloid leukemia (AML). I waged war on this disease that would have robbed my children of their mother, my husband of his wife, my parents of their daughter, and my sisters of their middle. During the course of writing this book, I underwent four rounds of chemotherapy while Michelle Johnson at the transplant center at the Arthur G. James Cancer Hospital and Richard J. Solove Research Institute at the Ohio State University Medical Center coordinated the search for a bone marrow donor. After a worldwide search, a match was found. In May 2011, I underwent a myeloablative bone marrow transplant, perhaps the most dangerous and miraculous medical procedure that exists. The chemotherapy ablates one's blood-cell system, and then the donor cells are infused. The cells make their way to the marrow and start producing a whole new system.

I now have the blood cell system of the generous (then) twenty-five-year-old man who was my match. I would not be alive today without the remarkable altruism of this most remarkable ally. The other ally without whom I could not have survived this journey is the amazing and wonderful Dr. William G.

Blum. I knew he was the right doctor for me when he sanctioned the start of my treatment on the day we met, December 13, 2010. I also knew he exercised exceptional judgment when I discovered he had a son named Jonah three months apart in age from my own son Jonah. Dr. Blum did not save my life once, he saved it repeatedly, and he continues to do so as he guides me on my journey back to a functioning immune system and navigates the sometimes-perilous path of graft versus host disease. Dr. Blum never failed to see me or call me or email me at a moment's notice, no matter the hour or day of the week. He tracked my progress constantly when I was in the hospital for transplant. When I was readmitted with multiple pulmonary embolisms—a condition he diagnosed by phone in the middle of the night and ordered me to the nearest emergency room—he was in my room within the hour despite his many other obligations and the fact that he was not on in-service duty. Any time he changed my medications and did not hear from me, he emailed—just one line: "how are you doing?" He is constantly managing my care; it is clear he is deeply invested in ensuring my long-term survival. One simply cannot ask for more from one's best and closest allies. And he is that. I am alive today because of him. I will be alive tomorrow and next year and five years from now because of him. He taught me a lot about the many different types of white blood cells and the complexity of the transplant process. But he also probably taught me more than anyone about alliances. He is an exceptional physician and a truly remarkable man.

Two other people are directly responsible for my being alive today. The first is one of my oldest and closest allies, David Wasser. David and I have been friends since 1981, when we spent the summer working together on kibbutz in Israel. I saw David in Providence, Rhode Island, for the first time in fifteen years in October 2010 while attending a conference. When I told him that I was struggling with inexplicably falling blood-cell counts, and had been trying without success to find a diagnosis despite hundreds of labs drawn and trips to multiple doctors multiple times, he demanded that I speak to his sister, Andrea (Andi) Wasser-Schindler, a nurse-practitioner who had worked in bone marrow transplantation for fifteen years. At the time, I believed the hematologist I was currently seeing, who told me emphatically that I was not experiencing a bone marrow problem. However, as my condition deteriorated, in late October 2010, I finally heeded the increasingly strident demands of David to call his sister. Andi became the most important person on my road to a second chance at life. After our first two-hour phone conversation, she told me she was certain I had a bone marrow problem and that I was not to leave my next hematologist appointment without scheduling a bone marrow biopsy. Because I had asked for a bone marrow biopsy several times to little avail, I was concerned once again that this request would be refused. Fortuitously, I had an appointment with Dr. Wael Jarjour in the Division of Rheumatology and Immunology at Ohio State University Medical Center the day before my next hematology appointment. Dr. Jarjour called my hematologist to insist I have a bone marrow biopsy. I met Dr. Jarjour only once, but he is among the heroes I have to thank for my life. I had the biopsy done immediately and was diagnosed a week later. Had I not listened to David or Andi, had Dr. Jarjour not intervened on my behalf, my MDS would surely have transformed to AML, and the fight would have been even more challenging, if not impossible, to win.

One other person needs to be mentioned: the rabbi who encouraged my donor to go through with the extraction process, Binyomin Forst. Not having any idea how rare a match was, my donor had initially declined to go forward with the testing when contacted by the registry. Yet his conscience would not relent. He consulted Rabbi Forst, who guided him to a decision to donate. A stem cell donor's cells must match the recipient's cells as closely as possible for a transplant to succeed. My donor was my only 10/10 perfect match. Without him, my fight would have been much harder. I am honored to carry his DNA.

These lessons about the importance of allies and the web of friendships that extend across the globe were brought home to me as my friends and family rallied to my side during my time of need. My sister Deborah Ogawa, living in Europe, cracked the whip and organized the operation with as much efficiency and effectiveness as the most seasoned general. My sisters Stacy Young (living in California) and Susan Huter (living in North Carolina) rotated in to Ohio for weeks on end to ensure that I had someone staying with me every day and night for the month-long sojourn at the James Cancer Hospital (the "Hotel James"). Their families had to pick up all the slack they left behind; for that, I am deeply grateful as well. Without my sisters' care, love, and tending to my every need this battle would have been so much harder. They made the month-long stay at the James endurable. Survivable.

My family, both the Hoffmanns and the Weitsmans, dropped everything to cycle in to care for us. For five continuous months someone was at the house to help, and for the month-long stay at the hospital, two family members were always on hand. I do not know how my husband, children, and I would have made it through without this support, love, and sustenance of my most precious and important allies. My dad, Allen Weitsman, came in more times than I can count; he was a rock and unrelenting source of hope and strength, as was his wife, Wei Cui. My mom, Judy Evans, came and stayed for several weeks, Skyping in from the house to the hospital during my actual transplant, despite its occurring in the wee hours of the morning. Her husband, Barry Evans, who died too quickly and unexpectedly before this book was in press, supported her despite the long absence my care demanded. We miss him terribly. My mother-in-law, Irene Hoffmann, came for multiple visits to bring calm to chaos and take care of the essential components of existence we struggled to maintain while my father-in-law, George Hoffmann, had to tend to affairs in Indianapolis because of her repeated visits. My sisters-in-law, Jill Hoffmann and Karen Hoffmann, with the support of their families, also took their turns caring for us. My aunt, Carol Franco, flew in and took charge. My beloved friends David Wasser, Ginger Moodie-Woodward, and Susan Varisco flew in from distant locations to make meals, do laundry, clean the house, and tend to our extensive needs. Even my guardian angel, Andi, flew in from Utah, visiting me in the hospital at the time she knew would be the most precarious. My sister Deborah arranged this— the most precious gift imaginable. Even though I met Andi only that one time, she is and will always be one of my most cherished allies. She will be in my life forever.

The ally above all others is my husband David Hoffmann. During this embattled period, he never failed to let me know that I was the strongest person he had ever known and that I would prevail in the fight for my life. He never wavered in any way or expressed any doubt throughout this extended period of successive hurdles. In addition to providing essential emotional support, he, more than anyone, ensured my day-to-day survival. He learned to care for my central line, flushing it every night, hooking me up to IVs every day, and changing the dressing every other day for months on end, maintaining a sterile environment all the while. It certainly took our love and partnership to a whole new level. He did all of this while running the house, taking care of the children, taking me to the hospital constantly, coordinating my care. He never complained. He was never resentful. He was just unfailingly loving, supportive, and strong. I could not have made it through without him. I am grateful to him every second of every day. He has taught me the true meaning of love.

Our children, Sarah Hoffmann-Weitsman and Jonah Hoffmann-Weitsman, a mere nine and seven, respectively, at the time of transplant, not only supported me in heart-melting ways; they provided me with the daily reminders that my survival was paramount. Just a few days before I went into the hospital, I took a walk with Sarah and warned her that I would get weaker before I got stronger. She turned to me and said, "Mom, your weak is everyone else's normal." I held on to those words over the course of the most difficult days, as I did Jonah's card, fashioned in my shape, which said, "Built to survive." This support saw me through my darkest moments.

The list of key allies goes on—Jacquie Moku, "Yogi Extraordinaire," who trained me for months on her day off, who brought my mind and body together while lifting my spirit and teaching me to believe. She was instrumental in facilitating the return of my strength and my belief that I could withstand the transplant process and the transition in mind and body it demanded. Lori Dunlap, who did Reiki and guided meditations throughout my initial treatment, giving me moments of peace that were as precious as they were scarce— and then doing the key formatting that saw this manuscript become a book! Her husband, Scott Dunlap, has also been an amazing supporter and friend as I traversed this hazardous path.

I must also thank my department colleagues and friends who carried me when I was unable to carry myself—especially Ly Burnier, whose continuous love, support, and companionship, as well as constant visits, maintained my morale, as did the cookies from her husband and my dear friend, David Descutner. They are Unparalleled Pals. Jay Ryu's continually reminding me of the strength of the dragon kept me moving forward. Vince Jungkunz, Julie White, Jim Mosher, and his wife, Christie Truly, were amazing in their unrelenting kindness and care. Patti Richard, Barry Tadlock, Andrew Ross, Susan Burgess, Kathleen Sullivan, Maria Fanis, John Gilliom, Sharell Arocho, Deena Proffitt, and Judith Grant encouraged me throughout the trial. Patricia Black copyedited the manuscript. Nina Sharpe provided support on every front—bureaucratic, administrative, emotional, and psychological. The process of getting through this past year and a half would have been much harder without her help.

My Fox Family YMCA family was instrumental in seeing me enter this process in peak condition and patiently nurturing me back to full strength: Laurie Swyers, Michiko Campbell, Karen Whitlach, Mike Lieber, Anita Morehart, Carrie Woody, Annie Weaver, Melinda Gossett, Linda Lally, Karen Shull, Sheila Heath, Jennifer Hughes, Linda Palmer, Michelle Purcell, Tammy Sharb, Amy Kabel, Peggy Griffin, and Judy Willison, among many, many others.

Essential other friends supported me in so many ways it is impossible to recount them all: Rabbi Danielle Leshaw, Dr. Timothy Lavelle, Jean Wince, Ava

Edmonds, Ed Gould, Carole and Fred Weiner, Linda Zionkowski, Terre Vander-voort and David Rader, Jodi and Paul Baxter, Scott Levi, Birgitte Soland, Robin Judd, and her son Jesse Steinman, whose bar mitzvah project was a swab drive in my honor. I am grateful to Robin and Jesse as well as my sisters, family, and friends who ran over twenty swab drives in my name. I would be remiss if I did not mention all of the wonderful people at the National Marrow Donor Pro-gram and at my registry, Gift of Life. Anyone reading these words who has not been swabbed—get to it! Someone's life may depend on it, as mine did.

Special thanks are necessary also to Tina Sessa and Chris Otter—who taught a class for David to give him the time he needed to care for me, yet another act of extreme generosity that allowed me and my family to reach this day. Ted Hopf not only brought me Jeni's ice cream while I was at Hotel James; he and Kavita Baireddy hosted me during the long days of treatment when it was too difficult to drive to and from Lancaster. The long walks with Marvelous Madge Vail were as important to my physical recovery as they were to my psychological revival. She is a treasure and I am privileged to know her. Her husband, Pete, picked up the kids from school too many times to count, interrupting the surreptitious naps he denies taking in the school parking lot. Their daughter Grace provided kindness and support, demonstrating that she was wise far beyond her years. The monthly hippos from Rachel Stohl were similarly an essential component of maintaining combat morale, as were the cheerful and caring notes from her parents, Cynthia and Michael Stohl. Many of my former students also rallied to support me—Michelle Frasher, Amy Geier Edgar, Beth Thompson, Balag'kutu Adivilah, Julie Garey, Kevin O'Hare, Gevorg Melikyan, and Saskia Van Wees. Thanks to my steadfast allies, Stacie Goddard, Jay M. Parker, George E. Sham-baugh, and above all J. Samuel Barkin, who not only withstood the repeated greetings from Mt. Laundry but also read this manuscript multiple times to ensure that, despite the quantity of pharmaceuticals I was ingesting during the course of its writing, it was, indeed, a book.

The tremendous intellectual debt I incurred while writing this book ex-tends to so many—individuals who not only served to form the ideas contained here but also were key supporters in the nonlinear process of seeing it through to fruition: David Baldwin, Warner Schilling, Robert Jervis, Jack Snyder, Stuart Kaufman, Nora Bensahel, Jason Davidson, Karl Mueller, Gale Mattox, Susan Sell, Martha Finnemore, James Lebovic, Chad Rector, and all of the members of the research seminar group at the Institute for Global and International Stud-ies, Elliott School of International Affairs, George Washington University. I am deeply grateful to Glenn Snyder, who died before this book was published. His intellectual imprint lives on within these pages.

Stephen Saideman's work was key as I progressed in this research, but the daily laugh he provided with silly photos as I traversed the rocky road of recovery made an enormous difference as well. The fact that he was a referee for the manuscript provides concrete evidence of my good fortune in allies. His comments, as well as the comments of the other referee, Daniel Baltrusaitis, improved the book in innumerable and immeasurable ways. I am deeply grateful to them for the care they took in reviewing the manuscript and for their exceptional feedback. I am also grateful to Mike Guillot at *Strategic Studies Quarterly* for his guidance and input. Many of the ideas developed in this book first appeared in "Wartime Alliances Versus Coalition Warfare: How Institutional Structure Matters in the Multilateral Prosecution of Wars," *Strategic Studies Quarterly*, Summer 2010. Geoffrey Burn at Stanford University Press encouraged me from the outset of the project; his suggestions shaped the book for the better in key ways. Most notably, Libya! He is a brilliant editor, and I am grateful for the opportunity to work with him. The rest of the Stanford team has been marvelous as well: James Holt, Patricia Myers, John Feneron, and Kate Wahl. I am grateful also to the Newgen Imaging team for *Waging War*'s production, most notably Jay Harward and copy editor Katherine Faydash. Without their collective effort and careful eyes, far more errors would languish among these pages. For research assistance, I am indebted to Matt Biddulph, Scott Jones, Asher Balkin, and above all Scott Bentley, who did the list of acronyms, essential formatting, and all of the research for the cost to allies of each operation. He reminded me repeatedly that China simply "wouldn't rise like that." The point was well taken.

For permissions to reproduce work, I am grateful to Trevor Stanley, Perspectives on World History and Current Affairs; Simon Rogers, of the Datablog at the *Guardian*; David Nokes and Adrien Starks at the Department of Defense; Chuck Young at the General Accountability Office; Jacob Poushter, Global Attitudes Project at Pew Research Center; Beth MacKenzie at the U.S. Army Center for Military History; Kamy Akhavan at ProCon.org; and Lauren Skrabala at the Rand Corporation. Neil Hall, deputy imagery editor, U.K. Ministry of Defense, deserves thanks for providing the rights to use the Royal Air Force photo that graces the cover of *Waging War*. As soon as I saw this image of an RAF VC10 K3 refueling two Canadian F18 aircraft—an incredible symbol of interoperability and coalition cooperation in Libya—I knew it was the one. Most authors must write in their acknowledgments that their greatest debt is to their family. In this case, while true, my family and I owe our greatest debt to my doctor, Dr. William G. Blum, David Wasser, and Andrea Wasser-Schindler. Words are simply inadequate to express my gratitude to them. Our greatest debt of all is owed to my donor, whose identity I learned on July 28, 2012. Out of 16.5 million people in the donor database, he was my only perfect match. I now carry his DNA. As such, this book is in large part his. Thank you, Yaakov M. Brisman, for heeding my call for help despite the fact that you did not know me. Words and expressions of gratitude will never be enough. Thank you, Miriam Brisman, for supporting and encouraging your husband to undergo this heroic act. My appreciation of you both knows no bounds. I cherish your altruism; I send you love and appreciation every single day. You are truly heroes. I am honored and blessed to know you, especially as I forge ahead. As this book goes to press, I learned that I have relapsed. I know that I will continue to wage this war successfully, armed as I am with the best possible coalition of supporters.

My last book was dedicated to my husband, David. This one I dedicate to our children, Sarah and Jonah—who appear to know a great deal about waging war—in the hopes that they will remember to be each other's closest ally as their lives unfold.

Waging War

1 INTRODUCTION

EVEN AS U.S. HEGEMONY reached its zenith in the late 1980s, the alarm of American decline was sounded in many influential circles. The volume of this alarm has grown in recent years, with the collapse of the financial system in 2008 and the rising economic power of China in the past decade. The declinist arguments pervading scholarly and policy-making circles focus a great deal on the economic components of U.S. power. Yet comparisons of economic or even military capabilities worldwide fail to account for the institutional dimension. Contemporary coalition warfare reveals that U.S. military might remains unrivaled and will be difficult for any other great power to match for some time to come. This has to do with the institutions of violence—not just with the technology, capability, and level of professionalism and training of the U.S. military, although these are essential ingredients of American hegemony as well.

Military alliances provide constraints and opportunities for states seeking to advance their interests around the globe. The two decades following the end of the Cold War are instructive in this regard. The active engagement of the United States and its partners in many corners of the world illustrates the distinctive nature of waging war in the contemporary age. War, from the Western perspective, is no longer—not that it ever was—a solitary endeavor. Partnerships of all types serve as a foundation for the projection of power and the employment of force. These relationships among states provide the foundation upon which hegemony is built.

The institutions of violence that promote U.S. interests include the web of military alliances that the United States has constructed worldwide. They include the coalitions that the United States culls in the face of crises. In addition,

1

they consist of the joint and unilateral command structures that span the globe. Together, these effective weapons of war augment U.S. fighting capacity and solidify the country's position as a global hegemon.

My argument here is not that military alliances provide a straightforward capability-aggregation effect. I have written extensively elsewhere that this is far from true. In this book, too, I show that allies may be a strategic liability in wartime. However, what does emerge here is that institutions of interstate violence serve as ready mechanisms for employing force. They are not always well designed, nor do they always augment fighting effectiveness as well as they could. They sometimes act as drag on state capacity. However, the net benefit of this web of partnerships, agreements, and alliances is great—it makes rapid response to crisis possible and facilitates countering threats wherever they emerge. As such, these institutions of interstate violence are facilitators of the realization of capability and a critical component of hegemony for the United States. My examination shows how and to what degree alliances and coalitions serve as vehicles for projecting U.S. power.

The purpose of this book is to determine which sorts of institutional arrangements lubricate states' abilities to advance their agendas and prevail in wartime and which components of institutional arrangements undermine effectiveness and cohesion, and increase costs to states. Not all institutions are the same—some provide more legitimacy than others, and some provide more efficient avenues for achieving goals. The two decades of trial and error from the Gulf War to Libya provide answers as to which arrangements foster fighting effectiveness and which inhibit the ability to prevail in wartime.

REALIST INSTITUTIONALISM

This book develops the theoretical approach of what I call realist institutionalism. Institutions are arenas through which states advance their goals and manifest their capabilities. Power matters tremendously. Institutions of war affect the operational execution of war: the way in which a mission is prosecuted and the cohesion and effectiveness of the fighting force brought to bear. In the study of contemporary warfare, it is not enough to say that power prevails; practitioners still have the difficult task of integrating forces, planning, and executing military operations because democratic warfare is multilateral. *Institution* "may refer to a general pattern or categorization of activity or to a particular human-constructed arrangement, formally or informally organized. . . . [Institutions] can be identified as related complexes of rules and norms, identifiable in space and time."[1] Rules that govern institutions or are embedded in them are essential to understanding those institutions' form and function. Institutions provide rules that prescribe behavior, constrain activity, and shape expectations.[2] Both military alliances and coalitions that are constructed to prosecute wars are institutions in this regard—they are a general pattern of activity, a humanly constructed arrangement formally organized with identifiable norms and rules for achieving participating states' objectives. There are principles, processes, and mechanisms. Thus, throughout this book I identify alliances and coalitions as institutions of war or interstate violence.

The analytical questions regarding multilateral versus unilateral operations or whether or not institutions matter in world affairs do not address the fundamental question of institutional design. Scholarship on multilateral warfare asserts the dichotomy and primacy of multilateral versus unilateral war fighting. Scholarship on the future of the North Atlantic Treaty Organization (NATO) assesses the importance or diminishing role of alliances in the contemporary age. Realist versus liberal literatures question whether or not institutions matter. Yet, in the end, these questions detract from the quest to understand which institutional mechanisms work in advancing state goals, power, and the ability to succeed in wartime. Viewing alliances and coalitions through the institutional lens they warrant allows us to generate important insights about their function in peacetime and war.

Realist institutionalism is unromantic: states are not preoccupied with moral command or moral imperative, with doing the right thing for the right reasons (witness Rwanda). States may, however, seek legitimation and international sanction for their actions; doing so may enhance their standing in the system.[3] States seek to exercise power in the Dahlian sense; that is, to get others do to their bidding, actions their targets would not otherwise undertake.[4] Institutions serve as vehicles for states to promote their agendas. Institutions augment power not by simply adding the power of others to their own, but rather through achieving ends that not only are rational but also enhance the power, soft or otherwise, of states.[5] This is why states will bypass a global organization if it is noncompliant. For example, the Gulf War slowed down the U.S. path to its goals and made the pursuit of those ends more challenging through a cumbersome multilateral apparatus, but it facilitated the ability of the United States to get others to do as it wished. By the time the UN sanction was forthcoming, the United States had already dispatched troops to Saudi Arabia, was already mobilizing, and would likely have proceeded with or without the UN authorization.

*Alliance Politics
White paper*

Well-established institutional structures may be overly rigid in advancing state objectives—more flexible and adaptable ad hoc institutional arrangements may be better suited for wartime application. Yet enduring institutional structures facilitate joint training, joint exercises, joint procurement, and familiar routines that may reduce the obstacles posed by friendly fire and interoperability that plague all multilateral war-fighting endeavors. The use of NATO over the course of the past two decades—fighting in Kosovo, peacekeeping in Afghanistan, and protecting civilians in Libya—allowed this deeply entrenched institutional structure to become more robust and permeable. From Kosovo to Libya, NATO undertook changes in the ways it approached war prosecution, particularly in regard to its decision-making structure but also in regard to procurement as well as its strategic mission and vision for the future.

Multilateral war-fighting frameworks benefit from a long history and established relationships, but they must also be flexible and adapt well to changing scenarios and demands. This is an essential difference between peacetime and wartime alliances, although the unintended consequences of both are the same: intertwining of command structures, joint operations and exercises, collective strategy, and forward planning all serve to inhibit member states from contemplating war with each other. Interests and strategies for pursuing those interests become interconnected.

The other side of enduring alliances and globe-spanning partnerships is that they advance a more ambitious agenda with more responsibilities and interests driven by partner states rather than just one's own strategic aims. Put another way, one's own strategic aims become enmeshed with the goals and strategies of others, with the potential to become entangling alliances, just as George Washington and Thomas Jefferson cautioned.

THE INSTITUTIONAL MECHANISMS OF WAR-FIGHTING CAPABILITY

The norm of multilateralism is entrenched in the American way of waging war. As the 2010 Quadrennial Defense Review Report indicates, "Our experience of operating as part of multinational coalitions in long-duration conflicts has demonstrated the importance of continually fostering long-term relationships with allies and partners."[6] Two decades of interventions have revealed the enduring importance of institutions of interstate violence. Some components of waging war multilaterally advance the strategic aims of partner states; other mechanisms inhibit efficiency in important ways.

Decision-making structures that foster clear chains of command and communication facilitate effectiveness in prosecuting wars. Structures that favor more egalitarian processes, such as consensus, inhibit efficiency and effectiveness. Long-standing institutional arrangements, such as those embedded in NATO, with emphasis on joint exercises, training, and transparency, reduce the likelihood of major interoperability challenges and friendly fire. Further, these relationships may not be as plagued by the alliance security dilemma, or intra-alliance threats, which coalitions, especially large ones, may experience. The size of an institution matters as well—small coalitions will experience fewer challenges than will the more unwieldy large ones that may require substantial work to maintain cohesion and fighting effectiveness. In other words, not all institutions of interstate violence are equal in their ability to prevail in wartime. There are both substantial costs and substantial benefits in the multilateral approach to interventions.

Allies may serve as strategic liabilities to states, even more in wartime than in peacetime. There will always be interoperability challenges, heightened threats of friendly fire, more cumbersome decision-making structures, more constituencies to satisfy, more burden-sharing conflicts, more intra-alliance or coalition bargaining that may produce additional costs. This is true in the absence of any guarantee of a legitimacy dividend. Which components of multilateral war fighting advance state objectives and which augment costs? Fears of abandonment and entrapment may mediate alliance and coalition activity, and less efficiency in war prosecution may result as well. And yet, having a broad foundation upon which power capabilities may be translated into the effective use of force is a critical benefit of waging war multilaterally.

INSTITUTIONS AND U.S. HEGEMONY

An important implication of viewing institutions as instruments of state power is that the arguments in the field regarding the continuation or decline of U.S. hegemony should prominently feature its institutions of war. Yet despite how consequential these institutions are for advancing U.S. objectives and projecting its power, declinist arguments focus most on economic indicators, though military capabilities and spending are often a component as well. The scholars who argue that the era of American hegemony will continue for a long time further neglect an assessment of these important vehicles of U.S. military might. The past two decades of active U.S. interventions and coalition and allied warfare dramatically underscore the centrality of the web of institutions advancing American interests. These include its military alliances that span the globe, such as NATO and the Australia, New Zealand, United States Security (ANZUS) Treaty, but also its command structures that represent deeply institutionalized frameworks of combat readiness that are unique worldwide. In any assessment of whether or not a great power such as China can anytime soon reach the level of the U.S. military must detail not only the military arsenals of the great powers in question, not only the economic indicators of growth, military spending, or even technological prowess in the area of weaponry, but also the standing readiness of these militaries to confront and combat threats as they arise.

There is no dearth of literature that addresses the extent to which the United States is or is not in decline. Almost from the moment of the Soviet implosion and the advent of unipolarity, scholars and practitioners have debated the future of American hegemony. These arguments gained even more traction in the aftermath of 9/11, in the age of American adventurist interventionism, and in the advent of global recession in 2008.[7]

Jack Snyder wrote in 2003 that the Bush doctrine of preventive war in Afghanistan and Iraq would culminate in imperial overreach and U.S. decline.[8] Charles Kupchan argues that the United States and the West are past their zenith and will ultimately be eclipsed by rising powers such as China and India, although ultimately the twenty-first century will be dominated not by any one country but rather by a plurality of ideologies and cultures:

> The collective strength of the West is, however, on the way down. During the Cold War, the Western allies often accounted for more than two-thirds of global output. Now they represent about half of output—and soon much less. As of 2010, four of the top five economies in the world were still from the developed world (the United States, Japan, Germany, and France). From the developing world, only China made the grade, coming in at No. 2. By 2050, according to Goldman Sachs, four of the top five economies will come from the developing world (China, India, Brazil, and Russia). Only the United States will make the cut; it will rank second, and its economy will be about half the size of China's. Moreover, the turnabout will be rapid: Goldman Sachs predicts that the collective economic output of the top four developing countries—Brazil, China, India, and Russia—will match that of the G-7 countries by 2032.[9]

Despite the fact that Kupchan repeatedly makes the critical point that U.S. hegemony emanates from the liberal democratic order and web of alliances, he does not take the argument to its logical conclusion by asserting the need for such institutional readiness to project power. The United States derives its power from its associations with other Western democratic states; yet the power of the developing nations Kupchan invokes derives from the economic output of the rising countries alone. Christopher Layne, too, invokes the rising power of China, India, and Russia in his assessment of U.S. decline, its inability to manage the international system effectively, and the end of Pax Americana.[10] Arvind Subramanian invokes economic indicators in anticipation of China eclipsing the United States.[11]

Some of the most important voices in the overlapping communities of scholarship and policy making echo these concerns regarding the decline of the United States' power, even though there are important, nuanced differences. For example, Fareed Zakaria argues that the United States may maintain its military hegemony even as it declines economically. David Calleo argues that regardless of the U.S. position, the perception of unipolarity has culminated in problematic foreign policy for the United States around the globe.[12]

Another key strand of argument surrounding the future of U.S. power is the narrative of the rise of China.[13] These fears are not pervasive only in the academic literature; they are also widely held views of international affairs by publics around the world.[14] A Pew survey in the spring of 2011 found that most Americans had a positive view of China, though most also expressed concern regarding China's economic growth and its increasing power relative to the United States.[15] As seen in Table 1.1, a Pew study from July 2011 shows that the publics of fifteen of the twenty-two countries queried expressed the view that China will replace or has already replaced the United States as the most powerful country in the system.[16]

The alarming economic indicators suggesting American decline and China's rise may be interpreted differently, however. As Ezra Klein points out, economic growth is hard to look at in a vacuum. What constitutes growth in one country impinges on heightened well-being in another.[17] Furthermore, as Joseph Nye indicates, even if China's gross domestic product surpasses that of the United States, its per capita income will not match that of the United States for a very long time. And even if American hegemony wanes in relative terms, it may well still stand above the rest for the foreseeable future.[18] Furthermore, the economic arguments cut both ways. Daniel Gross argues, for example, that the post-recession economic trends are, in fact, favorable to the United States and its future, as well as to the rest of the world. He points out effectively that economic growth cannot be assessed as a zero-sum game.[19]

Table 1.1 Public opinion on the rise of China

	Will China replace the United States as the world's leading superpower?			
	Has already replaced U.S. (%)	Will eventually replace U.S. (%)	Total: Has replaced or will replace U.S. (%)	Will never replace U.S. (%)
United States	12	34	46	45
France	23	49	72	28
Spain	14	53	67	30
Britain	11	54	65	26
Germany	11	50	61	34
Poland	21	26	47	31
Russia	15	30	45	30
Lithuania	11	29	40	40
Ukraine	14	23	37	36
Turkey	15	21	36	41
Palestinian territories	17	37	54	38
Jordan	17	30	47	45
Israel	15	32	47	44
Lebanon	15	24	39	54
China	6	57	63	17
Pakistan	10	47	57	10
Japan	12	25	37	60
Indonesia	8	25	33	46
India	13	19	32	17
Mexico	19	34	53	31
Brazil	10	27	37	47
Kenya	7	37	44	43

SOURCE: Pew Research Center. "U.S. Status as World's Superpower Challenged by Rise of China: U.S. Favorability Ratings Remain Positive." July 13, 2011. Accessed 7/9/2012. http://pewresearch.org/pubs/2059/-superpower-china-us-image-abroad-afghanistan-terrorism.

The idea that the United States is in decline has important strategic consequences. As Paul MacDonald and Joseph Parent argue, retrenchment may be a useful policy to manage the reduced relative capability of great powers.[20] Yet the profound difference between the web of institutions that translate U.S. capability to actuality and the imperial powers of the past does warrant a slightly more cautionary approach. The implicit assumptions about decline and retrenchment could be self-fulfilling; the United States dismantles its entrenched institutional framework to save money, which may improve economic indicators but undermine U.S. ability to translate military power to reality in the event of need. Friedman and Mandelbaum assume that U.S. decline stems from inattention to China's rise on various fronts, and that to preserve U.S. power, a rediscovery of American innovation, ingenuity in thought, and action needs to occur. The government must promote a strong domestic economy, private enterprise, an emphasis on education, and third-party competition as examples of the way forward.[21]

Recent arguments cite reasons for both optimism and pessimism about the future of American power. Robert Kagan, for example, is optimistic that the United States will sustain its hegemony and argues that its decline would culminate in more war and conflict;[22] Zbigniew Brzezinski, in contrast, is more pessimistic, citing the U.S. financial meltdown, interventions in Iraq and Afghanistan, the rise of China, and the political activism in the Middle East as profound challenges to prolonged American power. He sees the need for redoubled effort to regain and sustain U.S. standing.[23]

While the declinist arguments generally center on ebbing of U.S military and economic power and the rise of other countries such as China in comparison, the optimists' touchstone is American ingenuity, adaptability, and innovation.[24] The implicit assumptions that govern the literature on U.S. decline or sustained hegemony are the most important component of the arguments—they reveal what strategists believe are the most important components of power in the system, be they gross national product, the level of debt, military spending, or a culture of adaptability and innovation. The locus of the problem gives rise to the solutions as well. American overreach requires retrenchment; too much military spending demands reduced military spending; too little military spending demands increased military spending; economic decline requires fiscal conservatism and nurturing of entrepreneurship.

The argument here suggests that examining static indicators alone does not lend itself to understanding the full picture of U.S. power. There are important elements of military power that can be assessed objectively and analyzed. Yet it is equally important to explore the mechanisms through which that power may be realized. The web of institutions constructed to serve as conduits of American military might around the globe provide a unique dimension for exploring the future of U.S. hegemony. The United States literally rules the world via its command structures in all regions of the world and its alliances, which allow it a military presence far beyond its borders. In other words, basing does matter—it is easy in the contemporary age to view geography as playing a diminishing role at a time when technology closes the physical gaps. Yet in regard to the deployment of troops, responding to crises, and executing missions far from the homeland, location matters, and geography is highly consequential. In this way, the U.S. advantage over a country such as China is quite significant. As Yan Xuetong notes:

> America enjoys much better relations with the rest of the world than China in terms of both quantity and quality. America has more than 50 formal military allies, while China has none. North Korea and Pakistan are only quasi-allies of China. The former established a formal alliance with China in 1961, but there have been no joint military maneuvers and no arms sales for decades. China and Pakistan have substantial military cooperation, but they have no formal military alliance binding them together.[25]

Beyond alliances, the United States has a unified command structure that circles the globe. When the United States needed to respond to Saddam Hussein's invasion of Kuwait, it had U.S. Central Command (CENTCOM) at the ready to adapt to the mission. When the United States was called on to respond to the growing abuses by Muammar Gadhafi in Libya, it had U.S. Africa Command (AFRICOM) to use as the first line of defense. These existing institutions, coupled with advanced military technology and a highly professional, well-trained, and well-educated military give the United States a military edge that cannot be captured by straightforward assessments of capability, spending, or economic indicators alone. Map 1.1, the Unified Command Plan for the United States in 2011, illustrates the U.S. command structure worldwide.

As institutions are conduits of power, as they promote the realization of potential capability to actual exercise of influence in the military sphere, it is essential to know which institutional mechanisms serve to advance the strategic ends in question and which constrain the exercise of power. This is the central mission of this book—to achieve a better understanding of the ways in which institutions in the security realm facilitate the actualization of military power and of the ways in which they detract from or undermine war-fighting effectiveness. To realize this goal, in the next chapter, I examine the strategies of war prosecution, the different institutional types of war-fighting instruments, and the different mechanisms that inhere to those institutions that promote achieving strategic ends and to those that inhibit the ability to prevail in military conflict.

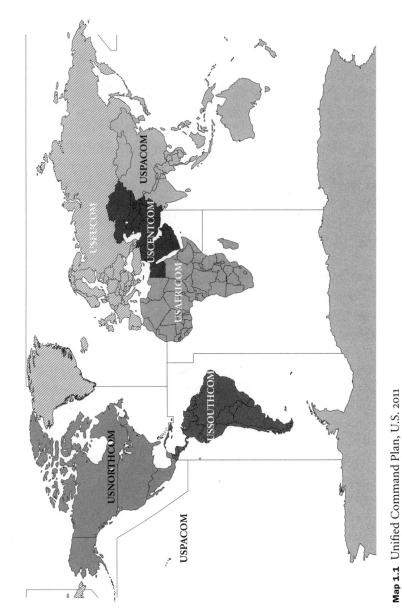

Map 1.1 Unified Command Plan, U.S. 2011

SOURCE: Department of Defense, Unified Command Plan. Last update as of April 27, 2011. http://www.defense.gov/home/features/2009/0109_ unifiedcommand. See also http://www.army.mil/info/organization. Both accessed 7/11/2012.

THE FUTURE OF AMERICAN HEGEMONY

In the absence of assessing institutions of war fighting, no true understanding of military might is possible. These institutions of interstate violence translate military capability into leverage or fighting effectiveness. They include military alliances as well as the command structures the United States has in place worldwide. These components of state power mean readiness in execution. U.S. technological prowess and its unparalleled military arsenal distinguish it as a hegemon. Its hegemonic foundation is provided not only by the B-2 bombers or precision bombs or unmanned aerial vehicles and other advanced weapons of war, but also by the strategic understandings it has with partners worldwide. This ensures that the United States has access to bases around the world, thus fostering its readiness to address threats wherever they arise. The U.S. command structures embodied in CENTCOM, AFRICOM, U.S. European Command (EUCOM), U.S. Pacific Command (PACOM), and U.S. Southern Command (SOUTHCOM) serve to ensure rapid deployment and readiness for combat in the event of a crisis or threat.

The web of institutions standing ready for the United States to wage war is thus an important component of the country's reach and hegemony. Any country seeking similar dominance would need not only the technology and capability of the United States but also its worldwide preparedness to launch war quickly and effectively. Although we tend to downplay the importance of geography in a world tightly knit by technology, when launching a war, where the targets are matters. The fact that the United States undertook missions over Libya with stealth bombers from Missouri is an exception. Geography does matter, and this example illustrates that technology does as well. In the past two decades most interventions, including that in Libya, required a closer basing of assets to execute the missions. Worldwide cooperation, even among noncombatant states, was central. It underscored the importance of the institutions of interstate violence as well as the interstate relationships that underpin those institutions. These are both central components of the foundations of state military power.

OUTLINE OF THE BOOK

In the following chapters I explore in more detail the notion that institutions advance the strategic ends of states in key ways while constraining efficiency in others. The next chapter lays out in detail the arguments regarding alliances and coalitions, as well as unilateralism, bilateralism, and multilateralism more generally. I advance the notion that alliances and coalitions are essential elements of pursuing state ends and preserving state power in the international system. More specifically, I outline a realist institutionalist agenda and the role these institutions of interstate violence play in the future of U.S. hegemony. I then discuss the central questions of institutional mechanisms prevailing in multilateral warfare—the use of alliances versus coalitions; the decision-making structures brought to bear; the interoperability, friendly fire, and burden-sharing challenges experienced; the internal balance of power and internal leverage and their effect on the way in which the coalition or alliance operated, as well as the way in which the alliance security dilemma manifests; how size affects cohesion, effectiveness, and costs; and the conditions under which multilateralism yields legitimacy. These are the central components of institutions of interstate violence that culminate in the key costs and key benefits of employing them.

In Chapters 2–7, I use specific cases to examine the core questions of the book regarding realist institutionalism and the mechanisms of institutions that advance or detract from efficiently achieving the strategic aims of intervention. I analyze these questions in the context of Operation Desert Storm and Operation Desert Shield, Operation Allied Force in Kosovo, Operation Enduring Freedom and the International Stabilization and Assistance Force in Afghanistan, Operation Iraqi Freedom and the war in Iraq, and Operation Odyssey Dawn and Operation Unified Protector in Libya. Each case has distinct lessons as well as important generalizations for contemporary multilateral war fighting. An overview of the findings and implications is presented in Chapter 8, the conclusion.

The mission of this book is to embed the study of wartime alliances and coalitions into the scope of institutional analysis, in order to better understand how these institutions serve as vehicles to actualize power, the ways in which they hamper power realization, and the extent to which they advance U.S. hegemony.

2 FIGHTING WITH FRIENDS

*Unlike Vietnam, we are joined by a broad coalition of 43 nations
that recognizes the legitimacy of our action [in Afghanistan].*
—**Barack Obama, U.S. Military Academy, West Point, New York,
December 1, 2009**

AS THE TWENTY-FIRST CENTURY unfolds, much has been revealed about the
nature of multilateral warfare. While the United States has never fought a major war alone, in the contemporary era, coalition size has grown dramatically.
The unthinking assumption that the larger the coalition is, the better, pervades
strategic planning and decision makers' rhetoric. This assumption goes hand in
hand with the idea that the more partners one has in war, the more legitimate
is the military action. Yet neither of these assumptions may be true. Large coalitions bring with them coordination problems in terms of taking action and
making decisions. Higher numbers of friendly-fire fatalities may result. Large
coalitions may result from small states seeking side payments for action rather
than being motivated by the legitimacy of the mission. Operation Iraqi Freedom had one of the largest coalitions in history, yet it was never widely viewed
in the international community as a legitimate enterprise.[1]

The principle that bigger is better underpins American military partnerships in war and peace. The North Atlantic Treaty Organization originally had
twelve signatories. During the forty years of its operation during the Cold War,
the alliance gained just four member states. Since the end of the Cold War, the
alliance has added twelve new members, with several others participating in the
Membership Action Plan, and future additions are likely.[2] The war-fighting coalitions that the United States constructed to fight its contemporary wars have
numbered between twenty-five and fifty partner states. Even during the era of
George W. Bush, when the international community condemned the United
States for being unilateralist, the coalitions it used to fight in Afghanistan and
Iraq were as big as the United States could possibly make them.[3]

Given how consequential these assumptions are regarding the size of coalitions and alliances and the implications for legitimacy, it is surprising that they have not been more closely examined. Even more foundational questions, such as how institutional design impinges on fighting efficacy, remain largely unexplored. I argue that growing, ever-larger military alliances and coalitions affect war-fighting effectiveness. In addition, I examine the idea that military alliances created in peacetime but called on to act in wartime may have significantly different institutional features—particularly in terms of decision-making procedures and command structures—than coalitions that are constructed in an ad hoc fashion to intervene in a crisis. Coalitions may be tailored to suit the needs of the mission at hand, while the more durable features of military alliances may not serve member states as well in times of war as they do in peacetime.

Whether the United States fights via wartime alliance or coalition, the size of the multinational operation and the structure of decision making are all highly consequential in regard to effectiveness, cohesion, durability, and whether the United States is likely to prevail in war.[4] The purpose of this chapter is to explore these issues theoretically, setting the stage for the empirical analysis that will come in subsequent chapters. I begin with a discussion about unilateral, bilateral, and multilateral strategies. This is important to bridge the gap between multilateralism and multinational war fighting. I discuss peacetime versus wartime alliances, as well as wartime alliances versus coalitions. I then proceed with a discussion regarding the relationship between institutional design and effectiveness, and I conclude with a number of questions that will guide the analyses in later chapters.

REALIST INSTITUTIONALISM

Military alliances illustrate the fact that states use institutions for power motivations. At their most fundamental level, even if not employed as such, military alliances are weapons of war. While they do not always or even most of the time actually augment war-fighting capability, and at times they even detract from it, the origins of alliances emanate from a desire for mutual protection and an enhanced ability to protect oneself or to advance national goals. Peacetime alliances often serve to manage relationships among states within the alliance, yet in doing so, they also serve strategic ends. This highlights the institutional component of realist theory.

For decades, the central debate of international relations was whether depictions of realism or of liberal institutionalism offered the best explanation for state behavior in the international system. The prevailing view of alliances largely emanated from the realist perspective, which suggested that power mattered above all and that multilateral war prosecution was merely unilateral action cloaked by multilateral design; power differentials among participating states are so great that all that really matters is the fighting force of the great power in the coalition or alliance.

In the past decade, however, a burgeoning literature has developed that seeks to incorporate institutions into the realist paradigm. In *Dangerous Alliances*, I argued that to achieve the best understanding of alliance formation and cohesion, one needed to synthesize and unify realism and liberal institutionalism by looking at different alliance behaviors, motivations, and cohesion, under conditions of varying degrees of threat. At lower threat levels, institutionalist arguments are more salient than realist ones; under conditions of moderate and high threats to states, realist insights are most relevant. Ikenberry's arguments regarding strategic restraint and Pressman's argument regarding the ways in which states constrain and control their allies are exceptionally insightful in advancing the literature in this regard.[5] Insights generated by the works of Schroeder, Grieco, Conybeare, Wallander and Keohane, Krebs, Duffield, Morrow, Sorokin, Gelpi, Leeds, Risse, Snyder, Schweller, Kreps, Baltrusaitis, Davidson, and Thompson take us even further along this path. Schroeder highlights the management function of alliances (as does Gelpi's scholarship on intra-alliance control via mediation), which Snyder further develops from a rational and strategic perspective. Schweller's work on bandwagoning for profit also underscores the need to understand the cost-benefit calculations above all in capturing alliance motivations, as does Conybeare's work. Grieco reveals to us the institutional incentives for states seeking heightened cooperation. The straightforward rational-choice literature is similarly helpful here. Morrow and Sorokin both enhance our assessments of the conditions under which states will signal their intentions, advance deterrence, or decide to arm themselves instead of creating or joining an alliance. Leeds has comprehensively addressed the causes and effects of alliance politics, moving beyond the capability-aggregation model. Wallander highlights the cost-benefit calculations in regard to the persistence of NATO after the Cold War. Krebs illustrates the extent to which the transparency of institutions may culminate in either heightened anxiety or cooperation. Duffield's work has been essential in building the foundation of our understanding of NATO's new era and the connection between alliances and regimes. Risse's work, too, has advanced Deutsch and colleagues' first delineation of security communities and has added to the institutional component of alliance politics. Thies analyzes the distinctiveness of NATO as an alliance and the robustness of the organization as a consequence of the democratic states that it comprises.[6]

More recent work is also extremely important and helpful in advancing a realist institutionalist perspective. Some key trends include, first, Crescenzi, Kathman, Kleinberg, and Wood's work illuminating the importance of commitments and reputation in alliance politics.[7] Second, Tierney scrutinizes the unintended consequences of alliance politics; he also delves more deeply into the ways in which the United States' culture and ideology affect the way it fights its wars. Third, Kreps's work highlights the legitimation effect of multilateral frameworks as well as the strategic components and costs. Fourth, Baltrusaitis builds on the literature on alliance burden sharing by identifying the conditions under which states contribute or not to coalitions. Fifth, Davidson's book on contemporary coalition warfare contains extremely valuable insights about burden sharing during wartime and the way in which valuing an alliance shapes decision making.[8] Sixth, Thies's work advances a more nuanced and thorough understanding of burden sharing—and burden shifting—within the NATO alliance than we previously had.[9] These recent works have elevated the study of contemporary alliances and coalitions in innumerable ways, each bringing different insights to bear. Collectively, they serve as an essential foundation of scholarship.

Above all, what brings these sometimes-disparate strands of thought together is the underlying argument that the strategic benefit of alliances extends beyond capability aggregation and highlights the institutional advantages of seeking security via coalition or alliance. In other words, military alliances offer constraining mechanisms, but they also offer opportunities to advance the agendas of states in ways that are not merely to augment power. Thompson's work illuminates this very effectively.[10] According to Thompson, institutions have varying degrees of neutrality, and therefore varying degrees of legitimating effect and political benefit for states that work through them to advance their own goals. Institutions serve as vehicles: to transmit information regarding the intentions of the policy purveyor; to determine the level of international support; and to seek endorsements from the international community.

More specifically, Thompson argues that in a number of ways international organizations provide political advantages to states seeking sanction for intervention. First, there is an informational component through which a coercive state can signal limited intentions that can be disseminated through working through the organization. There is also more transparency in regard to any operation subject to the sanction of the international community through the institution. The more global the institution, the more political benefit it yields; regional organizations with less diverse memberships have less neutrality and thus fewer political advantages.[11] Working through an international organization can also signal to domestic audiences at home and abroad that there are valid reasons for intervention, which heightens support for the mission. In other words, an international organization both legitimates action and contributes to heightened legitimacy. By the same token, a state's action is constrained when it operates through global organizations.[12] Additional costs include transaction costs and timing, less freedom of action, and slower speed.[13] While Thompson is less interested in military strategy than political strategy, his insights are extremely important from the perspective of multilateral war prosecution and foundational to the ideas of realist institutionalism.

Realist institutionalism posits that institutions are not simply separate bodies with independent influence; nor are they mere reflections of power. Instead, as states seek to exercise power and to influence the decisions and choices of others, institutions are one vehicle for them to do so. Institutions augment power not simply in the straightforward capability-aggregation manner, adding the power of others to one's own power, but also through achieving ends that are rational and strategic, and that advance the interests of the state in essential ways. This perspective underscores the insight that Robert Dahl, David Baldwin, and others have emphasized, which is that power is a relationship, the ability to get others to do one's bidding, not simply a static indicator of what one possesses.[14] In fact, Harold Sprout, in his review of Hans Morgenthau's *Politics Among Nations*, suggests that one of the missing components of this realist "bible" is an analysis of how institutions affect not only state policies but also power.[15]

I suggest that institutional design affects fighting effectiveness and is often a consequence not only of power and negotiation but also of quests for legitimacy. It represents a synthesis of realist and liberal institutionalist ideas. Central to the book is the question of what the strategic and military effects are if decisions regarding the institutional design in prosecuting wars are made for political and not military reasons. To what extent do decisions regarding institutional structure impinge on fighting effectiveness or cohesion? The answers to these critical questions should be elemental to the design of war-fighting strategies of the future.

STRATEGIES OF INTERVENTION

Unilateralism

During the eight years of the George W. Bush presidency, the international community was extremely critical of his administration for being overly unilateralist. Particularly in the aftermath of a controversial decision to go to war against Saddam Hussein's Iraq, there was a growing sense at home and abroad that the United States did not take other countries' interests into account as it formulated its foreign policy. This opinion prevailed even among the publics of several close U.S. allies.[16] But what does *unilateralist* mean? Here, it stands in for the extent to which other states' interests and perspectives matter in driving the foreign policy choices of a state.

Much of the criticism levied at the Bush administration domestically and internationally centered on the perceived unilateral approach that the administration took in its foreign policy—for example, not signing the Kyoto Protocol, not joining the International Criminal Court, and reneging on the Anti-Ballistic Missile Treaty.[17] And yet the administration went to great lengths and committed substantial resources to ensure that the United States would not be fighting alone in Afghanistan and Iraq. How do we reconcile these differences?

According to Ikenberry, unilateralism entails a "willingness to reject treaties, violate rules, ignore allies, and use military force on its own."[18] Yet although the United States rebuffed a number of international agreements during the Bush years, it remained unwilling to employ force alone. Despite the shift in declaratory policy to preemptive war,[19] in practice, the Bush administration did not abide by this doctrine, even allowing a new nuclear-weapons state, North Korea, onto the world stage.[20]

The norms of multilateralism are so embedded in the international system—what Ikenberry calls system and foundational multilateralism[21]—that few liberal democratic states wholly violate them.[22] As a consequence, even as the United States expressly eschewed the values of the international community in fundamental ways, it nevertheless abided by them. While the Bush administration did not rely on UN sanction to pursue its war in Iraq or Afghanistan—though it did attempt to gain that stamp of approval in its war in Iraq—the United States worked tirelessly to construct a broad international coalition to stand alongside it as the world's most powerful nation.[23]

Therefore, how we understand unilateralism in the contemporary system in the context of liberal democracies is still predicated on a complex system of multinational cooperation.[24] Unilateralism, one state acting alone to confront a foreign policy problem either by choice or by necessity, rarely wholly manifests among liberal democracies. Unilateralist posturing, when a country appears to reject the values of international collaboration, consultation, as well as international institutions, customs, and norms, certainly does exist in the contemporary system. In other words, there is a dramatic difference between the unilateralism of North Korea in pursuing its security ambitions and the United States doing the same.[25] In the event of a war decision, for example, Iran may take action without coordinating with another state in the system. The same could not be said of the United States, even if during the George W. Bush years the United States pursued its security objectives in ways that sometimes violated the norms of the international system. As Kreps argues, pure unilateralism does not really exist for liberal democracies in the contemporary era, given the essential practices of sharing intelligence, training, and coordinating closely among allies such as the United States, the United Kingdom, and Australia.[26]

Bilateralism

In international relations, bilateralism usually refers to policy dealings between two states rather than two states acting together in regard to a shared foreign policy objective. However, the term can be used either way. With respect to trade, for example, agreements that are negotiated bilaterally are negotiated between two states, where multilateral trade agreements are agreements negotiated among a group of states collectively, usually through an institutional mechanism such as the World Trade Organization. In the security realm, the concept can retain the meaning of two states seeking to come to a negotiated agreement, but it can also be understood as a shared understanding between two states in regard to their security affairs. Examples of important bilateral alliance relationships include that between the United States and Japan, and between the United States and Israel. Analytically, these are understood differently than are multilateral alliances such as NATO.

Bilateral alliances, or understandings that each party will jointly come to the other's aid in the event of a threat to the signatories' security, nevertheless represent a desire to take action with the aid of another rather than seeking a unilateral resolution to a problem. In this way, bilateralism is more closely related to multilateralism than either is to unilateralism. Bilateral relations render multilateral cooperation less complex. Further multilateral cooperation may be understood dyadically or in the bilateral relations that compose the whole.[27] Yet the operation of true bilateralism is simply the joint action of two states in tandem. The United States and Great Britain, for example, jointly undertook the early stages of Operation Enduring Freedom in Afghanistan in October 2001. Once the air campaign was underway, the Northern Alliance also became involved very quickly, thus moving the operation from a bilateral campaign to a multilateral one. Yet the joint U.S.-British action in the opening days of the war can be understood as bilateralism, even if the multilateral apparatus was salient (i.e., NATO with the Northern Alliance).[28]

Multilateralism

Multilateralism refers to collective responses to international problems: acting in concert with other states to manage a policy issue. Instead of acting alone, three or more states consult and confront a foreign policy situation together. International institutions are both manifestations of and vehicles for multilateralism. The broader debate within the field has centered on internationalism versus isolationism, or on unilateral versus multilateral strategies.[29] The arguments have developed along a number of lines.

A first line of inquiry has been to analyze whether or not multilateralism is a better approach for states than is unilateralism. Arguments here have ranged from exploring how or if multilateralism enhances security for all to assessing whether or not democracies, through the adoption of multilateral approaches to conflict, are more successful at winning wars than are other state types.[30] An important component of these arguments has been to assess whether or not multilateral approaches are better than unilateral ones as a consequence of the legitimacy they accord states availing themselves of these strategies and institutions.[31] Interestingly, despite the assertion of the connection between multilateralism and legitimacy, the link is not usually examined but simply assumed. For example, Kreps argues that although multilateralism is "cumbersome, slow, and sometimes unnecessary," it accords enormous value in terms of legitimacy.[32] Other arguments revolve around the degree to which American foreign policy is characterized by unilateralism or multilateralism and the implications of the United States' policy choices, particularly under the George W. Bush administration.[33]

Scholars who explore the dynamics of coalition warfare in particular often do so in the context of specific wars.[34] Some of the findings of these authors are significant and worthy of exploration in the broader context of coalition dynamics.[35]

Ruggie provides a detailed discussion of the meaning of multilateralism. He powerfully argues that multilateralism is not simply institutional design but principle as well. Principles give meaning and life to the institutional arrangement at hand. In other words, multilateralism contains within it a commitment to acting in concert with others, "without regard to the particularistic interests of the parties or the strategic exigencies that may exist in any specific occurrence."[36] Ruggie's ideas are foundational to ideological multilateralism. But what happens in the cases of states acting in concert with one another because they believe that doing so will best serve their interests? This is not unilateralism, because in this case states are not acting alone or even autonomously. In addition, Ruggie argues that "*multilateral* is an adjective that modifies the noun institution."[37] Yet this leaves less formal institutional arrangements such as coalitions unexamined.

Multilateralism is frequently understood as states acting via an international institution rather than alone. Yet ultimately, unilateralism and multilateralism are labels that should center on behavior—how states act, either alone or in concert with others. From this perspective, the Bush administration, unwilling or unable to act against Saddam Hussein without constructing a large coalition at great expense to the United States, actually appeared very committed to multilateralism.[38]

Yet there is a difference between acting together with one's close allies or partner countries and taking action via a global organization, such as the United Nations. When states take multilateral action via the United Nations, they can do so in many different ways. Examples include a UN peacekeeping operation or other action sanctioned by the UN Security Council but directed by one of the major powers in the international system.

With the advent of the Bush doctrine, more scholarly attention focused on unilateralism rather than multilateralism.[39] For example, Brooks and Wohlforth cogently argued that the Bush administration used multilateralism only strategically, never as an end in and of itself, at great potential cost, including the possibility of counterbalancing against the United States, reduced potential gains from institutionalized cooperation, and reduced international legitimacy of American hegemony.[40] Carter argued that the perils of unilateralism included reduced credibility abroad, increased resentment by allies and adversaries, and a reduced likelihood of U.S. foreign policy success.[41] Buzan catalogs

American unilateralism from the Reagan administration through the administration of George W. Bush, arguing that unilateralism is not simply correlated with unipolarity.[42] Kreps successfully looks at U.S. choices to employ multilateralism despite the associated costs and the fact that the United States could easily have undertaken its missions alone.[43]

While Brooks and Wohlforth suggest that multilateralism and unilateralism are opposite points on a spectrum, most treatments of the concepts suggest a dichotomy between them.[44] Carter and Buzan both list examples of American unilateralism. For Carter, the U.S. rejection of the Kyoto Protocol, the Ottawa Convention, the Comprehensive Nuclear-Test-Ban Treaty, and the verification procedures of the Biological Weapons Convention, as well as its rejection of the International Criminal Court, among many others, serve as illustrations.[45] Buzan's examples include the U.S. refusal to join the International Criminal Court and to abide by the 1949 Geneva Conventions with regard to prisoners held at Guantánamo Bay, tariffs on steel and agriculture subsidies, and its decision to go to war against Iraq without a UN Security Council resolution authorizing the action.[46] In contrast, Kreps makes the important point that multilateralism should be examined both quantitatively and qualitatively; the numbers of states are easily manipulated, which allows unilateralism to "masquerade as multilateralism."[47] This suggests that the qualitative dimension is more important than the quantitative one, even though the latter clearly matters in regard to coordination.

The paradox of American unilateralism in the Bush era is that the international community widely perceived the administration as unilateralist, and yet in the most important arena of foreign policy making, the prosecution of the wars in Afghanistan and Iraq, the United States opted—at great cost, at least in Iraq—to fight via coalition.[48] This has several important implications. First, the labels of "multilateralist" and "unilateralist" may indicate the general orientation of an administration in its approach to foreign policy making—in essence, how consultative an administration is with the rest of the international community and how concerned it is perceived to be with the interests of other states, regardless of the actual decisions the administration makes to act alone or in concert with others. In other words, the labels of "multilateralist" and "unilateralist" may be used to indicate the general perception of the international community of a country in the system, or the general perception the country wishes to project, rather than the actual behavior of the country in question. Even if a country tends to act in concert with others, the perception of it in the international system may nevertheless be unilateralist. Finally, and perhaps most importantly, while the meaning of multilateralism may be action taken by more than two states in the international system to address a foreign policy issue, it is often construed as something broader and deeper. Reading between the lines of public-opinion polls and scholarly literature on multilateralism, the concept of multilateralism is often constituted more as an ideology—one of collective action, with an emphasis on shared norms and values—and a belief that acting through international organizations in the system is preferable to organizing collective action outside the main global institutions in the system. In this view, multilateralism is a desire for shared governance.

A genuine desire on the part of the international community to deal collectively with an issue in the international system constitutes one understanding of ideological multilateralism. Burden sharing is less likely to be a problem in these coalitions than in strategic multilateral frameworks, which one country may initiate to serve its own interests.[49] In these strategic multilateral coalitions, the country whose interest is being served assumes the majority of costs. As Brooks and Wohlforth observe, multilateralism is strategic when "doing so is easier or especially advantageous, but never as an end in itself, and certainly not one whose pursuit merits bearing high costs."[50] In other words, strategic multilateralism represents a course of action taken for calculated, self-serving reasons. It is not undertaken out of a sense of commitment to the international community or a desire to forge international consensus, but rather as a means to reach wholly strategic ends.

Yet multilateral war fighting may be instrumental in both ideological and strategic ways. States may undertake multilateralism to allow a coalition or alliance to represent or manifest international legitimacy, that is, for ideological purposes. This constitutes a second understanding of ideological multilateralism.[51] States may also seek to form a coalition or act via alliance to augment the resources brought to bear in prosecuting a war, that is, for strategic purposes. There may be a tension between these two instrumental motivations in regard to institutional design. The design most likely to promote strategic ends (e.g., efficiency in war fighting) may be in conflict with the institutional design that manifests global support. States should be judicious in approaching this trade-off, and yet they often are not, instead seeking arrangements that signal legitimacy at the expense of effective war fighting, as in the second Iraq War.

War fighting may take place via a collective defense organization, such as NATO, or through a global organization, such as a UN-sanctioned coalition. In fact, each of these actions would be multilateral, yet UN-sanctioned coalitions are more likely to be perceived as more legitimate than collective defense operations (although missions that yield UN sanction may receive that sanction because they are deemed legitimate). In other words, UN-sanctioned operations may manifest predominantly ideological multilateral aims, whereas missions of military alliances may have a somewhat greater strategic multilateral component.

In essence, there is an analytical and a practical difference in the way countries fight wars multilaterally. While states may be instrumental in selecting institutional design, they may do so for ideological ends, to signal international legitimacy, or they may do so for strategic ends, to augment resources—or some combination of both aims. However, the tension between these considerations is apparent when assessing the relationship between institutional design and war-fighting effectiveness. In other words, states may seek broad institutional arrangements to fight their wars to signal widespread support for the endeavor, yet such arrangements may undermine war-fighting effectiveness by adding an unwieldy number of actors, each with different rules of engagement and a multitude of national constraints, generating cumbersome decision-making structures and introducing complex interoperability challenges. In other words, putting coalitions together for ideological purposes, or for the purpose of representing international support and legitimacy for an action, may detract from actual war-fighting capability.

Linking the institutional literature on multilateralism to multinational war-fighting operations also reveals that the literature on multilateralism often focuses on implementation rather than intention. For example, in both the Gulf War and the Iraq War, the United States desired to act through the United Nations but resolved to go to war in any event. It succeeded in gaining UN support in the first war but not the second. In each case, the United States' intention was to act in concert with other states in the system. The intention was not unilateral, as was the case, for example, in Operation Urgent Fury, the U.S. invasion of Grenada in 1983.[52]

Further, understanding the nuances in multilateralism also helps us understand the profound differences between fighting wars via long-standing alliance as opposed to ad hoc coalition. Just as multinational war efforts have largely been ignored in the context of studies of multilateralism, so too have military alliances been neglected in the context of understanding the way international institutions work[53]. And yet war prosecution and alliance institutionalization

Table 2.1 Typologies of state military action: Linking institutions to war fighting

Typology of action	Definition
Unilateralism	State confronts military threat alone
Bilateralism	Two states (or one state and one indigenous group) jointly intervene in military conflict
Multilateralism	Three or more states collectively confront a military threat
Global institution	Multilateral effort organized and sanctioned by global international institution such as the United Nations
Collective defense organization	Military alliance of three or more countries takes collective action against another state or set of states
Coalition	Ad hoc multinational understandings that are forged to undertake a specific mission and that dissolve once that mission is complete

NOTE: These typologies are restricted to state action rather than exclusively nonstate actors. This is not to say that nonstate actors do not undertake military action as above, but the focus of this book is on military alliances among state actors, rather than civil wars, ethnic violence, or other military engagements involving substate or transnational actors, although some of the arguments here may be generalizable to those types of engagements.

are highly consequential and worthy of scholarly attention. Since coalitions are generally formed with an eye to a specific mission, their purpose is more limited than long-standing alliances, even if their effects are consequential.[54] Understanding the effects of institutional design is fundamental to a realist institutionalist agenda. The typologies of action are summarized in Table 2.1.

Multinational war fighting, which has become predominant in U.S. military strategy, is a subset of multilateralism. Insights about multilateralism are relevant to understanding the dynamics of alliances in both peacetime and wartime, as well as coalition operations. How we understand multinational action in the security sphere can deepen our knowledge about the way institutions work more generally and can advance our understanding of the way in which institutions advance states' strategic goals.

Military alliances and wartime coalitions function as a key subset of multilateralism. While states act in concert with others in a number of different areas of international life, few are as consequential as multinational war fighting. I turn now to this particular component of multilateralism: the dynamics of alliances and wartime coalitions.

THE NORM OF COALITION WARFARE

One reason it is so important to understand multilateralism is that fighting alongside friends is a deep-seated tradition in the American way of war. Since the beginning of the twentieth century, the nature of American warfare has changed dramatically. While most of the United States' nineteenth-century wars were fought unilaterally, the advent of modern warfare brought with it a decidedly bilateral and multilateral element. At the end of the nineteenth century, the web of European military alliances represented interests across the globe.

At the dawn of the new century, those complex relationships and colonial entanglements heightened systemic insecurity and ultimately culminated in mass mobilizations and hegemonic war. Until World War I, the United States' experience in war was largely unilateral, having fought against Great Britain, France, North African states, and Spain, or it was civil in nature, which was crucial in forging the identity of the young nation (e.g., colonists fighting against Native Americans, the Union versus the Confederacy). With the onset of the twentieth century, however, coalition warfare became the norm for the United States—World War I and World War II, Korea, Vietnam, the Gulf War, interventions in the Balkans, Afghanistan, Iraq, and Libya. Only in its more minor incursions, in Cuba, Grenada, and Panama, did the United States opt to go it alone. Over time, the alliances and coalitions have grown—especially in the post–Cold War era. Further, the norm of fighting alongside others is now deeply entrenched.[55]

As the tradition of fighting with friends has evolved, the United States has heightened its efforts to routinize mechanisms that make coalition warfare more successful. As early as the immediate aftermath of World War II, in 1947, the American, British, and Canadian (ABC) armies' "Plan to Effect Standardization" was established; the Air Standardization Coordinating Committee was created a year later. Australia joined in 1964; New Zealand the following year.[56] In addition, even changes within the U.S. military had important ramifications for the architecture of coalition and alliance warfare.

Jointness became au courant, meaning change and transformation in the American military, particularly with the landmark Goldwater-Nichols Department of Defense Reorganization Act of 1986. At its core, the preoccupation with jointness was a commitment to coordinating the different branches of the U.S. Armed Forces, yet the jointness preoccupation spilled over into the arena of multinational operations as well, since at the same time the military was changing, the number of multinational operations was on the rise. Hence, dealing with increasing jointness meant heightened operational coordination and integration with alliance and coalition partners.

In the mid-1990s, these norms became increasingly institutionalized with the evolution of U.S. military doctrine to deal with the complexities of multinational operations. For example, in October 1996 a doctrine was established, under the direction of the chairman of the Joint Chiefs of Staff, governing the U.S. Armed Forces in joint operations to provide a doctrinal basis for U.S. military involvement in multinational and interagency operations. This document continues to be updated and revised. In addition, the process of strengthening interoperability deepened further in the 1990s with the establishment of the Multinational Interoperability Council in 1996 and the Multilateral Interoperability Program in 1998.[57]

As the nature of military technology has grown more complex, so have the requirements for interoperability. Technology has assisted coalition communication and has made the prerequisites for cooperation more involved than ever. With war's heightened rapidity and the augmented destructive power of contemporary weapons of war, close communications among allies have become ever more crucial. Once the structures for combined operations are established, routinized, and institutionalized, alliance and coalition warfare becomes easier. Once those structures are in place, routinized, and institutionalized, they are more likely to be used, suggesting that bilateral and unilateral operations become less likely in times of crisis. As a consequence, an extra dimension of strategic thinking pervades wartime decision making, and there are added constituencies to consider which influence the war process. For example, policy consistent with the domestic will in Spain culminated in that country's withdrawal from Iraq and dealt a significant blow to the Operation Iraqi Freedom coalition. Widespread domestic opposition in Poland to the Iraq War created a thorny political landscape for that country's leadership. The war-crimes case against seven Polish soldiers for killing Afghan civilians in August 2008 created even more turmoil. Actions and reactions in allied countries impinge directly on the wartime operations of others, often with great consequence. In an extreme case, war weariness in Russia during World War I was instrumental in yielding the Russian Revolution and Russian withdrawal from the war, thus dealing a tremendous blow to the Entente's war-fighting capacity, heralding the end of tsarist Russia, and ultimately culminating in the advent of the Soviet era.

Coalition and alliance warfare also present logistical and practical dangers, including lethal incidents of friendly fire. In March 2003, just north of Basra, Iraq, two American A-10 fighter pilots mistook a four-vehicle British reconnaissance patrol for the enemy, even though the vehicles were decorated with bright orange panels to signal that they were coalition forces. Diving from ten thousand feet to four thousand feet, the pilots bombarded the convoy with more than five hundred rounds a second of armor-piercing shells. The British tried in vain to raise the pilots on the radio, screaming for them to stop, but there was no response—the Americans were on a different frequency. The planes turned and headed inexorably toward the convoy again, strafing their coalition partners a second time. The American pilots never saw—or understood—the red smoke released by the British, another device used for coalition identification. The fratricidal, blue-on-blue incident killed one British soldier and wounded another.[58] This is just one of many friendly-fire incidents in Operation Iraqi Freedom. In the Gulf War, nearly a quarter of American battle deaths were a consequence of friendly fire; in that war, the United States killed as many British combatants as the enemy did.[59]

As the numbers of states involved in contemporary alliances and coalitions grow, the problems of coordination grow as well.[60] Certainly there are strategic benefits to fighting with friends, but there are liabilities as well. Given the evolution of the United States' commitment to fighting wars multinationally, it is useful to examine the costs and benefits as well as the institutional arrangements that work best for effective war fighting—above all, the best path to achieving war aims and prevailing over adversaries.

PEACETIME VERSUS WARTIME ALLIANCES

States are rarely idle in regard to preparations for military action. Even countries that have not been at war in centuries, such as Switzerland, nevertheless attend carefully to military affairs.[61] For some countries, such preparations include forging alliances with other countries in the international system to advance their security in some fashion, be it to counter a shared threat, to manage an internal threat, or to advance an interest of some kind.[62] The functions these alliances serve when nations are at peace are often fundamentally different from the ones they serve when at war.

Military alliances are generally formed to advance the strategic interests of participating states, in regard to hedging, tethering, balancing, or bandwagoning motivations. Security may be enhanced through the guarantees codified in an alliance treaty, through the intended or unintended consequence of keeping the peace among allies, or through the prospect of deterring one's enemies from encroaching on a core value. During peacetime, alliances may be forged to prevent war from happening—whether war among allies or war between the alliance partners and external enemies. Yet once wars occur and alliances do not dissolve, the ways in which the alliance functions are profoundly altered. Alliances then become vehicles through which states seek to prevail over their adversaries and achieve their war aims. This works more effectively in some cases than others.

PEACETIME FUNCTIONS OF ALLIANCES

Military alliances are most commonly considered strategies in a state's arsenal to counter an imbalance of power or to combat a shared external threat.[63] Inherent in this perspective is the idea that alliances allow states to add the power of their allies to their own to deter enemies or to prevail in the event of war. In contrast to pure military balancing, or "hard balancing," weaker states may undertake more limited measures short of military alliances to counteract a more powerful state, which some scholars have called "soft balancing."[64]

The way in which balancing behavior manifests differs depending on the distribution of capabilities in the system and perceptions of offense or defense dominance.[65] In multipolar systems, when states confront common threats in the system and perceive defensive strategies as dominant, their alliance choices will give rise to buck-passing, or relying on others to challenge the threatening country. According to Mearsheimer, buck-passing is preferable to balancing since it is cheaper. In bipolar systems, however, states must balance against their rivals; no other state is sufficiently powerful to effectively pass the buck.[66] According to Christensen and Snyder, when states face common threats under multipolarity and there is a perception that offensive strategies dominate, chain-ganging behavior will occur; states will "unconditionally tie themselves to reckless allies whose survival is seen to be indispensable to the maintenance of the balance."[67]

Tierney, elaborating on the chain-ganging behavior of alliances, argues that in tight alliance systems, states may engage in offensive chain ganging, in which states are rendered more bellicose by their alliance partners, or defensive chain ganging, in which bellicose states are restrained by their allies. The management function of alliances as an important alliance motivation has garnered increased interest, particularly in the post–Cold War era.[68]

Tethering: The Management Function of Alliances

While balancing is indeed a central role of alliances, it is by no means the only one. Scholars such as Schroeder have sought to understand the conflict management role of these institutions.[69] Elaborating on this perspective, I have argued that a military alliance may be forged to contain an adversarial relationship; that is, states tether their enemies to themselves to neutralize the threat.[70] From this point of view, alliances function as other international institutions do, to enhance transparency, increase the costs of defection, and make cooperation cheaper and therefore more likely. Long and colleagues further examine the institutionalization function of alliances and find that it successfully keeps the peace among member states.[71]

Viewing alliances as institutions generates insights into the ways in which threats within an alliance are managed. Thus NATO, in the words of its first secretary-general, Lord Ismay, was originally formed "to keep the Soviets out, the United States in, and the Germans down."[72] Examining NATO purely as a balancing response to the Soviet Union misses the important dynamics that exist within the alliance. Both Greece and Turkey are members of the NATO alliance despite the fact that they are each other's enemies; they are not adding the other's power to their own in the context of the alliance. Nonetheless, by being allied adversaries, they may gain important institutional advantages in transparency and conflict management.

One unintended consequence, however, of effective tethering alliances is that although they are formed to manage conflicts among signatories, they may appear threatening to nonmembers, thus heightening the level of threat and uncertainty in the international system. I call this dynamic the alliance paradox and argue that it culminates in a higher probability of war in the system.[73]

Pressman further develops the idea of alliances as mechanisms of restraint. Some states choose alliance partners to prevent war from occurring.[74] In a series of case studies, Pressman explores in detail two of the most important U.S. alliances, that with Israel and that with the United Kingdom.

Bandwagoning

Another alliance motivation that scholars have explored is when states seek to form an alliance to protect themselves from a very powerful and threatening enemy. Here, states bandwagon with the threatening state, capitulating to it to ensure survival.[75] Schweller persuasively argues that bandwagoning behavior may be viewed as something small states do for strategic gain, given their inability to counter the power capabilities of a strong state.[76] While bandwagoning behavior occurs more rarely than balancing, the bandwagoning logic is used often to explain or justify certain foreign policy objectives. For example, the fear of dominoes falling employs bandwagoning logic, or the belief that a hostile state will reap allies through victory culminating in a snowball effect. Realists generally posit that balancing is more prevalent than bandwagoning behavior, although Schweller argues that it is not as uncommon as earlier realists such as Waltz and Walt maintained.[77]

Hedging

I have described hedging behavior as states forming low-commitment alliances to draw other states into their sphere of influence. This allows the initiating state to consolidate its power and shut off avenues of potential rivals' expansion while not being overly provocative. Hedging alliances allow states more freedom of action in the international system, and they may set the stage for enhanced cooperation among signatories in the future. The Partnership for Peace initiatives and the Shanghai Cooperation Organization, which includes China and Russia among its signatories, are examples.[78] Robert Art uses the concept of hedging to understand European security policy in the post–Cold War period. Although less well developed than other alliance motivations, under conditions of reduced systemic threat, hedging options remain important.[79] Here, other motivations, such as ideology, regime type, identity, and domestic politics may come into play as well.[80]

Cohesion

The reasons states form alliances affect the degree to which they are able to agree on goals and strategies for attaining those goals.[81] In balancing alliances, in which states are driven by their mutual desire to contain a mutual adversary, cohesion is relatively easy to generate and maintain. In other types of alliances, especially tethering ones, cohesion is far more difficult to achieve. The proportion of external to internal threat determines the ease with which cohesion is generated.[82]

In wartime, cohesion is far more complex.[83] Agreement on war aims and strategies to achieve them translates into fighting effectiveness. Efficacious war fighting entails successfully coordinating troops and managing interoperability issues. The dictates of cohesion differ depending on the strategic environment. An essential aspect of that is whether or not states are at war. Thus, it is important to examine the prerequisites of cohesion under these different conditions.

FROM PEACE TO WAR

During peacetime, states may consult and plan together, thinking ahead in the event that war comes.[84] Once at war, every aspect of states' deployment decisions needs to be jointly considered and understood; tasks must be divided, and command, control, communication, and intelligence mechanisms must work effectively. It is much easier to function as a peacetime ally than one at war. Symbolic and verbal expressions of alliance are not as costly, nor the consequences as potentially lethal, as when allies are at war. In addition to close consultation, which requires an enormous amount of transparency and trust, allies at war must intertwine their political and strategic aims to ensure the alliance endures. The cost of defection during war can be devastating. Once blood is spilled—states pay the price of friendship with their lives—the complexities of alliance politics grow.[85]

This is not to say that allies in peacetime do not intertwine their policy making and strategic thinking. Yet peacetime military alliances vary a great deal in the degree to which states coordinate their military strategies—in other words, the degree to which they prepare for joint fighting. For example, despite the fact that the alliance preceded World War I by thirty-five years, the Central Powers' joint war planning prior to war was minimal. The Entente powers, in contrast, had consulted and coordinated their military planning before World War I much more closely.[86]

Contemporary military strategists understand the importance of close consultation and coordination. As a consequence, NATO has become the most institutionalized alliance in history.[87] For fifty years before its first active mission, NATO member states consulted on a command structure and developed detailed integrated military plans in the event of war. Despite that detailed planning, once NATO embarked on its first wartime mission in the former Yugoslavia, the decision-making structure proved itself more appropriate for peacetime than wartime functioning. The onerous decision-making structure was not well suited to quick and responsive action necessary during war, especially since it was not the same war as that for which it had planned.[88]

Because the dynamics of alliances are so different in peacetime from in wartime, the prerequisites of cohesion are different as well. Cohesion—the ability to agree on goals and strategies toward attaining those goals—derives from different sources in peacetime than wartime.[89] During peacetime, cohesion will result from the different levels of threat, both within the alliance and external to it.[90] During wartime, cohesion is more complicated.

First, threats that are compatible during peacetime may not be so during wartime. For example, two states equally threatened by an external alliance may balance together and form a cohesive alliance during peacetime. Once war comes, exactly from where the threat derives matters powerfully. A compatible external threat during peacetime may not be so during wartime—for example, Austria-Hungary and Germany were threatened by the Franco-Russian alliance in the pre–World War I period. Yet once war came, the fact that Austria-Hungary was principally threatened by Russia and Germany by France created enormous problems for the Central Powers in maintaining the cohesion of their alliance.[91] When states face external threats in peacetime, alliance cohesion will be easy to foster and maintain. Yet during wartime, the source of the threat matters.[92]

Second, because peacetime alliance costs are often not as great in terms of lives and treasure, second image constraints may not be quite as operative as they are during wartime. Particularly in countries with electoral accountability, states will be highly sensitive to the costs and benefits of military action in terms of leadership, the paying public, and the media. In July 2009, when fifteen British soldiers were killed in ten days in Afghanistan—eight on the bloodiest day of the war for the British—the media immediately raised the question of Britain's commitment to the war effort.[93] This sensitivity heightens the complexity of wartime alliances, as witnessed by President Obama's tribute to the British role in Afghanistan in the aftermath of the battle deaths.[94]

Third, capability asymmetries within alliances during peacetime matter much less in fostering cohesion than they do during wartime. While burden sharing affects cohesion in both peacetime and wartime, during wartime the costs are much greater in terms of lives and treasure.[95] Table 2.2 outlines the different effects of symmetry in capabilities on peacetime and wartime alliances, ceteris paribus.

Because long-standing, highly institutionalized alliances are usually established during peacetime, their wartime operation may be unwieldy and prob-

Table 2.2 Effect of capability distribution on the cohesion of peacetime and wartime alliances

	Symmetrical capabilities	Asymmetrical capabilities
Peacetime alliances	Some jockeying for preeminence in alliance, which creates problems for cohesion, especially in pluralistic alliances	Alliance is controlled by most powerful state, and cohesion is fostered by security benefits provided to smaller states
Wartime alliances	May be conflict over war aims, but when burden sharing is relatively egalitarian, cohesion is enhanced	Lack of symmetry gives rise to more dependence on most powerful country, which creates problems for achieving and maintaining cohesion

lematic. These alliances generally have rigid structures that are not suitable for effective or efficient wartime operation. Further, the demands on member states in regard to integration of forces are high, which creates a natural tension with states' desires to maintain national control of their troops. Hence, long-standing military alliances may actually be less cohesive in wartime than are ad hoc coalitions.

Furthermore, during wartime, power asymmetries will be felt more acutely in alliances than in coalitions, since ad hoc coalitions are driven by an immediate threat that will foster cohesion and make internal power disparities less important than in preexisting alliances with decision-making structures constructed during peacetime. Peacetime alliances that function during wartime will experience threats in a more diverse and diffuse way than ad hoc coalitions, which in turn will undermine their wartime effectiveness.

In addition, the institutional arrangements designed by policy makers and strategists impinge greatly on cohesion and fighting effectiveness. Selecting a long-standing peacetime alliance to function in wartime or building a coalition to meet the challenges at hand will have varying effects on cohesion.

Moreover, the ways in which power is distributed within the coalition or alliance may culminate in according disproportionate leverage to smaller states during wartime to maintain continued involvement. During peacetime, fears of entrapment may dominate the lead power's alliance and coalition choices, yet during wartime, fears of abandonment may mediate the lead power's decision making—the reverse is true for smaller states. This grants significant leverage to smaller states during wartime operations. In other words, instead of being coerced or bullied, coalition or alliance partners may be begged and bribed.[96]

Finally, selecting broad multinational arrangements for war prosecution to signal global support and legitimacy may actually undermine the ability of states to effectively fight and may not culminate in augmented legitimacy.

WARTIME ALLIANCES VERSUS COALITIONS: INSTITUTIONS OF INTERSTATE VIOLENCE

Not all wartime partnerships are created equal. In some cases, an alliance concluded during peacetime is called on to prosecute a war. In other instances, once war is imminent or has already begun, states come together in an ad hoc coalition designed for the express purpose of fighting. Preexisting alliances benefit from preexisting decision-making structures and joint planning, yet coalitions benefit from being tailored for the express purpose for which they are to be used.

In terms of effective fighting capability, military alliances have the advantage of providing opportunities for joint war planning; stable relations among allies; the opportunity to create effective command, control, and information structures; and agreed-on decision-making mechanisms. All of these factors should make coordinating action during wartime easier than in coalition operations. Yet because alliances that operate in war are usually created during peacetime, the transition is not so easy. This is true for several reasons. First, egalitarian decision-making structures that foster cohesion during peacetime create onerous procedures not well suited to the quick, decisive action necessary during war.[97] Second, not all alliance partners will be equally threatened, nor will they be likely to all desire wartime action equally. In other words, during wartime fears of entrapment are likely to outweigh fears of abandonment.[98] Finally, threats that are compatible during peacetime do not necessarily translate into compatible threats during wartime.

Coalitions and wartime alliances are both subsets of multinational operations, which may include other forms of multilateral cooperation, such as peacekeeping missions. Coalitions are ad hoc multinational understandings that are forged to undertake a specific mission, and they dissolve once that mission is complete. They are not wholly analytically distinct from wartime alliances, although the latter may have a greater degree of institutionalization and may exist before a specific wartime operation. Coalitions may be mandates of the international community and authorized by international organizations such as the United Nations. Others may be charged with missions that stem from one state or set of states in the system, frequently great powers.

Wartime alliances are formal or informal agreements between two or more states intended to further (militarily) the national security of the participating states, usually in the form of joint consultation and cooperation to prevail in war against a common enemy or enemies. Such alliances are usually concluded in peacetime in order to prevent or to prevail in war, but they continue to operate under wartime conditions. States augment their joint planning and consultation, and sometimes integrate their forces as their plans for war unfold and are implemented. Member states usually expect that the alliance will endure beyond any specific war or crisis.[99] There is a range of commitment levels that alliances may provide. I identify six: (1) a promise to maintain benevolent neutrality in the event of war; (2) a promise to consult in the event of military hostilities with an implication of aid; (3) promises of military assistance and other aid in event of war but without prepared or explicit conditions specified in advance; (4) a promise to come to the active assistance of an ally under specific circumstances; (5) an unconditional promise of mutual assistance, short of joint planning, with division of forces; and (6) an unconditional promise of mutual assistance in the event of attack with preplanned command and control and the integration of forces and strategy.[100]

Coalitions forged to combat a specific threat come in various forms. Contemporary coalitions formed by the United States to fight in the first Gulf War, Afghanistan, and Iraq have many features in common, yet many differences as well. The advantage of creating such coalitions is that they can be tailored for the specific needs of the mission at hand. Some of these coalitions—namely the first Gulf War—are forged as a consequence of a genuine desire to collectively address the wishes of the international community.[101] In reality, contemporary coalitions are often constructed in ways that are not always conducive to the national interest of the country initiating them.

First, the large scale of contemporary coalitions may actually reduce fighting effectiveness by creating additional complexities in regard to decision making, interoperability, and burden sharing. Second, contemporary coalitions are being formed with an eye to legitimize international operations rather than to increase war-fighting effectiveness, even if those efforts at establishing legitimacy may meet with varied success.

Fighting effectiveness of multinational forces requires a clear chain of command, decision making, interoperability, equitable burden sharing, technology, human power, and resources. The larger the coalition is, the more difficult it becomes to maintain effectiveness along these lines. In addition, as the size of a fighting force grows, managing the differences in rules of engagement becomes more difficult. For example, during the invasion of Iraq in March 2003, fourteen Australian Hornet pilots defied the orders of their American commanding officers. These pilots independently aborted forty bombing missions at the last minute because they believed that the objects of attack were not valid military targets or that dropping their bombs would result in an alarming number of civilian casualties. None of the pilots was reprimanded—they were following Australian rules of engagement.[102]

Contemporary coalition warfare differs from its historical counterparts in that coalitions formed by the United States in the post–Cold War and post–9/11 eras contain a significant number of American allies. Because the experience of NATO in the former Yugoslavia revealed that the unwieldy nature of the decision-making structure was at odds with the need for quick, decisive action during wartime, the United States opted to construct coalitions in the succeeding missions. Even with its longtime allies, the United States concluded bilateral agreements rather than using the preexisting multilateral framework available through NATO.[103] These agreements have the advantage of allowing the United States to fight alongside allies with shared experience in training and enhanced interoperability while maintaining flexibility in decision-making arrangements available through coalitions.[104]

INSTITUTIONAL DESIGN AND EFFECTIVENESS

The prerequisites of fighting multilaterally are substantial. When states fight alone, the demands of command, control, coordination, and intelligence are tremendous; multilateral operations multiply those concerns. The most pressing issues are interoperability, effective decision making, size of the multilateral operation, war aims, durability of the institutional structure, and cohesion and fighting effectiveness.

Interoperability

States fighting together during wartime represent one of the deepest forms of cooperation in the international system. At a minimum, states must coordinate their military activity; at a maximum, they must ensure that their communication and weapons systems are compatible and able to work together, including standardizing weapons systems, war tactics, and the training of military forces.[105] More specifically, interoperability refers to "the ability of systems, units or forces to provide services to and accept services from other systems, units, or forces and to use the services so exchanged to enable them to operate effectively together."[106]

The level of interoperability varies according to institutional arrangement. NATO member states emphasize interoperability, yet there is variation even within the alliance. For example, the partnership of the United States, Great Britain, Canada, Australia, and New Zealand is the "interoperability standard bearer."[107] This partnership, now more than sixty years old, grew out of World War II cooperation among the ABC states. In 1946, a decision was made to attempt to standardize the weapons, tactics, and training of the three states. This arrangement evolved over time. Despite close cooperation and communication, however, even U.S. and British interoperability did not approach the level that U.S. joint regulations required.[108] In other words, even without language barriers, and even among the closest of allies, interoperability issues matter.

Multinational war fighting is distinctive from unilateral endeavors. While blue-on-blue incidents occur even when fighting alone, the risks of friendly fire grow as the number of coalition partners increases. The expense of harmonizing equipment grows as well. For example, the United States created a $200 million coalition solidarity fund in 2005 to support such harmonization for its allies fighting in Iraq and Afghanistan. In addition, because of its incomparable size, the United States paid to airlift Polish troops to Iraq, built their camps, and provided them with equipment.[109]

In summary, there are degrees to which interoperability challenges confront partners on the battlefield. Long-standing alliances have an advantage of taking interoperability issues into consideration before military operations. Coalitions that include long-standing allies may similarly benefit. But new allies and coalition partners may be especially costly to incorporate into an effective and harmonious fighting institutional structure.

Prerequisites for Decision Making

As with interoperability, the need for a coherent, legitimate decision-making structure for war decisions may be complicated during wartime operations of alliances and coalitions. Long-standing, highly institutionalized alliances such as NATO have a standing decision-making structure, which may be adapted for wartime in the event of military hostilities. Coalitions have the advantage of flexibility—the decision-making structure that develops will be specifically tailored to the task and countries at hand.

A decision-making structure needs to specify a chain of command as well as the mechanism of governance and rules guiding collective decisions. While a chain of command generally suggests a hierarchical decision-making system, in order to preserve sovereignty, states often retain some element of decision-making authority. This can run the spectrum from insisting that decisions are made by consensus, giving all states an effective veto over critical decisions, to allowing troops to operate under the command of another state while still observing their own national rules of engagement.

Size

The size of a military alliance or coalition in wartime matters for the ease with which interoperability issues are resolved and the efficiency with which decisions may be made. Intuitively, the larger the coalition, the more challenging coordination will be. The United States in particular has increasingly used coalition warfare as its strategy to prosecute wars, and coalition warfare has been an enduring feature of the international system.[110]

In the past two centuries, the number of states involved in any one war has grown dramatically. Coalition size has exploded as the number of the states in the international system has grown. The trend line is documented in Figure 2.1, which draws from the Militarized Interstate Disputes (MID) data.

The size of multinational operations plays a key role in affecting the complexity of coalitional dynamics. It matters in influencing the intracoalition negotiations that occur, and it impinges upon the war termination process, as I discuss below. The trend in increased overall size of coalitions also matters. It is important to note, however, that while the absolute number of states involved in coalition warfare has grown over time, when weighted as a percentage of total number of states in the system, it has not. In other words, coalition size as a proportion of states in the system has remained fairly fixed over the past century.

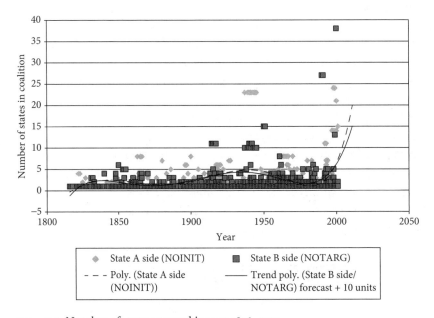

Figure 2.1 Number of states engaged in war, 1816–2001

SOURCE: Patricia A. Weitsman and Asher E. Balkin, "(W)hither Unilateralism? Coalition Warfare in the New Millennium," paper presented at the annual meeting of the American Political Science Association, Philadelphia, September 2006.

NOTE: NOINIT = number of initiating states; NOTARG = number of target states.

What has changed, however, is the size of coalitions that the United States has forged. Figure 2.2 depicts a graph of the size of the coalitions for wars in which the United States was classified as the initiator, drawn from the MID data.

The trend in the past century for the United States has been very noticeably away from unilateralism. The United States has become less inclined to engage in war making in the absence of coalition partners. According to a comprehensive list of all U.S. multinational operations, there were eleven operations between 1900 and 1982 and thirteen operations from 1991 to 2005.[111] While not all of these operations required a significant amount of military intervention and joint planning, what is clear is that the operations have become increasingly complex. As a consequence, the "doctrine for the Armed Forces of the United States when they operate as part of a multinational force" on the part of the chairman of the Joint Chiefs of Staff suggests that coalition warfare is likely to continue to figure significantly in decisions to employ force in the future.[112] What is particularly noteworthy here is that the United States has become increasingly multilateral in its war-fighting strategy despite the fact

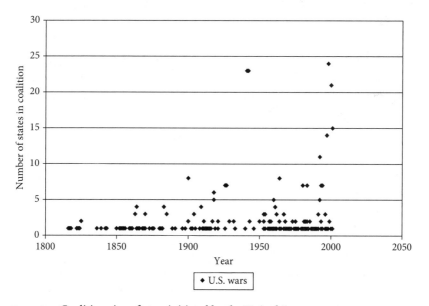

Figure 2.2 Coalition size of wars initiated by the United States

SOURCE: Patricia A. Weitsman and Asher E. Balkin, "(W)hither Unilateralism? Coalition Warfare in the New Millennium," paper presented at the annual meeting of the American Political Science Association, Philadelphia, September 2006.

that the overall trend in the system has stayed the same. Coalitional wars—defined as wars involving at least one alliance—as a percentage of the total number of militarized interstate disputes in the system have shown little change from 1816 to 2004. According to the MID data, coalition warfare represents about 58.8 percent of all wars in the international system throughout that time period.

A number of implications for reliance on coalition warfare as a key element of prosecuting wars require close examination. The war process will be affected along a number of dimensions. First, the larger the coalition or alliance, the more complex the decision-making procedures will be and the more difficult achieving consensus will be. Second, the more actors that are involved, the more challenges states will face in achieving interoperability and coordination in action, and friendly-fire incidents will be difficult to avoid. Finally, as the number of states in an alliance or coalition grows, the less autonomy states have in action.

Duration of Institution

The length of time an institution has endured may affect its operation in wartime. Long-standing alliances are usually established during peacetime.[113] When called on to act in wartime, the decision-making mechanisms and chain of command may not be well suited to the mission, or they may be unwieldy and inefficient when quick and nimble processes are necessary. In addition, there is an inevitable tension between states' desires to retain control of their troops and the necessities of troop integration during wartime. As a consequence, even if an alliance was institutionalized long before it operates in wartime, this history does not guarantee fighting effectiveness. In some ways, a coalition that is put together with a particular mission in mind has the advantage of being tailored to the goals of the member states.

LEGITIMACY

Defining international legitimacy is a complex endeavor. Legitimate action, behavior, and/or ideas are largely considered historically variable.[114] Ultimately, action or ideas that are deemed legitimate entail an element of "moral appropriateness" and/or are consistent with intersubjective understandings of just or correct principles, or those principles, institutions, norms, or rules that are deemed worthy in themselves of pursuing or obeying.[115] My purpose here is not to determine the substance of what is or what is not legitimate, although such questions are interesting and important. Evaluating the substance of the operation or the moral appropriateness of its mission is not my agenda; rather, I assess the extent to which the international community perceives the operation as legitimate. Thus, the relevant component of legitimacy for the purposes of this study entails the perceptions and public opinion of the international community regarding a military operation. Do they support it? Do they deem the operation legitimate? Hence, public opinion polls can serve as an appropriate measure of the legitimacy of any given operation, while understanding that the idea of legitimacy in international relations is a more complex and nuanced package.

Given that the literature on multilateral war fighting almost uniformly asserts that coalitions, alliances, and global institutions accord legitimacy to action, I explore the extent to which this is true. Ultimately, I argue that legitimacy—or favorable international public opinion—hinges on the mission of an operation, not on the number of states involved in its prosecution. In other words, had the United States intervened unilaterally in the Rwandan genocide, that action may have been received more favorably internationally than was the U.S.-led multinational operation to affect regime change in Iraq. In assessing the legitimacy component of institutions, we can determine whether indeed this is an institutional mechanism that effectively advances a strategic end.[116]

TOWARD AN UNDERSTANDING OF ALLIANCES AND COALITIONS IN WARTIME: CENTRAL QUESTIONS

Wartime alliances and coalitions function as a subset of multilateralism. They entail varying degrees of international cooperation to address or manage a problem in the international system. While states may be strategic with regard to their wartime obligations, by opting to take on these tasks with other nations, their choice necessitates complex institutional design questions, such as command structures, and the need to adapt to other states' strategic decisions. The norm of multilaterally embarking on war is deeply embedded in the American military doctrine and tradition. Vast resources have been applied to deepening military cooperation among traditional allies and augmenting interoperability for new ones.

Institutional design matters powerfully in understanding cohesion and warfighting effectiveness. I argue that coalitions, which may be more adaptable and malleable during wartime, may be a more effective fighting instrument than long-standing alliances called on to act in wartime.

At the center of this book are questions regarding the costs versus benefits of waging war via alliance or coalition. I explore the ways in which institutional structure impinges on war-fighting effectiveness and alliance or coalition cohesion. More specifically, the central questions I explore are the following:

- Did the operation entail the use of an alliance or coalition?
- What were the decision-making structures employed to manage the operation?
- To what extent did fighting multilaterally culminate in challenges in interoperability, burden sharing, and/or friendly fire?
- What was the power distribution within the coalition or alliance? Did it affect the cohesion, fighting effectiveness, and/or leverage of states within the coalition or alliance? In other words, did small states have disproportionate leverage over powerful states in negotiating participation and continued involvement in the operation? Did fears of abandonment mediate U.S. actions, and fears of entrapment dominate its partners' actions?
- To what extent did the size of the alliance or coalition affect cohesion and costs associated with multilateral war fighting? Did interoperability challenges grow with coalition or alliance size?
- Finally, does legitimacy really inhere in the size of the coalition or alliance? Or does it inhere to the mission of the operation?

To assess these questions, I examine five contemporary cases of multilateral warfare: the Gulf War, Operation Allied Force (Kosovo), the second Iraq War, the war in Afghanistan, and the Libyan operation. The cases make the assessment Western and U.S.-centric. However, these are the central post–Cold War cases of multilateral war fighting and are thus the most relevant in advancing policy prescriptions for contemporary warfare and for military alliances formed in peacetime that are brought to bear in wartime. But it does mean that generalizations may be limited to U.S.-centered missions and the unipolar system that has endured since the end of the post–Cold War world. However, these cases provide variation in the independent variable—there is a case of a preexisting alliance, a case of a UN-sanctioned coalition, a case with a coalition that is not UN sanctioned, and a case with a modified institutional alliance structure. Seeing how these differences in institutional design and size affected cohesion, war-fighting effectiveness, interoperability, internal leverage, and legitimacy is critical for advancing our understanding of waging war effectively.

Doing so illuminates the strategic ends of institutions more broadly as well as the components of U.S. power today and in the future. Further, understanding the ways in which contemporary American warfare takes shape in ways that make victory—especially rapid victory—elusive is also essential to understanding larger questions of military strategy.

METHODOLOGY

To answer the central questions of the book, I explore the formation of the alliance or coalition and its duration before the operation in question; the decision-making structure associated with the alliance or coalition; the distribution of power capabilities within the coalition or alliance; the size of the coalition or alliance; and the connection between these factors and war-fighting effectiveness, cohesion, interoperability, internal leverage, and the legitimacy of the operation. More specifically, I qualitatively analyze the relationships among the central concepts, using both primary and secondary sources. The issue of whether or not an alliance or coalition is employed has implications for the decision-making structure that is employed for the operation (Table 2.3), as does the size of the alliance or coalition (Table 2.4). These variables also impinge on the power distribution within the alliance or coalition and the leverage within the institution in question (Table 2.5). The way in which the

Table 2.3 Decision-making structure and alliance and coalition effectiveness

	Hierarchical structure (unity in command)	Egalitarian structure (decision authority diffuse)
Alliance	Operations will be executed efficiently, effectively, and cohesively. There are fewer interoperability and friendly-fire episodes	Operations may suffer from inefficiency, there may be challenges in cohesion, and effectiveness may be inhibited, though interoperability and friendly fire episodes are still contained
Coalition	Operations are executed more efficiently, effectively, and cohesively, although there may be interoperability and friendly-fire challenges; size may mediate outcome	Operations may suffer inefficiencies, challenges in cohesion, and effectiveness. Coalition may be vulnerable to friendly-fire and interoperability challenges

Table 2.4 Size effects

	Small	Large
Alliance	Reduced interoperability and friendly-fire challenges	Some interoperability and friendly-fire challenges
Coalition	Potential for interoperability and friendly-fire challenges depending on exercise and training history	Likely interoperability and friendly-fire challenges

Table 2.5 Internal distribution of capability and the alliance security dilemma

	Asymmetrical power distribution	Symmetrical power distribution
Alliance	Small states may fear abandonment and participate in operation as a consequence	Fears of entrapment may govern decision making
Coalition	Small states may have disproportionate leverage; fears of entrapment by small states prevail, and fears of abandonment by large state dominate	Fears of abandonment may dominate for most member states

Table 2.6 UN sanction and mission legitimacy

	UN sanction	No UN sanction
Alliance	Legitimacy enhanced; public opinion supportive	Legitimacy diminished; public opinion unfavorable to intervention
Coalition	Legitimacy enhanced; public opinion supportive	Legitimacy diminished; public opinion unfavorable to intervention

decision-making structure is constructed and the alliance or coalition power symmetries or asymmetries affect cohesion, war-fighting effectiveness, interoperability, and the legitimacy of the operation in question. Furthermore, Table 2.6 outlines the effect UN sanction should have on the legitimacy of an operation, if the conventional wisdom in regard to this relationship holds.

Alliances generally have egalitarian decision-making structures that frustrate cohesion and war-fighting effectiveness in wartime; coalitions may have more hierarchical decision-making structures, which may enhance cohesion in wartime, even if war-fighting effectiveness and interoperability remain as challenges. Furthermore, the larger the coalition or alliance, the more difficult cohesion, fighting effectiveness, and interoperability become. Alliances may have more symmetrical distributions of power, and coalitions more asymmetrical ones, thus giving disproportionate leverage to partner states in coalitions than in alliances. Finally, the literature overwhelmingly asserts that the fighting multilaterally augments legitimacy—there is no distinction here between alliances and coalitions—which suggests that the larger the coalition or alliance, the more legitimate it is. I explore this relationship qualitatively in each case.

I assess these arguments in the context of five qualitative cases—Operations Desert Storm and Desert Shield, Operation Allied Force, the war in Afghanistan, the second Iraq War, and the Libyan operation. Both wars in Iraq were fought via coalition; Kosovo, Afghanistan, and Libya relied largely on NATO forces. In the subsequent chapters, I qualitatively examine the power symmetries and asymmetries within the coalitions and alliances, the institutional design, the alliance and coalition size, and the consequences for cohesion and fighting effectiveness. Understanding the complexities and consequences of the United States' commitment to multilateral war fighting is critical. The subsequent chapters of this book are intended to deepen our knowledge of the implications of waging war multilaterally.

Alliances and coalitions are critical mechanisms for states to augment power and security. They provide numerous benefits to states, as stalwarts against encroaching threats and as devices to manage conflicts of interest. To preserve these valuable aspects and to maximize the efficiency and efficacy of these instruments of statecraft, it is essential to examine the conditions under which alliances and coalitions serve to advance states' interests and the situations in which they serve as strategic liabilities. More specifically, understanding the variables of wartime and peacetime as well as institutional structure will give us meaningful information on how to best construct multinational operations to advance states' security agendas. As we gain answers to these critical questions, we have a better sense of the institutional mechanisms that serve as conduits of power; how alliances, coalitions, and standing command structures facilitate the actualization of military capability, and those mechanisms that detract from the ability to prevail in conflict. The importance of this web of security institutions forged by the United States to project power becomes a critical component of understanding its future as a hegemon.

In the coming chapters, I explore the central questions in the context of the qualitative cases. Chapter 3 addresses Operation Desert Storm and Operation Desert Shield; Chapter 4 explores Operation Allied Force; Chapter 5 discusses Operation Enduring Freedom and the war in Afghanistan; Chapter 6 focuses on Operation Iraqi Freedom and the war in Iraq; Chapter 7 assesses the Libyan operation. I then provide the central findings and conclusions in Chapter 8.

3 OPERATIONS DESERT STORM AND DESERT SHIELD

THE GULF WAR HERALDED a new era in world politics. It punctuated the end of the Cold War and represented the advent of an age in which global challenges could be met with global solutions. The international community could come together to enforce the norms—in this case, sovereignty—of the system and to punish violators. Following so closely on the heels of the demise of bipolarity and East-West rivalry, the Gulf War suggested that global governance was accessible. The new world order proclaimed by George H. W. Bush seemed to be dawning.

Strategic context mattered powerfully in this case. It was the first unipolar case of intervention in the contemporary era, and it unfolded in the shadow of the end of the Cold War, with the attendant uncertainties and insecurities among states about the system that would ensue. The new epoch offered opportunities and constraints—opportunities for the United States to signal the kind of system it would oversee, the kind of hegemon it would be; it gave other countries opportunities to signal their continued allegiance to the United States and the chance to press the United States for sustained patronage. The Gulf War, more than any other case examined in this book, speaks to the post–Cold War world as much as it does to the eviction of Saddam Hussein's forces from Kuwait. After fifty years of bipolarity, what would the new order bring? What constraints and opportunities would follow? It became evident, for example, that the absence of enduring Soviet-U.S. hostility meant that the United Nations could serve as a vehicle through which international problems could be managed, instead of a politicized arena in which Cold War politics played out. The United Nations need not be stymied by great power rivalry.

The use of the United Nations in this case thus becomes important in several ways—not only to foster support and lend legitimacy, as will be discussed, but also to signal the advent of this new era in world affairs. The Gulf War is a seminal case, one that became a touchstone for the interventions that followed. It was the model—even if no subsequent global problem could be managed in quite the same way and beliefs about global governance dissipated over time.

Working through the United Nations and via multilateral coalition definitely slowed the United States' path to accomplishing its objectives, although the logistics were time consuming as well. The sheer number of forces that had to be mobilized and moved in theater was tremendous. In addition, achieving the goals of the coalition became far more difficult as a consequence of the cumbersome multilateral apparatus through which it prosecuted the war. However, as realist institutionalism reveals, working in this way facilitated the United States' ability to get others to do as it wished and heightened U.S. stature in the system in the process. The United States had already dispatched troops to Saudi Arabia, was already mobilized and mobilizing, and would likely have proceeded with or without UN authorization. Building a coalition and gaining UN authorization in this case illustrates that the United Nations and the multilateral coalition were not simply separate bodies with independent influence, nor were they mere reflections of power. Instead, the United States sought to exercise power through those institutions. This is why the United States would have bypassed the United Nations and the multilateral coalition had it been unable to gain compliance.[1]

This chapter explores the central arguments of the book in the context of Operations Desert Storm and Desert Shield. The purpose is not to provide a detailed account of how the war unfolded,[2] but rather to understand how institutional design affected fighting effectiveness, as well as the extent to which the coalition faced challenges of interoperability, burden sharing, and/or friendly fire. I also explore the power distribution within the coalition, the coalition security dilemma, whether size mattered, and the extent to which the operations were deemed legitimate—and if so, from where that legitimacy derived. I assess the extent to which political, rather than military, logic dominated operational decisions. In other words, which institutional mechanisms advanced strategic ends, and which constrained the achievement of strategic ends? To what extent did the institutions of interstate violence serve as a conduits through which the United States could project power? The case underscores the importance of the United States' standing institutions of power projection, the centrality of institutions in achieving strategic ends, and the areas in which working through multilateral frameworks inhibits effectiveness as well as the spheres in which those frameworks advance states' abilities to prevail in their goals.

THE COALITION

Operations Desert Storm and Desert Shield involved a coalition of almost fifty countries. The coalition was sanctioned by the United Nations, so although constructed at the behest of the United States, these were operations that were in practice global in nature. Desert Shield was designed to deter additional Iraqi aggression, particularly against Saudi Arabia; Desert Storm was an offensive mission intended to expel Iraq from its occupation of Kuwait.[3] The size of the coalition was daunting in regard to constructing a fighting force and to coordinating the agendas and militaries of the participating states. It was highly successful in some areas and less so in others.

The fact that a coalition and not an alliance prosecuted the war in the Persian Gulf was consequential. For example, because the coalition and not NATO fought the war, the NATO airborne warning and control system (AWACS) aircraft, stationed conveniently on Iraq's border in NATO ally Turkey, could not be used. These aircraft could be used only to protect Turkey, not to prosecute Desert Storm. Instead, the United States had to deploy an American AWACS for offensive command and control of the operation.[4] In other words, political decisions regarding the form and function of the war-fighting force had direct military (and economic) implications.

I turn now to an analysis of the primary institutional components of the coalition and its effects to foster greater understanding in regard to which institutional mechanisms promote power projection, which elements do not, and which constrain the actualization of power.[5]

Institutional Design

The institutional structure of the coalition, its decision-making apparatus, had far-reaching implications for war-fighting effectiveness, cohesion, and the management of interoperability challenges. To a large extent, while the institutional design was constructed to perform in the Gulf War, it borrowed from existing structures, particularly U.S. Central Command (CENTCOM). It also had formal ad hoc components as well as informal channels of communication. The bones of the institutional structure, however, came from CENTCOM. The fact that the United States had this standing structure was critical for it in realizing its military goals.

CENTCOM was established during the waning years of the Cold War. Following the Iranian hostage crisis, it became clear to U.S. decision makers that it was necessary to have a rapid deployment force that could be quickly dispatched around the globe in response to such developments. In 1983, the newly established Rapid Deployment Joint Task Force (RDJTF) was transformed into a permanent unified command. Its area of responsibility was the Middle East, East Africa, and Central Asia. Once the Cold War ended, CENTCOM commander in chief (CINCCENT), General Norman Schwarzkopf, began focusing on regional threats; when Saddam Hussein invaded Kuwait in 1990, CENTCOM responded quickly by dispatching troops to Saudi Arabia to deter an Iraqi attack, thus highlighting the importance of these institutions for actualizing power.[6]

In the immediate aftermath of Saddam Hussein's invasion of Kuwait on August 2, 1990, the United States spearheaded an effort to construct a multinational coalition to respond. The United Nations played an important role; the UN Security Council passed a series of resolutions condemning the invasion, demanding Iraq's withdrawal, establishing sanctions, and authorizing the use of force if Iraq did not comply.[7] With the international community unanimously condemning the invasion, and enormous effort on the part of President George H. W. Bush and Secretary of State James Baker, a large coalition of states was forged. The coalition was built beyond countries that were threatened by the invasion, though Iraq's attack did pose a tremendous threat to many. In the region, Saudi Arabia was especially vulnerable. The Gulf Cooperation Council (GCC) countries of Saudi Arabia, Bahrain, United Arab Emirates, Qatar, and Oman (and Kuwait) were alarmed and reacted strongly against the invasion. As Cairo became a center for Kuwaiti refugees, Egypt was also affected by Saddam Hussein's invasion, although Egyptian participation in the coalition culminated in substantial side payments.[8] Tensions had already been running high between Egypt and Iraq concerning Egyptian workers in Iraq; the attack on Kuwait deepened tensions. Syria, also threatened by the attack, responded quickly to the crisis, deploying troops in October.[9] The attack was also perceived as threatening to Western countries that were highly sensitive to the vagaries of the oil markets. This high level of threat effectively galvanized the international community, as did President Bush.

President Bush was instrumental in forging the coalition. He used personal diplomacy and ongoing relationships with world leaders to bring the member states together. Despite Bush's centrality, the coalition manifested ideological

multilateralism. While Bush took a leadership role, there was widespread sentiment in the international community that action needed to be taken and taken
collectively. The shared norm of sovereignty and the value of its preservation
was predominant regarding the decision to intervene. Bush made a point of
constructing a coalition that extended beyond the frontline states. Yet constructing a coalition definitely complicated the operational mission. By the end
of both Desert Shield and Desert Storm, thirty-eight countries, including the
United States, had contributed nearly eight hundred thousand troops.

The Joint Directorate of Planning (JDOP) between the United States and
Saudi Arabia was established in the two weeks following Saddam Hussein's
invasion. The United States took the lead in planning and executing the operations. As General Sir Peter de la Billière, commander in chief of the British
forces in the Gulf War, reported, Norman Schwarzkopf was the person who
"got things done . . . efficiently, and helped and enabled us to win this war."[10] De
la Billière said of Schwarzkopf, "I mean he ran the whole operation and it stood
or fell on his management of it."[11]

Ultimately, command and control of coalition forces was established with
"separate, but parallel lines of authority with U.S. and Saudi Arabian forces
remaining under their respective national command authorities."[12] French land
forces remained under French command, but they were under the operational
control of the Saudis. British forces remained under British command, but operational and tactical control of air and ground forces was given to the United
States. The number of personnel in Desert Storm's tactical air-control system
ultimately reached nearly five thousand.[13] Eventually, Egyptian and Syrian divisions were integrated into the defense.[14] The headquarters for CENTCOM,
as per its request, were located in the same building as the Saudi Ministry of
Defense and Aviation to facilitate coordination of the two staffs.[15] The parallel
command structure allowed largely Arab and Islamic countries' troops to remain under Islamic Arab control and Western countries to maintain control of
the majority of Western troops. In practice, however, to a large extent, coalition
partners had significant autonomy in decisions regarding the deployment of
their own troops and the execution of their missions, even if technically there
was a unified command over the various components of Desert Storm.[16]

The Gulf War coalition decision-making structure was effective—in large
part because of the conscious efforts on the part of the United States and its
key partners, but also because critical aspects of the operations were firmly
within the confines of exclusive U.S. control and within its standing institu-

tional structure, with a direct mission, set of responsibilities, and geographic area of concern for key commanders of combatant commands.[17] In December 1990, for example, as the planning for the first phase of Desert Storm unfolded, most non-U.S. coalition forces were not even included in the initial attacks because the secret of the operational plan was so closely guarded.[18]

The Coalition, Coordination, Communication and Integration Center (C3IC) was established, and later became the cornerstone of the combined operations. It provided the link between the two parallel command structures as well as the place where conflict could be aired, negotiated, and resolved.[19] At first, too few experienced personnel, an absence of mutual operating procedures, and inadequate communications interoperability posed problems, and these relationships changed continuously as more and more countries deployed troops to Saudi Arabia in advance of Operation Desert Storm.[20]

A separate planning cell was established to begin planning Operation Desert Storm. A planning team with representatives from the United States, the United Kingdom, Egypt, and France were at the heart of the effort. "As with everything else in this war, the development of this plan was a team effort involving literally hundreds of people at every echelon of command across the entire coalition."[21] However, the process did not always unfold smoothly.[22] In addition, much of the work was done by the United States, with one British representative in the planning cell.[23] Command and control were definitely a significant challenge throughout the war, and much depended on personal contact among key actors. De la Billière alone reports to have seen Schwarzkopf twice a day for a long period.[24] The challenges among coalition partners were only part of the story. There were also the usual difficulties and tensions among the branches of the military.[25]

During Operation Desert Shield the rift between the operational planners and intelligence widened, and the relationship became so problematic that it was easier for the central planning group "Black Hole" (consisting of joint and allied representatives—though only British planners participated until late 1990, when Saudi planners joined the group) to call Washington, DC, for intelligence rather than rely on in-theater intelligence sources.[26] Washington intelligence often knew when a target had been hit before in-theater sources did. Black Hole ultimately did its own target planning and had its own sources of information.[27]

Ultimately, the complexities of the organizational structure that executed Operations Desert Shield and Desert Storm make an easy summary almost impossible. The air war alone culminated in "a very complicated organizational architecture that combines technology, compartmented information, many people having myriad occupational specialties and perspectives—sometimes with conflicting organizational responsibilities—and numerous agencies, all of which have so many linkages and pathways that naming, let alone tracing, all the connections may be impossible."[28] Further, many of the critical components of the institutional structure relied on informal communication and ad hoc organizations.[29]

To illustrate the unwieldy nature of coalition decision making, the daily air tasking consisted of

> 200 pages in standard message format or approximately 800 pages on the Computer-Assisted Force Management System. It contained times, targets, altitudes, call signs, radio frequencies, and other necessary mission information. CENTAF found its daily construction and dissemination to all units concerned a massive task. The Services and Coalition Forces accepted the need for a single authority to coordinate an air campaign and to provide safe separation of the 2.000 to 3.000 aircraft sorties flown per day in the theater's limited airspace.[30]

The complexity of executing coalition operations was tremendous. From January 17 to February 28, around 120,000 sorties were flown; a daily average of 2,780 with a peak of 3,330 on February 24, 1991.[31] Lieutenant General Horner, joint force air component commander (JFACC), was instrumental in putting together the U.S.-Saudi plan for joint and combined military operations, but there were competing centers of power in running the air war. All central military planners needed to tend to coalition dynamics and developments on the ground, in addition to working with civilian and military leadership in the United States and essential allies.[32]

In principle, prosecuting a war with partners makes sense—there are more states available to advance the objectives at hand. In practice, however, there is an operational burden of communicating within the coalition, dividing the labor effectively, gathering and disseminating information, and negotiating differences in opinion. Tending to the often-competing centers of authority can be complicated, particularly as the number of coalition partners grows.

In summary, the coalition decision-making structure was highly complex and cumbersome, with both formal and informal channels operating simultaneously. At the heart was the parallel decision-making structure and liaisons functioning between the two command chains. In practice, the United States took the lead, with gaps filled by ad hoc and informal mechanisms. The existing institutional structure, namely CENTCOM, provided the base upon which the coalition could be forged and the operations executed. The central military actors remained in close contact and military plans were ever changing and evolving, depending on developments on the ground. The coalitional aspect, agreed on for political reasons, definitely complicated the war effort militarily in numerous ways, thus illustrating the ways in which institutional mechanisms may promote the achievement of strategic ends, but their effects may also culminate in constraining military effectiveness. The national institution that fostered fighting effectiveness may culminate in greater interoperability challenges; the multilateral institution of interstate violence advanced the strategic ends of member states, but there were also inhibiting effects, most particularly interoperability and friendly fire.

Interoperability and Friendly Fire

Large multinational coalitions present problems with interoperability, that is, the synthesis of the diverse military systems of associate states. These coalitions also pose difficulties in terms of friendly fire, or casualties that result from troops inadvertently killing or wounding soldiers from a coalition or allied state. These complications are magnified as the number of countries seeking to coordinate their military operations grows. These issues did, indeed, come to the fore in the Persian Gulf War. These complications are the consequence of opting to prosecute wars via multilateral frameworks.

Friendly-fire incidents generally arise from challenges in command and control. Coalition partners must communicate effectively at all levels to prevent lethal friendly fire. Fratricidal incidents were a key problem in the Gulf War. The United States killed as many British soldiers during the war as the enemy did. In addition, nearly a quarter of all American casualties during the Gulf War were a consequence of friendly fire.[33] In subsequent wars, in Afghanistan and Iraq in particular, friendly fire posed a significant hurdle to task cohesion on the ground.[34] Friendly-fire challenges grow as the number of states participating in a war effort grows. There are more obstacles in identification of friendly troops because of differences in national approaches and technologies of war fighting, in languages, and in communication routines.

Technology did facilitate fighting effectiveness, with a reduced likelihood of fratricidal incidents. For example, E-3 Airborne Warning and Control Systems (AWACs) allowed coalition forces to prevail in air-to-air combat against

Iraqi forces with beyond-visual-range shots without risking accidental friendly fire.[35] Costs were also a factor in reducing the number of friendly-fire incidents. As de la Billière said in reflecting on the incident in which an American missile killed nine British servicemen, the bottom line was costs—it would be possible but exorbitant to equip every coalition partner with identification friend and foe (IFF), thus enabling aircraft to identify electronically whether or not equipment was friendly or hostile. The cost would run in the millions or billions of British pounds, which no one was prepared to pay. Choices were made instead to invest resources elsewhere, by implication accepting the risk of friendly fire.[36]

Friendly-fire incidents are an inherent part of the war landscape. The complexities of operations on the ground coupled with the challenges of coordinating those operations with airpower make them nearly impossible to avoid. As the number of participating states grows, those coordination and communication challenges grow as well because of the differences among the participating states in their national methods of waging war. Long-standing allies with experience in joint exercises may serve to reduce those incidents, but even so, friendly-fire incidents are very difficult to eliminate from the multilateral warfighting experience. The lethality of modern armaments only exacerbates the problem. When asked about friendly fire in the Gulf War, General Horner, commander of all air assets during Desert Shield and Desert Storm, said that there had been a number of friendly-fire incidents, episodes in which the command and control system broke down. He explained that how to limit these occurrences became an obsession within the coalition, particularly given the deadly nature of contemporary weapons of war.[37]

As expected, fighting via coalition in the Gulf War culminated in numerous intracoalition friendly-fire incidents. While the coalition was very effective in achieving its military and political objectives, there were significant costs in the form of accidental killing of allied units. While it is difficult to eradicate such incidents even from unilateral war fighting, it is nearly impossible to eliminate them in cases of multinational war fighting.

The Gulf War coalition experienced challenges of interoperability and complexities in the operational aspects of the war as well. Maintaining the coalition required a great deal of effort, particularly on the part of the United States. Careful thought went into crafting the decision-making structure as discussed in the previous section—a system that could absorb differences of opinion, resolve them, and keep avenues of communication open.

Jurisdiction conflicts over the selection of aim points were, however, rife.[38] The complexities of the operational aspects of the war can also be illustrated through the air-tasking orders (ATOs). With more than two thousand sorties per day being run in the Arabian Peninsula and Iraq during Desert Storm, it was essential to communicate detailed information to each coalition partner about who would be flying where and when, and refueling where and when. However, the ATOs were so overwhelming that some units said it would take five hours or longer for the transmission and printing of the day's ATOs.[39] In addition, the ATOs changed constantly, which further complicated execution of the air war.[40] Another area that posed challenges was radio frequencies and the volume of communication that took place on the radio waves. More than nine hundred frequencies were used in the daily ATO, which meant that the standard practice of changing those frequencies daily was impossible to implement. Further, Saudi Arabia did not have a policy of assigning certain frequencies to communication, thus further complicating the enterprise.

Another interesting way in which technology and interoperability concerns affected, and to some extent even dictated, tactics and targeting in the air war was through allied partners' arsenals. In one case, for example, the British (Royal) Air Force (RAF) manifested a strong preference for the JP233, an anti-runway weapon designed for low-altitude attacks. Despite the fact that military planners did not necessarily think such attacks on Iraqi runways were vital, the RAF preference for these missions and munitions culminated in a number of such attacks in the early days of the operation.[41] The British took heavy losses as a result of these tactics, and this could have undermined the coalition if allowed to continue.[42]

While the joint training of many of these countries' militaries made the coalition operate more smoothly than one might anticipate,[43] a number of problems arose, such as the fact that France, Kuwait, and Iraq all flew the French F-1. These aircraft had to be grounded and their use restricted during the war to prevent misidentification of the enemy.[44] Technology costs also dictated operational decisions—the use of cruise missiles, for example, was curtailed as a consequence of their expense. General Colin Powell called General Norman Schwarzkopf during Operation Desert Storm and said, "I hope you realise that every time you fire another one of these cruise missiles, you know, it's two million bucks flying off into the air there and I wish you'd consider other ways of accomplishing the same mission if you can."[45] As a consequence, the United States reduced its reliance on cruise missiles in the operation.

Interoperability challenges cropped up repeatedly throughout the Gulf War. As Major Dean S. Mills reported in *Air and Space Power Journal*, the Gulf War underscored the imperative of coalition interoperability and the challenges associated with meshing the forces of a multitude of states into an effortless and effective operating military force. Despite the fact that many of the coalition partners already participated in interoperability forums, the realities of executing the military operation underscored the difference between principle and practice. For example, Mills pointed out, Australia did not send some of its F-111C aircraft because they posed serious interoperability challenges that were too difficult or too costly to overcome.[46]

In summary, the large coalition fighting in the Gulf War illustrates the challenges associated with multilateral war fighting, with the effects of advancing strategic ends via coalition. Interoperability and friendly fire are central challenges to institutions of interstate violence. In this case, the coalition framework created difficulties in regard to operational execution, friendly fire, and interoperability. Despite the fact that many of the countries participating in the war effort had deep connections to one another in regard to their military enterprises, it was still a struggle to maintain effective communication to prevent fratricidal or blue-on-blue episodes and to integrate equipment and forces. This illustrates that continued work in this area during peacetime is critical to successful wartime execution. It also shows that ad hoc coalitions that include partner states that have not trained with each other or addressed equipment compatibility issues pose a unique challenge in multilateral war fighting, though we also see that even when partner states do train together, it does not prevent blue-on-blue episodes from occurring. The within-coalition differences in power capabilities similarly pose a potentially challenging effect of opting to prosecute the war multilaterally.

Balance of Power, Burden Sharing, and Leverage Within the Coalition

The power distribution within the Gulf War coalition was markedly asymmetric. This is apparent from examining the Correlates of War data for 1991 for the five countries that contributed the most troops, shown in Table 3.1. The data include military expenditures, military personnel, and annual value for the Composite Index of National Capability (CINC). These values provide a rough indicator of power.

The United States had roughly ten times the capabilities of the second-largest contributor of troops in the coalition. In terms of burden sharing within

Table 3.1 Power capabilities of top-five contributors of troops to first Gulf War coalition

State abbreviation	Military expenditures (in millions of U.S. 2012 dollars)	Military personnel (in thousands)	Composite Index of National Capability
USA	26,200,000	2,110	0.136481
SAU	35,500	191	0.013034
UKG	40,430	301	0.02589
EGY	1,650	434	0.008457
FRN	37,340	554	0.020871
SYR	4,500	408	0.004824

SOURCE: Correlates of War Data. Version 3.02. See Singer 1987. Accessed 12/13/2012. http://www.correlatesofwar.org/COW2%20Data/Capabilities/nmc3-02.htm.

NOTE: The Composite Index of National Capability is computed by summing observations for total population, urban population, iron and steel production, energy consumption, military personnel, and military expenditures for the year, converting each country's absolute component into a share of the international system, averaging across the six component parts. USA refers to the United States; SAU to Saudi Arabia; UKG to the United Kingdom; EGY to Egypt; FRN to France; and SYR to Syria.

the coalition, however, the power disparity was not felt quite as keenly as it could have been.[47] There were more than 300 combat and combat-support battalions, more than 225 naval vessels, and nearly 2800 fixed-wing aircraft.[48] The operation included combat flying units from the United States, Great Britain, France, Canada, and Italy, as well as air forces from Saudi Arabia, Kuwait, Bahrain, Qatar, and the United Arab Emirates. South Korea, New Zealand, and Argentina provided transport aircraft. The United States flew more than 85 percent of the sorties during the war and provided nearly all of the command and control systems, the electronic warfare aircraft, heavy bombers, cruise missiles, and stealth capability.[49] The burden was shared somewhat more equally in air-to-air combat missions, with the United States' share at about 66 percent, and Saudi Arabia, Canada, the United Kingdom, France, and Bahrain, in that order, making up for the rest. Coalition partners proved invaluable in providing jet fuel. The U.S. Air Force alone used fifteen million gallons of fuel a day at the war's peak; Saudi Arabia, Oman, and the United Arab Emirates provided all of the fuel, at a value of approximately $2 billion.[50]

Many countries contributed to the coalition financially—in addition to the billions of dollars in economic aid to affected countries, an estimated $54 billion was given the United States to offset the projected incremental costs of $61 billion.[51] More precisely, the incremental costs to the United States, estimated by the Office of Management and Budget (OMB), were $61.1 billion.[52] According to the U.S. General Accountability Office, by September 1992, the United States had received this money in aid to offset what the United States spent on Operations Desert Shield and Desert Storm. Table 3.2 provides a country-by-country summary.

Thus, in terms of funding the war, burden sharing was handled fairly effectively. The United States by far provided the largest deployment of troops—540,000 of the nearly 800,000 total.[53] Saudi Arabia was the next-largest contributor, with troop levels around 50,000, followed by the United Kingdom, with approximately 45,000 troops.[54] Other contributions to the coalition included observing the embargo against Iraq, despite significant lost revenues.[55]

While opinions vary on the equity of burden sharing in the Gulf War,[56] of the post–Cold War coalitions formed by the United States, the first Gulf War coalition was funded most broadly. In contrast to the first Gulf War, the United States had to pay its coalition partners in the subsequent war in Iraq for their continued participation.[57] However, Alexander Thompson notes that a multitude of favors and side payments were undertaken by the United States to Egypt, Poland, Syria, Turkey, Security Council members, Colombia, the Ivory

Table 3.2 Foreign government pledges and contributions to the United States, dollars in millions

| Contributor | Pledges | | | Contributions | | | |
	1990	1991	Total	Cash	In kind	Total	GDP (%)
Saudi Arabia	$3,339	$13,500	$16,839	$12,809	$4,046	$16,855	21
Kuwait	2,506	13,550	16,056	16,015	43	16,058	81
United Arab Emirates	1,000	3,088	4,088	3,870	218	4,088	15
Japan	1,680	8,332	10,012	9,441	571	10,012	5
Germany	1,072	5,500	6,572	5,772	683	6,455	6
South Korea	80	275	355	150	101	251	1
Others[a]	3	26	29	8	22	30	—
Total	**$9,680**	**$44,271**	**$53,951**	**$48,065**	**$5,684**	**$53,749**	—

SOURCE: U.S. General Accountability Office. Report to Congress: Financial Management Fiscal Year 1992 Audit of the Defense Cooperation Account. GAO-NSIAD-93-185. August 1993. 1990 pledges are August–December; 1991 pledges are January–March. GDP data from CIA *World Factbook*, 1991. Accessed 5/15/2013. http://nodedge.com/ciawfb.

[a]Includes Italy, Oman, Qatar, Bahrain, Belgium, Denmark, Norway, and Luxembourg.

Coast, Ethiopia, Malaysia, the Soviet Union, and Zaire. The side payments included forgiving debt, giving loans, and making concessions in trade agreements. Egypt received loans from the International Monetary Fund amounting to $372 million, and $20 billion in debt was forgiven; the United States forgave 70 percent of Poland's $3.8 billion in debt for its coalition participation.[58]

Thompson goes on to discuss the political rewards the United States bestowed on numerous countries, as well as the punishments levied against countries such as Yemen, which voted against the UN authorization of the use of force against Iraq.[59] This implies that overt leverage was exercised within the coalition, even in a coalition that was populated by highly motivated members. In this case, it would appear that although smaller countries exacted payment from the United States to ensure cooperation, the United States received international community largesse for undertaking the mission of expelling Saddam Hussein's forces from Kuwait. In other words, leverage was reciprocal—exercised in both directions, from great powers to smaller powers and from smaller powers to the great powers.

Studies of burden sharing in the Gulf War also universally acknowledge the importance of the position of the United States in successfully constructing the coalition. Terasawa and Gates, for example, argue that intense lobbying by the United States culminated in Germany and Japan contributing more to the coalition than their return would warrant.[60] Similarly, Bennett, Lepgold, and Unger argue that alliance dependence makes states receptive to contributing to coalitions beyond the immediate gains they may reap.[61] What this suggests is that even in ideological multilateral endeavors, a powerful state's influence and regard in the international system may be essential to success in forging such coalitions—threat or moral imperative alone is not enough. Rational, pragmatic, and strategic benefits dictate coalitional dynamics to a large extent.

The reciprocal leverage exercised in this case also demonstrates the realist institutionalist insight that states may use institutions and multilateral frameworks to advance their objectives; they facilitate the ability of countries to do their bidding. The use of such vehicles increases a state's ability to exercise power over others. This stands in contrast to the wholly realist perspective that this was a unilateral action "cloaked" by multilateral design or that all that mattered was the power differential, which was so great that all that really mattered was the fighting force of the great power in the coalition or alliance. It also diverges from the neoliberal institutionalist perspective that the institution itself is the independent center of power or agency in achieving the goals sought.

The states prosecuting the war in the Persian Gulf were highly motivated and followed the American lead. This meant that concerns over burden sharing were less pressing than other subsequent post–Cold War interventions and that the wrangling to keep member states on board or to bring them into the coalition in the first place was more limited than we will see in the cases to follow. In the next section I examine the alliance security dilemma within the coalition—an additional potential challenging effect of prosecuting wars multilaterally.

Security Dilemma Within the Coalition

The alliance security dilemma concerns, of entrapment or abandonment, mediated coalition activity during Operations Desert Shield and Desert Storm. Allaying fears of entrapment were repeated U.S. assurances to Saudi Arabia that it would not maintain troops in Saudi Arabia beyond what was necessary to expel Iraq from Kuwait. Also mitigating immediate entrapment fears was the United States' swift call to end the war in advance of any pressure from its partners to do so.[62] A combination of limited and clear war aims, a clear violation of the international norm of sovereignty in a country that provided a significant amount of oil to the rest of the world, and the regional threat helped mitigate the alliance security dilemmas within the coalition.[63]

The broader strategic landscape, the end of the Cold War, did impinge upon the coalitional dynamics of Operations Desert Shield and Desert Storm. In some ways the alliance security dilemma played out even more as a result of the end of the Cold War than in the context of the crisis itself. The post–Cold War setting offered opportunities for the United States to exercise power in a vacuum. It also presented uncertainty and insecurity for U.S. allies, particularly in Europe. The Gulf War became an avenue through which countries such as the United Kingdom, France, Germany, Turkey, and Japan could allay anxieties regarding their fears of abandonment in the post–Cold War world.[64] In this way, the Gulf War was an important informational exercise, signaling continued allied connectivity to the United States that was motivated out of fears of abandonment.

Had the Gulf War taken place at a different point in time, it is likely that fears of entrapment would have dominated coalitional dynamics in a more meaningful way. To some extent, these fears did exist, and they culminated in the negotiations described in the previous section: side payments to countries such as Egypt for participating in the war. Receding fears over allied—primarily U.S.—abandonment in the post–Cold War era as time unfolded presented deeper fears of entrapment in subsequent cases.

The potentially challenging effects of prosecuting the war multilaterally in regard to interoperability, friendly fire, within–coalition asymmetries in capability, and the alliance security dilemma were not as problematic as they could have been, even though there were significant tribulations. The question, then, becomes, to what extent were the strategic ends of the coalition effectively realized—particularly in regard to prevailing over the enemy and maintaining cohesion and the perceived legitimacy of the operation?

Fighting Effectiveness

One element of the Persian Gulf War that is contested is the extent to which the reliance on airpower to prevail fundamentally altered the terrain of military strategy for subsequent wars. What is not contested is the sheer dominance of coalition forces in the Gulf War and the relative ease with which those forces prevailed over Saddam Hussein's military. The devastation wrought, the swift victory, and the limited casualties all speak to a highly effective fighting force.[65]

One interesting element of the effectiveness of the coalition in prosecuting Operations Desert Storm and Desert Shield is that although the U.S.-Saudi Joint Directorate of Planning (JDOP) was established in August 1990, and its planning continued throughout both Desert Storm and Desert Shield, ultimately the focal point of offensive planning lay firmly with CENTCOM. The JDOP was a highly effective forum for identifying and resolving problems cropping up with the coalition, and it was an excellent resource for swift access to Saudi policy makers, but in regard to the operational planning for missions, it simply did not fulfill those roles.[66] This underscores the importance of the United States' standing unified commands in serving to realize military ends. Possessing capabilities is only one aspect of prevailing in war. Effective structures are essential to the execution of operational missions.

Further, as mentioned earlier, war-fighting effectiveness was not compromised in the interest of broad inclusion of coalition partners.[67] There were differences of opinion within the coalition that had the potential to undermine effectiveness, but ultimately intracoalition conversation and negotiation culminated in a successful operation. For example, at the outset of operations, French airpower was to be used only to support French troops, but ultimately the French government expanded this mission.[68] In the end, the clear political and military objectives and a resilient coalition structure—as well as a weak enemy[69]—enabled the partners to prevail.

The overwhelming success of the coalition in ejecting Saddam Hussein's forces from Kuwait is well documented.[70] Would the United States have been equally successful in prevailing had it prosecuted the war alone? Given that U.S. forces undertook the largest operational components of the war, perhaps it would have been, particularly in light of how weak the Iraqi forces ultimately proved to be.[71] In fact, as discussed earlier, the central challenges to fighting effectiveness came from the coalitional dynamics. That is, the issues of friendly fire, interoperability, and unwieldy command and communication apparatuses degraded the fighting effectiveness of the coalition, even if at the end of the day the coalition was highly successful in achieving its military objectives and expelled Saddam Hussein's forces with rapidity. The case clearly illustrates that institutions of interstate violence facilitate the achievement of important strategic ends, even if certain effects of working multilaterally increase the costs to participating states.

In summary, the Gulf War manifested substantial fighting effectiveness, despite the obstacles posed by coalitional dynamics. In large part, fighting effectiveness stemmed from the overwhelming superiority in quality and quantity of coalition forces, and the manifest weakness of the Iraqi military. The Gulf War became instructional for subsequent wars, particularly in terms of the use of airpower. It also served as a model for effectively managing goals and strategies toward attaining those goals, that is, coalition cohesion.

Cohesion

A behavioral conceptualization of cohesion, the ability of states to agree on goals and strategies toward attaining those goals, would imply that it is necessary for coalition members to be able to agree on their objectives and construct effective command and control systems to allow them to pursue those objectives. It was relatively easy to come to agreement on deterring the Iraqis from invading Saudi Arabia. It was slightly more difficult to achieve consensus on pushing Saddam Hussein's forces out of Kuwait and back into Iraq.[72] However, ultimately, consensus was reached and cohesion maintained. The command and control system that emerged enabled the coalition to pursue those objectives effectively, thereby enhancing the cohesion of the coalition. Close contact and discussion were essential to maintaining coalition harmony.[73] General Norman Schwarzkopf was essential to maintaining coalition cohesion. As General Sir Peter de la Billière, senior British commander, said afterward in regard to a difference over where British troops would deploy and with whom:

> One of [Schwarzkopf's] great strengths is that he was a diplomat, as well as a
> soldier and why he was so successful in holding that coalition together, is that

when he saw that another nation had an over-riding need to do something that didn't meet his military priorities of the moment, he was prepared to give way to that nation in order to keep them on [sic] side. And he did it not just with the British, with a lot of other nations as well. . . .

And I think that says a lot for the man that he can get this balance right between diplomacy that is necessary to keep a coalition force together, on the one hand, and develop a military fighting capability with that coalition despite having to let diplomacy give way at times to military correctness.[74]

De la Billière goes on to describe Schwarzkopf's similar management of the Syrians, recounting a time in which they were unhappy with their designated role. Schwarzkopf changed their role in response, which kept the Syrians on board at a time they might otherwise have abandoned the war effort.[75]

The ability of coalition partners to agree on their common goals and strategies in large part, then, hinged on the United States, and on Schwarzkopf in particular and his ability to hear others out and accommodate diverse views and perspectives. Schwarzkopf had a unique ability to discern the critical components of the operational plan and to simultaneously integrate and synthesize coalition partners' agendas into the overall operation. He became the linchpin for Operations Desert Shield and Desert Storm; he also became the focal point for fostering, nurturing, and advancing coalitional cohesion. The main problem, though, with Schwarzkopf's centrality in being responsible for coalition cohesion was his temper.[76]

Despite the difficulties associated with working with him, Schwarzkopf managed to bring the coalition together and viewed the coalition as a whole. In fact, coalition cohesion was manifest in this unified view of the forces. For example, as discussed earlier, the question of low-flying aircraft in the early days of Operation Desert Storm was an issue, particularly for the RAF. In an interview, General Buster Glosson, chief of CENTCOM's offensive air campaign, was asked why he cared so much about the inherent danger to coalition forces in taking on that mission. He replied:

I've often been asked the question why General Horner and I really cared if it was a coalition aircraft and it wasn't a U.S. forces aircraft. And that's a very basic, fundamental issue with both of us. It stems from one thing, human life.

We never ask ourselves when we put any aircraft against a target what nation's flying that airplane, but that was a member of the coalition, a living breathing human being and when he went down the pain was the same no matter where he came from or what nation or who he represented in the coalition.

To try to have different rules for different members of the coalition is just totally absurd to my way of thinking.[77]

The threat perceived by the international community from the Iraqi invasion was also instrumental in fostering cohesion in the coalition. At the outset, in the first briefing the United States had with Saudi Arabia, when the United States outlined the need for Saudi permission to deploy U.S. troops to Saudi Arabia and to use Saudi airfields, ports, and equipment, King Fahd of Saudi Arabia agreed immediately, to the surprise of the Americans. Ambassador Charles W. Freeman Jr., who was at the meeting and understood Arabic, said that the discussion among the Saudis included a comment that they should not act too hastily. The king replied, "Yes, and the Kuwaitis are all living in our hotels right now because they weren't willing to make a decision in this matter and I'm not going to have that happen."[78] Saudi Arabia felt the threat acutely, and it was motivated to act as a consequence. Exacerbating that threat for Saudi Arabia, according to Schwarzkopf, was the fact that the Iraqis already had tanks on Saudi Arabian soil.[79]

Enormous efforts were taken to ensure that cultural sensitivities were observed. For example, U.S. personnel deploying to Saudi Arabia had to undergo extensive indoctrination programs aimed at educating them about the history, customs, religions, and laws of the region. Alcohol was prohibited in the CENTCOM area of operation, and a civilian dress code was established as well. Broadcasts on the U.S. Armed Forces radio and television services were monitored to avoid offense. American women were briefed extensively regarding Islamic and Saudi expectations of female conduct, although the Saudis did lift the prohibition against women driving, providing that it was part of their official duty.[80] Tending to cultural differences was essential in fostering and maintaining coalition cohesion, as was containing Israeli involvement in the conflict.[81] Further, as the coalition shifted from Operation Desert Shield to Operation Desert Storm, the parallel decision-making structure was augmented by upping the number of liaison officers, as well as changing the Coalition Coordination Communication and Integration Center (C3IC) to strengthen it and make it more effective.[82] Joint training also enhanced cohesion. Most CENTAF staff, for example, who deployed for Desert Shield had just completed a joint warfare center exercise, called Internal Look 90, which focused on the defense of Saudi Arabia.[83]

Personal relationships played an extremely important role in maintaining the cohesion of the coalition. Brigadier General Glosson (chief of CENTCOM's offensive air campaign), for example, had close connections with other U.S. military and intelligence officials, as well as with leaders of the Arab world. This facilitated communication among key players, even if it created other problems, such as keeping others out of the informational loop.[84]

The United States and its coalition partners worked very hard to keep the coalition together. The consequences of failure loomed. The "inherent fragility" of the coalition meant that a great deal of effort had to go into negotiating, compromising, and maintaining its cohesion.[85] Tension surfaced particularly among the force commanders, who did not always agree on operational or tactical implementation decisions. In the end, however, the coalition maintained cohesion because of the efforts undertaken by the main coalition partners.[86] This is not to say that the coalition partners always agreed; however, many times differences were effectively managed.[87] The desire to maintain the cohesion of the coalition even guided decision making regarding when to end the war. President George H. W. Bush "liked the idea of pressing for peace before it was pressed on him and staying one step ahead of calls from the coalition and Democrats that we cease operations."[88]

An additional component of cohesion was the Scud hunt, which required significant attention and resources during the Iraq campaign. This was necessary to maintain the coalition, despite the fact that the hunt diverted attention from the primary mission of the operation. Iraqi Scud attacks were launched into Saudi Arabia, Israel, and Bahrain, threatening coalition solidarity. Although the attacks did not pose an overwhelming military challenge, they nevertheless posed a tremendous threat to the coalition because of fears that Israel would counterattack. In this event, the coalition would be perilously divided, thus undermining the capacity of the coalition to function in a united way. If Israel counterattacked, it would be very difficult for the Arab countries to maintain their commitment to the coalition, particularly as Israeli response would likely entail air-space violations of Jordan, Saudi Arabia, or Syria. Because of the threat that key Arab countries would drop out of the coalition if this were to occur, the urgency to bring an end to the Scud attacks was far greater than straightforward military consequences would dictate. The Scud hunt became an extremely important component of coalition maintenance. Air assets, as well as British and U.S. Special Forces, were deployed to root out the Iraqi Scuds and destroy them before they could pose an additional threat.[89] The United States undertook 2,493 missions to hunt Scud missiles in Iraq.[90]

Scud missile attacks were lethal—including the loss of U.S. military personnel stationed in Saudi Arabia in an attack on al-Khobar that killed twenty-seven people—yet the real threat they posed was on coalition cohesion.[91] The capacity of the member states to agree on goals and strategies to attaining those goals was in peril in the event that Iraqi Scud attacks incited Israeli retaliation. As a consequence, more resources than would otherwise have been warranted were devoted to searching and destroying Iraqi Scud missiles. The dictates of coalition cohesion trumped straightforward strategic considerations in regard to the allocation of resources.

In summary, the cohesion of the coalition was modest; it hinged on the common purpose emanating from the threat the Iraqi invasion posed and the substantial efforts put forth by key actors in the war. Disagreement over goals and strategy occurred but were addressed directly by the United States, and by Norman Schwarzkopf in particular. Certainly, the large number of states in the coalition made this process more complicated and challenging than it would have been had the United States been fighting alone or with its closest allies. However, the shared goal of ejecting Iraqi forces and the speed with which that goal was achieved went a long way in fostering coalitional cohesion. Working multilaterally—through the coalition and through the United Nations—also had implications for the legitimacy of both Desert Shield and Desert Storm.

Legitimacy

It is important to disentangle a number of competing strands of thought that have become enmeshed in popular discourse. Was it the use of a coalition or the UN sanction that granted legitimacy to the Gulf War? Or did the legitimacy of the operation derive from its mission rather than from either the UNSC sanction or the size of the coalition? Or is the connection mutually reinforcing? These are some of the principal questions that need to be addressed to understand whether the Gulf War was deemed legitimate, and if so, why.

Certainly, the assumed connection between legitimacy and multilateral war fighting is pervasive. As General de la Billière said:

> It was essential to have a coalition. Otherwise it was going to be one major Western country imposing its will over less military effective Arab and Islamic countries and that would have been totally unacceptable. It would changed [sic]

the whole balance of power in the world. And, the Americans would never have done it. . . .

It could never have been an American operation[;] it wouldn't have worked. It would have worked, they put lots of forces there, but they would have had to invade Saudi Arabia to do so effectively. They would have had to . . . stand up against all their allies. And, war is only an extension of politics. They had to bring the coalition along, or get out. . . .

The Arab forces, in this war, were absolutely critical to its success. Without them and without having them along, then we would not have been welcome. If we had won a military battle, we'd have lost a political peace, and I think that is the great success of Norman Schwarzkopf, that he brought the whole of this coalition together and it fought as an entity. It wasn't just the American forces. It was Arab forces, Islamic forces, British forces, French forces, Italian. Thirty-one different countries.

So we had to have a coalition. We had to have as many forces as possible, gathered together to challenge this invasion of a minor country by Saddam Hussein. And of course, the threat that it posed to a substantial part of world oil supplies.[92]

In other words, the coalition in and of itself was a source of legitimacy for the Gulf War. Others, however, argue that the legitimacy of the Gulf War stemmed from its UN endorsement. Richard Haass, for example, argued that while many Americans might not respect the United Nations, others around the world do and deem it an important source of authority and legitimacy. This means that UN endorsement may actually be a prerequisite for joining a coalition and engaging in policy endeavors or actions that the United Nations indicates are appropriate.[93] The Bush administration pursued UN support from the beginning to forge international consensus—it was a political measure intended to strengthen domestic and international support for the operation.[94]

In the Gulf War case, there were numerous audiences and opinions to consider in assessing the legitimacy of the operation to deter further Iraqi aggression and then subsequently to expel Iraqi forces from Kuwait.[95] Because of this, global organizations such as the United Nations could help. They could function as neutral arbiters (because of the heterogeneity of their memberships and all-inclusiveness) within which states could act to communicate intentions and disseminate information, thereby enhancing public support for action and legitimating action.[96] What is interesting about the Persian Gulf case is that, coming on the heels of the end of the Cold War, an opportunity to use the United Nations in this way was possible. In the bipolar contest between East and West, the United Nations was an arena for Cold War politics to play themselves out, via vetoes by the United States or Soviet Union in the UN Security Council or through General Assembly debate. The use of the United Nations in the Persian Gulf case was significant not only in terms of managing this particular crisis but also in terms of what it meant for the advent of the post–Cold War era. Working through the United Nations, the United States was able to communicate and signal information about its intentions in regard to the Gulf War; it also communicated a broader intentionality of the kind of hegemon it would be.[97] In this way, we see that institutions of interstate violence may solidify and even augment power, in addition to serving as mechanisms to achieve strategic ends.

Public opinion both in the United States and abroad is another effective indicator of the legitimacy of action. A Gallup poll of Americans on January 20, 1991, found 80 percent believed that the coalition was justified in intervening in Iraq.[98] This is in contrast to the 55 percent of Americans polled in the last Gallup poll before the Gulf War took place, which suggests that the legitimacy of the operation derived not only from the mission but from its execution as well.[99] A distinct rally around the flag dynamic was at work, and support for the mission does not stand in perfectly for "legitimacy" of the operation, but nevertheless, the fact that most Americans supported the war effort, as did their European counterparts—70 percent polled supported the war[100]—suggests a high degree of legitimacy, or at least approval of the intervention. This was especially true as a consequence of the UN authorization.[101] According to Mueller's exceptionally thorough scholarship on this topic, in the aftermath of the vote in the United Nations on November 29, 1990, support for the war increased significantly. In addition, polls that specifically mention the United Nations' resolution yielded higher support for war than ones that did not.[102] Public audiences around the world viewed military action against Iraq as legitimate and desirable, even if in many instances those same publics preferred other countries to undertake the mission rather than their own.[103]

In summary, UN support for the Gulf War enterprise both reflected the legitimacy of the mission of expelling Saddam Hussein from Iraq for violating Kuwaiti sovereignty, and augmented legitimacy by signaling limited intentions on the part of the United States in regard to the Gulf War and its hegemony. Approval from the United Nations also allayed more specific fears that might otherwise have developed regarding a long-standing occupation by Western troops in the Arabian Peninsula.[104]

The legitimacy of the Gulf War, then, derived from sanctioning a violator of a widely accepted international norm, sovereignty—that is, the mission of the operation. But the way in which the war was prosecuted, via coalition, and sanctioned by the United Nations, fostered support for the war worldwide. The United Nations' authorization of force was more effective in generating support than the simple fact of the development of a multilateral war-fighting coalition designed to execute these operations. In fact, most of the polls indicating support for the war in the Gulf focused on the United States going to war, with no mention of the coalition partners.[105] Politically, UN involvement was an essential component of these operations, even if militarily the institutional design of the coalition that prosecuted the war was far more salient. The fact that public opinion was unchanged during this period, that intervention was favored with a broad international consensus, supports this idea.[106] As suggested in the previous chapter, components of institutional design are often constructed for political reasons, despite the gravity of their military consequences. International consensus was paramount for the Bush administration, which believed that in the absence of international support, domestic support would be lost as well. Using the United Nations to forge this consensus and to seal the coalition was essential in the administration's view,[107] although public opinion was remarkably unchanging in the period before and after the decision to go to war was made.[108]

In the Gulf War, the dynamics of the mission of punishing Saddam Hussein's Iraq for invading Kuwait and the use of the United Nations as a vehicle for communicating the intentions and actions of the international community were mutually reinforcing, thus making Operations Desert Shield and Desert Storm highly legitimate endeavors. While the use of a multinational coalition to prosecute the war was an emblematic component of the enterprise, legitimacy did not hinge on it alone.

CONCLUSION

The central questions of this book revolve around whether or not institutional structure affects multilateral war-fighting capacity. More specifically, does the use of alliance versus coalition structure matter, and if so, how? To what extent does the institutional architecture affect fighting effectiveness, interoperability, cohesion, and burden sharing? How does the size of the multilateral fighting force create obstacles to prosecuting war? Does the alliance security dilemma mediate such coalition activity, and if so, how? And finally, does multilateral war fighting affect the legitimacy of an operation?

All of these questions were answered by this case in a very straightforward fashion. The coalition that was designed to prosecute Operations Desert Shield and Desert Storm was large and unwieldy, with a highly complex decision-making structure, thereby creating challenges for the operational components of the war. And while these challenges did undermine fighting effectiveness, they did not do so to a degree that would prevent the coalition from achieving its central objectives. Further, the large size of the coalition culminated in significant interoperability problems as well as friendly-fire tragedies. We also saw that small states wielded substantial leverage over the United States in negotiating participation in the coalition, which was asymmetric in its power distribution, although burden sharing concerns were light in comparison to most interventions. And finally, legitimacy of the enterprise inhered to its mission, as well as its multilateral design and UN authorization. A summary of each variable is found in Table 3.3.

The theme of realist institutionalism here is quite apparent. Coalition partners came together to project influence and prevail in military conquest. Their mechanism of choice was an institutional framework that would allow them to pursue and achieve their objectives. We see very clearly in this case that there is no dichotomy between realism and institutionalism but rather a synthetic understanding of world politics. Institutions become a vehicle for promoting power and strategic aims. In the realm of war fighting, this is very consequential. Power projection entails more than simply manifesting military capability, but instead doing so in a community of allies, which augments authority and effectiveness in achieving one's goals. In other words, exercising power is about not only the end of winning but also the means of achieving that victory in

Table 3.3 Overview of variables in the Gulf War case

Independent variables	Mediating variables	Dependent variables
Coalition	Decision-making structure: hierarchical but dual	Cohesion: moderate
Size: large	Power distribution: asymmetrical	War-fighting effectiveness: effective
	Internal leverage: rests with lead powers	Interoperability: challenges
		Legitimacy of operation: legitimate

the company of others. Simultaneously, we note that the United States' institutional arrangements for war prosecution, namely CENTCOM in this case, provided an important vehicle for translating its capability from potential to actual power.

The Gulf War was a unique case, coming as it did in the immediate aftermath of the end of the Cold War. The informational opportunities were thus very substantial. The Gulf War was a way of signaling how the sole remaining superpower would manage the international system, and it gave an important affirmation to advocates of global governance. The war also presented opportunities for U.S. allies to signal their continued desire for American patronage. This suggests the central theme of this book, that the design of multilateral war fighting enterprises is often more about politics than they are about military dictates.

4 OPERATION ALLIED FORCE

IN LATE FEBRUARY 1998, government forces of the Federal Republic of Yugoslavia (FRY) and the Kosovo Liberation Army (KLA) began to clash. As the KLA began making advances in June and July of that year, the government launched a major counteroffensive, which continued through September. More than a quarter of a million people were displaced, thousands of homes were destroyed, and the makings of a humanitarian disaster confronted the international community.[1] Despite attempts to negotiate a cease-fire through the Holbrooke Agreement in October 1998 and negotiations at Rambouillet, France, in February 1999, the fighting on the ground in Kosovo escalated in March 1999.[2] By January 1999, the North Atlantic Treaty Organization empowered its secretary-general Javier Solana to authorize air strikes with the intention of compelling Serbian leader Slobodan Milošević into compliance.[3]

U.S. and NATO planning for war began earlier, in 1998. Above all, the strategic concern of turmoil in NATO's immediate sphere of influence was at issue. The European member states were unable to take action without the strategic assets of the United States. By early spring of 1999, more than forty air campaign options had been considered.[4] It was clear that the United States was unwilling to commit ground forces and that plans for fighting an air war were a political necessity.[5] On March 23, 1999, Operation Allied Force (OAF) began. The air campaign lasted until June 10 and ended with Serbian capitulation.[6]

Operation Allied Force is a seminal case for understanding alliance politics. NATO is the most institutionalized military alliance in history, with an enduring commitment to member states' security. The transformation from peacetime NATO to wartime operations illustrates the challenges of adapting institutions for such different purposes. NATO's central role in its first fifty years was to manage relations among member states while deterring Soviet encroachments. Over the course of the Cold War, the internal benefits of the alliance were manifold. Joint military planning, exercises, increased communication, and heightened transparency among member states all served to foster a sense of community and cooperation. These activities over the life span of the alliance reduced and relieved tensions among historical adversaries and kept the peace among active rivals.[7] When the alliance was called to action in Kosovo, it was the first real test of how the organization would operate in wartime.

This transition was difficult. Policy makers struggled to agree on the central objectives of the mission, and military strategists strived to develop plans agreeable to all. The operation revealed wide gaps in capabilities and underscored the challenges of burden sharing. Above all, the long-standing decision-making mechanisms that served well in peacetime impeded prosecution of the operation. During peacetime, states benefit from a high degree of organizational institutionalization; in wartime, those institutional mechanisms can constrain action at a time when swift response is required. By the same token, Kosovo demonstrated the advantages of using an enduring alliance to prosecute a war in that there were fewer difficulties with interoperability and friendly fire than could have been the case with an ad hoc coalition. The realist institutionalist implications here are that the standing alliance provided a framework for prosecuting the war, which is very important in regard to advancing the strategic ends of the member states. At the same time, the institutional effects did hamper efficiency in a number of ways—in regard to cohesion, communication, decision making, and burden sharing. Costs must always be balanced with benefits, and Operation Allied Force highlights the advantages of having an institution such as NATO at the ready for the United States to promote its strategic goals.

This chapter explores the use of an alliance as the mechanism to prosecute the war in Kosovo; the decision-making structure brought to bear; the interoperability, burden-sharing, and friendly-fire challenges; the power distribution within the alliance; the alliance security dilemma; and the legitimacy of the operation, as well as its source and value. In so doing, we see the ways in which institutions for interstate violence serve to advance strategic goals, despite the institutional effects and mechanisms that undermine efficiency.

THE ALLIANCE

The ongoing violence in the Yugoslav area in the 1990s posed a tremendous challenge to NATO member states. The continuing instability in the Eastern European region, repeated diplomatic and negotiation failures, and a growing humanitarian crisis dictated a European response. Despite European leaders' discussion of the problem in regional forums such as the Organization for Security and Cooperation in Europe (OSCE) and the European Union, only NATO had the capacity to formulate a comprehensive military response, thus highlighting the institutional dimension of power. The newly enlarged NATO took on this task on the eve of its fiftieth anniversary, thereby securing the post–Cold War alliance's future. However, using an alliance established in peacetime for wartime purposes created challenges that would haunt the alliance throughout the mission. Using an alliance structure instead of having any one state take unilateral action meant that in addition to reaping the benefits of advancing states' agendas via an institution, navigation of the expected multilateral hazards was simultaneously required. There were advantages and disadvantages to employing NATO in this way, as summarized by Secretary of Defense William Cohen and Chairman of the Joint Chiefs of Staff General Henry H. Shelton, who argued that NATO may have constrained the U.S. military forces from achieving their objectives efficiently and effectively. However, according to them, OAF could not have been conducted without NATO—its infrastructure, transit and basing access, member states' contribution of forces, as well as political and diplomatic support. They indicated that the allies and partners near the theater of conflict, Hungary, Macedonia, Bulgaria, Albania, and others, were especially important, as was a "dividend of sustained U.S. and NATO engagement with those nations over the last few years."[8]

Shelton and Cohen admitted that trying to achieve consensus among the nineteen member states was challenging, but they argued that building consensus would lead to better decisions. Further, they indicated that had NATO as an institution not responded to the crisis, it would have dealt a blow to the alliance—not addressing a major threat on its doorstep. In their view, NATO met the challenge and succeeded in achieving its goals.[9]

Using NATO to prosecute the war against Serb militias in Kosovo was a stroke of brilliance in ensuring the alliance's future and employing it in an adaptable, flexible way. In addition, it was the only standing institution available to deploy and project power for member states' ends. China's and Russia's opposition to military intervention stymied the United Nations, and other regional organizations in Europe did not have sufficient military capacity to bring to bear in the growing crisis. However, transitioning from peacetime to wartime and relying on the consensus of the nineteen member states posed huge obstacles to the military objective of defeating Milošević's forces and shaped strategic planning in less-than-optimal ways.

Decision-Making Structure

Article 9 of the Washington Treaty of 1949 established the North Atlantic Treaty Organization and created a council of member states that would implement the treaty. The North Atlantic Council (NAC), which developed from the Washington Treaty, governed by consensus on all of the most important strategic decisions confronting the signatories. From the creation of the NAC, an elaborate military and command structure evolved, culminating in a civil as well as a military decision-making structure.[10] NATO's Military Committee (MC) comprises representatives from every member state and is predicated on consensus-based decision making. The International Military Staff (IMS) is a supportive body that ensures appropriate implementation of NATO decisions.[11]

Within the integrated force structure is an integrated command structure under the Military Committee and the IMS. In July 1994, this structure was streamlined, and the major NATO commands were reduced from three to two: Allied Command Europe (ACE) and Allied Command Atlantic (ACLANT). Allied Command Channel was disbanded and subsumed by Allied Command Europe. There is, in addition to these two commands, a Regional Planning Group for Canada and the United States. This group develops plans and makes recommendations to the Military Committee for the U.S.-Canadian region. NATO commanders develop plans for defense of their areas, determine force requirements, and deploy and exercise the forces under their control. The supreme allied commander Europe (SACEUR) makes recommendations to NATO authorities on military matters in his area; he is the principal spokesperson for the Supreme Headquarters Allied Powers Europe (SHAPE), located near Mons, Belgium, which houses the Allied Command Europe (ACE). The SACEUR is an American four-star general. The three major subordinate commands responsible to the SACEUR are Allied Forces North West Europe, which encompasses Norway, the United Kingdom, and the adjacent seas; Allied Forces Central Europe; and Allied Forces Southern Europe, in Naples, Italy. The subordinate commands are under the authority of a British four-star general, a German four-star general, and an American four-star admiral, respectively.[12]

Despite this elaborate, integrated military and force structure, when NATO opted to intervene in Kosovo, the United States advanced a parallel command structure to avoid placing its troops under the command of others (see Figure 4.1). Unlike the parallel command structure in the Gulf War, although many individuals in the structure served two masters, there was less structured interface between the two. The chain of command was confusing, with unsuitable organizational structures and insufficient staff integration.[13] According to Secretary of Defense Cohen and Chairman of the Joint Chiefs of Staff Shelton, because the command relationships within NATO had not been used before to plan or manage combat operations, the parallel U.S.-NATO command and control structure that emerged made operational planning more complicated and degraded unity of command.[14] In the end, although NATO was necessary to prosecute the war, it "came at the cost of a flawed strategy that was further hobbled by the manifold inefficiencies that were part and parcel of conducting combat operations by committee."[15]

Because NATO decisions have to be made by consensus, waging war collectively was extremely difficult. At the start of the campaign, only 51 targets had been approved by the allies. By June 1999, the list included 976 targets. Each additional target had to be proposed, reviewed, and approved by NATO and national authorities before it could be added to the list.[16] Target requests were denied by some of the allies and the United States. Delays in approving target lists were rampant across the alliance. In some cases, targets were subjected to a domestic legal review to guarantee compliance with international law.[17] In fact, according to Paul Strickland, a member of the NATO Combined Air Operation Center (CAOC), in the initial forty days of the campaign, a number of fairly insignificant targets were bombed repeatedly into rubble because of an absence of new approved target sets.[18] The Pentagon estimated that some 80 percent of the targets hit in the first month of the campaign had been hit at some point before.[19] Targeting became a significant source of tension within the alliance. Lieutenant General Michael C. Short, who directed NATO's air operations against Serbia, serving as NATO's joint air force component commander, was a vocal critic. He stated explicitly that it was unacceptable for one nation to veto a target set that other states deemed important, meaning then that no one could strike it. In his view, this allowed the interests of one state to trump the interests of the whole alliance. To Short, this prolonged the war, since key target sets were kept off the table, and placed other member states' air crews at "unacceptable risk."[20] Further, Short indicated that NATO was unable to prosecute

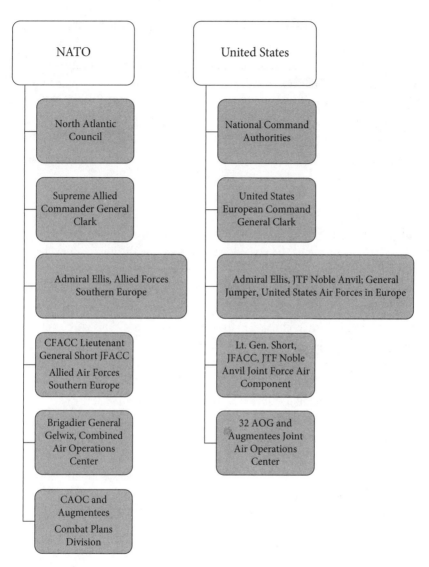

Figure 4.1 Decision-making structure, Operation Allied Force

SOURCE: Adapted from Benjamin S. Lambeth. *NATO's Air War for Kosovo: A Strategic and Operational Assessment.* Santa Monica, CA: Rand, 2001, 208.

NOTE: For tables that compare the command structure before and during Operation Allied Force, see "Report to Congress: Kosovo/Operation Allied Force After-Action Report," January 31, 2000, 18–20.

the war without the United States; according to him, if the United States had to provide 70 percent of the effort, leadership, command, control, and enabling force, then the United States should have more than one of the nineteen votes in the alliance. In his view, it was incumbent upon the United States to make this clear from the outset—that if the United States was going to run the war, it should have done so unencumbered by the alliance apparatus that gave other states a veto over targets. To him, this should have been a condition on U.S. participation—that the U.S. design the grand strategy, set the targets, and fight the war as it believed it should have been fought.[21]

The frustrations that arose as a consequence of the complex and burdensome decision-making structure, compounded by burden-sharing disparities, not only made the operation more difficult to prosecute but also impeded cohesion.[22] This theme of the United States working with allies with far less capacity to wage war persists throughout the era of intervention from Kosovo to Libya. And while the call for additional resources by non-U.S. allies in NATO to be brought to bear in military affairs met with limited success post–Operation Allied Force, changes in the ways in which decisions were made during wartime were implemented in subsequent operations, in large part because of the Kosovo experience.

The parallel decision-making structure also meant that states, the United States in particular, did not always keep their allies informed of their actions. In some instances, the United States withheld information about missions involving the use of "F-117s, B-2s, and cruise missiles, to ensure strict U.S. control over those U.S.-only assets and to maintain a firewall against leaks from any allies who might compromise those operations."[23] This created potentially dangerous situations when, for example, U.S. aircraft showed up on NATO radars without advance notice.[24] Even when the United States opted to share information, the process was complicated and cumbersome, thus impeding the alliance's ability to act effectively.[25]

In addition to being unwieldy and slow, the alliance suffered from other troubles as well.[26] According to Supreme Allied Commander Europe General Wesley Clark, who led NATO's campaign, leaks were a constant source of trouble. As early as October 1998, one of the French officers working at NATO headquarters had leaked key portions of the operational plan for the campaign to the Serbians.[27]

Even after Operation Allied Force ended, difficulties in NATO's decision making persisted. The fractures within the alliance were especially clear in the

dispute over the Pristina airport in June 1999, just after the NATO air operation had concluded. As the NATO-led Kosovo force (KFOR) was deployed
to Kosovo to occupy Serbia, Russia—fellow Slavs and in collusion with the
Serbians—moved to occupy the Pristina airport and enlarge a sphere of influence in the north, thus putting KFOR's mission at risk.[28] Fearing an expanding
sphere of influence for the Russians or a partition, Clark requested that enter-
ing troops block the runways at the airport and seize it ahead of the Russians.
Sir Michael Jackson, the British general in charge of the operation, balked at the
orders.[29] According to Clark, Jackson told Clark that Jackson "would no longer
be taking his orders from Washington."[30] When Clark countered by saying the
orders did not come from Washington, but rather from him as SACEUR, Jackson responded by saying that Clark did not have that authority. When Clark
responded that he did indeed have the authority, Jackson replied that he would
not be starting World War III for him. Jackson said that as a three-star general,
he should not have to take orders from Clark; Clark's response was that he,
himself, was a four-star general, and indeed Jackson did have to take orders
from him.[31] The difference resulted in numerous phone calls to various British
and American officials.[32] Above all, the incident revealed the difficulties among
the allies in agreeing on goals and strategies for attaining those goals. It also
illustrates the problems associated with multinational command structure,
even in long-standing, highly institutionalized alliances such as NATO.

NATO, constructed in peacetime and deployed to intervene in Kosovo, represented the best and worst of military alliance politics. The advantages of using a well-established institution with set decision-making mechanisms meant
that it could be employed at a time when constructing a coalition through a
global organization was not possible. However, because the alliance decision-
making apparatus was developed to function in peacetime, the execution of
wartime plans was obstructed by the need for consent by all member states
and the attenuating problems of managing nineteen domestic audiences. The
decision-making structure became an obstacle for NATO, one that required
constant amending and ultimately hampered the institution's ability to prosecute the war efficiently. The parallel decision-making structure degraded unity
of command and created its own challenges in communication. Operation
Allied Force underscores the difficulties of structuring a military alliance in
peacetime for wartime operation, especially when the details of any particular
operation are undetermined. The advantage of using an alliance structure to
prosecute a war is the source of its principal disadvantage as well. The highly

institutionalized nature of the organization, as well as the history of joint training and exercises, all facilitate employing such a weapon in war. However, those institutional rigidities, even if they can be amended ad hoc, can be paralyzing when quick reflexive action is necessary. This institution of interstate violence stood ready to implement war decisions. Yet although NATO offered advantages in realizing power, the effects were inhibiting with regard to efficiency in achieving the military ends. For this first NATO wartime operation, the institutional mechanisms that constrained the alliance were very apparent. Ad hoc coalitions have the advantage of having a more adaptable and flexible design for the task at hand; however, a standing framework for a relatively swift response to crisis provides an important platform for capabilities to be realized. Further, as the alliance was deployed in future cases, adjustments were made that demonstrated a crucial element of robustness and adaptability. In the Kosovo case, however, those institutional effects were quite pronounced and stood as important lessons for the institution as the member states moved forward from Operation Allied Force. Certainly, the benefits of the long-standing relationships in NATO fostered fewer friendly-fire episodes and reduced interoperability challenges; the latter in particular nevertheless served as a reminder of the problems associated with multilateral war prosecution.

Interoperability and Friendly Fire

Not a single friendly-fire incident developed despite the more than thirty-eight thousand sorties flown in OAF. NATO lost only two men in a training exercise in the eleven-week intensive operation.[33] Because there were no ground troops associated with OAF, friendly-fire episodes are not comparable to the Gulf War case (or the Afghanistan or Iraq cases). However, the absence of air-to-air fratricide in OAF (and, as we will see, in Operation Odyssey Dawn and Operation Unified Protector) demonstrates the effectiveness of joint training and effective communication.[34]

There were high-profile collateral-damage errors, such as the bombing of the Chinese embassy on May 7 and the bombing of a refugee column on April 15, 1999. However, despite the long-standing nature of NATO, a number of critical interoperability challenges (and capability disparities) arose and frustrated fighting effectiveness. These hinged principally on communication systems. As Secretary of Defense Cohen and Chairman of the Joint Chiefs of Staff Shelton indicated after the operation, Operation Allied Force underscored a number of profound disparities between the United States and its allies in regard to precision strike, mobility, command, control, and communications abilities. The gap between the United States and its allies hampered the alliance's ability to operate effectively. As an example, they described a situation in which very few NATO members could use precision munitions. As a result, the United States had to conduct the overwhelming number of strike sorties, particularly in the early days of the operation. Furthermore, the absence of a secure interoperable communications system meant that the allies had to rely on nonsecure methods that compromised operational security. Cohen and Shelton urged, in the face of these obstacles, the implementation of the Defense Capabilities Initiative in order to enhance allied capacity in the areas of deployment and mobility; sustainability and logistics; effective engagement; survivability of forces and infrastructure; and command, control, communication, and information systems.[35] As we will see in the chapters ahead, these problems of unequal capability have persisted within the alliance throughout the contemporary era and impinged on NATO's fighting effectiveness even through the Libyan operation. Kosovo gave the first hint of the profound disparities in capabilities between the United States and the rest of the world in the capacity to wage war.

The difficulties associated with interoperability and discrepancies in capabilities between the United States and the other NATO member states were so substantial that they culminated in a more urgent commitment to the Defense Capabilities Initiative following the operation. NATO's first active mission shined a light on those areas that debilitated the alliance during its wartime operations.[36]

Overall, however, the use of the preestablished alliance helped mitigate friendly-fire and interoperability problems. The nature of this operation, as it was exclusively an air war, played an important role as well. The problems associated with air-to-ground friendly-fire casualties were obviously averted. The nature of the operation matters in regard to institutional effects, in terms of friendly fire, interoperability, and burden sharing and leverage within the institution.

Balance of Power and Burden Sharing Within the Alliance

The top-three contributors to Operation Allied Force in terms of sorties and aircraft deployed were the United States, France, and the United Kingdom.[37] During the operation itself, most of the contributions by allies were made in terms of allied airfields, overflight rights, logistical support, and peacekeeping troops after Operation Allied Force concluded.[38] Thirteen of the nineteen member states contributed aircraft to the operation. Of the approximately 38,000 sorties flown, including those flown by airlifters, the United States flew more than 29,000 and deployed more than 700 aircraft. France deployed about 100 aircraft and flew approximately 2,414 sorties; the United Kingdom was the second-largest contributor of aircraft of all of the European allies and flew about 1,950 sorties. The Netherlands flew approximately 1,252 sorties; Italy was the third-largest contributor of aircraft of the European allies and flew about 1,081 sorties; Germany flew about 636 sorties.[39] Fourteen of nineteen alliance members contributed forces to the operation, totaling 305 aircraft that flew more than 15,000 sorties.[40] According to Secretary of Defense Cohen, the United States flew most of the sorties, with 400 planes in the allied force of just over 600 aircraft, flying about 60 percent of the sorties, with the remaining allies flying the other 40 percent. Similar proportions applied to other components of the operation, such as support, reconnaissance, and tankers.[41]

In his statement to the Armed Services Committee, Secretary Cohen said that he had approved an expanded air package and that the United States' role in the operation would only be growing. Table 4.1 summarizes the power capabilities data for the top six nations contributing to Operation Allied Force. While the United States was by far the most powerful country of the six in regard to capability share, the power differentials are not nearly as divergent as they were in the first Gulf War.

Table 4.1 Power capabilities of top-six contributors to Operation Allied Force

State abbreviation	Military expenditures (in millions of U.S. 2012 dollars)	Military personnel (in thousands)	Composite Index of National Capability
USA	29,200,000	1,490	0.149701
FRN	37,811	421	0.022813
UKG	36,368	218	0.024657
NTH	6,193	54	0.005624
ITA	22,664	391	0.019634
GMY	31,182	331	0.02941

SOURCE: Correlates of War Data. Version 3.02. See Singer 1987.

NOTE: The Composite Index of National Capability is computed by summing observations for total population, urban population, iron and steel production, energy consumption, military personnel, and military expenditures for the year, converting each country's absolute component into a share of the international system, averaging across the six component parts. Accessed 12/14/2012. http://www.correlatesofwar.org/COW2%20Data/Capabilities/nmc3-02.htm. USA refers to the United States; FRN to France; UKG to the United Kingdom; NTH to the Netherlands; ITA to Italy; and GMY to Germany.

Operation Allied Force cost the United States $3.1 billion in incremental funds.[42] The United States provided about 70 percent of the aircraft for the operation and about 60 percent of the sorties during the operation,[43] while the Europeans provided 56–70 percent of the peacekeeping troops after the air campaigns.[44] The Europeans, in summary, consistently provided the largest share of ground troops for NATO operations and specialists trained for post-conflict crisis intervention. The non-U.S. NATO European allies also took the lead in development assistance. The European Commission (EC) and European NATO member states provided approximately $10.2 billion of the almost $15 billion paid into the Balkans between 1993 and 1999. These funds were used for humanitarian and reconstruction purposes, and for rebuilding infrastructure such as airports, bridges, and roads. During this same period, the United States paid approximately $1.2 billion, mostly for institution building and emergency relief. Furthermore, the European allies provided a large contingent of civilians for programs to rebuild, such as two thousand UN civilian police.[45]

The challenges associated with burden sharing in Operation Allied Force were mirrored by burden-sharing problems in the alliance more generally. Burden sharing in NATO was an issue of contention throughout the history of the alliance. As the Department of Defense reported in its annual assessment of allied contributions to defense, the United States paid one-quarter of the NATO common-funded budgets in which all nineteen members contributed to at the time of Operation Allied Force.[46] Table 4.2 reports these data regarding NATO's common-funded budgets.

The enduring differences in military spending on the part of the United States and its European allies meant that once planning for Operation Allied Force was underway, the capability differential would be exceedingly apparent. For example, the absence of a strong European strategic transport and logistics capability alone meant that the United States had to undertake the bulk of the work of the Kosovo campaign. Operation Allied Force also revealed a serious technology gap between the United States and Europe, given that more than 70 percent of the firepower deployed in the operation was American. The United Kingdom was able to provide cruise missiles, but only a few European member states had laser-guided bombs. In addition, only 10 percent of European aircraft were capable of precision bombing, and only France could contribute in a meaningful way to high-level bombing raids at night. U.S. superiority in military technology and equipment was overwhelming. Only the United States could provide strategic bombers and stealth aircraft. The

Table 4.2 NATO's common-funded budgets, 2000 (2000 dollars in millions, 2000 exchange rates)

Member	NATO Security Investment Program	Percentage of NATO Security Investment Program	Military budget	Percentage of total military budget[a]	Civil budget	Percentage of total civil budget	Total NATO common budget	Percentage of total NATO common budget[a]	Percentage of national GDP in 2000
Belgium	23.2	4.3	13.9	3.1	3.6	2.8	40.7	3.6	0.020
Canada	20.4	3.7	25.6	5.7	7.0	5.4	53.0	4.7	0.007
Czech Republic	3.1	0.6	4.5	1.0	1.2	0.9	8.8	0.8	0.007
Denmark	18.6	3.4	8.2	1.8	1.9	1.5	28.7	2.6	0.020
France	29.1	5.3	28.2	6.3	20.0	15.3	77.3	6.9	0.006
Germany	126.7	23.2	76.9	17.1	20.2	15.5	223.8	19.9	0.010
Greece	5.4	1.0	1.9	0.4	0.5	0.4	7.8	0.7	0.005
Hungary	2.3	0.4	3.3	0.7	0.8	0.6	6.4	0.6	0.008
Iceland	0.0	0.0	0.2	0.0	0.1	0.1	0.3	0.0	0.005
Italy	46.2	8.5	29.7	6.6	7.5	5.8	83.4	7.4	0.007
Luxembourg	1.1	0.2	0.4	0.1	0.1	0.1	1.6	0.1	0.009
Netherlands	25.7	4.7	13.9	3.1	3.6	2.8	43.2	3.8	0.010
Norway	15.9	2.9	5.7	1.3	1.4	1.1	23.0	2.0	0.020
Poland	8.6	1.6	12.4	2.8	3.2	2.5	24.2	2.2	0.009
Portugal	1.9	0.3	3.2	0.7	0.8	0.6	5.9	0.5	0.004
Spain	13.8	2.5	17.6	3.9	4.6	3.5	36.0	3.2	0.005
Turkey	5.8	1.1	8.0	1.8	2.1	1.6	15.9	1.4	0.004
United Kingdom	61.1	11.2	80.4	17.9	22.5	17.3	164.0	14.6	0.010
United States	136.3	25.0	115.6	25.7	29.2	22.4	281.1	25.0	0.003
Total	545.2	100.0	449.6	100.0	130.3	100.0	1,125.1	100.0	—

SOURCE: Department of Defense, Report on Allied Contributions to the Common Defense, March 2001 (a report to the U.S. Congress by the secretary of defense). Data on percentage of GDP taken from the CIA World Factbook. Accessed 5/15/2013. http://nodedge.com/ciawfb.

NOTE: As a result of rounding, the numbers shown may not add up to the totals.

[a]Calculation does not include contributions to the NATO Airborne Early Warning and Control Program.

European deficiency in reconnaissance and surveillance aircraft was painfully acute in this case, as it would be in the Libyan case to come.[47]

The United States' dominance in information systems actually made it difficult to communicate with its allies.[48] In other words, despite the fact that NATO was a long-standing alliance, the actual implementation of a war plan was problematic as a consequence of these differences in capability. In the Department of Defense's After-Action Report, Secretary Cohen and General Shelton asserted that even though the United States shouldered the primary military burden, NATO did provide aircraft and flew a significant number of strike missions. The Europeans provided ground forces in Albania and Macedonia, and their air bases and facilities providing communication, intelligence, and logistics support were instrumental in executing the operation. In addition, the Europeans provided much in the way of humanitarian relief and also took on the largest share of the peacekeeping effort.[49]

On the one hand, OAF is a burden-sharing success story in that NATO member states contributed proportionately to the operation in terms of, for example, their available aircraft. Further, NATO military infrastructure such as bases, airfields, and airspace were essential for the operation's success. However, OAF revealed the great disparity in capabilities between the United States and its European allies, and the United States ultimately shouldered by far the biggest share of the burden.[50] The alliance was very effective in uncovering the benefits of ready institutions of interstate violence—the mechanisms that hampered efficient attaining of goals were highly visible as well.

Alliance Security Dilemma

The question of the alliance security dilemma in NATO's operation in Kosovo is an important one. The inability of Europe to respond to a European security crisis without U.S. initiative could demonstrate a level of U.S. entrapment in the context of the alliance. The case demonstrates the continued European need for American security capabilities, even if the case itself simultaneously illustrates some allies' unhappiness with U.S. hegemony.[51] The United States in this case, however, took the lead in forging a military solution to Serbian aggression, driven by factors that were not only strategic but also personal and internal. President Clinton was affected by his inaction in Bosnia and Rwanda, as well as shattered by domestic scandal. Secretary of State Madeleine Albright was highly motivated as a consequence of her personal experience and the Bosnian legacy.[52] As a consequence, the alliance security dilemma did not mediate U.S. decision making to the degree one might expect in the face of European impotence as the crisis unfolded.[53] However, the commitment to action was constrained by Clinton's staunch opposition to U.S. troops being deployed for a ground war, and certainly congressional tepidness did not signal a strong strategic commitment to European stability. A more forceful commitment to war against Yugoslavia, the unwillingness to incur American casualties, and ambivalence about the war were manifestations of weak United States' fears of entrapment.[54] Great Britain worked hard to bolster U.S. resolve and commitment to the operation.[55]

Not all European allies viewed participation in the operation in the same way. Pierre Martin and Mark Brawley call the categories of NATO allies "the front runners," "the faithful," and "the frustrated." The front-runners, such as the United Kingdom and Canada, were strongly motivated by principle to act; the faithful, such as Spain and Germany, were motivated to act to demonstrate alliance reliability; and the frustrated, such as France, desired decisive action but were unable to supply an alternative to U.S. leadership in the operation.[56] The preeminence of U.S. capability was apparent in this case. The NATO alliance facilitated the United States' ability to bring capabilities to bear even though institutional effects hampered efficiency.

The need by many alliance partners, including the newest ones at the time—Poland, the Czech Republic, and Hungary in particular—as well as more enduring ones, such as Germany and Spain, to demonstrate reliability and utility to the United States suggests that they were at least in part motivated by general fears of abandonment. There would be no need to demonstrate utility to the lead power if long-term viability of the commitment were not at risk. The theme of new Eastern European NATO member states underscoring their loyalty and reliability to the United States punctuates the era of post–Cold War NATO expansion. Poland and Hungary supported the NATO operation despite the fact that Hungary incurred costs as a consequence of the turmoil. The Czech Republic was less favorable to the operation, which generated tension within the country as well as within the alliance.[57] The Kosovo operation highlighted Europe's strategic dependence on the United States, thus raising abandonment fears within the region.[58] The operation underscored the importance of NATO to European security and the need to preserve it.[59] In a more indirect way it also illuminates the importance of NATO to advancing U.S. interests. The web of institutions of interstate violence that the United States has constructed enables it to respond and react more easily to situations in principle and practice than any other state in the international system. It not only has the capability to do so; it has the platform from which it can launch its objectives and realize its goals. In other words, the military might of the United States is projected via these institutions that exist, such as NATO. In some ways these institutions augment fighting effectiveness, though in others, effectiveness is hampered. This is explored more fully in the following section.

Cohesion and Fighting Effectiveness

Operation Allied Force was effective in achieving the goals it set out to achieve at minimal human cost to the alliance. This was not always an easy undertaking; the airspace in which the operation took place was extremely challenging, with thousands of combat sorties flying in hostile airspace over territory with a significant integrated air defense network, where commercial, private, and humanitarian relief flights were all taking place. In addition, the weather conditions were often less than ideal for identifying targets, and the rugged terrain further complicated the mission, thus creating additional hazards. Despite this environment, NATO was able to execute a precise air operation with precision munitions and well-trained forces.[60]

As in the Gulf War, airpower prevailed. As Lieutenant Colonel Lamb wrote, OAF was successful; it achieved is primary objectives. With a total of more than thirty-eight thousand sorties flown, all but two aircraft returned safely during seventy-eight days of around-the-clock operations. Ultimately, the Serbs left Kosovo, NATO peacekeepers ensured stability, and refugees were able to return to their homes.[61] Echoing these positive sentiments regarding NATO's achievement, Secretary of Defense Cohen, in a joint statement with General Shelton, chairman of the Joint Chiefs of Staff, speaking to the Senate Armed Services Committee in October 1999, asserted that OAF demonstrated NATO's "unrivaled military prowess." The use of new systems and capabilities was effective. According to Cohen and Shelton, NATO demonstrated both political cohesion and military capacity in the face of new threats confronting states in the twenty-first century.[62]

NATO did prevail in the air war against Milošević and his forces, and it fought effectively in this regard, with minimal loss of life on the part of NATO troops. However, there were many obstacles in terms of running the war and efficiency. Further, as in the Gulf War case, NATO's easy victory had as much to do with its fighting capability as it did with the weakness of its adversary.[63]

It was a challenge to develop and maintain cohesion of NATO during the Kosovo campaign. Despite the fact that NATO was a preexisting alliance with a command structure and decision-making mechanisms in place, the Kosovo campaign was a seminal moment in NATO history. The nineteen member states struggled to determine how to confront Milošević's brutality in Kosovo. In fact, the U.S. General Accountability Office identified the absence of clear military objectives as one of the principal departures from military doctrine in Operation Allied Force.[64] The ambiguity of the alliance's goals was the result of divergent perspectives within the alliance. The member states had different perspectives on the conflict and on what action should be taken and how. As the General Accountability Office reported in summary after the Kosovo mission, one state shared religious and cultural background with the Kosovo Albanians, while another had historic and religious connections to the Serbian Yugoslavs. In another NATO member state with a coalition government, part of the coalition supported the operation, whereas the other part did not and threatened withdrawal from the government in the event of a ground war. Poland, the Czech Republic, and Hungary supported the operation, though to varying degrees, and Hungary feared Serbian retaliation against an ethnically related minority population in the Yugoslav area.[65]

The alliance grappled principally with how to stop the Serbian government. In essence, while alliance partners agreed on their overall objectives, achieving consensus on strategies toward attaining those goals was far more difficult. Exacerbating this problem was that as the air war, an operation designed to stop the killing and expulsion of Albanian Kosovars, got underway, the situation on the ground worsened. This heightened criticism in some countries such as Germany regarding the war, and tension within the alliance grew.[66]

Further, as General Wesley Clark noted in an interview after the operation, there was international concern regarding the possibility of a ground war, resulting in fears that it would not be possible to sustain domestic support from participating countries for such an operation and that the costs of a ground war would not correspond with the interests at stake.[67] According to British Prime Minister Tony Blair, these differences were at the heart of the challenges to NATO consensus.[68] Most NATO countries were adamantly opposed to a ground war, which meant that operation planning was constrained; no NATO consensus would emerge on how to fight a land war in Kosovo.[69] There was, however, a common belief that something needed to be done, particularly in the aftermath of the Gornje Obrinje massacre in September 1998, which culminated in a UN Security Council resolution.[70] The Račak massacre in January

1999 further galvanized the NATO community to act, particularly as diplomatic efforts to end the Serb militia's brutality failed.[71]

In the aftermath of Gornje Obrinje and Račak, the core goal of halting the destruction of Milošević's forces in Kosovo became paramount, even if wide differences existed among the allies in terms of strategy for attaining that goal.[72] Ultimately, NATO agreed to a number of goals: to signal NATO opposition to Milošević's continuing aggression and to deter him from continuing or escalating his attacks and to undermine Serb military capacity. To achieve those goals, a strategy of attacking targets throughout the Federal Republic of Yugoslavia and fielded forces in Kosovo would be undertaken.[73]

Because of the differences among the allies in regard to preferred strategies for confronting Serbia, significant effort went into maintaining alliance cohesion both leading up to and during the operation. General Wesley Clark describes talking to political leaders at home and abroad, as well as diplomats and defense chiefs, and having to bargain, negotiate, and cajole to get the NATO operation underway.[74] During the operation, similar coaxing was necessary. The United States in particular worked hard to keep the alliance together. There was constant communication among the U.S. president, the secretary of state, and various other U.S. officials with their NATO counterparts every single one of the seventy-eight days of the operation. This was essential to NATO unity. On April 23, 1999, at the NATO Summit in Washington, DC, alliance member states approved of intensifying the air war, they expanded the target set, and they deployed additional aircraft, as well as articulating the political conditions that needed to be met to end the war.[75]

The need to manage the alliance, keep it together, maintain it in every way, never dimmed throughout the operation. It was apparent to all that in order to prevail, the alliance had to finish what it started. As Secretary of Defense Cohen said at an Armed Services Committee hearing, NATO was determined to prevail and to remain united. The goals of the operation were clear—Milošević needed to withdraw, to allow refugees to return to their homes, to allow humanitarian assistance to flow into the area, and to see the deployment of a NATO-led international security force. Cohen also indicated that Kosovo should be given the right to democratic self-governance. He was adamant that NATO would stand together, stand united, and be strong in its determination to prevail.[76]

Operation Allied Force underscored the challenges of keeping a large alliance on task in wartime. Constant communication and negotiation were necessary in maintaining cohesion. Once underway, the goal of prevailing over Serb militias became paramount, which helped foster unity of purpose. The United States adjusted its strategic thinking to get the alliance to agree to the operation.[77] In other words, cohesion dictated the design of the air campaign. The United States originally put together a completely different air plan, which was more extensive and intensive than the one to which NATO ultimately agreed. As Secretary Cohen indicated, had the United States acted unilaterally, it would have hit "hard and fast," crippling Milošević's forces immediately. But it was not easy to implement such an operation, given the need to achieve consensus among all nineteen NATO member states. Furthermore, basing needs, supplies and logistics, airspace, and the like all meant juggling various demands and perspectives. According to Cohen, acting unilaterally would have culminated in a far more "robust, aggressive, and decapitating type of campaign." But the dictates of alliance unity altered the configuration and execution of the operation in critical ways.[78]

The alliance operation represented strategic multilateralism—using NATO for this mission was the only way to approach the issue, as no one country was willing to take action alone. In this way, we see the insights of realist institutionalism very clearly. The ends were worth pursuing, yet could be advanced only through an institutional framework. In other words, institutions are essential in promoting states' agendas, militarily and otherwise. Further, unity offered NATO an opportunity to bolster its image in the early post–Cold War years, when its mission and continuance were being questioned. It also gave the United States a chance to strengthen the alliance in the aftermath of the Bosnia experience.[79] The institution was a benefit to the United States in facilitating the actualization of power. A unilateral approach to the Kosovo crisis would have proved far costlier politically and militarily than any country was willing to bear; in this case, multilateralism was easier and more advantageous, even if the problems within the alliance during the operation culminated in reviews outlining how to improve alliance performance.[80] The operation was motivated by a shared commitment to NATO and to keeping the alliance active.[81] In this case, as in many of the operations discussed in this book, member states valued the alliance itself, perhaps even more than the conflict at hand.[82] Further, because of the countries' reluctance to act alone, acting via NATO was the only viable and least costly option. Again, the case highlights the theme of realist institutionalism, of using organizations and multilateral frameworks to advance a strategic agenda. It showcases the importance of these institutions of interstate violence for U.S. hegemony and the calculated enhancement to member states' abilities to achieve their goals.

In summary, NATO struggled mightily with cohesion, particularly in the tactical operational aspects of the war. The decision-making mechanism requiring consensus paralyzed the organization and was the opposite of what a flexible fighting force requires. The challenges associated with maintaining the cohesion of the alliance provided critical lessons for the institutional design constructed for future operations. The case clearly demonstrates the difficulty in converting a peacetime organization to wartime endeavors; achieving consensus on how to prosecute war, and even the mission's ultimate objectives, were not easily reached. According to the General Accountability Office, cohesion was so difficult to maintain that it resulted in profound departures from U.S. military doctrine, which further complicated the campaign.[83] Operation Allied Force underscores the many inherent challenges to alliance war fighting. It also reveals the ambiguity in the relationship between the multilateral prosecution of war and the inherent legitimacy in those operations.

Legitimacy

The decision to undertake the Kosovo operation via alliance was motivated out of a desire to enhance the legitimacy of the undertaking. Unilateral action was not politically feasible for the United States, the United Nations was unavailable because of the opposition of China and Russia to employing force, and Europe was unable to act on its own. Even within the context of NATO, questions regarding the legitimacy of the operation emerged repeatedly. The legal ramifications and repercussions of such an operation were evaluated and discussed at length among European policy makers in particular while they tried to decide how to address the human rights violations taking place in the former Yugoslavia. As Secretary Cohen recalled, one if his major concerns was whether or not NATO would be on board, since he strongly believed that the United States could not undertake the action alone. The long internal debate over whether or not NATO had the legal authority to intervene thus ensued. According to Cohen, he spent an enormous amount of time with his European counterparts addressing and allaying concerns over a contagion effect of instability as a result of refugee flows. Further, he indicated that most NATO member states stipulated that they would not take action in the absence of a UN Security Council resolution sanctioning action. This discussion of legal authority began in early 1998 and continued until action was finally taken in the spring of 1999.[84]

Because the Kosovo intervention was motivated by humanitarian concerns, the issue of the form the intervention would take was very important.[85] The role of moral imperative has been explored in depth in this case.[86] Scholars of international law indicate that unilateral interventions in cases of humanitarian crises are illegal. The authority and judgment of a single state cannot stand in for global opinion as to whether or not intervention is warranted. Thus, collective involvement is required.[87] Again, this highlights the importance of institutions in actualizing power capabilities and advancing specific strategic ends.

In the case of Kosovo, the UN Security Council (UNSC) did condemn the Serb militia's brutality and humanitarian abuses, even if it did not condone external military intervention. UN Resolution 1160 imposed an arms embargo on the Federal Republic of Yugoslavia on March 31, 1998. The UNSC then called for a halt to the "indiscriminate force" being employed by Serb militias in Kosovo and demanded a cease-fire in Resolution 1199 on September 23, 1998.[88] The following month, UN Resolution 1203 invoked growing concern regarding the humanitarian crisis.[89] The United States took the position that the resolutions were sufficient for legitimating action in the area.[90] Because it was clear to the United States and its European allies that an explicit resolution from the UN Security Council sanctioning intervention would be vetoed by Russia and by China, the question was never submitted.[91]

To some, the absence of a UN resolution explicitly condoning the operation undermined the legitimacy of NATO's action.[92] UN Secretary-General Kofi Annan was conflicted over UN Security Council inaction in the face of humanitarian abuses in the former Yugoslavia. In the midst of OAF, he said, "Unless the Security Council is restored to its preeminent position as the sole source of legitimacy on the use of force, we are on a dangerous path to anarchy."[93]

NATO Secretary-General Javier Solana contextualized the alliance's intervention through the United Nations' position to reconcile NATO members who were divided over the need for UN sanction. More specifically, Solana noted the failure of Yugoslavia to heed the UN Resolutions (1160 and 1199); the unraveling of the situation in Kosovo posing a threat to stability in the region (1199); the growing humanitarian crisis in the area, which had even been documented by the UN secretary-general in fall of the previous year; and the inability to speedily get a UNSC resolution authorizing force in the region.[94] Ironically, this is suggestive of the UN legitimating authority, even in the absence of its express sanction. A number of participating countries had strong reservations about bypassing the United Nations.[95]

The extent to which the United Nations resolutions legitimated action in Kosovo is in some ways secondary to the question of whether or not the operation was widely viewed as motivated by global concern. In addition, the issue of legitimacy with OAF rested not only on the ends of the intervention but on its means as well. In other words, there was worldwide support for stopping the humanitarian abuses promulgated by Serb militias, but the use of a strategic air bombing campaign to do so was widely perceived as culminating in a rise in displaced refugees and increased humanitarian abuses at the outset of the campaign. However, simultaneously, particularly within the participating states, there was no widespread public support for a ground war to end the violence,[96] although that support grew in the United States from 31 percent at the time the air strikes began to 52 percent by April 13–14, 1999, as a consequence of the highly publicized Kosovar refugee problem. Most people in favor of committing ground troops believed that the United States had a moral obligation to help the refugees.[97] In some countries, such as Canada, support for the air war was 79 percent early on in the operation, and 57 percent even approved of launching a ground operation.[98] It is also noteworthy that even though most NATO member states' citizens were against committing to a ground war, when polled, these constituencies also believed that if a land offensive unfolded, their countries' troops should be dispatched to serve in the operation.[99]

Public opinion in the United States weakly supported intervention in Kosovo a month before the air strikes began, as the peace talks in Rambouillet unraveled, standing at just 43 percent polled. Once the mission was underway, support grew to 61 percent in a poll conducted on April 13–14, 1999.[100] This was true across most of the states involved, with about 61 percent in favor and 31 percent against the NATO operation, with higher support in some countries, such as the United Kingdom, Denmark, Norway, the Netherlands, and Canada.[101] In Eastern Europe, among the new NATO member states, popular support for the intervention was more mixed. In the Czech Republic, citizens opposed NATO intervention 57 percent to 35 percent.[102] In polls in many countries around the world, Milošević was overwhelmingly perceived as a war criminal.[103] Opposition in the international community to the NATO air strikes was also present. This was very true in Russia, Ukraine, Slovakia, and to a lesser extent, Sweden.[104] By and large, however, publics around the world supported NATO action to bring an end to the persecution of Albanian Kosovars, although there was much uncertainty regarding the political objectives to be served by employing force.[105] This culminated in a mixed legitimacy score for Operation Allied Force.

Further, in this case, there is a distinction between the legitimacy of the operation and the means through which it was accomplished.[106] For example, the Hungarians thought the region was worse off after the air strikes began than before, as did the French and the Germans.[107] While intervention was largely regarded as warranted, the air strikes were met with mixed opinion. On the one hand, member states' leadership and domestic populations did not support the commitment of ground troops; on the other hand, there was a sense that once the operation was underway, the air war itself exacerbated the crisis on the ground.

The interventions not taken, especially in Rwanda and Bosnia, also played a role in determining legitimacy and support for the intervention. Inaction of the international community in these crises culminated in a heightened stimulus for action in Kosovo. Six years had passed since the United States' withdrawal from Somalia after the loss of eighteen U.S. Rangers. The well-documented atrocities in Bosnia and Rwanda drew significant international and media attention. The fact that Serb militias were then at work in Kosovo, again in NATO's immediate sphere of influence, lent legitimacy to the operation.

The thesis that institutions have varying degrees of "neutrality" and therefore varying degrees of legitimating effect and political benefit is certainly at work here. Not only was there a hit to legitimacy in the operation because there was no UN sanction; there were also more questions regarding U.S. motives.[108] In addition, the wrangling and hand-wringing within the alliance over how to proceed in the absence of UNSC authorization affected the cohesion of the alliance. It made agreeing on goals and strategies of the operation more challenging. It is not, however, clear that a UN Security Council Resolution advocating a military response to the Serbian government would have altered worldwide public opinion.

The strategic context played an important role in this case as well. In the early post–Cold War years, scholars and policy makers alike questioned the ongoing role of NATO. Academics and practitioners tend to neglect the singular importance of alliances in peacetime beyond their deterrent value. The conventional wisdom suggests that the value of alliances derives exclusively from their capacity to prosecute wars and their capability-aggregation effect, thereby missing the beneficial institutional effects such as transparency and conflict management. These beneficial institutional effects should suffice to justify or legitimate an enduring peacetime alliance such as NATO in the post–Cold War era, but they do not because of the pervasive view that alliances merely serve to deter or prosecute wars. Undertaking an operation of this kind on the eve of NATO's fiftieth anniversary and days after its first post–Cold War expansion was a huge symbol of NATO's continuing importance and purpose. In fact, some argue that NATO's legitimacy was on the line while confronting the crisis in Kosovo.[109] This case illustrates the complexity of the relationship between legitimacy and multilateralism. It is not necessarily a linear relationship or even a unidirectional one. On the contrary, multilateralism is both a product of legitimacy and a catalyst in building legitimacy; the type of institutional response will be determined by the legitimacy inherent in the mission. The type of institutional response will determine the legitimating effects as well.

The legitimacy of Operation Allied Force was not incumbent upon the alliance undertaking the mission—legitimacy inhered principally to the belief that action needed to be taken to allay the growing humanitarian crisis in Kosovo. Legitimacy was curtailed by the fact that the operation was not sanctioned by the United Nations and by the means employed to secure Serbian capitulation. In addition, public opinion polls in Europe suggested that there was some skepticism toward President Clinton's motivations, given the domestic turmoil and internal scandals he was facing. However, this was clearly not a majority opinion.[110] Overall, legitimacy did not inhere to the multilateral framework used to prosecute the war; interestingly, it was NATO legitimacy that was bolstered by the operation rather than the other way around. Operation Allied Force was not as legitimate as the Persian Gulf War; public support for it was decidedly lower.[111] The fact that action was taken through NATO rather than the United Nations is both representative of reduced legitimacy and a product of it.

CONCLUSION

Operation Allied Force dramatically underscores the institutional component of military alliances. The use of a peacetime alliance structure to prosecute a war was challenging. Ultimately, even though NATO apparatus was employed, the United States cultivated a parallel decision-making structure, which further undermined the credibility of NATO as a wartime actor. It also suggests that while some elements of institutions advance strategic goals, other components and effects diminish the efficient quest to achieve those ends. In addition, the United States shouldered the biggest burden of action, and interoperability challenges still confronted the allies despite the long-standing nature of the institution—though likely fewer than there could have been in an ad hoc coalition of nonallied states without joint training and exercise experience. These issues,

Table 4.3 Overview of variables in Operation Allied Force

Independent variables	Mediating variables	Dependent variables
Alliance	Decision-making structure: hierarchical but dual	Cohesion: low to moderate
Size: medium	Power distribution: asymmetrical	War-fighting effectiveness: effective
	Internal leverage rested principally with lead power	Interoperability: few challenges
		Legitimacy of operation: mixed

particularly the decision-making mechanisms, hampered the cohesion of the alliance in a very significant way. Legitimacy of the mission was undermined by the absence of a sanction by a neutral global arbiter such as the United Nations, though NATO's pursuit of humanitarian objectives and the defeat of the Serb militias were not condemned by the international community writ large, even if they were condemned by China and Russia. Legitimacy, thus, did not inhere to NATO; in some ways, NATO's legitimacy hinged on the operation. Table 4.3 provides an overview. Operation Allied Force illustrates again the importance of institutions in advancing power-seeking objectives and the use of multilateralism for political benefit. In this case, not only was NATO instrumental in taking action to fulfill the will of many of its member states; it also served to underscore the ongoing meaning and legitimacy of the organization itself.

Operation Allied Force illustrates the realist institutionalist theme of providing a framework through which member states can achieve their goals in a way that they would not otherwise be able to accomplish. The standing institutional framework advanced the goals of the states while simultaneously hampering efficiency along many dimensions. The existing alliance, with long-standing relationships and a high degree of institutionalization, provided a foundation from which member states, and particularly the United States, could realize their power. In the absence of such institutions, there could not have easily been a military response to Milošević's humanitarian abuses in Kosovo.

5 OPERATION ENDURING FREEDOM AND THE INTERNATIONAL SECURITY ASSISTANCE FORCE

IT IS ESPECIALLY important to explore the meaning of multilateralism in the context of the war in Afghanistan. This war decision by George W. Bush and his administration was widely perceived as unilateral.[1] And yet a close examination of the way in which the war in Afghanistan unfolded makes clear that wholly unilateral operations are rarely feasible in the contemporary age and are profoundly un-American. Multilateralism was undertaken in Afghanistan for both strategic and ideological reasons that persisted for the duration of the war. The central question of American warfare is not whether it is unilateral or multilateral, but rather how the multilateralism manifests. The Afghanistan case is instructive in this context; it reveals the spectrum of multilateral action even in the space of one target country. The institutions available to promote American hegemony are many; some of these instruments of war facilitate the projection of American power; others hinder its realization. We see evidence of both in this case. As realist institutionalism instructs, certain institutional mechanisms facilitated the United States' swift and effective response post–9/11; other institutional effects undermined cohesion, efficiency, and effectiveness in pursuing U.S. military ends.

This chapter offers an examination of the Afghanistan case and the multilateral character of the operation, both in regard to Operation Enduring Freedom (OEF) and to the International Security Assistance Force (ISAF). I analyze the institutional arrangements, decision-making structure, size, burden sharing and balance of power within the alliance and coalition, and effects on cohesion and efficacy of the coalition and alliance used to prosecute the war and to maintain the fragile peace in the less turbulent regions in Afghanistan.

IN THE BEGINNING: THE ALLIANCE, SORT OF

In the immediate aftermath of the 9/11 attacks, the United States began shoring up support for war. The day following the attacks, President Bush spoke with UK Prime Minister Tony Blair, French President Jacques Chirac, Chinese President Jiang Zemin, and twice to Russian President Vladimir Putin. These individuals, representing the UN Security Council permanent members, provided support for the United States, before the coalition canvass broadened. Bush warned that the coalition might not be as wide or as representative as in the first Gulf War. Meanwhile, Secretary of State Colin Powell approached NATO Secretary-General George Robertson to ensure that article 5 of the Washington Treaty, the mutual defense clause, would be invoked, which it was for the first time in the alliance's fifty-two-year history. Both Britain and France immediately committed military planners to work with U.S. officials as plans to respond to the 9/11 attacks unfolded.[2] While Colin Powell undertook most of the heavy lifting in regard to assembling the international coalition, President Bush himself spoke with the leaders of Russia, France, Germany, Canada, and China.[3] In the words of President Bush, "My attitude all along was, if we have to go it alone, we'll go it alone; but I'd rather not."[4]

At the outset of the war in Afghanistan, OEF was publicly considered a largely unilateral exercise.[5] If anything, however, the war demonstrates that contemporary interstate warfare prosecuted by democracies is rarely pursued in the absence of coalition and allied cooperation. It also highlights the institutional mechanisms that facilitate power projection and those that hinder the efficient achievement of war aims. The United States was the principal architect of the war in Afghanistan, although the operations called for substantial cooperation from neighboring countries and the United States' closest allies. The need for allies even in an operation that was largely designed by the United States highlights the less visible yet consequential aspect of maintaining, projecting, and sustaining American hegemony, that is, its web of alliances and institutions of interstate violence that span the globe. With the lessons of Operation Allied Force burned indelibly into the minds of U.S. strategic thinkers, despite NATO's invocation of article 5 of the Washington Treaty, the arrangements made by the United States with other countries cooperating in the war effort were bilateral. In the early days of OEF, American allies were eager to help, and cohesion was high—states agreed on goals and on strategies toward attaining those goals. Yet as the insurgency grew and the commitment to

Afghanistan grew with it, cohesion declined and the dynamics of NATO in particular became more complex.

In the beginning of Operation Enduring Freedom, on October 7, 2001, the United States, with the United Kingdom and Northern Alliance forces, undertook the attack against the al-Qaeda network in Afghanistan and ultimately the Taliban government. On October 7, both the United States and the United Kingdom reported the use of military force to the UN Security Council, invoking UN article 51 regarding the right to self-defense. The United Kingdom was the only country other than the United States to participate in the military action in Afghanistan at the very outset of Operation Enduring Freedom. Only ten days following 9/11, Prime Minister Blair had U.S. war plans as they stood at that time so he could coordinate the British plan, Operation Veritas, which would use the British Army Special Forces; the parachute regiment; Royal Marines; and the Royal Air Force's aircraft, including four C-17 transports.[6] British Special Forces operated in country, and UK submarines fired Tomahawk cruise missiles into Afghanistan. In addition, the United Kingdom played a supporting role by making the air force base at Diego Garcia available and providing daily air-air refueling and reconnaissance operations. The Royal Air Force aided the United States in other ways as well—deploying to support U.S. carrier-borne assets. Further, British forces from the Saif Sareea II training exercise in Oman in October 2001 remained in theater to contribute to Operation Veritas.[7] According to Adam Ingram, UK armed forces minister from 2001 to 2007, on October 26, 2001, UK forces were configured to assist the air campaign and would develop over time, as would the capabilities assigned to them. Thus, a large and rebalanced force was created in the area, with a total of 4,200 personnel in theater, in addition to the substantial military assets brought to bear.[8]

The British reaction to the 9/11 attacks and the desire to support the United States militarily was uniform in the United Kingdom. In addition to the supportive reaction from Tony Blair, the head of the opposition in Great Britain, Conservative Party leader Iain Duncan Smith, assured Prime Minister Blair that the Conservatives would demonstrate "full support for his immediate pledge to stand shoulder to shoulder" with the United States and would give their "total backing throughout in maintaining his position of unflinching support for the United States in its search for the perpetrators and its subsequent action."[9] Because more than twenty thousand British troops were in Oman on September 11, 2001, there was a quick deployment to Afghanistan, illustrating the strategic benefit of long-standing alliances poised and ready to advance shared strategic ends. Even before the onset of Operation Veritas and Operation Enduring Freedom on October 7, British and American Special Forces were already on the ground in Afghanistan.[10]

Numerous countries and organizations offered support to the United States in the earliest days of Operation Enduring Freedom.[11] Most notably, Australia pledged 1,000 troops, including 150 Special Air Services troops, as well as permission for the additional deployment of 295 Australian troops from the 120th Special Air Services Division already stationed in the United States, as well as tanker and refueling planes and an Australian warship.[12] Canada sent 2,000 troops to join the coalition, as well as significant assets, warships, helicopters, planes, fighter jets, and more.[13]

France immediately sent a navy air-defense frigate and a command and logistics vessel to the Indian Ocean to support the U.S. armada. French Special Forces were put on notice to deploy and France agreed to commit forces for the Afghan offensive. Further, French satellites and intelligence agents worked with the anti-Taliban opposition to scout out counterattack targets.[14] Most other countries' and organizations' contributions included permission for overflight, intelligence sharing, and the use of infrastructure and bases—that is, the institutions and foundation from which military power could be projected.[15] In the words of President Bush on October 7, 2001:

> We are joined in this operation by our staunch friend, Great Britain. Other close friends, including Canada, Australia, Germany and France, have pledged forces as the operation unfolds. More than 40 countries in the Middle East, Africa, Europe and across Asia have granted air transit or landing rights. Many more have shared intelligence. We are supported by the collective will of the world.[16]

While the United States clearly took the lead in designing and executing the attack against al-Qaeda networks in Afghanistan, it did so with the close cooperation and support of key allies, especially Great Britain. Further, at the outset of the mission in Afghanistan, the United States and its closest allies had clear objectives and strategies for attaining those objectives.[17] Above all, among the earliest goals of Operation Veritas were to eliminate terrorism, to bring Osama bin Laden to justice, and to prevent al-Qaeda from continuing to pose a terrorist threat. Ultimately, goals came to include regime change in Afghanistan; reintegrating Afghanistan into the international community; and deterring states from supporting, harboring, or cooperating with terrorists.[18]

While the Bush administration consolidated support from the international community for its unfolding war plans in Afghanistan, it would rely principally on coalition partners to provide critical base support and air-space transit approvals. The military campaign would be undertaken by U.S. forces and by only the closest of U.S. allies, so as to avoid the treacherous problems experienced by NATO in Operation Allied Force only two years earlier.[19] This hub-and-spokes mode of war planning provided a far more efficient model for prosecuting war than reliance on rigid institutional procedures, as had been the case in Operation Allied Force.

The first phase of Operation Enduring Freedom involved airpower and precision weapons, aided on the ground by U.S. Army Special Forces working in tandem with members of the Northern Alliance. A coordinated series of offensives to drive the Taliban regime from government and disrupt al-Qaeda networks was successful.[20] This is not to say that there were no operational challenges in the early days of the war in Afghanistan. Coordination problems between the army and the air force, in particular during Operation Anaconda in March 2002, after the major initial combat operation in Afghanistan was winding down, culminated in bitter recriminations.[21] In addition, conflicting objectives of the United States and Northern Alliance leaders posed problems in the war effort.[22] This was especially important when the Northern Alliance entered Kabul and the United Nations did not want Kabul in the hands of the Northern Alliance. This precipitated the Bonn process—the political process to create stable, democratic government in Afghanistan articulated in the Bonn agreement of December 2001—and the establishment of the new government in Afghanistan.[23] The Northern Alliance itself was a strained alliance of numerous subfactions, a "coalition of sometimes common interests."[24] By the end of 2001 and early 2002, the war in Afghanistan transitioned from principally aerial bombardment to a ground-dominated campaign.[25]

At the very beginning of OEF, the countries involved were the United States and Great Britain, along with fairly small contributions from Turkey, Canada, and Australia. Just weeks into the war, allies such as Germany, Italy, and France, eager to participate, were included in operations. Ultimately, in addition to U.S. forces, Special Forces from Australia, Canada, Denmark, France, Germany, Great Britain, Norway, Poland, and Turkey were part of Operation Enduring Freedom.[26] Phase 2 of the operation was intended to implement the initial combat operations; phase 3 entailed conducting decisive combat operations, building coalitions, and organizing operations throughout Afghanistan.[27]

At the outset of the war, allies clamored to join Operation Enduring Freedom. This enthusiasm did not last. By 2005 and 2006, the deployment of international forces to the provinces revealed tremendous disagreement over burden sharing concerns;[28] by 2008, burden sharing and frustrations regarding deployment levels, placement of troops, and concerns over the duration of the war were a constant in the coalition.[29]

In 2010, the Pentagon allocated an additional $350 million to improve counterterrorism operations of U.S. allies, particularly smaller coalition partners in Afghanistan. The targets of the aid were principally Georgia, Croatia, Hungary, Latvia, Lithuania, and Estonia, whose national contingents at the time all together totaled fewer than 1,300 in Afghanistan. The aid was viewed as a mechanism to offset political pressure to withdraw troops from Afghanistan.[30] This money was in addition to the Coalition Solidarity Fund allocated to subsidize countries with troops in Afghanistan and Iraq's expenses, ultimately at a fairly steep rate per troop.[31] This impinged on cohesion, as is discussed later in the chapter.

The standing alliance system facilitated the United States' ability to respond to the 9/11 crisis swiftly and effectively. Other countries stood ready to respond with the United States: its closest allies accustomed to operating with the United States were able to lend capabilities, and others offered locational resources that were invaluable in constructing a military response in Afghanistan. As we would expect, there were also important drawbacks to moving forward with allies, particularly in regard to efficiency, friendly fire, interoperability, and burden sharing, as we will see later in the chapter.

International Security Assistance Force

The Bonn Conference in 2001 established the International Security Assistance Force (ISAF) framework. After OEF brought down the Taliban government in Afghanistan, UN Security Council Resolution 1386 called for the creation of the ISAF to help the interim Afghan government maintain security.[32] Originally designed to provide security in and around Kabul, the mandate extended north, then west, then south, and finally came to include the entire country.[33] In contrast to Operation Enduring Freedom, Afghanistan, ISAF is NATO led; the alliance took over command of ISAF in August 2003.[34] Both OEF and ISAF operated under different mandates and distinct authorities, although they maintained coordination and support between the two missions.[35] In principle, OEF's mission was counterterrorism; ISAF's objective was stabilization:

to provide security for development projects and to promote governance and reconstruction activities. In practice, the difference between the missions was not always easy to distinguish.

From the beginning, ISAF was plagued by burden-sharing problems. NATO took over ISAF leadership because of ongoing challenges in finding new national leadership, which was supposed to rotate every six months. Furthermore, disagreements over rules of engagement became pervasive.[36] The varying degree of restrictiveness in regard to engagement and deployment embodied in national caveats quite dramatically undermined NATO cohesion in the context of ISAF and the coalition.[37] Frustration over the differences in casualty rates and hazards to some national forces and not others, as well as over a confusing chain of command, also undermined institutional cohesion.[38] In January 2012, fifty states were contributing a total of 130,236 troops and twenty-eight provincial reconstruction teams (PRTs).[39]

A German Marshall Fund survey in 2009 found wide disagreement among NATO member states about Afghanistan. While 63 percent of Europeans were pessimistic about stabilizing the situation there, 56 percent of Americans were optimistic. In addition, 55 percent of Western Europeans and 69 percent of Eastern Europeans wanted to see troop reductions or total withdrawals of their troops from Afghanistan.[40]

By 2010, disagreements were so entrenched among the allies that the CIA generated an analysis of public relations strategies designed to augment support in France and Germany for the work in Afghanistan.[41] Above all, however, the biggest burden-sharing challenge for NATO and ISAF was troop commitments.[42] In short, NATO in Afghanistan is an alliance in which member states struggle to agree on goals and strategies to achieve those goals. In other words, there were very clear institutional benefits but also significant costs in proceeding multilaterally.

In January 2010, the allies held a conference in London on Afghanistan. The conference objectives included outlining a security plan that involved financial incentives for Taliban fighters renouncing violence and changing over from war to peace. The plan was also aimed at transitioning military leadership in the more stable regions of Afghanistan from NATO to Afghan national authorities.[43] In addition to military transition, the Afghanistan conference in London called for an increase in civilian, rather than simply military, experts on the ground to support Afghan local governance and economic development. Further, an oversight office would be created to try to address rampant corruption.[44] The link between poppy cultivation, the narcotics trade, and the insurgency (in addition to other criminal activity) was also addressed.[45]

The London Conference allowed the allies to agree on the central goals confronting NATO in Afghanistan. This certainly helped paper over some of their differences, although operational challenges and burden-sharing issues remained. At the Kabul Conference on July 20, 2010, the emphasis was on social and economic challenges confronting Afghanistan as well as the continuing transition from ISAF to the Afghanistan National Security Force.[46] Map 5.1 shows the regional commands by area.

OEF and ISAF Command Structure and Coordination

A distinctive feature of the war in Afghanistan is the twofold institutional structures that coexisted: the U.S.-led OEF and ISAF, commanded by NATO. In Operation Allied Force, the Kosovo Force (KFOR) was constructed after OAF had finished the air war. In Afghanistan, OEF and ISAF coexisted in country for all but a few months of the war. The United States periodically pressed to merge the two structures, but NATO allies resisted doing so. From fall 2005 through early 2006, the Bush administration pushed hard to get NATO and ISAF to assume counterinsurgency and counterterrorism responsibilities, especially in the southern and eastern parts of Afghanistan. At a minimum, this would involve a joint NATO command structure with one commander to oversee the counterinsurgency mission and another commander who would assume leadership over those troops engaging in peacekeeping and noncombat roles. Both of those operations would fall under a single NATO commander in charge of all operations in Afghanistan. The allied response, especially in Germany, France, and Britain, was that combat operations were OEF's mission; the UN resolution that governed ISAF called only for stabilization.[47]

The Afghanistan case highlights the ways in which institutions of interstate violence may promote the realization of military ends, but it also highlights the costs and strategic liabilities of allies. Multilateral war efforts are often impeded by interoperability challenges, unwieldy decision-making structures, and difficulties in maintaining cohesion—Afghanistan was no exception. Exacerbating the situation in Afghanistan were the myriad structures operating there and the confusing differences in national capabilities and rules of engagement. For example, in 2002, the concept of provincial reconstruction teams (PRTs) first surfaced; by early 2003, the first PRTs had been established in Afghanistan. In the beginning, PRTs consisted of sixty to one hundred soldiers; ultimately,

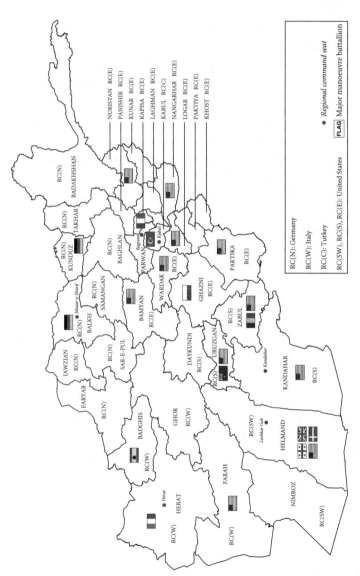

Map 5.1 ISAF regional commands and major units

source: NATO-ISAF, http://www.isaf.nato.int/images/stories/File/2012-01-23%20ISAF%20Placemat-final.pdf. Accessed 4/28/2012.

note: Fair use according to NATO webpage, http://www.nato.int/cps/en/natolive/68162.htm. "Photos, videos and articles are released under the legally recognized terms of 'Fair Use' to members of the press, academia, non-profits and the general public."

Afghan advisers and representatives from civilian agencies such as the U.S. State Department, the U.S. Agency for International Development, and the U.S. Department of Agriculture became part of the teams.[48] These civilian-military units were effective at undertaking reconstruction and development projects in Afghanistan, although they posed their own unique challenges given national restrictions on these forces. For example, in 2006, in a normally stable area of Afghanistan, a Norwegian-Finnish PRT came under attack. At the time, no NATO combat forces were in the region to protect ISAF personnel. Furthermore, other NATO forces in the vicinity had caveats prohibiting their use in combat operations. Ultimately, a British force had to be found to help end the attack.[49] This lack of coordination hampered PRT functioning and made the jobs of the PRTs even more perilous in many parts of the country. Map 5.2 details the positioning of the PRTs in January 2012.

The reliance on Special Operations Forces (SOFs), especially U.S. SOFs, with a significant degree of autonomy added another layer of complexity to the command situation. Ultimately, in the spring of 2010, General Stanley A. McChrystal brought most U.S. SOFs under his control.[50] At the outset of Operation Enduring Freedom, ultimate control for the operation was with the commander of U.S. Central Command. CENTCOM also took the lead role in managing the coalition.[51] This was clear from the outset and facilitated war decision making, although the widely dispersed command structure posed challenges in the beginning.[52] In essence, at the start of ISAF's mission, three parallel command structures had evolved, one emanating from the United States and the secretary of defense, one through NATO and ISAF, and a third through coalition partner countries, with some support of coordination linkages among the command structures (see Figure 5.1).

Over time, this structure became more complex, with the addition of PRTs and counternarcotics operations (see Figure 5.2). The lack of unity of command created major inefficiencies; for example, ISAF had to negotiate diplomatically through U.S. channels to request and secure CENTCOM assets.[53] Not only did this frequently endanger ISAF and OEF missions and forces, perpetuating the incentives for caveats among allies and coalition partners, it also undermined NATO cohesion.

The Obama administration's decision to unify the command structure, appointing General McChrystal to oversee both NATO and U.S. forces in Afghanistan as well as Special Operations Forces, demonstrated an understanding of the complexities of the hybrid multilateral structures at work in the

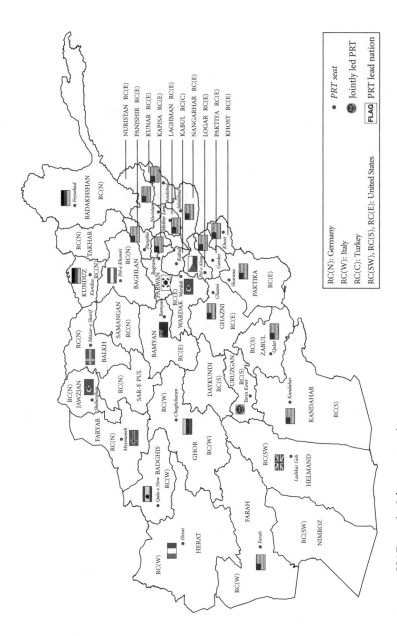

Map 5.2 ISAF provincial reconstruction teams

SOURCE: NATO-ISAF, http://www.isaf.nato.int/images/stories/File/2012-01-23%20ISAF%20Placemat-final.pdf. Accessed 4/28/2012.

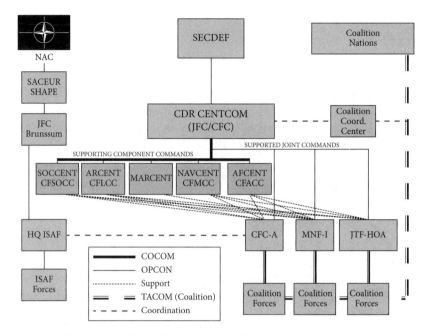

Figure 5.1 Command relationships, CENTCOM 2003

SOURCE: Ian Hope. *Unity of Command in Afghanistan: A Forsaken Principle.* Carlisle, PA: U.S. Army War College, 2008, 9. http://www.strategicstudiesinstitute.army.mil/pdffiles/pub889.pdf.

Afghanistan area.[54] In the aftermath of McChrystal's interview with *Rolling Stone* magazine that culminated in the article "The Runaway General" and led to his dismissal, the Obama administration replaced him with General David Petraeus in June 2010.[55] WikiLeaks revelations suggest that there were still U.S. SOFs operating outside the coalition structure, reporting directly to the Pentagon.[56] NATO decided that by August 3, 2009, ISAF's command structure should have ISAF's day-to-day operational functions separated into new intermediate headquarters, ISAF Joint Command (IJC) Headquarters (see Figure 5.3). The command structure actually became operational in October 2009.[57]

The complexity of the command structure in Afghanistan highlights both the strategic advantages and the liabilities of fighting with friends. There are clear institutional benefits in regard to swift and immediate responses to crises and the ability to bring allies' capabilities to bear to advance military goals. However, the consequences for more unwieldy decision-making and command structures, as well as the implications for cohesion and burden sharing, may inhibit the benefits of multilateralism from being fully realized.

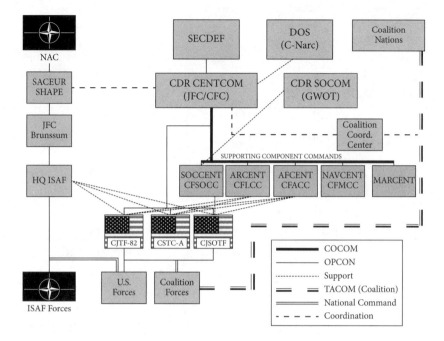

Figure 5.2 Command in Afghanistan, 2008
SOURCE: Ian Hope. *Unity of Command in Afghanistan: A Forsaken Principle.* Carlisle, PA: U.S. Army War College, 2008, 11.

Interoperability and Friendly Fire

By 2007, American forces were responsible for the deaths of about 10 percent of the Canadian troops who perished in Operation Enduring Freedom, including an Olympic contender who was killed when American forces accidentally strafed their own NATO allies in 2006.[58] In late November 2007, yet another British soldier's death in Afghanistan was attributed to friendly fire.[59] Friendly-fire fatalities became a significant source of friction between American troops and their Canadian and British counterparts.[60] Complex communication often culminates in disaster for allies. For example, British troops who were just beginning to install themselves in Helmand Province in 2006 became embroiled almost immediately in a blue-on-blue situation. Local police in Afghanistan opened fire on UK forces, thinking they were Taliban. The UK convoy attacked in response, killing one and wounding thirteen other police officers. Believing themselves to be under attack by the Taliban, the UK forces called in a U.S. air strike.[61] Map 5.3 documents the friendly-fire incidents in Afghanistan.[62]

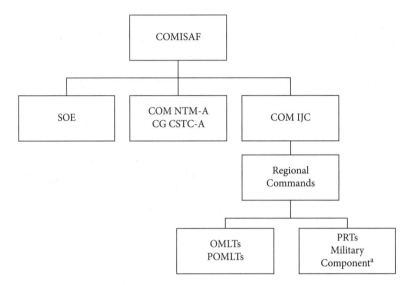

Figure 5.3 ISAF upper-command structure

SOURCE: NATO, ISAF. Accessed 8/26/2010. http://www.isaf.nato.int/en/isaf-command-structure.html.

NOTE: OMLT = operational mentoring and liaison teams; POMLT = police operational mentoring and liaison teams.

^aThe civilian component of a provincial reconstruction team (PRT) is run by the ISAF nation leading the PRT.

In the early years in Afghanistan, nationally oriented communications systems impeded interoperability to a great degree. For example, land mines that killed troops were documented in one national system but not in others because of firewalls. The emphasis on national control over troops in Afghanistan[63] exacerbated interoperability challenges. By 2009, with the surge of U.S. troops into the area, confronting and resolving these issues became paramount. As a consequence, a number of serious technical planning conferences were held in the United States and the Netherlands, and the combined technical teams of NATO and the United States developed the design of the future network.[64] In January 2010, the Afghanistan Mission Network (AMN) evolved with the mission of enabling more than forty countries to conduct network-enabled operations.[65]

The use of PRTs and NATO's operational mentoring and liaison teams (OMLTs) in Afghanistan also made interoperability challenges more profound. This was a consequence of the independence and autonomy of the PRTs, as well as the differences in national cultures regarding civil-military relations among the various countries that served in the OMLTs.[66]

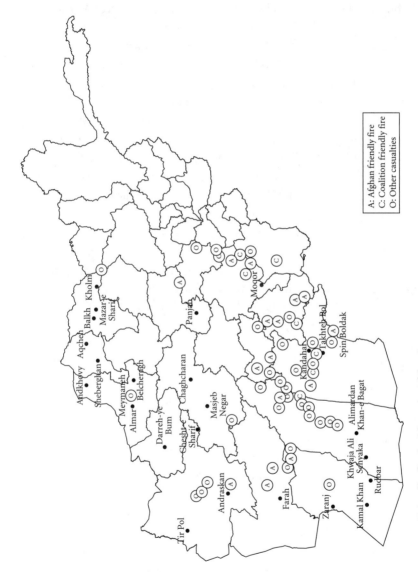

Map 5.3 Friendly-fire incidents in Afghanistan

SOURCE: http://wikileaks.org/afg/sort/type/friendly_fire_o.html. Accessed 4/27/2012.

A: Afghan friendly fire
C: Coalition friendly fire
O: Other casualties

Tir Pol

Andraskan

Farah

Zaranj

Kamal Khan
Rudbar
Khaja Ali
Safiyaka

Ahdkhøvy
Sheberghan
Meymaneh
Almar
Belcheragh
Darreh-ye
Bum

Aqcheh
Balkh
Mazar-e
Sharif
Kholm

Chaghcharan

Shesht-e
Sharif

Masjeb
Negar

Panjad

Moqor

Kandahar
Takhteh-Pol
Spin/Boldak

Alimardan
Khan-e Bagat

The coalition and NATO faced interoperability trials throughout the duration of the war. In fact, the basing transportation and support systems made it difficult for the United States to accept allied forces even at the outset of the war, thus highlighting the problems associated with multilateral war fighting. In addition to the lack of a common language, there were problems with synchronizing command and control, as well as with symmetry in training in the use of particular equipment, techniques, combat rescue, and force protection capacities.[67] However, by early 2002, the United States was accepting support from well over two dozen partners, and this number grew over time.[68] By 2009, between OEF and ISAF, more than forty countries had troops on the ground, though there was a wide disparity between the number of troops various countries dispatched and the freedom of action those national troops had, or rather the restrictions their national governments placed on them. In January 2012, more than fifty countries had troops in Afghanistan. By the end of 2014, most combat troops will be gone.[69] (See Tables 5.1 and 5.2)

On the one hand, operating via alliance in Afghanistan meant that the United States did not have to be the sole provider of troops and had a ready platform from which to launch Operation Enduring Freedom. In April 2012, approximately 90,000 of the total 128,961 troops in Afghanistan were from the United States.[70] On the other hand, the price of paying for those 38,961 remaining troops, many of which were not allowed in the more dangerous regions and whose rules of engagement were quite limited, resulted in substantial intra-alliance negotiation and a reduction in U.S. autonomy. This may have been a small price to pay to have the presence in Afghanistan be NATO rather than the United States alone. The strategic benefits and liabilities of proceeding multilaterally are apparent.

In summary, despite the deep institutionalization manifest in NATO and the constant attention to resolving interoperability challenges, even under the best of circumstances, friendly fire and interoperability are institutional effects of a multilateral exercise, particularly one as complex as Operation Enduring Freedom and ISAF, along with the PRTs and OMLTs. The myriad tasks and missions of the coalition and NATO in Afghanistan brought numerous hazards to the fore. In addition, the war's long duration and the sensitive nature of fighting an insurgency only exacerbated those problems. As expected, then, interoperability issues mediate alliance and coalition dynamics and dramatically complicate the prosecution of the war in Afghanistan.

Table 5.1 ISAF troop-contributing nations

Country	Number of troops	Country	Number of troops
Albania	286	Latvia	185
Armenia	126	Lithuania	237
Australia	1,550	Luxembourg	11
Austria	3	Malaysia	46
Azerbaijan	94	Mongolia	114
Bahrain	95	Montenegro	39
Belgium	520	Netherlands	167
Bosnia & Herzegovina	55	New Zealand	189
		Norway	487
Bulgaria	604	Poland	2,472
Canada[a]	510	Portugal	117
Croatia	310	Romania	1,876
Czech Republic	626	Singapore	39
Denmark	750	Slovakia	330
El Salvador	24	Slovenia	77
Estonia	150	Spain	1,502
Finland	156	Sweden	500
France	3,832	Former Yugoslav Republic of Macedonia	163
Georgia	935		
Germany	4,715	Tonga	55
Greece	154	Turkey	1,846
Hungary	412	Ukraine	23
Iceland	4	United Arab Emirates	35
Ireland	7		
Italy	3,956	United Kingdom	9,500
Jordan	0	United States	90,000
Korea (South)	350	**Total**	**130,236**

SOURCE: NATO-ISAF, http://www.isaf.nato.int/images/stories/File/2012-01-23%20ISAF%20Placemat-final.pdf, accessed April 28, 2012.

NOTE: Figures are calculated by Allied Command Operations on the basis of the military personnel required for the mission. Figures do not include troops deployed on a bilateral basis, personnel above minimum requirements, or those serving in a national support or command capacity. Number of troops should be taken as indicative, as they change daily.

[a]To train Afghan National Security Forces.

Table 5.2 Troops in Afghanistan

Country	Troops, July 31, 2009	Troops, June 6, 2011
Albania	140	260
Armenia	0	40
Australia	1,090	1,550
Austria	3	3
Azerbaijan	90	94
Belgium	510	507
Bosnia & Herzegovina	2	55
Bulgaria	470	602
Canada	2,800	2,922
Croatia	295	320
Czech Republic	340	519
Denmark	700	750
Estonia	150	163
Finland	110	156
France	3,160	3,935
Georgia	1	937
Germany	4,050	4,812
Greece	145	162
Hungary	310	383
Iceland	8	4
Ireland	7	7
Italy	2,795	3,880
Jordan	7	0
Korea (South)	0	426
Latvia	165	139
Lithuania	200	237
Luxembourg	9	11
Macedonia	165	163
Malaysia	0	31
Mongolia	0	74
Montenegro	0	36
Netherlands	1,770	192
New Zealand	160	191
Norway	485	406

(*continued*)

Table 5.2 (*continued*)

Country	Troops, July 31, 2009	Troops, June 6, 2011
Poland	2,000	2,560
Portugal	90	133
Romania	1,025	1,938
Singapore	8	21
Slovakia	230	308
Slovenia	80	80
Spain	780	1,552
Sweden	430	500
Tonga	0	55
Turkey	730	1,786
Ukraine	10	22
United Arab Emirates	25	35
United Kingdom	9,000	9,500
United States	29,950	90,000
Total	**64,495**	**132,457**

SOURCE: The Guardian Datablog; NATO. "Afghanistan Troop Numbers Data." *The Guardian*. Accessed 5/14/2012. http://www.guardian.co.uk/news/datablog/2009/sep/21/afghanistan-troop-numbers-nato-data.

Balance of Power Within the Alliance Hybrid and Burden Sharing

There are always costs of fighting multilateral wars, and the war in Afghanistan is no exception. The disproportionate leverage that small allies bring to the table can be challenging. For example, the demands by Uzbekistan at the beginning of the Afghanistan war made it difficult for U.S. Secretary of State Colin Powell to forge a deal for cooperation.[71] The costs to the United States alone were substantial. Table 5.3 provides a summary of the U.S. costs in Afghanistan from 2001 through 2012. Even as troops have been drawn down, the budget for the war in Afghanistan has still been very high, at $455 billion total in fiscal year 2011 and $107 billion in fiscal year 2012.[72] The average monthly spending of the Department of Defense between fiscal years 2009 and 2010 increased from $4.4 billion to $6.7 billion when the troop strength nearly doubled (44,000 to 84,000). This increased further in fiscal year 2011, when troop strength in Afghanistan averaged about 102,000.[73]

Table 5.3 U.S. costs in Afghanistan in billions of dollars, fiscal years 2001–2012

FY 01–02	FY 03	FY 04	FY 05	FY 06	FY 07	FY 08	FY 09	FY 10	FY 11	FY 12	Total 03–11	Total with 12
20.8	14.7	14.5	20	19	39.2	43.5	59.5	93.8	118.6	113.7	**443**	**557.1**

SOURCE: Congressional Research Service. "The Cost of Iraq, Afghanistan, and Other Global War on Terror Operations Since 9/11." CRS Report for Congress No. 7-5700. March 29, 2011, 3. Congressional Research Service estimates in billions of dollars of budget authority. Accessed 4/29/2012. http://www.fas.org/sgp/crs/natsec/RL33110.pdf.

By contrast, according to UK Defense Secretary Philip Hammond, the total costs for the United Kingdom for the war in Afghanistan were about £17 billion (or about US$27.66 billion) at the end of March 2012.[74] For Australia, anticipated total expenses by June 2013 are estimated at more than $7.4 billion.[75] While estimates of the cost of the war to Germany vary, the official estimate is $11.8 billion.[76] For France, the cost of the war in Afghanistan was approximately $2.6 billion.[77] As Table 5.4 demonstrates, there is a significant differential in shouldering the burden of costs in the war in Afghanistan. This is not surprising, given the singular importance of the mission to the United States above all others. In contrast to Operations Desert Storm, Desert Shield, and Allied Force, the objectives of the war were less a collective or common good and more directly connected to the specific security challenges confronting the United States. The burden-sharing issues that plagued the coalition and alliance throughout the war were mostly in regard to the refusal of NATO and coalition members to augment troop levels when, according to the U.S. government, there was clear need for larger deployments.

Table 5.5 provides the 2007 data on power capability for countries with more than one thousand troops in Afghanistan. It reveals that while the United States commands far and away more capabilities than other states, a number of great powers were contributing.

In summary, as expected, burden-sharing problems and disproportionate leverage have marked the campaigns in Afghanistan. The United States, as the most powerful country in the coalition and alliance, shouldered a significant portion of the burden. Also, as the lead state, it had the most at stake, which made it more vulnerable in regard to the alliance security dilemma over time.

Alliance Security Dilemma

It is difficult to make sweeping assessments about fears of entrapment versus fears of abandonment in the context of the war in Afghanistan. The circumstances from the immediate post-9/11 era to the present day are different for

Table 5.4 Military expenditures by coalition member, Afghanistan operations

Coalition member	Expenditures (in millions of U.S. 2012 dollars)	Percentage of national GDP
United States[a]	562,000	4.0
United Kingdom[b]	27,660	1.0
Germany[c]	11,800	0.4
Canada[d]	11,300	0.8
Australia[e]	7,400	0.8
Spain[f]	4,000	0.3
Italy[g]	3,900	0.2
France[h]	2,600	0.1
Poland[i]	2,000	0.3
Total	**636,660**	

SOURCE: Compilation from official estimates, newspaper articles, and CIA *World Factbook*. Accessed 5/15/2013. http://nodedge.com/ciawfb.

[a]Amy Belasco. "The Cost of Iraq, Afghanistan, and Other Global War on Terror Operations Since 9/11." Congressional Research Service. CRS Report for Congress No. 7-5700. March 29, 2011, ii, Accessed 4/29/2012. http://www.fas.org/sgp/crs/natsec/RL33110.pdf.

[b]"Afghan War 'Has Cost the UK £17 bn.'" *Defence Management Journal*. April 25, 2012. Accessed 4/29/2012. http://www.defencemanagement.com/news_story.asp?id=19568.

[c]Tilman Brück, Olaf J. de Groot, and Friedrich Schneider. "The Economic Costs of the German Participation in the Afghanistan War." *Journal of Peace Research*, vol. 48, no. 6, November 2011, 3. Accessed 11/23/2012. http://www.econ.jku.at/members/Schneider/files/publications/2011/groot.pdf. The number used in the text is the official German government estimate of spending up to 2012, though unofficial estimates place the number as high as €47 billion (or US$62.28 billion).

[d]Government of Canada. "Cost of the Afghanistan Mission 2001–2011." Accessed 11/20/2012. http://www.afghanistan.gc.ca/canada-afghanistan/news-nouvelles/2010/2010_07_09.aspx?lang=eng&view=d.

[e]Ian McPhedran. "Each Soldier in Afghanistan Costs Taxpayers a Million Dollars." *The Daily Telegraph*. January 18, 2012. Accessed 4/29/2012. http://www.dailytelegraph.com.au/news/each-soldier-in-afghanistan-costs-taxpayers-a-million-dollars/story-e6freuy9-1226246792609.

[f]"Spain Forces to Begin to Leave Afghanistan in 2012—Pm Zapatero." *Eurasia Review*. June 24, 2011. Accessed 11/15/2012. http://www.eurasiareview.com/24062011-spain-forces-to-begin-to-leave-afghanistan-in-2012-pm-zapatero.

[g]"Afghanistan, War Will Cost More Than $2 Million a Day." *Libre* (Madrid). January 20, 2011. Accessed 11/25/2012. http://www.libreidee.org/en/2011/01/afghanistan-la-guerra-ci-costa-oltre-2-milioni-al-giorno.

[h]John Irish. "France Won't Cut Force in Afghanistan Despite 500 Million Euro Cost." Reuters. August 3, 2010. Accessed 11/28/2012. http://www.reuters.com/article/2010/08/03/idUSLDE6720DA. This number is based on official estimates of $500 million for fiscal 2010 provided by the French defense minister and reports of similar levels of spending for fiscal 2009–12.

[i]"Afghanistan Operations Cost Poland Dear." Polskie Radio. April 7, 2012. Accessed 11/21/2012. http://www.thenews.pl/1/10/Artykul/104781,Afghanistan-operations-cost-Poland-dear. This number is an estimate based on available official estimates for spending between 2007 and the end of 2011 provided by the Polish armed forces general staff for the Defense Ministry.

each country involved. The domestic landscapes have changed, the strategic environment has changed, and the economic climate has changed. Bearing this in mind, it is possible to observe that entrapment fears, which did not govern U.S. allies or coalition partners in the beginning of the war in Afghanistan, have grown over time. Countries willingly made their contributions available to the

Table 5.5 Power capability data of countries with more than 1,000 troops in Afghanistan

Country	Military expenditures (in millions of U.S. 2012 dollars)	Military personnel (in thousands)	Composite Index of National Capability
United States	552,568	1,506	0.1421487
Australia	20,216	52	0.0071125
France	60,662	255	0.0189237
Germany	42,108	246	0.0240815
Italy	37,770	191	0.0174203
Poland	7,983	142	0.0069389
Romania	3,044	70	0.003213
Spain	17,495	147	0.0113889
Turkey	13,643	515	0.014317
United Kingdom	63,258	191	0.0211575

SOURCE: National Military Capabilities Data. Version 4.0, extended to 2007. Accessed 4/28/2012. http://www.correlatesofwar.org/COW2%20Data/Capabilities/nmc4.htm; J. David Singer, Stuart Bremer, and John Stuckey. "Capability Distribution, Uncertainty, and Major Power War, 1820–1965." *Peace, War, and Numbers*. Bruce Russett, ed. Beverly Hills, CA: Sage, 1972, 19–48.

NOTE: The Composite Index of National Capability is computed by summing observations for total population, urban population, iron and steel production, energy consumption, military personnel, and military expenditures for the year, converting each country's absolute component into a share of the international system, averaging across the six component parts. Accessed 12/14/2012. http://www.correlatesofwar.org/COW2%20Data/Capabilities/nmc3-02.htm.

United States in the early days out of a desire to stand shoulder to shoulder with the United States in the aftermath of the 9/11 attacks. This initial support was very important in facilitating the U.S. response to the attacks and the war in Afghanistan. Entrapment fears weighed on many participating member states and manifested in the caveats they placed on their troops.[78] In 2006, when President Bush implored NATO allies to match the U.S. commitment to augmented force levels in Afghanistan, most countries, with the exception of Denmark, France, Britain, and Canada, informed Bush that their parliaments would not accept such a mandate.[79] Ultimately, in Bush's own words, "the multilateral mission proved a disappointment."[80] And yet in the absence of this multilateral foundation, a swift reaction to the 9/11 attacks may have been thornier. The United States benefited from the solidity of its alliance relationships, from knowing that it was standing shoulder to shoulder with others. However, the United States had sufficient capabilities to bring to bear even without its allies, although this became more challenging as it became enmeshed in planning for the Iraq War.[81]

While fears of entrapment among NATO and coalition partners grew, abandonment fears on the part of the United States grew as well. This is particularly notable in the context of its relationship with the United Kingdom. During the 2010 British election campaign, U.S. media coverage focused a great deal on fears of abandonment, particularly in light of the wars in Afghanistan and Iraq, with conflicts simmering in the background in Iran, Syria, and potentially North Korea.[82] From the outset of the war in Afghanistan, the United Kingdom was essential to the mission and to support for the United States. Tony Blair was the first head of state with whom Bush spoke post-9/11, and he was a central figure whom Bush consulted as he planned the initial OEF operation.[83] A similar dynamic was at work during the French national elections in 2012; the U.S. media focused on abandonment fears.[84] The United States has been deeply concerned about keeping NATO member states on board in Afghanistan until the 2014 drawdown.[85]

In contrast, while U.S. fears of abandonment, particularly toward its closest allies, may have grown over time, entrapment concerns grew dramatically in the context of its relationship with the Afghan government, and with Afghan President Hamid Karzai in particular.[86] Even the Vietnam analogy being applied to Afghanistan is emblematic of fears of entrapment dominating strategic thought regarding the war and the alliance with Afghanistan.[87] Karzai's alleged and actual ineffectiveness, corruption, fraud, and mental instability created challenges for the United States in the context of its alliance with him; growing concerns regarding Karzai's effectiveness were similarly manifest. And yet the United States was not able to functionally disconnect or detach itself from continuing support of the Karzai government, even if media reports constantly depicted the relationship as one of entrapment.[88] In fact, in July 2012, as the United States announced its plans to draw down troops by 2014 and declared Afghanistan the newest major non-NATO ally to the United States, Secretary of State Hillary Clinton said, "We are not even imagining abandoning Afghanistan,"[89] suggesting that the United States was, indeed, managing entrapment concerns and that Afghanistan was confronting abandonment issues. The alliance security dilemma has also been manifest in the discussions regarding military bases and basing rights allowing U.S. forces to remain in Afghanistan beyond 2014.[90]

In essence, then, the United States has been preoccupied with concerns of abandonment by its closest allies; coalition partners and NATO members have been more preoccupied with entrapment concerns and have thus focused on their own national interests, such as by limiting their troops in number and mandate. In the context of the U.S. relationship with Afghanistan, however, there has been a growing sense of entrapment in more recent years. These findings are consistent with our expectations that the lead state would be more concerned with abandonment, although they raise an interesting point that over time the lead state may ultimately fear entrapment over abandonment in regard to its most central ally in the fight. These institutional effects impinge on the capacity of the member states to come together with shared goals and strategies for attaining those goals.

Cohesion and Fighting Effectiveness

Cohesion refers to the ability of states to agree on goals and strategies to attain those goals.[91] A key component of such a conception of cohesion is the capacity of an alliance to work efficiently and effectively. At the outset of OEF, key states' goals and strategies were consistent.[92] The primary ally with which the United States and its partners had periodically to negotiate goals and strategies was the Northern Alliance, the resistance force against the Taliban government in Afghanistan. The Afghan model—using indigenous allies on the ground along with select Special Forces, combined with U.S. airpower[93]—meant that joint goals and strategies were paramount. The immediate joint goal of unseating the Taliban made the alliance effective. Yet even so, internal divisions made maintaining meaningful cohesion difficult. For example, some tribal leaders still maintained close relationships with the Taliban—local rivalries were an important aspect of the conflict.[94] Pakistan's opposition to northern Uzbeks and Tajiks advancing on Kabul without any Pashtun forces similarly created tensions among the allies.[95] In addition, when Northern Alliance fighting came to a stalemate, an absence of sustained U.S. air strikes further demoralized Afghan opposition forces. The Northern Alliance requested bombing on the front lines to break the lines and take control over territory held by the Taliban.[96]

Other examples of the difficulties of agreement among participating states on goals and strategies include when the Taliban captured the resistance leader Abdul Haq. The United States denied his request for help, and he was subsequently tortured and executed by the Taliban. At the outset of the war in Afghanistan, many local tribal leaders simply waited to see who would prevail before committing themselves to one side or the other.[97] These are all indications that divergence among the actors' goals was significant, as was the uncertainty. Constant negotiating over goals and how to proceed was necessary.

As frequently occurs in multilateral war fighting, reaching consensus over goals was elusive. In December 2001, representatives of the four Afghan opposition groups negotiating in Bonn accepted a UN proposal regarding interim governance in Afghanistan and recommendations regarding permanent arrangements.[98] Force levels in post-Taliban Kabul were similarly subject to intense negotiation.[99] In Tora Bora, the United States was interested in capturing Osama bin Laden; local Afghan ally forces were interested in controlling territory. This culminated in the U.S. bombing of areas that jeopardized Afghan military fighters. Once al-Qaeda was driven from the local areas, village leaders considered that their main objectives had been met. The United States, however, was interested in capturing fleeing al-Qaeda fighters—a goal the local allies were uninterested in pursuing. Once Afghan forces expelled al-Qaeda from their strongholds, they saw the role of the United States and its great power allies as complete—a view profoundly different from the American desire to capture and bring to justice as many al-Qaeda operatives as possible.[100] So while opposition fighters wanted to drive out Taliban forces and assume power themselves, hunting down al-Qaeda operatives was not their objective. In fact, some Afghan opposition fighters accepted large bribes from al-Qaeda members to ensure safe passage to Pakistan, thus foiling the United States' goal and allowing large numbers of al-Qaeda members to elude capture.[101]

From the outset, the United States struggled with its indigenous allies over goals and strategies. As the war unfolded, substantial divisions among its great-power partners also arose. A significant component of this conflict centered on risk sharing. Forces from the United States, Canada, Denmark, the Netherlands, and the United Kingdom were stationed in the most dangerous areas in the southern and eastern parts of Afghanistan, engaged in most of the fighting, and sustained most of the fatalities. In addition, allies disagreed over the central objectives of the Afghanistan mission and the appropriate strategies for achieving those objectives (e.g., military versus nonmilitary means, combat versus reconstruction missions).[102] These issues became much more problematic in the context of the International Security Assistance Force in Afghanistan. The institutional effects hindering cohesion were considerable.

Coalition cohesion in OEF appeared greater than NATO cohesion in ISAF. In the former, a strong sense of purpose and American leadership facilitated unified goals and strategies. In the latter, disagreements over burden sharing, caveats, and troop levels marred NATO's ability to act cohesively. Even when the states agreed on goals, they differed widely on how to achieve those goals.[103]

Within NATO and ISAF, the viewpoints most closely aligned with the United States were those of countries such as Canada and Great Britain, which were also part of the OEF coalition.[104]

The cohesion of OEF and ISAF was interconnected with resentments that existed among countries in regard to the Iraq operation, which is discussed in the next chapter. Because a number of key NATO allies were adamantly opposed to the Iraq War, this inhibited their participation in OEF and culminated in caveats in regard to their participation. As a consequence of these resentments, Germany and the Netherlands, for example, were not to cooperate with OEF even as they participated in ISAF. Furthermore, U.S. commitment to Operation Iraqi Freedom meant that non-U.S. forces committed to ISAF were especially important in numbers and with regard to their tasks. The inability to bring more U.S. forces to bear in ISAF may have impinged on its effectiveness in essential ways. Furthermore, some countries, such as the Netherlands and Canada, left combat early in the operation, an indication of challenges in reaching agreement on goals and strategies for attaining those goals.[105]

In long wars, institutional effects may be felt more keenly as the political and economic landscapes both within member states and across the international system change over time. This was certainly true in Afghanistan in regard to the challenges in burden sharing and cohesion, as well as the legitimacy of the operations.

Legitimacy

In the aftermath of the 9/11 attacks, the United States had significant worldwide support and sympathy. Under the circumstances of a direct and immediate threat, the United States did not seek authorization through the UN Security Council to target al-Qaeda networks in Afghanistan in retaliation. Instead, President Bush garnered support among close allies and gave the Taliban government an ultimatum to close terrorist-training camps, hand over al-Qaeda leaders, and return detained foreign nationals. When the ultimatum went unmet, the United States launched OEF.[106]

One of the broadest global public-opinion polls undertaken at the outset of OEF, the Gallup International End of Year Terrorism Poll 2001, was conducted between November 7 and December 29, 2001, with more than sixty thousand people from sixty-two countries polled.[107] Results indicated that only twenty-five of those sixty-two countries had 50 percent or greater support for the U.S.-led military action in Afghanistan. This is without polling Arab countries in the Middle East and including only four African and seven Asian countries.[108]

It is counterfactual to assert that had the United States sought UN Security Council support, which could have facilitated information transmission regarding U.S. intentions, legitimacy and global public opinion may have been enhanced.[109] Working through a global organization such as the United Nations would have slowed down the process of embarking on a retaliatory war in Afghanistan and may have increased worldwide support for the United States' operation. However, in the case of OEF, signaling strength was more of a priority than was signaling limited intentions. Had the Bush administration taken to the United Nations its desire to launch an attack on the Taliban government and al-Qaeda training camps in Afghanistan in the aftermath of an attack on the United States, this may have signaled weakness to the U.S. public. The choice of moving forward with a hub-and-spokes framework engaging the closest U.S. allies was a middle path, even if it did not generate global support for the operation. Institutional design matters particularly in determining the effects felt in regard to some of the central costs to achieving goals through a multilateral framework. In this case, using existing institutions to adapt to the mission at hand helped the United States project power, although there were costs in regard to efficiency, friendly fire, interoperability, burden sharing, and cohesion. Strategic advantages do come with costs and liabilities.

To what extent did the operation provide legitimacy to NATO? The 9/11 attacks brought the first invocation of article 5 of the Washington Treaty. Did acting on the dictate that an attack on one is deemed an attack on all augment the legitimacy of the organization? Given that the United States opted not to call on NATO in its first response, did this undermine the legitimacy of the institution? Perhaps. This may have been a central reason OEF was considered largely unilateral. However, if public-opinion polls are the main indication, then the war in Afghanistan was not widely viewed as legitimate.

By 2007, in a poll conducted by the Pew Global Attitudes Project, populations in only four of forty-four countries indicated that they believed that the United States and NATO should continue operations in Afghanistan. Those four countries—Ghana, Israel, Kenya, and the United States—were the only ones with 50 percent or more of respondents agreeing that the military presence should be continued until the situation was stabilized. The same study indicated that populations in thirty-two of the forty-four countries had more than 50 percent of respondents indicating that troops should be removed from Afghanistan as soon as possible, regardless of the political stability of the country. By 2011, populations in six of twenty-two countries polled had less than

50 percent of respondents indicating that troops should be removed straight away, and only three of the twenty-two countries (Spain, Kenya, and Israel) had more than 50 percent of respondents indicating that the United States and NATO should maintain their troops in Afghanistan.[110] By 2012, only 24 percent of Americans polled believed that the current timetable to leave Afghanistan was acceptable; 50 percent believed that the United States should speed up its withdrawal, although 59 percent believed that going into Afghanistan was the right thing to do.[111] Although this is not a mirror of legitimacy, it gives insight into the transformation in domestic and global opinion on the United States' war in Afghanistan.

While worldwide public-opinion polls are not the only indication of the legitimacy of an operation, they do give a window into public perception of Operation Enduring Freedom and the war in Afghanistan more generally. Further, the length and complexity of the war, with substantial costs in the midst of global recession, made publics inclined to favor withdrawal and reduced military and reconstruction obligations even if the operations were perceived as legitimate.

Another interesting feature of the war in Afghanistan was the strong commitment by the coalition and NATO to the PRTs. These teams focused on enhancing stability in Afghanistan through economic development and augmenting the host government's ability to provide public and social services throughout the country, including health care, governance, and security. The teams were first put together in 2002 and have expanded in number and mandate over the course of the past decade.[112] While one might speculate that the emphasis on reconstruction and development could augment legitimacy of the operation, particularly as this aspect of the Afghanistan operation was mandated and supervised by the United Nations, these missions have also culminated in increased casualties and counterterrorism operations.[113] The UN Security Resolutions 1378, 1383, and 1386, all from 2001, sanctioned and encouraged the development of the PRTs and supported efforts to root out terrorism in Afghanistan.[114] In addition, the UN talks on Afghanistan culminated in the "Agreement on Provisional Arrangements in Afghanistan Pending the Re-Establishment of Governmental Institutions," which spelled out the role of the international community in fostering stability, law, and order in Afghanistan.[115] This use of the United Nations—as a global, neutral arbiter to demonstrate resolve in aiding the reconstruction and stabilization of the country—did not augment the legitimacy of the ISAF mission. Public opinion, despite this role of the United Nations, was not positive. Over time, civilian casualties, as well as the costs in lives and treasure to the participating states, further eroded whatever support the mission may have had at the outset. The use of the United Nations in this case had a legitimacy-neutral effect, neither enhancing nor detracting from the legitimacy of the operations.

As President Bush reflects in his memoirs, he was motivated to act to signal resolve and determination—he was not interested in signaling limited or benign intentions. On the contrary, his desire was to signal strength, willpower, and fortitude. And yet this could not have easily been done alone, which highlights the value of standing institutions of interstate violence. Working to generate global support for action would be open to interpretation as weakness. President Bush sought to change what he believed was a perception of the United States as weak and passive in the face of terrorist threats, although he was concerned that the United States not come off appearing as occupiers.[116] Above all, Bush desired to bring Osama bin Laden to justice.[117]

In the aftermath of a direct attack, the United States was less concerned with pursuing legitimacy than strength. While Bush did not worry about this aspect of decision making on Afghanistan, it did matter to him that the United States had its close allies by its side. This was essential for practical and ideological reasons. From the earliest moments after 9/11, Bush was in close contact with Tony Blair, and he was comforted by the fact that "America's closest ally in the wars of the last century would be with us in the first war of a new century."[118]

From the outset of the war in Afghanistan, the United States brought together as many countries as possible to focus on reconstruction and rebuilding the country devastated by war. "A multilateral approach would defray the financial burden and invest nations around the world in the ideological struggle against extremists."[119] The network of allies was critical to this end, despite the costs in regard to institutional effects. Capturing this inherent tension was the fact that Bush viewed Afghanistan as a war that the world viewed as "necessary and just," despite the persistent frustration at the lack of willingness on the part of NATO member states to match U.S. troop commitments and to reduce caveats. Many troops sent had so many restrictions on them that U.S. generals complained, "They just took up space."[120]

Another factor damaging the legitimacy of the war in Afghanistan was the ongoing support of Hamid Karzai, with his attendant charges of corruption and problematic governance. Karzai's legitimacy both at home and abroad was undermined by chronic scandals, charges of fraud regarding elections, his inability to govern effectively in the provinces, and bribes and complicity in illicit activity.[121] The continuing relationship among Karzai, the coalition, and NATO culminated in degraded legitimacy for the Afghanistan missions. The OMLTs, which provided training and mentoring to the Afghan National Army while simultaneously serving as liaisons between the Afghan National Army and ISAF,[122] helped foster governance in distant reaches of the country, but not sufficiently to affect the legitimacy of operations in Afghanistan.[123]

While legitimacy dividends may not have been paramount for U.S. decision makers in making the decision to undertake OEF, certainly the United States and its allies have been aware that the means of the operation play to legitimacy concerns worldwide. For example, in a WikiLeaks cable from the U.S. NATO mission, it was clear that the Spanish were painfully aware of the problems that collateral damage in Afghanistan were causing for the ongoing legitimacy of the coalition and alliance's operations there. The cable emphasized the impact of collateral damage on public opinion. Spain's NATO permanent representative, Pablo Benavides, urged that OEF be mindful of the political effect of the operation and to abide by the principles of proportionality, necessity, and discrimination. Benavides indicated that his position was driven by Spanish Prime Minister José Luis Rodríguez Zapatero's alarm over civilian casualties, particularly after seeing the negative reporting in the press. This served as a "reminder of the fragility of public opinion in some key Allied capitals."[124]

Civilian casualties undermined the legitimacy of operations in Afghanistan and the worldwide image of the international troops serving there.[125] Further damaging the legitimacy of the operations were the episodes of problematic behavior among international troops stationed there. For example, in March 2012 a U.S. serviceman killed sixteen Afghan civilians, and there were reports of some U.S. soldiers burning Qur'ans and others urinating on the corpses of Taliban soldiers.[126] The civilian deaths from unmanned aerial vehicles, or drones, were also a continuing problem. The ethical challenges posed by the use of drones in Afghanistan (and Pakistan) undermined legitimacy in a profound way. While the numbers of civilian casualties are debated furiously, it is clear that collateral damage has been significant. The use of remote weapons of war undermined the legitimacy of the operations.[127]

The fact that the war in Afghanistan was ongoing for more than a decade culminated in major challenges to its enduring legitimacy. This is despite the unprecedented level of attention to mentoring, reconstruction, development, and civil-military practices all designed to promote effective governance and enhance the quality of life for the people of Afghanistan. For short operations such as Operations Desert Storm, Desert Shield, and Allied Force, the legitimacy of the mission may inhere to the form and function of the institutional framework. In a longer war, such as the one in Afghanistan, the conduct in the war theater matters as much as the multilateral framework used to pursue the strategic ends of the operation. In other words, at the outset of a war, the mechanisms of fighting matter a great deal; in its duration, it is the means employed that become more salient in determining the mission's legitimacy.

CONCLUSION

In principle, states make important decisions regarding how to confront challenging foreign policy objectives, especially when the possibility of war looms. However, for states—particularly advanced industrial and democratic states deeply embedded in the web of a highly interdependent and complex international system—wholly unilateral action in the face of military challenges is increasingly unlikely. Instead, a spectrum of choices faces states with respect to the degree to which they will embrace multilateralism, from cooperating with a few close allies to accepting the contributions of many countries across the international system. In many ways, the United States was actually pressured to accept the offerings of its allies as the post-9/11 decision to invade Afghanistan unfolded. It was never a question of unilateralism or multilateralism; it was a question of what the multilateral effort would look like, which countries would contribute what and to what degree, and what the decision-making structure would look like. The planning and execution of the Iraq War affected these decisions in important ways. Many partner countries, unable to support the Iraq War for domestic reasons, opted instead to lend support in Afghanistan. In addition, because NATO was employed, the solidity of these alliance relationships provided an important adhesive in the war effort in Afghanistan.[128] The United States did not need to stand alone. Tables 5.6 and 5.7 provide a summary of the variables discussed here. The results largely mirror the expectations laid out in chapter 2.

The simultaneous use of NATO and the coalition in Afghanistan is distinctive. While forging a limited coalition at the outset of OEF allowed the United States to retain substantial control over the mission and execution of the war, over time managing two different and unwieldy institutional structures became problematic. The absence of unity in command, and struggles over burden sharing and risk taking, undermined the cohesion of the alliance and

Table 5.6 Overview of variables in Operation Enduring Freedom

Independent variables	Mediating variables	Dependent variables
Coalition	Decision-making structure: hierarchical	Cohesion: moderate
Size: small	Power distribution: asymmetrical	War-fighting effectiveness: moderately effective
	Internal leverage rested principally with lead power	Interoperability: some challenges
		Legitimacy of operation: higher at the beginning of the war, lessening over time

Table 5.7 Overview of variables in ISAF

Independent variables	Mediating variables	Dependent variables
Alliance	Decision-making structure: decentralized but hierarchical; much emphasis on national priorities and caveats	Cohesion: low to moderate
Size: large	Power distribution: asymmetrical	War-fighting effectiveness: moderately effective
	Internal leverage rested principally with lead power	Interoperability: significant challenges
		Legitimacy of operation: declines over time from moderate to low

coalition in ISAF and OEF. The contemporary American way of war is multilateral war fighting; as a consequence, it is essential to understand the added layers of complexity and the prerequisites of cohesion.

Above all, it is clear from examining the war decision making in Afghanistan that it was far from unilateral. While at the outset of the war in Afghanistan the United States was highly selective in determining how it would use its OEF coalition partners, the fact is that the United States did rely on coalition partners, and that reliance grew over time. Ultimately, both a coalition structure and an alliance structure operated in Afghanistan, which resulted in a highly complex and often confusing command structure. The use of this dual structure undermined cohesion and efficacy, thereby raising issues of burden sharing and variances in rules of engagement and a pervasive system of caveats. While strategists are always fighting the last war—in this case lessons from Kosovo were at the forefront of U.S. policy makers' minds as they designed the Afghanistan operation—from Afghanistan strategists will learn that unity of command is essential in wartime, and that the prerequisites of alliance and coalition cohesion often come at the expense of integrity of mission.

Another principal lesson of the war in Afghanistan will be the value of employing smaller numbers of highly trained units, such as Special Operations Forces, from close allies such as Great Britain, Australia, Canada, and Germany.[129] Interoperability challenges may be reduced in this case. But above all, contemporary warfare should reveal the depth of U.S. commitment to fighting multilaterally, and long-term planning to shape coalition warfare into its most efficient form should be undertaken through continuing interoperability efforts and decision-making simulations that best suit effective war fighting.

The case of Afghanistan also illustrates how much the United States and NATO learned from their experiences in the Gulf War and Kosovo. The hub-and-spokes decision-making structure and the containment of combat forces to closely connected states with substantial experience in training and fighting together was realized in this case. The Afghanistan case also set the stage for the Iraq War that followed.

The Afghanistan experience highlights a number of important realist institutionalist insights. Institutions of war facilitate the projection of power; they are vehicles or conduits for strategic ends. Yet the effects may hinder efficiency and cohesion. Having allies at the ready made it possible for the United States to deliver a swift blow to al-Qaeda networks in Afghanistan. This network of friendships provided the basis on which the United States could realize and project its power. Even if the military capabilities brought to bear at the outset by allies were redundant, the solidity of these relationships and the support they offered were beneficial and meant that the United States did not need to undertake the intervention alone. The tightly interconnected world in which we live makes it virtually impossible to act alone, and the presence of strategic partnerships is critical to pursuing military objectives. However, we also see the strategic liability of inclusion; it affects nearly every aspect of war conduct, in regard to decision making, friendly fire, interoperability, burden sharing, the alliance security dilemma, cohesion, and effectiveness.

6 OPERATION IRAQI FREEDOM AND THE WAR IN IRAQ

IN SEPTEMBER 2000, the think tank Project for a New American Century, produced a report, "Rebuilding America's Defenses," which advanced the thesis that, given U.S. hegemony, the opportunity was present to build and secure an international system conducive to its long-term strategic interests. The neoconservative document provided a road map for the new administration to expand American influence abroad. Shortly after George W. Bush was elected, several key neoconservatives from the Project for a New American Century joined his advisory team. The aftermath of the 9/11 attacks provided an opportunity to intervene in Iraq, to promote regime change, and to attempt to construct a region that would secure U.S. interests in the long term.[1]

On September 20, 2001, in his speech to the Joint Session of Congress, President Bush announced: "We will pursue nations that provide aid or safe haven to terrorism. Every nation in every region now has a decision to make: Either you are with us or you are with the terrorists. From this day forward, any nation that continues to harbor or support terrorism will be regarded by the United States as a hostile regime."[2] The Bush doctrine continued to evolve with his State of the Union address in January 2002, in which he identified Iraq, North Korea, and Iran as the "axis of evil."[3] At his West Point commencement address in June 2002, President Bush alluded to the dangers of proliferation and the failure of deterrence. He indicated the need for preemption to wage the war on terrorism.[4] In September 2002, Bush's national security strategy was released, outlining more fully the Bush doctrine.[5]

Momentum for the Iraq intervention continued to build throughout 2002 in the U.S. government in the context of Iraq's alleged program of weapons of mass destruction and noncompliance with weapons inspections. In November 2002, the UN Security Council adopted Resolution 1441, which recalled earlier resolutions calling on Iraq to comply with International Atomic Energy Agency (IAEA) and UN Monitoring, Verification, and Inspections Commission (UNMOVIC) inspections and to disclose completely all aspects of its programs pertaining to ballistic missiles and weapons of mass destruction. The resolution demanded full Iraqi compliance with UN weapons inspections. It concluded with the warning that Iraq "will face serious consequences as a result of its continued violations of its obligations."[6] In October 2002, the U.S. Congress passed the Joint Resolution on the Authorization for Use of Military Force Against Iraq.[7]

The confluence of neoconservative advocacy of regime change in Iraq for strategic reasons, the Bush doctrine of preventive war, and the targeting of Iraq's alleged program of weapons of mass destruction were mutually reinforcing; they culminated in the United States seeking support for an invasion of Iraq. By early 2003, momentum had grown. In his 2003 State of the Union address, Bush detailed the Iraqi threat in terms of weapons of mass destruction and links to terrorists, even alluding to a connection between Saddam Hussein and the 9/11 attackers:

> Before September the 11th, many in the world believed that Saddam Hussein could be contained. But chemical agents, lethal viruses and shadowy terrorist networks are not easily contained.
>
> Imagine those 19 hijackers with other weapons and other plans, this time armed by Saddam Hussein. It would take one vial, one canister, one crate slipped into this country to bring a day of horror like none we have ever known.
>
> We will do everything in our power to make sure that that day never comes.[8]

The neoconservative perspective, far from eschewing multilateral frameworks, embraces allies as essential to American power projection. In fact, the core principles that the Project for a New American Century lists as central include strengthening ties to democratic allies and challenging regimes hostile to American interests and values.[9] Acting with allies to confront or contain enemies is undertaken for pragmatic and strategic reasons, even if the United Nations and its sanction are immaterial to the agenda.[10] On March 19, 2003, the United States, together with the United Kingdom, Australia, and Poland, undertook the attack that launched the Iraq War. The combat phase of the Iraq War lasted until May 1, 2003; the stabilization and rebuilding phase continued from May 2003 until U.S. forces departed Iraq in December 2011. The overwhelming number of states participating in the Iraq coalition were unable to provide combat power. Further, many of them had restrictions and caveats in regard to the way in which their troops could be employed.[11]

THE COALITION

The coalition the Bush administration put together to prosecute the war in Iraq culled more than forty countries that supported the operation in some manner. In November 2002, President Bush was already forging the coalition; in advance of the NATO summit in Prague, which culminated in the invitation of seven new Eastern European states into the NATO alliance,[12] he stated explicitly that, should Saddam Hussein "choose not to disarm, the United States will lead a coalition of the willing to disarm him and at that point in time all our nations . . . will be able to choose whether or not they want to participate."[13] The symbolism of this call on the eve of the NATO summit, which heralded the biggest expansion of the organization, is significant. The strategic use of partnerships was paramount to the Bush administration. Not surprising, all but one of the seven invited states were part of the initial coalition of the willing, as were the first three post–Cold War NATO-expansion member states: Poland, the Czech Republic, and Romania. The benefits of such participation and support of the United States led effort were immediately realized, in terms of aid and equipment.

In his speech declaring the war, President Bush announced: "More than 35 countries are giving crucial support, from the use of naval and air bases, to help with intelligence and logistics, to the deployment of combat units. Every nation in this coalition has chosen to bear the duty and share the honor of serving in our common defense."[14]

Most of the countries involved provided nonmilitary assistance; those that did contribute troops did not have many on the ground. In addition, many of the United States' traditional allies, such as Germany and France, were absent from the coalition. Others, such as Italy, supported the United States and participated in the coalition, although this support came after the combat phase of the operation was over.[15] Those countries that did send troops often had significant constraints on how those troops could be used. "The Dutch did good patrols, on foot. The Italians only patrolled by vehicle. . . .The Japanese didn't patrol at all. . . . [U]nder their rules of engagement which provided only for self-defense, the Japanese weren't permitted to secure their own perimeter and had to rely on the Dutch to do it. . . .The Thai battalion's rules didn't even allow them to leave their camp near Karbala."[16] Many of these rules were known at the outset. For example, Prime Minister José María Aznar of Spain said that although Spain would send nine hundred troops and three ships to the Iraq War effort, those would not be combat troops, but rather troops for medical and antimine support.[17]

In summary, the coalition of the willing that followed the United States into the war with Iraq was largely composed of small countries with small military contributions, many of which had very strict constraints on how those contingents could be deployed. Only a few countries brought real firepower to the war effort. The United Kingdom, Australia, and Poland were the largest contingents of troops except the United States. NATO could not be deployed, as most member states did not approve of the U.S.-led action. The United Nations was not used as an organizing framework since the UN Security Council did not sanction the initial combat operation. As a consequence, the coalition of the willing was largely composed of states with something to gain by standing shoulder to shoulder with the United States, rather than being motivated by outright fear or threat generated by the Hussein government. The exception was the United Kingdom, which perceived a threat from Saddam Hussein's Iraq. However, even in the case of the United Kingdom, its close connection with the United States was a paramount consideration regarding its participation in the Iraq War.[18]

Decision-Making Structure

The initial invasion of Iraq consisted principally of the participation of the United States, the United Kingdom, Australia, and Poland. As such, coordination of forces was not overly complex at the outset. The multinational forces that were involved in the invasion were under the command and control of General Tommy Franks, commander of U.S. Central Command (CENTCOM), although national chains of command were maintained.[19] In fact, in his memoirs, Bush describes video conferencing with General Tommy Franks, and the lead U.S. Army, Navy, Marine, Air Force, and Special Operations commanders, as well as their counterparts from the British and Australian militaries, in the moments leading up to his order to execute Operation Iraqi Freedom. He wanted to ensure that each commander was prepared to implement the strategy.[20] That he was on the line with the United States' closest allies at the time the order was given is suggestive of the command structure of the operation.

CENTCOM, which figured prominently in the prosecution of Operation Desert Storm and Operation Desert Shield, similarly implemented the strategy for war in this case. It had joint command of the land, sea, air, and Special Operations Forces, underscoring the importance of this standing institutional structure for the exercise of U.S. military power.

The U.S. and coalition forces' organization took a number of different shapes. At the outset, the U.S. and coalition ground forces were part of the Coalition Forces Land Component Command (CFLCC), led by Lieutenant General David McKiernan, and directed the U.S. Army V Corps and the I Marine Expeditionary Force. The British First Armoured Division served under this latter force, while Special Operations Forces comprised the U.S. Combined Forces Special Operations Component Command (CFSOCC).[21]

In June 2003, the CFLCC was replaced by the Combined Joint Task Force 7, which was then replaced by the Multinational Force–Iraq (MNF-I) in May 2004 (which was replaced in turn by United States Forces–Iraq in January 2010). In 2004, the NATO Training Mission in Iraq (NTM-I) was established and operated through December 2011.[22] Within the United Kingdom, authority for the command and control relationships was delegated by the Chief of Joint Operations (CJO) to the National Contingent Command (NCC), which in turn delegated tactical command to the British environmental contingent commanders, who could then delegate tactical control to their U.S. counterparts.

The British NCC was based along with Tommy Franks in Qatar for the duration of the initial invasion. Informal channels of communication and dialogue among coworkers, individuals who had experience dealing with one another, and the many who wore more than one hat in their designated roles, fostered harmony and allowed the coalition to operate effectively.[23] There was far more flexibility in decision making, which encouraged efficiency, thus averting the problematic and cumbersome processes that characterized some of the larger coalition and allied operations in the post–Cold War period.[24] Figures 6.1–6.3 illustrate the evolution from CFLCC to MNF-I as well as the NTM-I decision-making structure.

In summary, through each evolution of the force composition in Iraq, the hierarchy remained largely within the United States' control, with a fairly straightforward and clear-cut chain of command, along with informal communication mechanisms that enhanced the coalition's ability to operate. The clarity and reduced number of partners engaged militarily, particularly at the outset, offered a far more conducive environment for coalition operations than

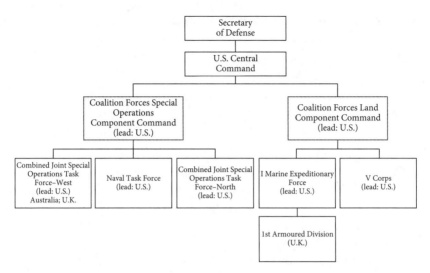

Figure 6.1 Decision-making structure, Operation Iraqi Freedom

SOURCE: Stephen A. Carney. *Allied Participation in Operation Iraqi Freedom.* Washington, DC: Center of Military History, U.S. Army, 2011, 8.

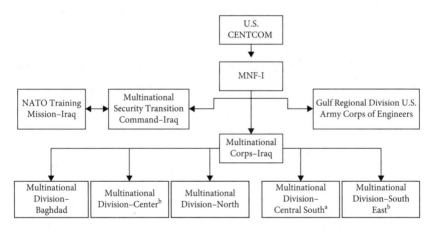

Figure 6.2 MNF-I chain of command

SOURCE: U.S. Forces in Iraq. "MND-C, MND-SE Operating Areas Combine to Create MND-South," U.S.F-I. April 1, 2009. Accessed 11/6/2010. http://www.usf-iraq.com/?option=com_content&task=view&id= 25981&Itemid=128.

NOTE: MNF-I: U.S. commander; U.S. troops. MNC-I: U.S. commander; U.S. and Georgian troops. MSTC-I: U.S. commander (same commander as NTM-I). Gulf Regional Division U.S. Army Corps of Engineers: U.S. commander. MND-Baghdad: U.S. commander; U.S., Romanian, Estonian troops. MND-Center: U.S. commander; U.S. and Georgian troops. MND-North: U.S. commander; U.S. troops. MND-West: U.S. commander; U.S. troops. MND–Central South: Polish commander; Polish, Nicaraguan, Dominican, Ukrainian, Mongolian, Honduran, Salvadoran, Romanian, Spanish, Bulgarian, Danish, Hungarian, Latvian, Lithuanian, Kazakh, Dutch, Thai, Norwegian, Slovakian, Filipino, and American troops. MND–South East: U.K. commander; U.K., Danish, South Korean, Dutch, New Zealander, Norwegian, Portuguese, Lithuanian, Australian, Romanian, Italian, and Czech troops.

[a]MND–Central South dissolved in October 2008 with its areas of responsibility falling mostly under U.S. control.

[b]In April 2009, MND–Center and MND–South East combined to form MND–South under U.S. command.

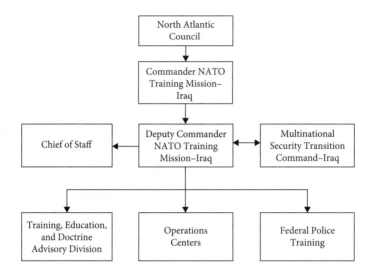

Figure 6.3 NTM-I chain of command

SOURCE: NATO. "NTM-I Outline," Accessed 11/6/2012. http://www.aco.nato.int/resources/10/documents/NTMI.pdf.

did allied military endeavors such as Operation Allied Force.[25] The ability to launch the war using existing institutional structures enabled efficient translation of capability to manifest military power. Nevertheless, there were challenges in regard to interoperability and friendly fire.

Interoperability and Friendly Fire

As described in chapter 1, during the invasion of Iraq in March 2003, fourteen Australian Hornet pilots defied the orders of their American commanding officers and independently aborted forty bombing missions at the last minute, believing that the objects of attack were not valid military targets or that dropping their bombs would result in an alarming number of civilian casualties. None of the pilots was reprimanded—they were following Australian rules of engagement.[26]

Later that same month, as described in chapter 1, just north of Basra, two American A-10 fighter pilots mistook a four-vehicle British reconnaissance patrol for the enemy, even though the vehicles were decorated with bright orange panels to signal that they were coalition forces. As the pilots bombarded the convoy, the British tried unsuccessfully to raise the pilots on the radio. They got no response, however, since the Americans were on a different frequency. The planes turned and strafed their coalition partners a second time.

The American pilots did not see or understand the red smoke released by the British, another coalition identification device. This incident killed one British soldier and wounded another.[27] Friendly-fire challenges plagued the Iraq coalition.[28]

Lieutenant General Conway, commander of the First Marine Expeditionary Force (I-MEF), when asked about the anger friendly fire engendered, said, "I think at this point there's just more anxiety that [friendly fire] continues to happen. In the last war, we lost Marines to A10s. We believe we've lost Marines through A10s in this war. And it's one of our major efforts now, in the wake of it all, to find a better IFF—Identification of Friend or Foe—system that will allow a shooter to realize that that target is a friendly or enemy vehicle."[29]

In yet another instance early in the operation, a U.S. Patriot took down a British Tornado, culminating in the loss of the entire crew.[30] Over the summer, as the war gathered momentum, a series of friendly-fire incidents unfolded— U.S. troops fired on civilians rushing home before curfew; a Reuters cameraman was killed because the device on his shoulder looked like a launcher for a rocket-propelled grenade to the soldier who shot him. In September, a firefight with Iraqi police near Fallujah resulted in ten deaths.[31]

These episodes pockmarked the coalition experience in Iraq and damaged coalition standing in the country as well. The manner in which they were managed also mattered in regard to lasting resentments within the coalition. While employing force multilaterally may be undertaken for strategic ends, the consequences may be costly—friendly fire is very difficult to avoid within national forces; it is much harder still to avert within a coalition because of the differences in practice that exist among participating states.

WikiLeaks reports 1,328 episodes of friendly fire between January 2004 and December 2009. The breakdown by type is reported in Table 6.1.

The most common friendly-fire episodes were coalition on coalition, although there were many Iraq-Iraq cases as well as Iraq-coalition cases. Despite the sophisticated Blue Force Tracking System (BFT) designed to track friendlies, provide emergency communication, and identify and locate troops, in the early stages of the war these technologies did not work as effectively as they did later in the operation.[32]

Language often poses challenges in coalition warfare; Operation Iraqi Freedom was no exception. For example, Georgia's troops largely managed checkpoints in the fortified section of the Green Zone in Baghdad, but few of the troops spoke anything but Russian or Georgian.[33]

Table 6.1 Friendly-fire incidents in Iraq, January 2004–December 2009

Type of incident	Number
Blue-Blue	364
Blue-Green	141
Blue-White	93
Green-Blue	225
Green-Green	307
Green-White	135
White-Blue	26
White-Green	10
White-White	27

SOURCE: WikiLeaks. Accessed 5/28/2012. http://wikileaks.org/irq/sort/type/friendly_fire_0.html.
NOTE: Blue represents coalition forces; Green represents Iraqi forces; White represents civilians.

Interoperability and information sharing were also pervasive problems in Iraq. As an RAF squadron leader indicated, sharing information was the greatest interoperability challenge, which created tremendous frustration. The system was extremely slow. In addition, the United States operated on a superior computer information system, not releasable to the United Kingdom without U.S. supervision, and the United Kingdom operated on a number of systems, but the transfer of information was manual, thus requiring the United States to find the time in a high-paced environment to decide on and implement the transfer. There was a definite cost in regard to efficiency.[34]

Although the technology was impressive, there were continuing problems in surveillance and communication, and challenges in getting on the ground information in real time. Even in the initial invasion, tracking friendlies was easier than tracking hostile forces, via the BFT.[35] Given how pervasive the problem is in regard to friendly fire in coalition warfare, effective technologies to reduce it are welcome and warranted. Sharing information and communicating regarding the location of hostiles as part of deepening interoperability among coalition partners needs to continue to develop along these lines as well.

In summary, interoperability and friendly-fire challenges confronted the coalition from the outset of its operation in Iraq. Despite the relatively contained nature of the initial combat mission, there were a number of fatal tragedies. The frequency of these episodes increased as the complexity of the mission increased. Attention to the technologies and the fraught nature of the incidents for maintaining coalition cohesion meant that heightened attention was paid to avoiding such costly problems. But this case again illustrates that interoperability and friendly fire are an inherent component of multilateral war fighting. Although institutions of interstate violence provide a foundation for the projection of state power, there are institutional effects that hinder the operations. The dynamics of the wartime alliances and coalitions are complex and not always straightforward. This is certainly true in the Iraq case, and it is very visible in regard to burden sharing and intracoalition leverage.

Balance of Power and Burden Sharing Within the Coalition

Coalition warfare, and indeed multilateral operations in general, require the harmonization of military equipment. If any U.S. coalition partners have out-of-date equipment ill suited for joint operations, it often falls to the United States to provide up-to-date replacements or at least help provide them. For example, the United States paid approximately $240 million to Poland for equipment, meals, transportation, and medical supplies when Poland first deployed troops to Iraq in 2003. In the 2005 fiscal year, the amount the United States paid the Czech Republic amounted to about $43,478 per soldier. The costs of coalition warfare are high, even when the rewards are small: the 138 total Czech troops in Iraq and Afghanistan in 2005 did not really affect the security needs in either country. Further, because the United States is one of the few countries in the world with significant airlift capacity, the burden of flying in allies fell to the United States as well.[36] The disproportionate capability of the United States was apparent in all of the interventions under review in this book, and certainly very visible in the Libyan operation analyzed in the next chapter.

The United States offered numerous incentives to entice states to join the cause in Iraq—cooperation was worthwhile for partner states at the outset of the war because of these inducements. The United States reportedly lobbied India with promises to sanction the sale of the Arrow 2 missile defense system by Israel and to relax restrictions on other state of the art military equipment. Pakistan was offered more than $3 billion in military and economic aid.[37] Turkey received $1 billion in aid and $8.5 billion in U.S. loan guarantees (it was originally offered $6 billion in aid and $24 billion in loan guarantees before Turkey's Parliament voted on March 1, 2003, to reject U.S. troop access to Turkish bases). U.S. subsidies, in addition to contracts to help rebuild the Iraqi infrastructure, were among the enticements offered to coalition partners.[38]

Allies and partner states contributed troops at the United States' behest in large part because the side payments made it worthwhile. For example, Moldova's troops to Iraq earned it a visit from Secretary of Defense Donald Rumsfeld, who thanked the country for its contribution to the war on terrorism and promised support in the face of continued Russian military presence in the Transnistria region of Moldova.[39] Poland and the Czech Republic earned a promise for an antimissile shield, and Poland received additional U.S. pledges of support in the event of an attack on it by a third party.[40] Mongolia's contribution of approximately 180 troops yielded its first U.S. presidential visit, as well as negotiations for a free-trade agreement.[41] In the Operation Iraqi Freedom coalition in particular, small states that brought few military capabilities to the table won disproportionate leverage over the most powerful country in the international system.

In 2005, Congress established the $200 million Coalition Solidarity Fund (CSF) to support coalition partners in Iraq and Afghanistan. As examples of how this money was disbursed, Estonia received $2.5 million for its then 40 troops in Iraq and 80 in Afghanistan. Albania received $6 million to support 120 troops in Iraq and 35 in Afghanistan; the Czech Republic similarly received $6 million for its 100 troops in Iraq and 60 in Afghanistan at the time the money was granted. Furthermore, because of its overwhelmingly asymmetrical capability, the United States paid to airlift Poland's 2,400 troops to Iraq, as well as build their camps and provide equipment. In addition, Poland received $57 million in CSF monies.[42] According to the General Accountability Office, by April 2007, the United States had spent approximately $1.5 billion to transport, sustain, and provide services for military troops from twenty countries other than the United States and Iraq. Approximately 66 percent of this total was used to support Poland and the countries under its command; about 20 percent went to Jordan for border operations among other activities. On top of the support for the operation in Iraq, the State Department provided approximately $1.9 billion in security assistance for military training and equipment to ten coalition members and Jordan between 2003 and 2007.[43]

The countries that did send troops mostly sent low numbers of them in brief rotations, with limiting rules over engagement. For example, Japan sent troops, but they were not allowed to fight; Dutch troops were deployed to guard the Japanese contingent. Iceland sent two individuals at its peak deployment. In regard to lives lost, the United Kingdom endured 179 casualties, and the United States more than 4,300; the rest of the coalition combined lost on the order of 139.[44] Georgia had a fairly large contingent, about 2,000 at peak, but they had to be quickly withdrawn to confront the Russian invasion in August 2008.[45]

Despite the large number of countries participating in the Iraq War, most deployments were very, very small. In March 2003, the United States had about 250,000 troops deployed; the British about 45,000; and approximately 2,000 Australian troops were present.[46] By March 2004, the United States had about 130,000 troops in Iraq; the United Kingdom, 9,000; Italy, 3,000; and Poland, 2,460. Table 6.2 provides a snapshot from 2004 in regard to troop contingents by state; Table 6.3 provides comprehensive data on national participation.

Table 6.4 demonstrates that the power distribution within the coalition was relatively asymmetrical, with, as in Afghanistan, a very powerful United States operating with other great powers which were, nevertheless, significantly weaker than the United States. The leverage within the coalition, however, may have fallen disproportionately to the weaker states, as the United States did all it could to maintain the coalition.

On the flip side, as of April 2007, $15.6 billion was forthcoming from other countries, including those that did not participate in the Iraq operation, for reconstruction and state building. Most of these funds (70 percent), however, came in the form of loans rather than grants.[47] The costs of the war in Iraq to the United States have been substantial, in addition to the costs of reconstruction and development, which continue even after the operation ended. The United States shouldered the burden of the war in Iraq.[48] It paid nearly 98 percent of the total cost, as Table 6.5 shows.

By July 31, 2009, all countries but the United States had withdrawn their forces from Iraq, although the United Kingdom had some remaining troops.[49] In January 2010, the coalition was renamed U.S. Forces in Iraq; in September 2010, Operation Iraqi Freedom was renamed Operation New Dawn. It became a singularly U.S. operation designed to address Iraq's political and economic transition through continuing work targeting terrorist networks, but it focused principally on strengthening Iraqi political, military, and economic capacities and stability. In December 2011, the United States formally ended its military operations in Iraq.

In summary, the balance of power in regard to capabilities was asymmetrical in that the United States was by far the most powerful country in the coalition. The Iraq war was a U.S.-initiated operation, and thus it is not surprising that the United States shouldered the largest share of its cost. Within the coalition, however, small states contributing very little to the coalition in terms of

Table 6.2 Troop contingents in Iraq by country of origin,
March 2004

Country	Troops	Per 100,000 population	Per 1,000 military
United States	130,000	47.7	94.8
United Kingdom	9,000	15.2	42.4
Italy	3,000	5.3	11.3
Poland	2,460	6.7	10.2
Ukraine	1,600	3.2	5.1
Spain	1,300	3.3	7.0
Netherlands	1,100	7.0	19.5
Australia	800	4.3	14.5
Romania	700	3.1	3.4
Bulgaria	480	5.9	5.9
Thailand	440	0.7	1.4
Denmark	420	7.8	17.3
Honduras	368	6.1	5.4
El Salvador	361	6.2	14.7
Dominican Republic	302	3.7	12.3
Hungary	300	2.9	6.9
Japan	240	0.2	1.0
Norway	179	4.0	5.8
Mongolia	160	6.1	17.6
Azerbaijan	150	1.9	2.1
Portugal	128	1.3	2.6
Latvia	120	5.1	20.9
Lithuania	118	3.3	9.7
Slovakia	102	1.9	2.3
Czech Republic	80	0.8	1.4
Philippines	80	0.1	0.7
Albania	70	2.1	7.0
Georgia	70	1.4	2.7
New Zealand	61	1.7	6.4
Moldova	50	1.1	4.7
Macedonia	37	1.8	2.3
Estonia	31	2.2	6.5
Canada	31	0.1	0.5
Kazakhstan	25	0.1	0.4

SOURCE: Perspectives on World History and Current Events. Accessed 5/16/2012. http://pwhce.org/willing.html.

Table 6.3 Coalition members, March 27, 2003–August 31, 2010

Nation	Mar. 27, 2003	Dec. 2003	2004	2005	2006	2007	2008	2009	Mar. 1, 2010	Aug. 31, 2010
Total coalition countries	49	37	37	32	30	28	26	6	1	1
Afghanistan	X									
Albania	X	X	X	X	X	X	X (12/18/08)			
Angola	X									
Armenia				X	X	X	X (10/6/08)			
Australia	X	X	X	X	X	X	X	X (7/31/09)		
Azerbaijan	X	X	X	X	X	X	X (12/3/08)			
Bosnia & Herzegovina				X	X	X	X (11/29/08)			
Bulgaria	X	X	X	X	X	X	X (12/17/08)			
Colombia	X									
Costa Rica	X									
Czech Republic	X	X	X	X	X	X	X (12/4/08)			
Denmark	X	X	X	X	X	X	X (2008)			
Dominican Republic	X	X	X (2004)							
El Salvador	X	X	X	X	X	X	X	X (1/22/09)		
Eritrea	X									
Estonia	X	X	X	X	X	X	X	X (2/7/09)		
Ethiopia	X									
Georgia	X	X	X	X	X	X	X (10/20/08)			
Honduras	X	X	X (2004)							
Hungary	X	X	X (2004)							
Iceland	X									
Italy	X	X	X	X	X (2006)					
Japan	X	X	X	X	X	X	X (12/6/08)			
Kazakhstan		X	X	X	X	X	X (10/20/08)			
Kuwait	X									
Latvia	X	X	X	X	X	X	X (11/8/08)			
Lithuania	X	X	X	X	X	X	X (12/16/08)			
Macedonia	X	X	X	X	X	X	X (11/08)			
Marshall Islands	X									

(*continued*)

Table 6.3 (*continued*)

Nation	Mar. 27, 2003	Dec. 2003	2004	2005	2006	2007	2008	2009	Mar. 1, 2010	Aug. 31, 2010
Micronesia	X									
Moldova		X	X	X	X	X	X (12/18/08)			
Mongolia	X	X	X	X	X	X	X (10/4/08)			
Netherlands	X	X	X	X	X	X (2007)				
New Zealand		X	X (2004)							
Nicaragua	X	X	X (2004)							
Norway		X	X	X (2005)						
Palau	X									
Panama	X									
Philippines	X	X	X (2004)							
Poland	X	X	X	X	X	X	X (10/4/08)			
Portugal	X	X	X	X	X (2006)					
Romania	X	X	X	X	X	X	X	X (7/23/09)		
Rwanda	X									
Singapore	X	X	X	X	X	X	X (2008)			
Slovakia	X	X	X	X	X	X	X (2008)			
Solomon Islands	X									
South Korea	X	X	X	X	X	X	X (12/1/08)			
Spain	X	X	X (2004)							
Thailand		X	X	X (2005)						
Tonga	X	X	X (2004)							
Turkey	X									
Uganda	X									
Ukraine	X	X	X	X	X	X	X (12/9/08)			
United Kingdom	X	X	X	X	X	X	X	X (7/31/09)		
United States	X	X	X	X	X	X	X	X	X	X
Uzbekistan	X									

SOURCE: "U.S.-Iraq War." ProCon.org. Accessed 5/15/2012. http://usiraq.procon.org/view.resource.php?resourceID=000677; for December 2003–2007: U.S. Government Accountability Office. "Stabilizing and Rebuilding Iraq: Coalition Support and International Donor Commitments." May 9, 2007; for 2008–10: U.S. Department of Defense. "Measuring Stability and Security in Iraq." June 2009; Multi-National Force-Iraq and United States Forces-Iraq websites (various pages); Rod Nordland and Timothy Williams. "Iraq Force Soon to Be a Coalition of One." *New York Times.* July 28, 2009; BBC. "UK Troops in Iraq Moved to Kuwait." July 28, 2009; Associated Press. "Facts, Figures Related to the Iraq War." August 31, 2010.

NOTE: Withdrawal dates are in parentheses.

Table 6.4 Power capabilities of largest contributing countries in
Iraq War, 2004

Country	Military expenditures (in millions of U.S. 2012 dollars)	Military personnel (in thousands)	Composite Index of National Capability
USA	455,908	1,450	0.1431688
UKG	50,120	209	0.0211505
ITA	34,345	195	0.0185087
POL	4,630	152	0.0070501
UKR	1,013	241	0.0139714
SPN	12,746	149	0.0113157
NTH	9,440	53	0.0061963

SOURCE: National Military Capabilities Data. Version 4.0, extended to 2007. Accessed 5/26/2012. http://www.correlatesofwar.org/COW2%20Data/Capabilities/nmc4.htm; J. David Singer, Stuart Bremer, and John Stuckey. "Capability Distribution, Uncertainty, and Major Power War, 1820–1965." *Peace, War, and Numbers*. Bruce Russett, ed. Beverly Hills, CA: Sage, 1972, 19–48.

NOTE: The Composite Index of National Capability is computed by summing observations for total population, urban population, iron and steel production, energy consumption, military personnel, and military expenditures for the year, converting each country's absolute component into a share of the international system, averaging across the six component parts. Accessed 12/14/2012. http://www.correlatesofwar.org/COW2%20Data/Capabilities/nmc3-02. htm. USA refers to the United States; UKG to the United Kingdom; ITA to Italy; POL to Poland; UKR to Ukraine; SPN to Spain; and NTH to the Netherlands.

troops yielded significant benefits, emblematic of their disproportionate leverage within the coalition. The war in Iraq highlights the ways in which multilateral warfare advances strategic ends, yet in so doing states incur inevitable costs. As is often the case, challenges in burden sharing impinged on cohesion and fighting effectiveness.

Cohesion and Fighting Effectiveness

Operation Iraqi Freedom is an interesting case from the perspective of cohesion. The war in Iraq magnified differences among the NATO allies and exacerbated tension among them. The absence of NATO to hold the coalition together culminated in a continuous withdrawal of countries and their troops during the course of the operation, which stands in contrast to the Afghanistan experience. Key allies, such as Canada, Germany, and France, did not participate in Iraq, which is also a striking contrast to Afghanistan. Given that many NATO allies were not part of the operation, the impact of the war on NATO cohesion is entirely separate from the question of how cohesive the Operation Iraqi Freedom coalition itself was.[50] Despite how interesting the first question is, the

Table 6.5 Military expenditures by coalition members, Iraq operations

Coalition member	Expenditures (in millions of U.S. 2012 dollars)	Percentage of national GDP
United States[a]	806,000	5.00
United Kingdom[b]	14,000	0.60
Australia[c]	3,000	0.30
Poland[d]	500	0.06
Spain[e]	489	0.03
Denmark[f]	365	0.20
Romania[g]	90	0.03
Total	**824,444**	

SOURCE: Compilation from official estimates, newspaper articles, and CIA *World Factbook*.

[a]Amy Belasco. "The Cost of Iraq, Afghanistan, and Other Global War on Terror Operations Since 9/11." Congressional Research Service. CRS Report for Congress No. 7-5700. March 29, 2011, ii. Accessed 4/29/2012. http://www.fas.org/sgp/crs/natsec/RL33110.pdf.

[b]BBC News. "Iraq War in Figures." December 14, 2011. Accessed 12/6/2012. http://www.bbc.co.uk/news/world-middle-east-11107739.

[c]Mark Davis and Phillip Coorey. "$3b and Rising Rapidly: Cost of the War to Australian Taxpayers." *Sydney Morning Herald*. March 21, 2007. Accessed 12/5/2012. http://www.smh.com.au/news/national/3b-and-rising-rapidly-cost-of-iraq-war/2007/03/20/1174153066804.html.

[d]Jin Zhao. "How About Gain and Loss of Polish Military Mission in Iraq." *People's Daily*. October 7, 2008. Accessed 12/17/2012. http://english.people.com.cn/90001/90780/91343/6511014.html. This estimate is supported by earlier reporting in the Polish press that placed the amount spent by 2006 at "hundreds of millions of zlotys"; Warsaw Rzeczpospolita. "Highlights: Polish Press 18-19 Nov 06 Poland." OSC Report. November 20, 2006. Accessed 12/20/2012. World News Connection.

[e]"Iraq Operation Has Cost Spain over 369m Euros—Minimum." *El País*. May 25, 2004. Foreign Broadcast Information Service Translated Excerpt No. FBIS-WEU-2004-0526. Accessed 12/23/2012. World News Connection. Information available at http://wnc.fedworld.gov/index.html.

[f]AFP. "Denmark Has Spent 278.4 Million Euros on Iraq War." March 6, 2007; OSC Transcribed Text. Accession No. 240651039. Accessed December 23, 2012. World News Connection. Information available at http://wnc.fedworld.gov/index.html.

[g]"Romania Poised to Withdraw Its Troops from Iraq." *News Max Wire*. June 29, 2006. Accessed 1/10/2013. http://archive.newsmax.com/archives/articles/2006/6/29/113134.shtml. The Romanian defense minister was quoted in 2006 saying that the withdrawal of Romanian troops from Iraq would save Romania $90 million. Yet Romanian forces did not in fact withdraw; they stayed until 2009. This would suggest that that money was not saved and that Romania spent at the very minimum $90 million in Iraq.

primary focus of this section is the latter—to what extent were the coalition partners able to coordinate their goals and strategies toward attaining them?

According to George Bush, the central goals of the operation were "to disarm Iraq of weapons of mass destruction, to end Saddam Hussein's support for terrorism, and to free the Iraqi people."[51] In the aftermath of toppling Saddam Hussein's government, the objectives were to reconstruct and rebuild the country. It was this latter goal in particular that posed a tremendous challenge to the United States and the coalition: "the United States did not help its cause in Iraq by choosing haphazardly to 'reinvent' it, that is, by pursuing goals that severely strained available U.S. capabilities and by making grand decisions with inadequate deliberation."[52] For the major combat component of the war, coalition cohesion was easier to maintain than the longer, more arduous second phase of the operation to rebuild and restore Iraq, which was characterized by deepening contention within the coalition. In other words, removal of the Hussein government was easier in regard to cohesion than regime change was.[53]

The United States began planning for the war in Iraq in late 2001.[54] According to leaked British documents, war planning in the United Kingdom began in early 2002.[55] In advance of Operation Iraqi Freedom, launched in March 2003, the United States and the United Kingdom flew more than twenty thousand sorties in preparation for the potential invasion.[56] The two countries were very closely intertwined in the planning and execution of the operation. Cohesion in this regard was quite significant, though the countries did negotiate in regard to goals and strategy. As Sir Anthony Brenton, minister and at times chargé d'affaires between January 2001 and March 2004 in the British embassy in Washington, wrote in a now-declassified telegram on March 6, 2003:

> Barring a highly improbable volte face by Saddam, the US is firmly on track for military action in the very near future. This does not depend on the adoption of a second Security Council resolution. But the military planning does assume that the UK will act alongside US forces. Franks is advising the President that he is ready to go. Turkey is a complication with "operational consequences," but one that can be got round without imposing significant extra delay. If, however, there were any question about UK involvement it would be, according to [blanked]—"huge-like trying to play football without the quarterback."[57]

Sir Brenton also suggested in his interview for the British Iraq inquiry:

> The first thing I should say was Blair, as was also I, was firmly convinced of the desirability of getting rid of Saddam, we because we thought he would constitute a threat, and therefore we were not seeking to impose conditions for doing something which we thought was right.
>
> That said, we did have strong views on how we went about it, and Blair was very clear in getting those views over to Bush, and we were all clear at our different levels in getting them over.
>
> One was that we had to go through the UN route, which they did. Another was a renewed US attention to the Palestinian dispute, which there was. It didn't last very long, but they did that as well."[58]

During the initial assault, there was a give and take among the coalition partners. For example, as Lieutenant General Conway, commander of the fifty-
thousand-strong First Marine Expeditionary Force (I-MEF), explained in regard to the assault on Basra, American strategists were interested in British
tactics in Basra, as Basra was a large city, and the belief was that this was representative of what U.S. forces would face in Baghdad with the fedayeen and
Ba'athists. U.S. military leadership watched closely as the British confronted this
situation to observe their successes and failures. The upper echelons of the U.S.
military wanted ground forces to take Basra earlier than the British Lieutenant
General Robin Brims thought wise; Brims and Conway jointly convinced the
higher command to allow the British to go at the pace they believed was right.[59]

The United Kingdom hoped that the United Nations would take on a
greater role in the postwar reconstruction process in Iraq; the United States was
less keen on this tactic, which suggests that coalition cohesion on the broader
mission of rebuilding Iraq was problematic.[60] Further, the U.S.-UK relationship strained in Iraq over confronting the forces loyal to Muqtada al-Sadr. The
British favored accepting the reality of al-Sadr, while the United States continued to combat the Sadrist forces. This disagreement over goals in Iraq did
undermine the cohesion of the coalition.[61] The U.S. relationship with Poland
was also strong in the early invasion period, though fissures did emerge over
time, appearing as early as March 2004, when Poland's President Aleksander
Kwasniewski commented that he had been misled about the alleged threat from
Iraqi weapons of mass destruction.[62]

Shared goals with Australia similarly waned over time. Australia was another
early supporter of the war, deploying Special Forces to secure western Iraq at
the outset of Operation Iraqi Freedom. Prime Minister Kevin Rudd, making
good on his campaign promise, ended Australia's involvement and withdrew
its forces in 2009. At one time or another some fourteen thousand Australian
troops had served in Iraq, at a cost of $2.2 billion.[63] Australian commitment and
concerns regarding the Iraq War and its conduct surfaced as early as 2004, at
which point a letter from the minister of defense to the prime minister warned
that Australia may be "in breach of its international legal obligations in hand-
ing over individuals who might be subject to the death penalty."[64]

Italy, which did not send troops during the initial invasion of Iraq but deployed them in the aftermath of the fall of the Hussein regime, experienced
some tension over time with the United States as well.[65] In other words, among
key allies, coordination of goals and strategy was not always easy in the latter

years of the Iraq War. The lack of clarity in goals and strategy was even reflected in the fact that a new strategy for addressing the insurgency did not emerge until the middle of 2004.[66] In other words, despite the incentives and benefits of addressing the war in Iraq with allies, there were significant hurdles in executing a cohesive mission over time.

In this case, as with the previous ones, the target of the operation was a profoundly weaker country. The question of how effective a coalition of great powers would need to be to prevail over a weaker country such as Iraq is fairly straightforward. Reuters reported, for example, that British troops entered Iraq completely ill prepared—some soldiers had their weapons confiscated, as they had to fly civilian aircraft; others "went into action" with only five bullets. Supply-chain challenges culminated in episodes such as a container of skis being delivered. The intense desert heat meant that long-distance radios failed. But because of the profound capability asymmetry between the coalition and Saddam Hussein's forces, the coalition was nonetheless able to prevail handily. Leaked government reports that revealed these situations suggested that "the war phase was a 'significant military success' but one achieved against a 'third-rate army.' . . . 'A more capable enemy would probably have punished these shortcomings severely.'"[67]

The coalition fought very effectively in regard to its initial goal—as effectively, perhaps, as the Iraqis did ineffectively.[68] The advanced technology of the coalition forces culminated in a high degree of lethality and enabled military victory at a low cost to themselves. Iraqi errors compounded this effectiveness—their mistakes facilitated the effective use of this technology.[69]

However, once the initial military victory was secured, moving forward with the goal of reconstructing Iraq was far more difficult than anyone anticipated. As Lieutenant General William Scott Wallace, commander of the U.S. Army's Fifth Corps, who led the Army forces in the invasion of Iraq, said in an interview, the military component of the operation was the easy part, the reconstruction component was the hard part, and the military was not well prepared for the total collapse of the regime and the impact that would have on the state:

> When we arrived in Baghdad, everybody had gone home. The regime officials were gone; the folks that provided security of the ministry buildings had gone; the folks that operated the water treatment plans and the electricity grid and the water purification plants were gone. There were no bus drivers, no taxi drivers; everybody just went home.

I for one did not anticipate our presence being such a traumatic influence on the entire population. We expected there to be some degree of infrastructure left in the city, in terms of intellectual infrastructure, in terms of running the city infrastructure, in terms of running the government infrastructure. But what in fact happened, which was unanticipated at least in [my mind], is that when [we] decapitated the regime, everything below it fell apart. I'm not sure that we could have anticipated that.[70]

The military strategy in the long period following the toppling of Saddam Hussein was opaque, and the goals and strategies for attaining those goals elusive for the United States, not just the coalition. Thomas E. Ricks, who has written extensively on the Iraq War, addresses this. He quotes a Marine infantry officer, Captain Zachary Martin, who said that forces on the ground were less concerned with winning and more concerned with making it through their tours.[71] In his view, part of the loss of focus was the absence of clear guidance on the ultimate goals and strategies for achieving them.[72]

In short, the small coalition that prosecuted Operation Iraqi Freedom—the United States, the United Kingdom, Australia, and Poland—handily managed goals and strategies toward attaining the goal of toppling Saddam Hussein's government. However, coalition cohesion in implementing plans for countering the insurgency, managing regime change, and stabilizing Iraq were highly fraught. Differences over questions of torture, human rights, and the status of enemy combatants all wreaked havoc on coalition cohesion. These troubling aspects of coalition cohesion brought on growing entrapment fears within the coalition and culminated in the departure one by one of the U.S. partners from the coalition over time.

Alliance Security Dilemma

Analyzing the security dilemma in Operation Iraqi Freedom and the Iraq War more generally is very illuminating—the case underscores that the alliance security dilemma is perceptual, psychological, and not yoked to capability. The alliance security dilemma manifested most obviously in this case in the context of maintaining the coalition. Threats and fears of abandonment mediated nearly all coalition activity—these persisted for the duration of the war for the United States. At the outset, in determining whether or not to join the Iraq coalition, those states whose abandonment fears outweighed their entrapment fears opted to join the United States. However, over the course of the war, entrapment fears emerged and began to dominate for most states in the coalition.

Entrapment fears were present, too, for those U.S. allies that opted out of the coalition in the first place. For states that did fight the Iraq War, their entrapment fears manifested in their dropping out once the operation was underway. These considerations underscore the fact that states focus on the strategic and pragmatic components of their relationships with others, particularly in regard to military alliances and obligations.

As noted in Table 6.2, there were forty-nine countries in the coalition in March 2004. By the end of the calendar year, thirty-seven remained. By 2005, two additional countries dropped out of the coalition; two more in 2006, and again in 2007 and 2008. In 2009, twenty countries left the coalition, and by 2010 only the United States remained.

In each instance, the security dilemma was acute, but domestic pressures trumped loyalty to the United States. Spain's withdrawal from the Operation Iraqi Freedom coalition in 2004 had a dramatic backlash effect on public opinion in the United States and the United Kingdom, thus fulfilling U.S. abandonment fears. When Italian Prime Minister Silvio Berlusconi announced in March 2005 that he would begin the process of withdrawing Italian troops, the fourth-largest contingent of foreign troops, mostly peacekeeping troops in southern Iraq, it was apparent that he was capitulating to internal sentiment in the face of U.S. pressure to stay. Two weeks prior to the announcement, American soldiers had killed an Italian intelligence agent, Nicola Calipari, riding with a freed kidnapped journalist, Giuliana Sgrena. This episode heightened domestic pressure on the Italian government to abandon the coalition and dealt a keen blow to the Bush administration's failing attempts to maintain a broad coalition of international troops in Iraq. Domestic pressures percolated to the surface, putting pressure on the alliance relationships, and fostering and deepening the alliance security dilemma.

As domestic pressures pushed into the international sphere, they exacerbated the alliance security dilemma of others. After every announcement of departure, others would come flooding in, aggravating the abandonment fears for the United States and remaining countries. In the aftermath of the Italian announcement, British opponents of the war lauded the Italian decision and suggested that the United Kingdom should do the same. The Netherlands and Ukraine had already begun the withdrawal process; Poland announced it would it would do so as well. In other words, as one key ally signaled impending abandonment, others played into those fears even more.[73] The increase in the number of constituencies that needed to be satisfied is another consequence of adopting a multilateral plan of action.

The Spanish withdrawal intensified the security dilemma within the coalition, and these fears metastasized in the year that followed, as one central partner after another threatened departure and then ultimately withdrew from Iraq. Evidence of the fear of abandonment by the United States was the resources it allocated to try to keep partners in country. Yet domestic pressures, the political landscape, and electoral considerations in most of these partner countries ultimately eclipsed the desire to maintain a presence in Iraq for the sake of loyalty to the United States. In other words, entrapment considerations for Spain, Italy, the United Kingdom, and Poland, in addition to the countries contributing fewer forces, culminated in the unraveling of the coalition over time. It became more of a security challenge to be associated with the U.S.-led coalition in Iraq than to court American censure by abandoning the effort.

Democracies are especially vulnerable to abandonment fears. As each state withdrew from the war effort, it affected public opinion adversely. As coalition-partner publics read about states leaving, the sense of unfair burden sharing was heightened, and the will to fight and win waned. Troop reductions by the United Kingdom in Iraq affected discussions of American troop levels as well. Furthermore, states abandoning the coalition underscored the unpopularity of the war and mobilized public opinion in the United States and worldwide against it.

Because the Iraq War was deeply unpopular with many of the democratic countries that participated in it, it is not surprising that entrapment fears would mediate decision making, especially during periods leading up to election. The threat environment for the participating states was a central component in understanding the alliance security dilemma for those states opting not to participate, those that joined the coalition, and those that ultimately dropped out of the operation. Outside threats and other strategic benefits of closely aligning oneself to U.S. interests were essential in driving the countries on the verge of NATO membership to participate. The North Korean threat and perception in Japan of the essential nature of the U.S.-Japan security relationship was critical to its compliance with U.S. interests, despite the fact that public opinion was deeply opposed to the Iraq War. Countries such as France and Germany without such strong external threat environments did not experience the same compulsion to move forward with the United States in the face of such strong domestic opposition.[74] This suggests that the fear of abandonment did weigh on many U.S. allies' decision making in regard to participation in the Iraq War.

Those abandonment fears over time gave way to more serious entrapment concerns, particularly in the face of the potential loss of electoral support for the government opting in to the Iraq operation.

The alliance security dilemma was at work leading up to Operation Iraqi Freedom, as well as during it and as the war unfolded. Many traditional U.S. allies, such as Germany, France, and Turkey, were governed by fears of entrapment and opted out of the operation altogether. Decision making regarding participation was also marked by concerns over the country in question's relationship with the United States and the implications participating or opting out would have on their long partnerships. As Sir Anthony Brenton answered when asked if opting out of participation in the Iraq War would have undermined the U.S.-UK relationship:

> I think it would have been damaged. I think the parallel in a sense is the U.S./France relationship, which went into the deep freeze for a year after the French behaved as they did over Iraq. I don't know that we would have had [sic] suffered any material costs, but the US attention to UK political concerns in the wider world would have been significantly weaker. . . .
>
> I think the real concern was that if the U.S. had gone in with much more limited international support than they had gone in with and had then gotten into the situation we subsequently got into in Iraq, there would have been much more disposition in the United States to back away from other aspects of international involvement with the UK, Europe and others and move back into sort of semi-isolationism. Our involvement was a constraint on that happening.[75]

In other words, clear abandonment fears regarding its relationship to the United States were in play as the United Kingdom assessed its involvement in the Iraq War, even if it deemed Saddam Hussein's Iraq a threat that needed to be addressed. Similar dynamics were at work with the other partners. Poland's commitment to Iraq, for example, was motivated out a desire to deepen its relationship to the United States, though Poland, as had states that participated in the coalition, ultimately yielded to heightened entrapment fears as the war dragged on, withdrawing from Iraq and leaving the United States on its own until its own withdrawal in December 2011.[76]

The alliance security dilemma among coalition partners in the Iraq War illuminates the institutional effects of advancing military objectives multilaterally. While there may be strategic reasons for pursuing one's goals via coalition or alliance, the vulnerabilities to fears of abandonment or entrapment may become debilitating. Institutional benefits come at a price. States often pursue a multilateral approach to augment legitimacy; however, legitimacy dividends may not always be realized in wartime operations.

Legitimacy

From the outset, Operation Iraqi Freedom struggled with legitimacy. In fact, in the weeks leading up to the operation, the prospect of war generated the largest antiwar demonstrations since Vietnam. On the weekend of February 15–16, 2003, as momentum for the U.S.-led invasion of Iraq was building, millions of people worldwide came out in protest of such an attack.[77] The BBC News reported that between six million and ten million people from sixty different countries marched in opposition to military intervention.[78] This case suggests that legitimacy inheres to the mission of the operation, not exclusively to the multilateral framework that implements it.

Public opinion polls across the globe revealed a deep suspicion of the United States' motives in Iraq as well as profound opposition to the war. Even in countries that ultimately participated in the mission, public opinion was deeply opposed to the action. For example, a Gallup poll indicated that even if the action was sanctioned by the United Nations, in Romania, only 38 percent of the population supported the war, 28 percent supported it in Bulgaria and 20 percent supported it in Estonia. A British opinion poll undertaken by the *Times* reported that in the United Kingdom, the United States' closest ally, 86 percent of the population polled wanted additional time for weapons inspections, and only 25 percent believed in mid-February—just a few weeks before the invasion was launched—that there was sufficient evidence to justify an intervention.[79] These opinions became more entrenched over time; the view of the United States deteriorated dramatically. Most public opinion polls showed that people believed that the war in Iraq heightened the threat of terrorism rather than reducing it, that the United States was more of a threat to world peace than Iraq was.[80] Furthermore, the overwhelming number of people polled worldwide believed that the United States should withdraw from Iraq as soon as possible.[81]

Accentuating this dynamic, a poll released in September 2007 by the Pew Foundation found that of all of the Middle Eastern countries surveyed, NATO ally Turkey had by far the largest percentage of people who named the United States as the country that posed the greatest threat: nearly two-thirds (64 percent) of Turkish respondents named the United States as the most threatening state in the system.[82] In addition, a Pew Global Attitudes survey in 2007 indicated that few people worldwide believed that the United States paid attention to the interests of others in its policy decisions. In the international community, the perception of the United States as unilateralist was pervasive.[83] During the 2005 Iraqi elections, there was a small surge of support for the operations there, although it was not sustained.[84] The war in Iraq was largely unpopular even with participating states. There were, however, exceptions. For example, the deployment was popular with Georgians, "who often were seen buying reduced-price televisions and stereos at the PX [post exchange] to send home for resale."[85]

The legitimacy deficit in the Iraq operation had domestic consequences for the many U.S. allies who supported the war. Tony Blair suffered significant political fallout, which spilled over into the political standing of the Labour Party. The government that supported the United States operation in Iraq was voted out in Spain in the aftermath of tremendous domestic opposition to the war and the deadly terrorist attacks in Madrid on March 11, 2004. The socialist government that promised Spanish withdrawal from the coalition was voted in, ultimately leading to Spain's abandonment of the coalition in Iraq.[86] In Poland, widespread domestic opposition to the war in Iraq created a thorny political landscape for the leadership. In 2007, the war-crimes case against seven Polish soldiers for killing Afghani civilians heightened already-strident domestic criticism of Poland's troop deployments in Afghanistan and Iraq. Civic Platform leader Donald Tusk was able to successfully campaign with the promise of bringing Polish troops home from Iraq as soon as possible. In October 2008, Poland withdrew its nine hundred remaining troops.[87] The ongoing departures of coalition partners over time also punctuated the legitimacy deficit of the operation.[88]

Despite the vast resources that the United States committed to the coalition in Iraq, the legitimacy of the enterprise never increased; rather, it declined over time. Even in the United States, where there was more support for the war than other parts of the world, the operation eventually lost legitimacy and validity. In early March 2003, an ABC poll indicated that 65 percent of Americans polled favored U.S. forces taking military action to remove Saddam Hussein from power. By December 2011, 66 percent were opposed to the U.S. war in Iraq, with only 31 percent remaining in favor, according to a poll by CNN and Opinion Research Corporation International. In the same time frame, 78 percent of Americans polled approved of the decision to remove U.S. combat troops from Iraq in 2011.[89]

The lack of UN Security Council sanction further undermined the credibility of the OIF mission. In September 2002, President Bush delivered a speech to the General Assembly in an attempt to bring the international community on board regarding the need for a resolution to the Iraq situation. In the immediate aftermath of this speech, there was an increase in support for confronting Iraq. However, this ultimately culminated in UN Security Council Resolution 1441, which served U.S. interests in condemning Iraqi behavior and failure to comply with the IAEA and inspection activities but did not authorize the use of force in the event of noncompliance.[90] While the United States attempted to take the UN path to cultivate support for its actions and appeal to publics worldwide, it was largely ineffective in generating the desired results.[91] Trying to garner support from the United Nations failed. The costs of not working through the United Nations were significant in regard to legitimacy.[92]

In the United States, there was some indication that support for the war would have been bolstered by UN sanction. A poll by CNN, USA Today, and Gallup in February 2003 indicated that of those polled, 40 percent believed that the United States should send troops to Iraq only with UN approval; 38 percent indicated that they should be sent even in the absence of UN approval. However, in a poll by ABC News and the *Washington Post* in the same month, 56 percent polled indicated disapproval with the way the United Nations was handling the situation with Saddam Hussein; only 38 percent approved.[93] The UN effect on legitimacy in this case is not entirely straightforward. In a Gallup poll undertaken in February 2003 of Europeans, most people indicated that even with a UN sanction they were not in favor of military action against Iraq, with the exception of Ireland and the Netherlands (see Table 6.6).[94]

The consequences of failing to generate a UN mandate were manifest in UN Secretary-General Kofi Annan's remarks in an interview in 2004 in which he indicated that the lack of UN Security Council approval of the war and the fact that the decision to undertake it was not in conformance with the UN Charter rendered the war illegal.[95] It is counterfactual to query whether the United Nations could have fostered legitimacy for the operation in Iraq. It is, however, not unreasonable to assert that had the United States worked more closely with the United Nations to advance its objectives of regime change in Iraq, it may have garnered more global support. This is true in that it may have allayed the threat that aggressive action in Iraq represented to the international system and may have signaled more modest and limited motivations. However, indications were that Saddam Hussein was complying with UN demands

Table 6.6 Favorability toward intervention in Iraq

	Are you in favor of military action against Iraq?		
Country	No (%)	Only if sanctioned by the UN (%)	Unilaterally by America and its allies (%)
Spain	74	13	4
France	60	27	7
Luxembourg	59	34	5
Portugal	53	29	10
Germany	50	39	9
Denmark	45	38	10
Finland	44	37	6
United Kingdom	41	39	10
Ireland	39	50	8
Netherlands	38	51	7

SOURCE: Gallup Poll. February 14, 2003. Accessed 5/24/2012. http://www.usatoday.com/news/world/2003-02-14-eu-survey.htm. Copyright 2003 Gallup Inc. All rights reserved. The content is used with permission; however, Gallup retains all rights of re-publication.

and requests; as such, it is not likely that had Bush cultivated UN support, it would have been forthcoming. In essence, the motivations of the United States were not entirely modest or limited, and as a consequence, in this case, working though the United Nations would likely have meant no invasion at all. Thus, the United Nations did provide a forum for the United States to signal its intentions and motivations—they were ambitious, and the rejection of the UN format was an indication of that. The costs of pursuing UN approval were simply too prohibitive.[96]

The United States did hope that constructing an international coalition would augment legitimacy. As Sir Anthony Brenton responded when asked how important the United Kingdom's role was in the Iraq war from a political perspective:

> I think it was very important. I mean, they would have done without us, but our involvement gave a significant extra aspect of international respectability to the operation. It demonstrated that it was not just the U.S. acting against an international villain, but it was a wider community, and Blair, of course, was a very eloquent advocate for the action we took. That was very useful to them as well.[97]

Over time, the UN Security Council did pass resolutions to provide a mandate for a multinational force in Iraq, particularly to facilitate governance and stability within the country, via UN Resolutions 1511 in October 2003, and Resolutions 1546, 1637, 1723, and 1790 in each year following.[98] Resolution 1511 authorized

> a multinational force under unified command to take all necessary measures to contribute to the maintenance of security and stability in Iraq, including for the purpose of ensuring necessary conditions for the implementation of the timetable and programme as well as to contribute to the security of the United Nations Assistance Mission for Iraq, the Governing Council of Iraq and other institutions of the Iraqi interim administration, and key humanitarian and economic infrastructure.[99]

The subsequent UN Security Council resolutions sought to evaluate the mandate for the multinational force and check Iraqi progress toward self-governance. The mandate expired on December 31, 2008, with the last of the UN resolutions: 1790.[100]

Despite the UN mandate for a multinational stabilization force in Iraq, public opinion regarding the legitimacy of this enterprise did not improve. Furthermore, despite strides in openness and democratic governance, domestic turmoil, growing numbers of internally displaced Iraqis (which reached their peak in 2008 at 2,770,000) and civilian casualties (which peaked in 2006 with a total of 34,500 for the year), and the insurgency meant that the operation in Iraq did not garner widespread acceptability.[101] The election of President Barack Obama fostered enhanced views of the United States from abroad,[102] but it did not heighten legitimacy of the Iraq War.

In summary, legitimacy of the Iraq War was missing from the outset. A significant component of legitimacy—or lack thereof—inheres to the mission of an operation, not simply to the coalition that advances it. The absence of an initial UN mandate for war against Saddam Hussein's forces exacerbated the lack of legitimacy but was more emblematic of the absence of a legitimate mission in the first place than a factor in and of itself. In other words, legitimacy may precede UN sanction, which may in turn augment that legitimacy. Without legitimacy in a mission, UN sanction is not likely to be forthcoming. The use or nonuse of the UN framework provides information about intentions and motivations. That was as apparent in this case as it was in the first Gulf War. Public opinion was opposed to the second war in Iraq all around the world. A UN Security Council resolution allowing the war to unfold is not likely to have improved that outlook entirely. In addition, once the United Nations sanctioned use of multinational force, the legitimacy of the enterprise did not improve.

The strategic use of multilateral frameworks to advance military ends has limits. While institutions may be used for pragmatic reasons, there are costs associated with proceeding multilaterally. In the Iraq War, the inability of the United States to get the United Nations to authorize force in a timely way meant that it was unable to get the international community to agree with the U.S. approach. The launching of the war with coalition partners did not actually facilitate the perception of this mission as legitimate either. Multilateralism mattered, and it mattered powerfully in this case, even if it could not in the end legitimate a war plagued by challenges in international acceptance of its mission.

CONCLUSION

Operation Iraqi Freedom and the ensuing war in Iraq illustrate quite a bit about multilateral war fighting. The operation was never a wholly legitimate enterprise, and the multilateral framework for prosecuting the war did not augment legitimacy. It is questionable whether or not working through the United Nations would have facilitated the legitimation process in any but a few participating states. What this indicates is that legitimacy largely inheres to the mission of the operation—and neutral global organizations can be involved only to the extent that some legitimacy in mission is already present. In other words, undertaking a mission for regime change in a sovereign state that is not attacking another state or engaging in massive and egregious human rights violations may not generate a UN sanction—the mission itself must have legal grounding in the context of what is occurring in the country and in the region. At that point, multilateral frameworks may serve to increase information about intentions and motivations, as well as to deepen the legitimacy of the operation. There must be a baseline of legitimacy at the outset, however, given the mission and objectives of the operation. Table 6.7 summarizes the variables.

The decision-making structures constructed for Operation Iraqi Freedom evolved as the tasks of the war unfolded. They generally worked well as straightforward hierarchical chains of command augmented by informal channels of communication. This facilitated the cohesion of the coalition, particularly at the outset of Operation Iraqi Freedom. There were the usual challenges that multilateral war fighting poses, in regard to interoperability, intelligence failures, and friendly fire. Despite those, however, fighting effectiveness at the

Table 6.7 Overview of variables in Operation Iraqi Freedom and the Iraq War

Independent variables	Mediating variables	Dependent variables
Coalition	Decision-making structure: hierarchical	Cohesion: low to moderate
Size: large	Power distribution: asymmetrical	War-fighting effectiveness: moderately effective
	Internal leverage rests principally with lead power	Interoperability: some challenges
		Legitimacy of operation: low for the duration of the operation

outset of the operation was significant. As the goals of the operation became more opaque, and as the situation on the ground became more complex, coalition cohesion began to unravel as well. Nothing substitutes for clear objectives that enable the development of strategies to attain those goals. At the outset, with a clear military goal of taking down the Hussein regime, the cohesion of the coalition was fairly easy to forge and maintain. As this clarity degenerated in the aftermath of the chaos that ensued following military victory, coalition cohesion unraveled as well, despite the fact that the UN Security Council did legitimize the multinational stabilization force in October 2003.

In regard to burden sharing, the United States did the heavy lifting in Iraq. In addition to not receiving contributions to offset its costs there, it paid a great deal of money to secure the participation of coalition partners. In addition, small countries that participated reaped dividends that were not always proportionate to their military contributions. The alliance security dilemma reflected this dynamic as well—fears of abandonment weighed in states' considerations regarding participation, but gradually, as costs grew, entrapment fears began to eclipse those fears. For the United States, abandonment fears motivated its alliance behaviors in pursuing its partners' involvement and in trying to maintain the coalition. These aspects of coalition warfare emanate from multilateralism. Although the United States was motivated by a desire to augment the legitimacy of the operation through its pursuit of an international coalition to prosecute the war in Iraq, the strategy did not increase support for the operation.

The Iraq case illustrates the importance of allies in advancing strategic ends, as we would expect from a realist institutionalist perspective. Yet it also underscores the vulnerabilities and costs associated with proceeding multilaterally in a war endeavor. In addition, the Iraq case reveals that domestic pressures may come to trump international and strategic concerns, even when the alliance relationships are strong.

In the end, however, the United States was able to advance its goals as a consequence of the web of institutions and alliances crosscutting the globe even in the absence of a UN mandate and even in the face of significant worldwide disapproval of its actions. These institutions and relationships nevertheless provided a foundation through which American power could be realized. They served and continue to serve as a central component of U.S. hegemony in the contemporary era.

7 OPERATIONS ODYSSEY DAWN AND UNIFIED PROTECTOR

THE ARAB SPRING came to Libya in early 2011, bringing peaceful demonstrations against the long-standing repressive regime of Muammar Gadhafi. In the aftermath of the fall of Egypt's President Hosni Mubarak, calls went out on Facebook for a nonviolent protest in Libya against Gadhafi's government. When the government arrested human rights activist Fathi Tarbel on February 15, it triggered a demonstration in Benghazi in which the government used lethal force.[1] Thursday, February 17, 2011, had been designated a day of protests since it was the anniversary of the 2006 killing of protesters in Benghazi by security forces when the protesters attacked the Italian consulate. These demonstrations brought additional crackdowns by the government.[2] The violence and demonstrations escalated, bringing with them mounting consternation in the international community over the Gadhafi government's fierce reaction to the rebellion and protests. Libyan refugees began to flee the country.[3] Countries with noncombatant citizens began the process of evacuation.[4]

Alarm in the international system over the strident response by Gadhafi led France and the United Kingdom to take the initiative in sponsoring United Nations Security Council (UNSC) Resolutions 1970 (February 26, 2011) and 1973 (March 17, 2011).[5] They also advocated for the European Union to adopt sanctions against Gadhafi.[6] UNSC Resolution 1970 included an arms embargo and a call for a cease-fire. The situation continued to worsen, however, becoming ever more precarious and perilous for the civilian population. By early March 2011, conversations were underway in the international community as to how to enforce UNSC Resolution 1970 and ensure the safety of the Libyan civilian population.[7] On March 17, the UNSC passed Resolution 1973, which called for states to "take all necessary measures . . . to protect civilians and civilian populated areas" and called "upon all Member States, in particular States of the region, acting nationally or through regional organisations or arrangements, in order to ensure strict implementation of the arms embargo."[8] Two days later the U.S.-led coalition began its operation in Libya.[9]

COALITION AND ALLIANCE

The Libyan war follows the evolving model of contemporary Western multilateral intervention—a coalition executed the immediate combat aspects of the operation, followed by NATO participation, which coordinated and cooperated with rebel forces on the ground.[10] The initial Libyan campaign, called Operation Odyssey Dawn by the United States, Operation Ellamy by the United Kingdom, Opération Harmattan by France, and Operation Mobile by Canada, entailed the participation of Belgium, Canada, Denmark, France, Italy, Norway, Qatar, Spain, the United Arab Emirates, the United Kingdom, and the United States.[11] The subsequent NATO mission that took over the initial operation was called Operation Unified Protector (OUP). States participating in OUP included Belgium, Bulgaria, Canada, Croatia, Denmark, France, Greece, Italy, Jordan, the Netherlands, Norway, Qatar, Romania, Spain, Sweden, Turkey, the United Arab Emirates, the United Kingdom, and the United States.[12]

As the violence in Libya became more alarming, countries began evacuating their nationals, and the momentum to build a coalition grew. France and England, already in the process of evacuation operations, indicated their readiness to move forward; Italy and Germany agreed to logistical support for humanitarian assistance or continued evacuation operations, but they were not in favor of a military mission in the absence of a UN mandate. None of the African states within the U.S. Africa Command's (AFRICOM) area of responsibility were willing to participate; as a consequence, coalition partners had to be forged from the U.S. European Command (EUCOM) and U.S. Central Command (CENTCOM) areas of responsibility. This illustrates that having an international web of institutions designed to implement war plans makes it easier to respond to crises, even when adaptation is necessary. Forging the coalition, getting states to contribute and commit, getting agreements for basing rights, and so forth, was a labor-intensive job that had to be done quickly and in the absence at AFRICOM of experience in such endeavors.[13] In the words of an AFRICOM officer: "Building a coalition: We didn't know who to call and contact to make this happen. We sent LNOs [liaison officers] to the [United

Kingdom] and France to facilitate, and later sent an LNO to SHAPE [Supreme Headquarters Allied Powers Europe]. . . . 'Who do you talk to in order to find out who's going to play and how much they are going to bring to the fight?'"[14]

The coalition and alliance structures used to prosecute the Libyan operation were well established even if inexperienced in the direct military task entrusted to them. However, the existence of these multilateral frameworks that could readily be tailored to the tasks at hand was invaluable in pursuing the central objectives of the Libyan campaign. The ability to borrow from EUCOM facilitated achieving the tasks at hand. The structures employed were hybrids, a coalition at the outset and then the NATO alliance once the campaign was underway, although the alliance was modified to include non–member states' participation, and not all member states participated in the operation. The decision-making structures derived from the institutional design of the existing frameworks.

Decision-Making Structure

The United States took command of Operation Odyssey Dawn (OOD) via AFRICOM.[15] Admiral Samuel J. Locklear III coordinated the tactical operations. He undertook the task on the command and control ship, the USS *Mount Whitney*, and served as both commander of U.S. Naval Forces Europe and Africa, as well as commander of Allied Joint Force Command, Naples, which had the operational responsibility for NATO missions in the Mediterranean. The USS *Mount Whitney* hosted U.K. and French naval officers as well as the liaison officers from other coalition countries.[16]

Under U.S. command, the coalition forces undertook a campaign against the Libyan government to establish a no-fly zone and then took out Libya's long-range air defense to reduce the threat of Gadhafi's forces to its civilian population and to ensure access by international humanitarian organizations. The command structure was under the auspices of AFRICOM. Strategic command came under the authority of the AFRICOM combatant commander, General Carter Ham, and tactical control was under Admiral Locklear, commander, U.S. Naval Forces Africa, although they worked very closely with coalition partner leadership. On USS *Mount Whitney*, there was representation from the French and UK navies, as well as liaison officers from a number of other navies, to closely coordinate with coalition partners.[17]

General Carter Ham, the commander of U.S. Africa Command maintained control of AFRICOM; Admiral Locklear led the Joint Task Force Odyssey Dawn.

The command was then split between the air and naval aspects of the operation, and coalition partners maintained control of their assets and undertook the operations in compliance with their individual countries' rules of engagement, communicating and coordinating via liaison officers. More specifically, the command relationships included a joint commander, a foreign policy adviser, a deputy commander, a chief of staff, and a senior enlisted adviser. The joint staff for Odyssey Dawn had a number of directorates, and twenty-eight U.S. and ten foreign liaison officers from France, Italy, and the United Kingdom supported the joint staff, in addition to twelve members from the U.S. Joint Forces Command's Joint Enabling Capabilities Command's Joint Deployable Team.[18] Figure 7.1 demonstrates in broad strokes the command relationships.

NATO assumed the command of the arms embargo on March 23; it assumed responsibility for the no-fly zone operation on March 24, 2011. The alliance took sole command and control of the operation on March 31, 2011.[19] Admiral Locklear was very clear that a transition in command structure would be fluid and flexible. According to Admiral Locklear, the turnover and transition between organizational constructs was not difficult since there were similar procedures, and the forces operated, exercised, and spoke together.[20] In reality, however, there were more than a few challenges along the way.

Many of the individuals in question wore two hats; Admiral Locklear himself was not only joint task force commander of Operation Odyssey Dawn but also commander of U.S. Naval Forces Europe and Africa as well as commander of NATO's Allied Joint Force Command (JFC) Naples, Southern—the southern regional commander under the supreme allied commander Europe (SACEUR).[21]

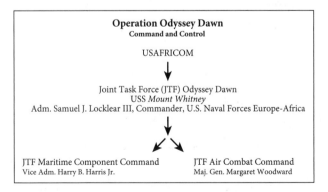

Figure 7.1 Command and control, Operation Odyssey Dawn

Once NATO took over the command structure of the operation, it became officially known as Operation Unified Protector (OUP). The decision-making structure thus emanated from the standard NATO hierarchy. The North Atlantic Council (NAC) exercised the overall political objectives, while Supreme Headquarters Allied Powers Europe (SHAPE) implemented NAC decisions militarily via the Joint Force Command (JFC) in Naples. Lieutenant General Charles Bouchard served as overall operational commander of the Combined Joint Task Force Unified Protector. NATO Maritime Command Naples directed naval operations in support of Unified Protector, and NATO's Air Command Headquarters for Southern Europe, in Izmir, Turkey, managed air operations. However, the air campaign itself was run from NATO's Combined Air Operations Centre in Poggio Renatico, Italy. Italian Vice Admiral Rinaldo Veri from NATO Maritime Command Naples led the maritime arms embargo; Rear Admiral Filippo Maria Foffi served as the task force commander at sea.[22]

Figure 7.2 illustrates the command structure; command emanating from U.S. Admiral James G. Stavridis, SACEUR, then to Canadian Lieutenant General Charles Bouchard, who oversaw the operation and maintained control of the air and sea assets, the former being commanded by an American general, and the latter being overseen by an Italian vice admiral. Despite the symbolism of the United States relinquishing primary control of the coalition operation

Figure 7.2 Command and control, Operation Unified Protector

SOURCE: NATO. "NATO and Libya: Operation Unified Protector, Command and Control." Accessed 6/7/2012. http://www.nato.int/cps/en/natolive/71679.htm.

to NATO, the SACEUR running the NATO operation was American Admiral Stavridis, although Lieutenant General Bouchard (Canadian) served as the overall operational commander of Operation Unified Protector.[23]

The decision-making structures of Operation Odyssey Dawn and Operation Unified Protector were adapted frameworks. AFRICOM had focused more on engagement than combat, but the United States was able to use EUCOM assets and experience to execute OOD. The institutionalization of U.S. doctrine enabled the adaptation, with a clear hierarchy and chain of command. Many of the participating countries maintained national command; the U.S. structure provided a coordination structure.[24] This in turn fostered a rapid response to the humanitarian crisis emerging in Libya, as did the acceptance by the coalition of U.S. leadership, which allowed for unity of command. Without the forward deployed forces, such a swift response would not have been as easy to execute.[25]

The transfer of command from the United States to NATO was not seamless, and ultimately unity of command in OUP was achieved, though it took some time to complete, and there was some disorganization in the first couple of weeks of the transition.[26] NATO was able to bring nonalliance states, such as Sweden and the United Arab Emirates, into the operation effectively. Their integration into the command chain was not always smooth, but here, too, it was greatly facilitated by years of joint training through a variety of NATO partnerships.[27] In this case, the use of preestablished multilateral frameworks also facilitated the containment of interoperability challenges and reduced the number of coalition and allied friendly-fire incidents.

Interoperability and Friendly Fire

The Libyan operation was an example of the importance of joint training, joint operability exercises, extensive consultation among allies, and the lessons of the previous decade in alliance and coalition warfare put to use. The allies and the coalition did a very effective job of coordinating the operations and executing them with a short preparatory time period. However, there were complexities as there always are—in particular, managing air attacks with local rebel forces on the ground.

In this case, the most pronounced friendly-fire problems involved several episodes in which the allies accidentally hit rebel troops on the ground as they pursued the objective of defeating Gadhafi's forces. The fluidity of the ground situation and insufficient knowledge of those events led to an episode in early

April in which five people were killed, fourteen injured, and six missing—NATO forces struck rebel tanks that NATO did not know the rebel forces had, tanks that had been taken from Gadhafi loyalists. This event occurred despite the fact that the rebel troops claimed that they had informed NATO of their situation and position.[28] Only a week before, another NATO air strike had killed thirteen rebel forces outside Brega.[29]

The coordination of air support with local forces on the ground is one aspect of contemporary coalition warfare that heightens the risk of friendly fire. The firing on rebel troops occurred again later the same month (April 2011), when a NATO air strike killed twelve rebel forces and injured three more in Misrata. Precautions had been taken to avoid this; NATO had asked the rebels to paint the roofs of their vehicles in a distinctive way for identification, which had been done—the roofs of the tanks were bright pink—and the forces were in position on order from their military council, believing themselves safe from friendly attack. The deadly incident nevertheless occurred.[30] In August 2011, NATO warplanes inadvertently attacked a tank that had been captured from Gadhafi's forces in Zawiyah; four rebels were killed.[31]

While the formula of supporting rebel forces from the air works well to contain allied causalities and fatalities, it does raise the likelihood of mishap between ground and air forces. These coordination issues will always be problematic, even when the ground forces are of the same military as the air assets.[32] The problems are magnified, however, when there are coalition forces on the ground and in the air. They are exacerbated even more when rebel forces are on the ground with no experience coordinating maneuvers with coalition or alliance partners, and without the technology or direct communication systems that exist within militaries and among close allies. In addition, when advances on the ground are nonlinear and unpredictable, the likelihood of mistaken identity rises.[33]

The other element of complexity in coalition operations is interoperability. While the coalition members were fighting alongside solid and long-standing partners with a tremendous amount of experience in joint exercises and attention paid to interoperability challenges, there were still a number of issues that came to the fore during the Libyan operation. Notably, as European stockpiles of laser-guided bombs began to wane very early in the Libyan operation, U.S. arsenals had to be tapped. However, American munitions did not fit the British- and French-made planes that flew most of the missions.[34]

In addition, significant challenges presented themselves in regard to sharing information. The requirements of "releasability," to whom information could be shared or distributed, were complicated, and they were further magnified by the changing nature of the operation, from U.S. control, to NATO, to coalition force—and these changes had to be mirrored in the releasability of information. In other words, the releasability requirements for sharing the information constantly challenged the foreign disclosure officers (FDOs). As a consequence, there were delays in release requests. There were additional challenges in regard to bandwidth sufficiency and network capability, which further restricted the information flow between the United States and its allies. Initially, a good deal of the information had to be passed manually from one network system to the other, revealing a weakness in alliance capability in sharing information and the imperative of building systems capable of transferring intelligence between the command, control, communications, computers, and intelligence systems of the United States and NATO.[35] The Naval Computer and Telecommunications Station (NCTS) in Sicily sought to find a solution for providing services to non-NATO coalition partners, since these units were prohibited from having access to coalition networks for security reasons. The NCTS provided connectivity independent of U.S. or NATO networks. It provided non-NATO partners with the connectivity they needed to stay in touch with their higher headquarters and to receive direct information from the coalition through approved channels, thereby facilitating more effective planning and execution of operations, and underscoring alliance flexibility and robustness.[36]

In regard to interoperability, the Libyan campaign revealed a number of additional strengths. Given the short time span in which action needed to take place, NATO, with its established command and control systems and the ability to integrate both standing members and coalition partners into its mission, was really the only organization that could respond quickly and effectively under the circumstances, even if it was not well suited to integrating U.S. intelligence. The operation also highlighted the fact that OUP would not have been possible absent American assets. This was true in that the initial assault in Operation Odyssey Dawn was dominated by U.S. forces, even after the United States ostensibly reduced its participation. U.S. aircraft were required for numerous essential tasks, such as surveillance and intelligence, air-to-air refueling, electronic jamming, and suppressing enemy air defenses.[37]

Given the concentration of air strikes and the rapidity from conception to execution of the operation, interoperability and friendly-fire challenges were rather contained. The Libyan operation did underscore a number of areas in which allied cooperation needed to evolve, and it demonstrated the challenges of coordinating an air operation with a ground operation, particularly one in which the ground operation was being executed by indigenous rebel forces and the air support was being conducted by coalition forces. The Libyan operation did benefit from the experience of the coalition wars that came before it, though there were inherent challenges that will always be present in multilateral war fighting, challenges that will endure regardless of the close relationships involved in executing such a campaign.

Balance of Power and Burden Sharing

The Libyan operation is an interesting case in regard to the internal balance of power and burden sharing in that it is largely considered a mission undertaken fundamentally at the behest of Britain and France, executed principally by NATO. British Prime Minister David Cameron and French President Nicolas Sarkozy acted in tandem to promote a resolution that would authorize NATO action via the United Nations in March 2011. The UN resolution established a no-fly zone over Libya and an arms embargo, and it authorized UN member nations to "take all necessary measures," bar a foreign occupation force to protect civilians in Libya, to pave the way for NATO action.[38]

In reality, however, the United States still undertook by far the largest share of the operation not only at the outset during Operation Odyssey Dawn but even once NATO assumed command two weeks after the operation was underway. The U.S. combat assets and personnel in the Libyan intervention far surpassed any other coalition partner, with 8,507 Americans deployed; there were 3,500 British troops, 4,800 Italian, 4,200 French, and 2,561 Canadian, after which point the state contributions drop to 1,200 Spanish, and twelve other countries in the range of 2 (Croatia) to 500 (the Netherlands).[39]

Furthermore, according to the Pentagon, from March through September 2011, the U.S. Defense Department spent roughly $1.1 billion in Libya, while the United Kingdom spent between $257 million and $482 million, and France between $415 million and $485 million.[40] Other countries, such as Denmark, spent approximately $110 million each.[41] Common NATO funds were about $52.3 million for seven months and $7.8 million for structural and personnel costs related to the operation.[42] Despite this wide disparity in costs, Vice President Joe Biden, in an interview with CNN in October 2011, said, "The NATO alliance worked like it was designed to do, burden sharing. In total it cost us $2 billion, no American lives lost, we carried the burden a lot of other places where NATO is—the primary burden like in Afghanistan—and this was really burden sharing."[43]

According to SACEUR Stavridis, "In Libya, NATO aggressively stepped up to lead that mission just three weeks after military operations commenced, conducting 75% of all sorties and 100% of the maritime operations."[44] The United States was the largest contributor, flying more than 25 percent of all sorties over Libya; France and Britain flew about a third of all of the missions, and the remaining coalition members flew approximately 40 percent. Italy flew the fourth-largest number of overall sorties, and it was instrumental in providing the basing necessary to manage the logistical components of the air strikes.[45] Only eight countries flew strike sorties—the United States, France, Great Britain, Canada, Italy, Denmark, Belgium, and Norway, although Norway withdrew its aircraft on August 1. Of these, France flew about 33 percent, the United Kingdom flew about 20 percent, and the United States about 16 percent, with Canada, Italy, Denmark, and Norway coming in between 5 percent and 10 percent of the total.[46]

According to Ivo Daalder, U.S. permanent representative to NATO, and SACEUR Stavridis:

> Smaller allies also punched above their weight. Denmark and Norway together destroyed as many targets as Britain; Denmark, Norway, and Belgium dropped as many bombs as France. Canada, too, was part of the strikers['] coalition. And Spain, the Netherlands, Turkey, Greece and Romania played useful parts, enforcing the no-flight zone and arms embargo at sea. Those NATO members that didn't contribute forces still supported the operation by staffing the command structure; not one of the 28 members balked at the challenge. Even Sweden, not a NATO member, was a crucial partner, contributing its own naval and air forces.[47]

Despite this optimistic rendering of the NATO enterprise, there are many elements of the Libya intervention that underscored the entrenched imbalance of power and burden sharing that exists within the alliance. While in the previous cases, the United States was the primary burden carrier, it was also the political agenda setter of the operation in question. In the Libyan case, the United States complied with its allies' wishes to intervene to prevent humanitarian disaster in Libya; however, it became clear very early on that U.S. assets were essential in meeting the mission's goals. In a speech delivered in Brussels in June 2011, Secretary of Defense Robert M. Gates was very pointed in his remarks on this topic. He condemned NATO for the fact that although all NATO countries were in favor of the operation, fewer than half actually participated. Fewer still flew strike sorties. He underscored that this was not only about willingness but also about capability—many of the NATO allies simply did not possess the necessary military capabilities. He brought out the particular weakness of NATO in regard to intelligence, surveillance, and reconnaissance assets, and the inability of the alliance to run the air campaign without U.S. capabilities in this area. He denounced the allies' waning of munitions early in the operation, and yet again their need to rely on the United States to fill the gap. He used this as evidence that NATO has turned into a two-tiered alliance in regard to capability and burden sharing, indicating that just five of the twenty-eight allies—the United States, United Kingdom, France, Greece, and Albania—actually exceed the 2 percent of gross-domestic-product spending on defense. He applauded Norway, Denmark, Belgium, and Canada for making major contributions to the Libyan air strikes, and he called for other NATO member states to prepare for the same in the future.[48] Gates was not alone in recognizing the disproportionate role the United States played in the Libyan operation. As Ivo Daalder said in remarks to the press, the United States took out the air-defense system in Libya, continued suppressing enemy air defenses throughout the operation, and provided the precision targeting capability by deploying armed Predators. The United States provided the essential ISR and refueling capability.[49]

The Libyan campaign highlighted the fact that countries such as France and Italy were unable to sustain the operation, for logistical and financial reasons. With reduced defense budgets in the two decades following the end of the Cold War, and the impact on the decline in military capacity of many European countries, the Libyan crisis illustrated that it was impossible to prevail even in a limited campaign against a weak opponent not far geographically from Europe in the absence of U.S. capability.[50] Further, the use of advanced technological military equipment such as Predator drones underscored the gap between the United States and its allies in regard to capability. It took the drones three weeks to reach Libya, but once there they undertook more than 145 strikes.[51] Several months into the Libyan campaign, NATO commanders requested more of them from the United States to bolster NATO capability in the campaign.[52] These remotely piloted aircraft armed with precision missiles have dramatically altered the landscape of warfare, and they will continue to do so in the future. They offer an opportunity to take out targets or gather information, and they play an essential role in reconnaissance and surveillance without risking U.S. loss of life.[53]

The technological prowess of the United States is a function of its allocating resources to military spending and the development of advanced weapons systems. It is also a reflection of the great differential in power capabilities between it and the rest of the world. The United States possessed the greatest amount of capability within the coalition and the alliance, as can be seen in Table 7.1. Table 7.2 reveals the differences in contributions by country.

Table 7.1 Power capabilities, Libyan intervention

Country	Military expenditures (in millions of U.S. 2012 dollars)	Military personnel (in thousands)	Composite Index of National Capability
Belgium	5,000	40	0.0038946
Bulgaria	881	51	0.0014218
Canada	18,491	63	0.0106829
Croatia	843	21	0.0005799
Denmark	4,028	22	0.0014931
France	60,662	255	0.0189237
Greece	8,653	147	0.0038126
Italy	37,770	191	0.0174203
Jordan	1,621	101	0.0014484
Netherlands	11,141	53	0.0056463
Norway	5,546	23	0.0016396
Qatar	1,099	12	0.0008841
Romania	3,044	70	0.003213
Spain	17,495	147	0.0113889
Sweden	6,773	28	0.0029788
Turkey	13,643	515	0.014317
United Arab Emirates	10,082	51	0.0029798
United Kingdom	63,258	191	0.0211575
United States	552,568	1,506	0.1421487

SOURCE: National Military Capabilities Data. Version 4.0, extended to 2007. Accessed 5/26/2012. http://www.correlatesofwar.org/COW2%20Data/Capabilities/nmc4.htm; J. David Singer, Stuart Bremer, and John Stuckey. "Capability Distribution, Uncertainty, and Major Power War, 1820–1965." *Peace, War, and Numbers*. Bruce Russett, ed. Beverly Hills, CA: Sage, 1972, 19–48.

NOTE: The Composite Index of National Capability is computed by summing observations for total population, urban population, iron and steel production, energy consumption, military personnel, and military expenditures for the year, converting each country's absolute component into a share of the international system, averaging across the six component parts. Accessed 12/14/2012. http://www.correlatesofwar.org/COW2%20Data/Capabilities/nmc3-02.htm.

Table 7.2 Military expenditures by country, Libya operations

Coalition member	Expenditures (in millions of 2012 U.S. dollars)	Percentage of national GDP
United States	1,100	0.01
United Kingdom	482	0.02
France	485	0.02
Turkey	300	0.03
Italy	200	0.01
Denmark	110	0.05
Canada	100	0.01
Spain	65	0.01
Sweden	50	0.01
Belgium	50	0.01
Norway	50	0.02
Total	**2,992**	

SOURCE: Compilation from official estimates, newspaper articles, and CIA *World Factbook*. Data on coalition members comes from the following sources cited in the chapter: United States, United Kingdom, and France: Rettig 2011 (for the United Kingdom, the higher end of the range of estimates provided by the Pentagon has been used given corresponding official British estimates as well as additional unofficial reporting that places the number as high as $2 billion); Turkey: Sabah and Chipman 2011; Italy: Agence France-Presse 2011; Denmark: O'Dwyer 2012; Canada: RT TV-Novosti 2012 (initial estimates by the defense minister of $50 million were contradicted by an official report released by the Canadian Department of National Security that put the total cost at $347 million, with an incremental cost of $100 million. Because this official report by the Canadian government suggests a higher figure, the incremental cost of $100 million—spending in addition to normal operating expenses—has been used); Spain: Diaz Valenzuela 2011; Sweden: Radio Sweden, 2011 (the Swedish government placed the official expenditures of the Libya operations at $50 million as of June 2011. While it is possible the actual number could be as high as $150 million, based on reports of spending $22 million dollars a month, this number could not be independently verified, and thus the lower official estimate has been used); Belgium: DMorgen.be 2012; Norway: O'Dwyer 2011 (number based on June 2011 request from the Norwegian Ministry of Defense to Parliament for a supplementary budget of $47 million to cover the cost of Libyan operations).

The power distribution among the states was certainly asymmetrical, most noticeably in the context of the Composite Index of National Military Capabilities (CINC). No participating state rivaled American hegemony, and this was pronounced in the context of the Libyan operation, although in regard to relative distribution of power, given the presence of a number of great powers in the alliance and coalition, it was not as asymmetric as other coalitions have been in the post–Cold War era. The differential in power, however, was very noticeable in this case, given the inability of the coalition or NATO to prosecute the war without U.S. capabilities and technology.

The Libya operation could not have been undertaken without the United States. However, other countries did play an important role, particularly in basing and logistics, as well as in air strikes. In addition, principally the United

Kingdom and France set the political agenda, even if the military burden was carried by the United States. The burden was less of a disproportionate load than the other NATO operations in Afghanistan or Kosovo.

Alliance Security Dilemma

The alliance security dilemma in the context of the Libyan operation was most pronounced in relations between the United States and its allies that were advocating most stridently for intervention. Fears of abandonment prevailed for those countries, most particularly the United Kingdom and France, while entrapment fears were prevalent for the United States. These sentiments culminated in U.S. participation that was labeled "leading from behind," however misleading the phrase. The United States' reluctance to assume the overt leadership role in the Libyan operation is an indication of its concerns regarding entrapment. A significant component of these entrapment fears stemmed from the U.S. operations in Iraq and Afghanistan.[54] The context of decision making mattered; linkage among these cases of post–Cold War intervention was powerful. War weariness played a significant role in magnified entrapment fears as well.[55] Entrapment considerations mediated German decision making as well.[56]

The United Kingdom and France were not motivated by abandonment fears alone, though these were certainly present. This was particularly true as it became ever clearer as the operations unfolded that it would be impossible to achieve the ultimate objectives of securing the civilian population's well-being in the face of Gadhafi's violence and of enforcing the no-fly zone in the absence of U.S. capabilities.[57] As a consequence, French and British behaviors had to be adjusted to accommodate U.S. wishes. For France, the Libyan operation ultimately displayed the utility of NATO for mitigating those abandonment fears, increasing fighting effectiveness, and for the rapidity of response.[58]

Other allies and coalition partners were not as forthright in their desire to pursue the UN mandate in Libya, and some, such as Germany, did in fact have fears of entrapment which governed their decision making. Interestingly, in the context of the German case, however, is the fact that it withdrew assets from the Mediterranean area to preclude their use in Libya, it took over command of AWACS surveillance operations in Afghanistan, and it increased its deployment by an additional three hundred military personnel to the country.[59] This demonstrates that even in the face of entrapment fears, the desire to manage alliance relationships was nevertheless present. It also highlights the contingent nature of decision making in regard to interventions—the reality of the long wars in Afghanistan and Iraq influenced decision making in regard to Libya.

The conflict over how to prosecute the war and who would do so were all manifestations of the alliance security dilemma preoccupations. The United States' fears of being dragged into another long, costly war; the reluctance of France to be enmeshed with NATO and yet unable to fulfill its objectives in the absence of that structure; the United Kingdom's passion regarding pursuit of the Libyan mission and fear that the United States in particular would not fulfill the necessary part of its obligation to acquit those goals; and Germany's deep fear of entrapment—all were very pronounced from the outset of the Libyan operation. To some extent, these concerns compromised alliance cohesion in regard to clear goals and strategies, as well as the burden-sharing component of the operation.[60]

Other NATO member states were similarly plagued by entrapment fears. Britain and France tried to pressure allies such as Italy, Spain, and the Netherlands to increase their level of involvement in the Libyan operation. Italy rejected the pleas, indicating that the assets it was providing were ample. It was unwilling to be entangled in the conflict beyond providing many of its air bases for alliance and coalition use and the sorties it conducted. Spain and the Netherlands were also driven by entrapment fears—in terms of the alliance but by the campaign in Libya more particularly.[61] U.S. Secretary of Defense Robert Gates identified Germany, Poland, Spain, the Netherlands, and Portugal specifically as having more resources to contribute to the Libyan campaign, but they opted not to. Germany and Poland had a combined possible four hundred combat jets at their disposal that they did not commit to the operation, largely as a consequence of fears of entrapment and escalating defense commitments and costs.[62]

The alliance security dilemma was clearly present in the Libyan case. It mediated decision making for most of the participating states. The complexity of the concerns regarding entrapment and abandonment is reflected in the relationship among the participating states, the way in which they viewed the future of those relationships, and the urgency with which they viewed both the situation and the context of the decision in light of the wars in Iraq and Afghanistan. These fears affected alliance cohesion.

Cohesion and Fighting Effectiveness

The primary goals of Operation Odyssey Dawn and then Operation Unified Protector were to enforce the no-fly zone over Libya, to impose the arms embargo on Gadhafi's government, and to protect the civilian population from government violence as well as from the rebels seeking to end Gadhafi's forty-two-year rule, despite the fact that regime change was not an explicit goal of the mission nor of the UNSC resolutions.[63] The ultimate initial goal of the military coalition was to prevent further attacks by Gadhafi's forces on Libyan citizens and to undermine Gadhafi's military ability through implementing a no-fly zone.[64]

Although NATO portrayed a united front, there was no unanimity in the North Atlantic Council regarding the Libya mission. According to Admiral Xavier Païtard, France's military representative in NATO, the NATO secretary-general had to "force consensus." Some countries were opposed to making contributions; the war effort was sustained by a small group of countries. The lack of consensus within the alliance on how to address the Libyan crisis was most obviously manifested by Germany's abstention in the UNSC on the vote to support intervention in Libya. In March, Germany withdrew its naval assets in the Mediterranean from NATO. France and Turkey vehemently disagreed on the flexibility NATO should have in targeting, with France insisting that ground forces be susceptible to targeting if civilian lives were in jeopardy, and Turkey opposing the targeting of any ground forces. Norway refused to deploy its fighter jets unless under NATO command, and it expressed, along with Italy, frustration with the inability of NATO to agree on goals and strategy. This discord hampered the alliance's ability to take on the operation from the outset.[65]

In addition, the operations, headquartered in Naples and Poggio Renatico, were understaffed and unable to turn to personnel in NATO's permanent structure for assistance.[66] The NATO command in Italy had severe shortages of political and legal advisers, intelligence analysts, logistics planners, linguists, and target specialists. Further, the target specialists there were inadequately trained.[67]

When the NATO member states and operational partners in Operation Unified Protector met in Berlin on April 14–15, 2011, to discuss the Libya mission, the countries reaffirmed their goals of protecting civilians and supporting the rebels in their fight against forces loyal to Gadhafi. However, the means to achieving those ends and the level of support by member states created friction within the alliance.[68] Furthermore, the early intervention of France in the absence of consultation with NATO revealed fissures within the alliance regarding goals and strategy.[69] Even more telling was the disagreement among allies about NATO's assumption of control of the operation. Germany recalled its frigates and AWACS to prevent entrapment if NATO took control from the United States; the United Kingdom advocated the assassination of Gadhafi, which culminated in conflict between the United States and the United Kingdom over goals and strategy; France was reluctant to give NATO political control; Turkey advocated limited involvement; Italy warned that it would not continue its air-base accessibility in the absence of an agreed-upon NATO coordination structure.[70]

The transfer of command from the United States to NATO underscored how institutional design impinged on effectiveness. According to a Danish Defense Force report that was inadvertently released in October 2012, the NATO command structure was unable to lead at the outset of the Libyan operation, in particular because of the lack of intelligence-gathering facilities and capabilities to glean the situation on the ground for targeting purposes. According to the report, the command change had a negative effect on the campaign.[71]

Operation Odyssey Dawn was very effective in achieving the immediate goals of embargo, destroying key elements of the Libyan air defenses, and protecting central civilian population centers. While the absence of a joint force land component in the Joint Task Force Odyssey Dawn could have inhibited the success of the operation in its fight against the enemy on the ground, liaison officers became very important in this regard. Furthermore, the Joint Task Force Odyssey Dawn team was composed of individuals who had not necessarily worked together on any previous active mission. However, the depth of experience and training mitigated this challenge, particularly on such joint maneuvers as the Austere Challenge events, which were major annual joint training exercises.[72] In addition, the fact that all of the primary commanders and staff responsible for implementing Operation Odyssey Dawn were all gathered on the USS *Mount Whitney*, a command ship featuring premier communications ability—the most advanced command, control, communications, computer, and intelligence (C4I) ship ever commissioned.[73] Having all of the necessary personnel aboard the USS *Mount Whitney* fostered effective communication, task management, and unity of command.[74] This was true once Operation Odyssey Dawn was redesignated Operation Unified Protector as well, and NATO assumed responsibility for it. U.S. Air Force Lieutenant General Ralph Jodice served as combined forces air component commander for NATO (CFACC), and he moved his operational headquarters from Turkey to Italy to be nearer to the center of action. "'Because of the dynamic environment,' requiring face-to-face discussions with NATO leaders and representatives of coalition partners, 'it was critical that we were all together,'" Jodice said in an October 2011 interview.[75]

Although once OUP was underway Britain and France undertook more of the air strikes, the United States remained the core enabler via ISR assets. Furthermore, the operation was still very dependent on U.S. contributions in addition to ISR, including air-to-air refueling, and unmanned drones, among additional key military assets other NATO members did not have. This dependence was a constant source of friction and underscored the problems once the transfer of command from the United States to NATO occurred. According to French pilots in the middle of the operation, getting targeting imagery through NATO commanders at the Combined Air Operations Center (CAOC) in northern Italy took too much time to coordinate. Instead, they would launch a reconnaissance plane, take photos, identify targets, and then launch a strike aircraft to the target in the space of five hours.[76]

Even before the end of Operation Unified Protector, in October 2011, "NATO Secretary General Anders Fogh Rasmussen described the mission as 'a great success' but acknowledged that it exposed Europe's need to invest in unmanned drones, intelligence assets and air-to-air refueling aircraft."[77] In addition, only a month into the operation, NATO allies began running low on precision munitions, and the United States had to intervene to replenish stockpiles.[78] Furthermore, only eight days after NATO assumed command of the Libyan operation, British and French decision makers were calling to intensify the air strikes against Gadhafi's forces, a call that NATO rejected, even though the pace of the air attacks did pick up a few days later.[79]

The differences among the member states in regard to their view of how to manage the Libya crisis were manifest in the dynamics of the alliance decisions on how to implement the strategies of achieving civilian protection and enforcement of the no-fly zone. The negotiated strategies ultimately were effective, even if fissures of disagreement existed within the alliance. The burden-sharing component of NATO came to the fore in the context of cohesion as well, in the ability of the member states to accomplish their goals, although ultimately the Libya operation did meet its military objectives handily. Once again, as in the previous cases, the campaign was directed against a weak opponent, although the operation's complex air component did highlight the strengths of alliance and coalition warfare among the prosecutors of the war.[80]

Legitimacy

Despite the fact that the international community worked through the United Nations and the Arab League to gain support for an intervention in Libya, global support for it was mixed.[81] Public opinion worldwide was more reserved than might be expected given the mechanisms of legitimation at work in moving toward intervention. This was especially true in the Middle East and North Africa, as seen in Table 7.3.

A survey of three thousand people in Egypt, Morocco, Jordan, Lebanon, and the United Arab Emirates in October 2011 indicated a slight increase in favorable opinion of the United States, improved from 2010, which could be an indication of tepid support for U.S. handling of the Libyan crisis.[82]

Public opinion in the United States indicated trepidation in regard to the intervention. In a poll by the Pew Research Center for the People and the Press conducted March 10–13, 2011, 27 percent of 1,001 Americans surveyed responded that the United States had a responsibility to intervene in Libya, and 63 percent responded that it did not. Barely half of those queried favored increasing economic and diplomatic sanctions, and 77 percent opposed bombing Libyan air defenses.[83] Once the air strikes were underway, 47 percent of 1,002 polled March 24–27, 2011, said that the United States made the right decision in conducting the air strikes; 36 percent said it was the wrong decision, and

Table 7.3 Favorability toward intervention in Libya in 2011

Overall, did you favor or oppose NATO's military intervention in Libya in 2011?			
	Favor (%)	*Oppose (%)*	*Don't know/Refused (%)*
Somaliland region	26	72	2
Algeria	14	70	16
Comoros	33	67	1
Palestinian territories	21	62	17
Mauritania	41	57	2
Egypt	13	52	35
Lebanon	29	41	30
Yemen	22	41	38
Tunisia	33	40	26
Morocco	12	26	62

SOURCE: Gallup Center for Muslim Studies. "Snapshot: NATO Intervention in Libya Unpopular in Arab World, Least Popular in North Africa." May 31, 2012. Copyright 2012 Gallup Inc. All rights reserved. The content is used with permission; however, Gallup retains all rights of republication.

17 percent expressed no opinion.[84] These attitudes remained fairly stable through the first weeks of the intervention.[85]

In the United Kingdom, a week before the initial air strikes in Libya began, public opinion was completely divided on whether the Cameron government was managing the Libyan crisis effectively, with 42 percent satisfied and 42 percent dissatisfied. By April, instead of increased support for the intervention, public support had actually declined, with 43 percent being satisfied with Cameron and his government's response and 57 percent dissatisfied, while 50 percent of those polled supported the intervention and 49 percent opposed it. In France, 63 percent supported the intervention, and 50 percent supported Sarkozy and his government in taking a hard line toward Gadhafi and the Libyan civil war.[86] In Germany, the government did not support the UN Security Council resolution to establish the no-fly zone and abstained from the vote, which reflected public opinion against intervention.[87]

Despite mixed global public opinion, the advocates of action in Libya proceeded via international institutional mechanisms designed to augment legitimacy, even if this did not culminate in overwhelming international support. On March 7, 2011, the Gulf Cooperation Council "demanded" that the United Nations take action to protect civilians in Libya, including a no-fly zone;[88] on March 8, 2011, the Organization of the Islamic Conference (OIC) indicated its support of a no-fly zone over Libya;[89] on March 12, 2011, the Arab League voted to support a no-fly zone over Libya. This helped legitimize a push in the UN Security Council for intervention, and it facilitated the passing of UN Resolution 1973 on March 17, 2011, which appealed to the international community to take any and all necessary measures to end the violent repression by the Gadhafi government in Libya.[90] All of these organizational calls for intervention both manifested the legitimacy of the operation and augmented it.

The impetus for acting in Libya emanated from the UN doctrine of responsibility to protect (R2P), which embodies the imperative by the international community to bring an end to mass atrocities and genocide, and even seek to prevent them. While R2P maintains the sanctity of sovereignty of a state, it calls for intervention despite invocations of sovereignty in the event that large-scale human abuses are unfolding. According to the United Nations, the three cornerstones of R2P are the following:

1. The State carries the primary responsibility for protecting populations from genocide, war crimes, crimes against humanity and ethnic cleansing, and their incitement;

2. The international community has a responsibility to encourage and assist States in fulfilling this responsibility;

3. The international community has a responsibility to use appropriate diplomatic, humanitarian and other means to protect populations from these crimes. If a State is manifestly failing to protect its populations, the international community must be prepared to take collective action to protect populations, in accordance with the Charter of the United Nations.[91]

The United Nations' initial reaction to the unfolding crisis in Libya was UN Security Council Resolution 1970 on February 26, 2011, which unanimously endorsed R2P as the motivation for imposing sanctions on the Gadhafi regime. This was the first explicit invocation of R2P by a unanimous UN Security Council vote.[92] The extent to which the R2P foundation legitimated the intervention is difficult to navigate. Connecting the legality of intervention to ethical legitimacy makes interpretation of any crisis challenging, particularly when foreign intervention is necessary to "liberate a country whose people have been unable to liberate themselves,"[93] although R2P is about protecting civilians, not about regime change.[94]

The Libyan operation had both local and international legitimacy, given the sanction of both regional and global organizations. These institutional frameworks allowed information about the intentions of the proponents of action to be seen and heard, thereby allaying any potential mistrust regarding the ambitions of the advocates of intervention.[95] These steps, seeking sanction from regional and global organizations, were vital in building support for international action. The operation augmented the capabilities of rebels on the ground fighting to overturn the government, and international support for the operation culminated in an effective mission that differed from previous interventions in the post–Cold War period.[96] The action was limited in scope and duration, and it was taken only after global and regional organizational sanction. In this way, OUP was most similar to Operation Desert Storm, and it diverged dramatically from the experiences of Kosovo, Afghanistan, and the second war in Iraq.

The legitimacy of the Libyan operation largely derived from the sense of the agenda setters in the international community that action needed to be taken, and decisions were made in the context of the global organizations of the international system. There was a disconnect between global public opinion and the moral imperative articulated by key decision makers in the system. R2P enforcement did not seem to affect legitimacy as represented by public opinion. This case underscores the difference in understanding legitimacy as a moral command as opposed to public support for a particular policy. In this case, too, we see that international institutions when used for strategic ends may both reflect and promote legitimacy. We also see that institutions are very much, as Alexander Thompson notes, channels of power.[97] The standing global, regional, and national institutions that exist as foundations for power to be actualized are very important—even if they are not as widely recognized as such in comparison to other capabilities, such as what weapons states possess, or the existence of a well-trained, highly educated, professional military.

CONCLUSION

The Libyan operations highlight important lessons regarding multilateral war fighting in the contemporary era. They illustrate that a robust decision-making structure facilitates rapid response during crises and goes a long way toward ensuring the mechanisms necessary to discuss goals and strategies toward attaining those goals. In other words, those decision-making structures by no means guarantee cohesion, but rather they set the foundation for building it. In both Operation Odyssey Dawn and Operation Unified Protector, the decision-making structures were clear and hierarchical, setting the stage for fighting effectiveness, though the U.S.-led coalition was more effective and efficient than the more unwieldy and cumbersome NATO structure.

Further, deep institutionalization of military relationships in the context of previous war-fighting experience, joint exercises, and well-established command structures all fostered fighting effectiveness and augmented interoperability, even if the latter can never completely be eliminated in a system of sovereign states. These institutional effects are a part of the costs associated with multilateralism, though the benefits may be substantial.

The Libyan operation also illustrates that asymmetrical capabilities and burden sharing may undermine cohesion and heighten the alliance security dilemma. In this case, if the United Kingdom and France had possessed sufficient capability to prosecute the war even under the auspices of NATO and augmented by NATO member states' capabilities, fears that the United States would abandon the effort would not have been as prevalent. Conversely, had the other NATO members possessed sufficient capability to prosecute the war absent the most substantial contribution by the United States, American fears of entrapment would have been less pronounced. The United States still wielded significant leverage within the coalition and alliance, particularly given the dependence of both multilateral institutions on it for the necessary capabilities to prosecute the war. Although this case is known as the one in which the United States "led from behind," and ostensibly France and the United Kingdom took the lead in regard to the political agenda, in reality the decision-making structures, capabilities, and fighting effectiveness still largely rested with the United States. An overview of the variables can be seen in Tables 7.4 and 7.5.

The Libyan operation indicates both the strengths and weaknesses of prosecuting multilateral wars—the ways in which institutions are mechanisms for achieving strategic ends, and the ways in which they serve as liabilities in pursuing state goals. The lessons of the operation for the NATO community and beyond indicated the intense reliance on U.S. capability but also revealed the durability and functionality of the NATO command structure and its enduring capacity to prosecute wars on short notice. The institutional dimension of the alliance was very pronounced and very important in this case. The Libyan operations certainly illustrate the importance of institutions in serving as foundations for power actualization as realist institutionalism asserts. The United States' ability to quickly respond using its unified command plan, drawing on

Table 7.4 Overview of variables in Operation Odyssey Dawn

Independent variables	Mediating variables	Dependent variables
Coalition	Decision-making structure: hierarchical with informal channels of communication	Cohesion: moderate
Size: small	Power distribution: moderately asymmetrical	War-fighting effectiveness: effective
	Internal leverage rested principally with United States, with United Kingdom and France setting the agenda	Interoperability: few challenges
		Legitimacy of operation: legitimate

Table 7.5 Overview of variables in Operation Unified Protector

Independent variables	Mediating variables	Dependent variables
Alliance with add-on countries	Decision-making structure: hierarchical	Cohesion: challenges
Size: medium	Power distribution: moderately asymmetrical	War-fighting effectiveness: challenges; less effective than Operation Odyssey Dawn
	Internal leverage rested principally with the United States, with the United Kingdom and France setting the agenda	Interoperability: a few challenges
		Legitimacy of operation: legitimate

the institutional framework of AFRICOM, EUCOM, and then NATO, illustrates how the web of institutions that spans the globe serves as an important component of American hegemony. The Libyan operation also benefited from the decade-long collaborations that twice unfolded in the context of the Gulf, in Kosovo, and in Afghanistan. NATO served as an institutional resource for the member states demanding a swift and effective response to Gadhafi. It advanced their power capabilities and objectives in a very straightforward way. Yet NATO also learned a piercing lesson in its deficiencies, which culminated in the aftermath of Operation Unified Protector, in the pursuit of deeper collaboration and increasing independence of the European partners.

The Pooling and Sharing Initiative through the European Union seeks to augment European capabilities; the Smart Defense Initiative tries to ensure reduced reliance on the United States for very expensive advanced military capabilities. The idea is to be strategic about where resources are committed, given times of reduced defense spending and military budgets, as well as worldwide economic contraction. These priority areas include the pooling of various resources, such as maritime patrol aircraft; force protection, such as equipment to counter improvised explosive devices (IEDs); the building of a universal armaments interface so that combat aircraft can actually use the same munitions and share specialized munitions; the construction of multinational field hospitals; and the potential joint acquisition of surveillance equipment, counter-IED devices, and radars; and the potential for building permanent joint ISR structures.[98] Other interrelated initiatives, such as the Connected Forces Initiative, seek to augment interoperability and capacity, with an emphasis on joint training, education, exercises, and the improved use of technology as well as the application of new technologies.[99] The Libyan operations in many ways capture the essence of the lessons learned from all the preceding cases. In turn, the lessons drawn from this intervention will shape the future of contemporary coalition warfare as well.

8 CONCLUSION

THE UNITED STATES has rarely fought alone in the past; it is even less likely to do so in the future. As a consequence, the meaning of multilateralism for war fighting is more important now than ever. In general, states embrace the military assistance of others for both strategic and symbolic reasons; ideological multilateralism and strategic multilateralism are two different logics that culminate in similar motivations and behavior. Yet despite the entrenched norm of multilateral war fighting in the U.S. context, the way in which it manifests is powerfully important, for symbolic as well as for pragmatic reasons, in regard to the effectiveness of war-fighting capability, efficacy, and alliance or coalition cohesion.

The wars studied here underscore the fact that partnerships may take many forms and that the decisions regarding coalition or alliance structure impinge on the outcomes of war. In these cases, the United States opted to accept practical, material, and symbolic contributions from a large swath of the international system, but in many cases, it fought alongside only its closest allies at the outset of the wars. This era of interventions reveals a reliance on the institutional structure of NATO both to prosecute wars and for peacekeeping purposes. Over time, the allies addressed interoperability challenges, and the alliance framework was rendered adaptable and robust, able to adjust to the crises and tasks at hand. At times, this produced convoluted, dichotomous institutional structures, but it demonstrates the many faces of multilateralism that surface in the context of contemporary warfare.

The American way of war was described in Russell Weigley's book of that title as a strategy designed to bring about overwhelming American victory through a strategy of attrition or annihilation of the enemy.[1] Max Boot argued that the contemporary American way of war is instead a quick victory with minimal casualties.[2] This emphasis on ends is important, but means matter as well. For Norman Friedman, the new way of American warfare is precision air attacks.[3] Dominic Tierney describes the American tradition of war as highly schizophrenic—the United States is attracted to crusades and overturning tyrants, but it is leery of the hard work and high costs that come with nation (re) building in the aftermath of intervention.[4]

One highly consequential and profoundly underemphasized element of contemporary American warfare is the reliance on allies. The North Atlantic Treaty Organization has been quite active in the post–Cold War world, and U.S.-forged coalitions have grown in size and importance in contemporary U.S. military strategy. The use of alliances and coalitions to prosecute wars creates a unique set of concerns and operational challenges—differences in rules of engagement, differences in languages, and problems with interoperability, to name a few. Yet the consequences of the highly interconnected international system where communication and media are instantaneous and give rise to transparency impinge on the way wars are fought. In democratic states with politically accountable executives, fighting multilaterally ostensibly gives the appearance of legitimacy.

The study of the American way of war requires more attention to the varied manifestations of multilateralism and the implications regarding the ability to prevail in wartime. Viewing these weapons of war through an institutional lens is essential. This will advance the literature on alliances and coalition warfare, as well as deepen our knowledge of the ways and means of waging war. Instead of focusing on the unilateral or multilateral character of U.S. foreign policy, we should be developing our knowledge of the implications of the different ways that multilateral strategies are employed and the effects of relying on allies to achieve wartime objectives.

In the cases studied here, NATO served as an important foundation of power and legitimacy, yet coalitions fostered fighting effectiveness. This was most transparent in the Libyan case as the coalition command transferred to NATO. It facilitated the bringing to bear of particular assets, yet unity of command was less optimal, and the United States still needed to play a central role in providing intelligence, surveillance, and reconnaissance for NATO to execute its mission.

Contemporary coalition and alliance warfare highlights the costs and benefits of pursuing strategic ends multilaterally. On the one hand, fighting with friends allows states to take advantage of an institutional foundation upon which they can execute their missions, thus reducing transaction costs and geographic burdens. On the other hand, there are costs—in regard to interoperability, friendly fire, and challenges to maintaining cohesion. The causal connections flow from whether the multilateral institution is an alliance or a coalition and its size, which affect the decision-making structure, power distribution, and internal leverage, which in turn affect cohesion, war-fighting effectiveness, interoperability, and legitimacy:

> Alliance or coalition, size → decision-making structure, power distribution, internal leverage → cohesion, war-fighting effectiveness, interoperability, legitimacy.

The findings of the empirical chapters are summarized in Table 8.1.

Institutional structure and size did impinge on cohesion, war-fighting effectiveness, and interoperability. Size mattered, but not as much as the number of actually deployed troops from the countries involved; hence size can be misleading when small deployments or constricting national caveats are involved.

In all but one of the four coalition cases, significant interoperability challenges hampered the interventions, and the larger the coalition, the more challenges the states faced. Decision-making structure definitely mediated this effect; straightforward, hierarchical decision-making institutions fostered effectiveness. With one exception (the second Iraq war again), the coalition wars were more legitimate than the wars prosecuted by alliance. This suggests that working through global institutional frameworks does enhance legitimacy, although we saw that the relationship works both ways: legitimacy produces the ability to work through those global institutions in the first place, and those global institutions may in turn produce heightened legitimacy.

In the alliance cases, we saw more effectiveness and fewer interoperability challenges, as expected. We also saw an unanticipated feature of alliance warfare, which was the increasing robustness, adaptability, and vitality of the organization, that is, NATO, as it underwent repeated missions during these two decades under review. Painful lessons were learned from Operation Allied Force regarding decision-making structure and execution; over time, the alliance adapted. By the Libyan operation, the alliance structure was permeable by other states, and it could work quickly and effectively to manage the crisis at hand.[5]

The internal balance of power was fairly asymmetrical in nearly all of the cases, and it did not impinge directly on cohesion or effectiveness. Without

Table 8.1 Overview of variables

Case	Independent variables	Mediating variables	Dependent variables
Gulf War	• Large • Coalition	• Decision-making structure: dual-hierarchical • Asymmetrical power distribution • Internal leverage with lead power	• Moderate cohesion • Effective war fighting • Interoperability challenges • Legitimate
Operation Allied Force	• Medium • Alliance	• Decision-making structure: dual-hierarchical military command structure, egalitarian consensus decision making • Asymmetrical power distribution • Internal leverage with lead power	• Low to moderate cohesion • Effective war fighting • Few interoperability challenges • Mixed legitimacy
Operation Enduring Freedom	• Small • Coalition	• Decision-making structure: hierarchical • Asymmetrical power distribution • Internal leverage with lead power	• Moderate cohesion • Moderately effective war fighting • Some interoperability challenges • Legitimacy waned over time from moderate to low
ISAF	• Large • Alliance	• Decision-making structure: decentralized but hierarchical; emphasis on national priorities and caveats • Asymmetrical power distribution • Internal leverage with lead power	• Low to moderate cohesion • Moderately effective war fighting[a] • Significant interoperability challenges • Legitimacy declined over time from moderate to low
Operation Iraqi Freedom and Iraq War	• Large • Coalition	• Decision-making structure: hierarchical • Asymmetrical power distribution • Internal leverage with lead power	• Low to moderate cohesion • Moderately effective war fighting • Some interoperability challenges • Low legitimacy
Operation Odyssey Dawn	• Small • Coalition	• Decision-making structure: hierarchical with informal channels of communication • Asymmetrical power distribution • Internal leverage with lead power: United States militarily, United Kingdom and France politically	• Moderate cohesion • Effective war fighting • Few interoperability challenges • Legitimate
Operation Unified Protector	• Medium • Alliance with add-on countries	• Decision-making structure: hierarchical • Asymmetrical power distribution • Internal leverage with lead power: United States militarily, United Kingdom and France politically	• Challenges to cohesion • Reduced effectiveness in war fighting • Some interoperability challenges • Legitimate

[a]ISAF was not intended to be a war-fighting institution but rather a stabilizing force. Nevertheless, in turbulent areas, it was not possible to stabilize without the capacity to employ force.

much variation in this area, it is not possible to come to hard-and-fast conclusions. The alliance security dilemma, in contrast, did have a distinct effect on coalition and alliance activity; the locus of threat affected whether fears of abandonment or entrapment prevailed. This was more telling than the distribution of power within the alliances and coalitions, thus suggesting that perceived threat is a more potent driving force than capabilities alone.[6]

Legitimacy was both a product of and a catalyst for working through global and regional institutions. However, working through these organizations did not always lead to greater international support as measured by global public opinion, even if it helped neutralize negative public opinion. Legal interventions and legitimate ones are closely intertwined. But analyzing cases in which states worked through standing organizations such as the United Nations and NATO does reveal the institutional benefits states reap from being members and participating in such forums, as does analyzing the specific institutions of war prosecution.

However, as raised at the outset, the downside of multilateral war fighting is that even at the most integrated level, interoperability challenges will remain as long as the sovereign state system endures. Friendly fire may be more likely with more countries involved, particularly in cases in which rebel forces are on the ground and coalition forces are in the air trying to support them, or in cases in which ground and air forces are committed. Multilateral war fighting is not always more cost effective than unilateral approaches, nor does it necessarily augment legitimacy—those aspects must be tended to strategically as war decisions unfold.

There is also a strategic liability of allies inherent in multilateral war fighting. It is inescapable, yet the existence of these relationships provides a platform to advance state goals, execute missions, and transform military capability into the use of force. There are important elements of this web of institutional commands, both national and international, which are essential to U.S. hegemony and allow for the projection of American influence, even if there are critical components of constraint at work as well. Once interests are defined broadly, so too are the dictates of intervention.

In the cases examined in this book, the web of institutions that spanned the globe, facilitating the translation of military capability into the use of force, was a vital resource for U.S. hegemony. This resource should be factored in when analyzing the decline of American hegemony. The United States' war-fighting capacity is a function of the American tradition of possessing a highly trained, highly professionalized military, along with its enduring institutional frameworks for command and control, and the most advanced technological weapons systems in the world. It makes rivaling that capacity fairly difficult. The Libyan operation underscored this differential in the capacity to wage war. The legacy of privileging defense spending and allocating those funds in a way that produced a strong technological edge in military capability may, in fact, sustain American hegemony for some time to come, even if U.S. relative economic prowess declines. The gap between the United States and the rest of the world is wide in regard to the ability to wage war quickly and effectively. No other country in the world could have undertaken operation after operation as the United States did in the two decades following the end of the Cold War. Repeated interventions may have taken their toll on the U.S. economy, but they also demonstrated the tremendous disparity between the United States and the rest of the world in regard to war-fighting capacity along many dimensions.

The possession of institutional command and control structures all over the world—ready to deploy rapidly in a crisis situation—is a key element of actualizing military power. No assessment of the future of American hegemony is complete without an analysis of its relationships at home and abroad, of the institutions that allow it to realize its strategic goals. The United States' ability to dispatch militarily in crises and threats wherever they emanate is at this point unparalleled. The advanced technological arsenal is critical, and the level of education and professionalism of the U.S. military is critical, but so is the foundation on which these bases of power can be realized. This capability also produces a permissive environment for adventurism and interventionism, particularly in an era when American power is unrivaled. At the same time, the active and interventionist role the United States has played in this era did affect the perception of it in the international community. The way in which hegemony and authority are conceptualized affects how those wars impinge on U.S. standing in the world today.[7]

What this suggests is that the era of U.S. hegemony has a particular manifestation—one of an active hegemon responding to threats and crises all over the world. In the first twenty years after the end of the Cold War, during its reign as hegemon, the United States has prosecuted five wars. Chinese hegemony would look vastly different—in large part because of the absence of institutional agreements and networks that span the globe. The inability of China to bring force to bear whenever and wherever it would like—would this impinge on its capacity to serve as a hegemon? The operationalization of hegemony is essential. Does it simply reflect power capabilities? Or does the capacity of the hegemon to bring those capabilities to bear affect how hegemony is constituted? If so, then China is not likely to challenge U.S. hegemony for a very long time to come.

Realists argue that institutions serve merely as a reflection of the distribution of capabilities. They do not have an independent effect on state behavior.[8] In the security sphere, alliances are constructed to counter threats, and they dissolve when threats fade. But this is not an accurate view of institutions and alliances. As states seek to exercise power and to influence the decisions and choices of others, institutions are one vehicle for them to do so. Institutions augment power not simply as tools for capability aggregation but also through providing the capacity to achieve ends that are rational and strategic and that advance the interests of the states in essential ways. The solidity of alliance relationships is a hidden yet vital aspect of capability and hegemony. The United States may be the most powerful country in the world, but it cannot bring that power to bear in the absence of its relationships with others. For example, U.S. drone capability is well known, and U.S. use of drones is growing. This could suggest a rise in unilateral action. But where are the drones? They are in Turkey, Afghanistan, Qatar, the Philippines, the United Arab Emirates, Yemen, Ethiopia, Djibouti, and the Seychelles.[9] Without strong partner relationships and agreements, it would not be possible to have such basing rights. These are the relationships that serve as a foundation for the exercise of power. It is not the same as capability aggregation, as realism would direct us to, nor is it the institutional drive to peace and stability that liberal institutionalists would suggest.

While realists argue that institutions have no independent effect on state behavior, liberal institutionalists argue that institutions alter state preferences, and thus state behavior. Yet the truth lies somewhere in between. International institutions—sets of interrelated regulative and procedural norms and rules that pertain to the activities of states and other actors in the system[10]—serve as conduits for the actualization of capabilities. Institutions are binding mechanisms that alter the strategic opportunities for states, but not simply in the ways that liberal institutionalists would suggest.[11] While liberal institutionalists demonstrate how institutions allow states to escape the prisoner's dilemma,[12] what they fail to recognize is that institutions may also provide a permissive environment for warfare. This is the unintended consequence of having institutions that span the globe at the ready to confront threats—interventions are possible; troops and assets stand at the ready. They can be brought to bear, and thus there is a greater likelihood that they will be. Institutions can serve as conduits for state power in ways that are not recognized by realists or institutionalists, yet both schools have important insights that shed light on security institutions in the contemporary age.

What happens within a coalition or alliance is as important as what happens outside of it. States seek multilateral approaches to crises not simply to yield a legitimacy dividend but also to know that they are standing shoulder to shoulder with another—they are not in it alone. This internal dimension is as important as the external component of seeking legitimation. These two issues are of course interconnected but still distinct enough that we should not focus on the latter at the expense of the former. The solidity of alliance relationships, this internal dimension, provides an important foundation for power realization. In the cases discussed in this book, NATO served as an important foundation for power actualization—for U.S. objectives but also for the objectives of other states, such as the United Kingdom and France in the Libyan operation. NATO provided the glue that held the Afghanistan operation together in a way that was absent in the Iraq case; the value the member states placed on their alliance relationships provided the landscape in which they made their decisions to participate in the operations at hand. The institution of NATO was more than just the sum of its parts—it was a mechanism through which states were able to realize their goals. This is in contrast to the realist idea alone that institutions are mere reflections of power; that NATO should have dissolved with the end of the Cold War, its viability derived only from mutual and common threats. It is contrary to the liberal institutionalist idea that institutions promote peace and stability in the international system.

The interventionist history of the past two decades culminated in more robust and adaptable multilateral frameworks for war fighting; prosecuting wars has done for the alliance what peacetime operations could not—it has brought to the fore the central obstacles of interoperability and promoted deeper collaborations in regard to procurement and exercises. The institutional components are more permeable and versatile and able to quickly respond to crises militarily, even if not politically. Policy directives following the alliance interventions seek to rectify shortcomings in the structure and capacity of the institution. The war context fostered deeper institutionalization in ways to promote fighting effectiveness. Furthermore, as this institutionalization deepens, as states must seek greater and greater integration of their systems and militaries, the likelihood of fighting one another drops dramatically.

A distinctive feature of this era is the view that encouraging non-U.S. NATO member states to augment their capability is a goal that even the United States wishes to see come to fruition. When states desire that their allies are strong enough to prosecute war without them, when they desire a reduced reliance on them, they are encouraging a reduction in their relative power capabilities, a significant observation from the perspective of realist thinking.[13] The 2010 U.S. Quadrennial Defense Review (QDR) features building the security capacity of partner states as a priority.[14] And yet from a realist institutionalist perspective this makes sense—given that the institution itself is a platform to advance strategic ends. Among the ends detailed in the QDR are to "strengthen and institutionalize general purpose force capabilities for security assistance," to "enhance linguistic, regional, and cultural ability," to "strengthen and expand capabilities for training partner aviation forces," to "strengthen capacities for ministerial-level training," to "create mechanisms to facilitate more rapid transfer of critical materiel," and to "strengthen capacities for training regional and international security organizations."[15] These are all institutional components that advance strategic aims and solidify the foundations of U.S. military power. But they do so in a way that simultaneously advances the interests of other states, which highlights the problem with viewing absolute versus relative gains in a dichotomous way.

In addition, it would appear that associated states are more rather than less secure as a consequence of their partnership with the United States. The relationships among the allied states allow countries to use the United States as an avenue to achieve their ends, although it also makes them vulnerable to compliance with U.S. interests even as those interests diverge. The twinning of these security interests is important—maintaining a strong U.S. overseas presence may allay security anxieties and threats to partner countries, as well as provide flexibility in responding to threats to U.S. interests wherever they emerge. More specifically, the web of partnerships and bases across the globe reassures allies, reduces fears of abandonment, and may strengthen deterrence as well as foster U.S. ability to respond rapidly to crises wherever they arise.[16] The trend in this regard may continue, although the complexities at work in Syria illustrate that it is not just capability that matters in regard to calculations about intervention. The potential costs in regard to lives and treasure matter deeply, particularly in the event that a crisis dictates the commitment of ground troops. Furthermore, the contingent nature of these decisions is very straightforward. In the aftermath of long costly wars in Afghanistan and Iraq, there is far more leeriness in regard to continued interventions, particularly in complex situations such as Syria. Any future Western intervention will likely follow the model of Libya—a UN mandate and a coalition execution, with NATO providing the foundation and ongoing base of assets and participants to advance the operation's mission.

Is the United States at its zenith? Or is it in decline? The past two decades suggest that U.S. ability to project power remains unprecedented in the international system. By the same token, the twenty years of military interventions have taken their toll in terms of costs, both materially and in regard to the way forward in waging war. The use of more remote technologies to prosecute underreported and undetected wars via unmanned aerial vehicles and cyberspace in the immediate future, in order to counter war fatigue and reduce costs in terms of dollars, human power, and the emotional costs that long and fraught deployments entail, is likely to continue for the foreseeable future. This will not diminish the importance of the web of institutions in place to prosecute war; those institutions remain a critical feature of the war landscape, as does any other weapon in states' arsenals to wage war. Institutions serve to advance strategic ends and preserve states' power positions in the international system.

NOTES

Chapter 1

1. Robert O. Keohane. "International Institutions: Two Approaches." *International Studies Quarterly*, vol. 32, no. 4, December 1988, 383.

2. Robert O. Keohane. *International Institutions and State Power: Essays in International Relations Theory*. Boulder, CO: Westview Press, 1989, 163.

3. See the foundational work of Alexander Thompson. *Channels of Power: The UN Security Council and U.S. Statecraft in Iraq*. Ithaca, NY: Cornell University Press, 2009; Alexander Thompson. "Coercion Through International Organizations: The Security Council and Logic of Information Transmission." *International Organization*, vol. 60, no. 3, January 2006, 1–34.

4. Robert A. Dahl. "The Concept of Power." *Behavioral Science*, vol. 2, no. 3, July 1957, 201–215.

5. Alexander Thompson, *Channels of Power: The UN Security Council and U.S. Statecraft in Iraq*. Ithaca, NY: Cornell University Press, 2009; Alexander Thompson, "Coercion Through International Organizations: The Security Council and Logic of Information Transmission." *International Organization*, vol. 60, no. 3, January 2006, 1–34.

6. Department of Defense. "Quadrennial Defense Review Report." February 2010, 62.

7. See, for example, Andrew J. Bacevich, ed. *The Short American Century: A Postmortem*. Cambridge, MA: Harvard University Press, 2012. See also John J. Mearsheimer. *The Tragedy of Great Power Politics*. New York: Norton, 2001; and, for more a more general argument, Paul Kennedy. *The Rise and Fall of Great Powers*. New York: Knopf, Doubleday, 1989; Robert Gilpin. *War and Change in World Politics*. Cambridge: Cambridge University Press, 1981.

8. Jack Snyder. "Imperial Temptations." *National Interest*, spring 2003, 29–40.

9. Charles A. Kupchan. "The Decline of the West: Why America Must Prepare for the End of Dominance." *The Atlantic.* March 20, 2012. Accessed 7/9/2012. http://www .theatlantic.com/international/archive/2012/03/the-decline-of-the-west-why-america-must-prepare-for-the-end-of-dominance/254779/. See also Charles A. Kupchan. *No One's World: The West, the Rising Rest, and the Coming Global Turn.* New York: Oxford University Press, 2012.

10. Christopher Layne. "Graceful Decline." *American Conservative.* May 1, 2010. Accessed 7/9/2012. http://www.theamericanconservative.com/articles/graceful-decline/.

11. Arvind Subramanian. *Eclipse: Living in the Shadow of China's Economic Dominance.* Washington, DC: Peter G. Peterson Institute for International Economics, 2011.

12. Fareed Zakaria. *The Post-American World.* New York: W. W. Norton, 2009; David P. Calleo. *Follies of Power: America's Unipolar Fantasy.* New York: Cambridge University Press, 2009.

13. See, for example, David C. Kang. *China Rising: Peace, Power, and Order in East Asia.* New York: Columbia University Press, 2007; Robert S. Ross and Zhu Feng, eds. *China's Ascent: Power, Security, and the Future of International Politics.* Ithaca, NY: Cornell University Press, 2008; G. John Ikenberry. "The Rise of China and the Future of the West: Can the Liberal System Survive?" *Foreign Affairs.* January–February 2008, 23–37; Alastair Iain Johnston and Robert S. Ross, eds. *Engaging China: The Management of an Emerging Power.* New York: Routledge, 1999. Cf. Thomas J. Christensen. "Posing Problems Without Catching Up: China's Rise and Challenges for U.S. Security Policy." *International Security,* vol. 25, no. 4, spring 2001, 5–40; Peter Hays Gries. "Correspondence: Response to Power and Resolve in U.S. China Policy by Thomas J. Christensen." *International Security,* vol. 26, no. 3, fall 2001, 155–165. For a compelling alternative perspective, see Victor Cha. "Winning Asia." *Foreign Affairs.* November–December 2007, 98–113.

14. See Department of Defense. "Quadrennial Defense Review Report." February 2010, 60.

15. See Pew Research Center. "Ask the Expert: Public Opinion About the U.S. and China." February 13, 2012. Accessed 7/9/2012. http://pewresearch.org/pubs/2194/ china-united-states-relations-xi-jinping-barack-obama-ask-the-expert.

16. Pew Research Center. "U.S. Status as World's Superpower Challenged by Rise of China: U.S. Favorability Ratings Remain Positive." July 13, 2011. Accessed 7/9/2012. http:// pewresearch.org/pubs/2059/-superpower-china-us-image-abroad-afghanistan-terrorism.

17. Ezra Klein. "American Decline a Mirage in a World That's Rising." *Bloomberg.* May 16, 2012. Accessed 7/9/2012. http://www.bloomberg.com/news/2012-05-16/ameri can-decline-a-mirage-in-a-world-that-s-rising.html.

18. Joseph S. Nye. "The Decline and Fall of America's Decline and Fall." *Project Syndicate,* October 6, 2011. Accessed 7/9/2012. http://www.project-syndicate.org/commen tary/the-decline-and-fall-of-america-s-decline-and-fall. See also Joseph S. Nye. "The

21st Century Will Not Be a 'Post American' World." *International Studies Quarterly*, vol. 56, no. 1, March 2012, 215–217.

19. Daniel Gross. *Better, Stronger, Faster: The Myth of American Decline . . . and the Rise of a New Economy.* New York: Free Press, 2012. Cf. Gideon Rachman. "Think Again: American Decline: This Time It's for Real." *Foreign Policy.* January–February 2011. Accessed 7/11/2012. http://www.foreignpolicy.com/articles/2011/01/02/think_again_american_decline?page=full.

20. Paul K. MacDonald and Joseph M. Parent. "Graceful Decline? The Surprising Success of Great Power Retrenchment." *International Security*, vol. 35, no. 4, spring 2011, 7–44.

21. Thomas L. Friedman and Michael Mandelbaum. *That Used to Be Us: How America Fell Behind in the World It Invented and How We Can Come Back.* New York: Farrar, Strauss, and Giroux, 2011.

22. Robert Kagan. *The World America Made.* New York: Alfred A. Knopf, 2012.

23. Zbigniew Brzezinski. *Strategic Vision: America and the Crisis of Global Power.* New York: Basic Books, 2012.

24. See Robert J. Lieber. *Power and Willpower in the American Future: Why the United States Is Not Destined to Decline.* New York: Cambridge University Press, 2012.

25. Yan Xuetong. "How China Can Defeat America." *New York Times.* November 20, 2011. Accessed 7/11/2012. http://www.nytimes.com/2011/11/21/opinion/how-china-can-defeat-america.html?pagewanted=all.

Chapter 2

1. Pew Global Attitudes Project. "War with Iraq Further Divides Global Publics." Released June 3, 2003. Accessed 7/14/2012. http://pewglobal.org/reports/display.php?ReportID=185.

2. NATO. "NATO Enlargement." Accessed 6/5/13. http://www.nato.int/cps/en/nato live/topics_49212.htm.

3. Pew Global Attitudes Project. "47-Nation Pew Global Attitudes Survey." Accessed 7/14/2012. http://pewglobal.org/reports/pdf/256.pdf, esp. 20–21. Multilateral war fighting gives rise to other problems as well, such as embedding caveats into the arrangements for burden sharing. David P. Auerswald and Stephen M. Saideman. *NATO in Afghanistan: Fighting Together, Fighting Alone.* Princeton, NJ: Princeton University Press, 2014; Stephen M. Saideman and David P. Auerswald. "Comparing Caveats: Understanding the Sources of National Restrictions upon NATO's Mission in Afghanistan." *International Studies Quarterly*, vol. 56, no. 1, March 2012, 67–84.

4. See Patricia A. Weitsman. "Wartime Alliances Versus Coalition Warfare: How Institutional Structure Matters in the Multilateral Prosecution of Wars." *Strategic Studies Quarterly*, vol. 4, no. 2, summer 2010, 113–136.

5. E.g., G. John Ikenberry. *After Victory: Institutions, Strategic Restraint, and the Rebuilding of Order After Major Wars*. Princeton, NJ: Princeton University Press, 2000. Jeremy Pressman. *Warring Friends: Alliance Restraint in International Politics*. Ithaca, NY: Cornell University Press, 2008.

6. Paul W. Schroeder. "Alliances, 1815–1945: Weapons of Power and Tools of Management." Klaus Knorr, ed. *Historical Dimensions of National Security Problems*. Lawrence: University Press of Kansas, 1976, 227–262; Christopher Gelpi. "Alliances as Instruments of Intra-Allied Control." Helga Haftendorn, Robert O. Keohane, and Celeste A. Wallander, eds. *Imperfect Unions*. New York: Oxford University Press, 1999, 107–139; Glenn H. Snyder. *Alliance Politics*. Ithaca, NY: Cornell University Press, 1997. Randall Schweller. "Bandwagoning for Profit: Bringing the Revisionist State Back In." *International Security*, vol. 19, no. 1, summer 1994, 72–107; John A. C. Conybeare. "A Portfolio Diversification Model of Alliances: The Triple Alliance and Triple Entente, 1879–1914." *Journal of Conflict Resolution*, vol. 36, no. 1, March 1992, 53–85; John A. C. Conybeare. "Arms Versus Alliances: The Capital Structure of Military Enterprise." *Journal of Conflict Resolution*, vol. 38, no. 2, June 1994, 215–235; John A. C. Conybeare. "The Portfolio Benefits of Free Riding in Military Alliances." *International Studies Quarterly*, vol. 38, no. 3, September 1994, 405–419. Joseph M. Grieco. "The Maastricht Treaty, Economic and Monetary Union and the Neo-Realist Research Programme." *Review of International Studies*, vol. 21, no. 1, January 1995, 21–40. James D. Morrow. "Alliances and Asymmetry: An Alternative to the Capability Aggregation Model of Alliances." *American Journal of Political Science*, vol. 35, no. 4, November 1991, 904–933; James D. Morrow. "Arms Versus Allies: Trade-Offs in Search for Security." *International Organization*, vol. 47, no. 2, spring 1993, 207–234; James D. Morrow. "Alliances, Credibility, and Peacetime Costs." *Journal of Conflict Resolution*, vol. 38, no. 2, June 1994, 270–297; Gerald L. Sorokin. "Alliance Formation and General Deterrence: A Game Theoretic Model and the Case of Israel." *Journal of Conflict Resolution*, vol. 38, no. 2, June 1994, 298–325. E.g., Jesse C. Johnson and Brett Ashley Leeds. "Defense Pacts: A Prescription for Peace?" *Foreign Policy Analysis*, vol. 7, no. 1, January 2011, 45–65; Brett Ashley Leeds, Michaela Mattes, and Jeremy S. Vogel. "Interests, Institutions, and the Reliability of International Commitments." *American Journal of Political Science*, vol. 53, no. 2, April 2009, 461–476; Brett Ashley Leeds and Burcu Savun. "Terminating Alliances: Why Do States Abrogate Agreements?" *Journal of Politics*, vol. 69, no. 4, November 2007, 1118–1132; Brett Ashley Leeds and Michaela Mattes. "Alliance Politics During the Cold War: Aberration, New World Order, or Continuation of History?" *Conflict Management and Peace Science*, vol. 24, no. 3, July 2007, 183–199; Andrew G. Long and Brett Ashley Leeds. "Trading for Security: Military Alliances and Economic Agreements." *Journal of Peace Research*, vol. 43, no. 4, July 2006, 433–451. Celeste A. Wallander. "Institutional Assets and Adaptability: NATO After the Cold War." *International Organization*, vol. 54, no. 4, autumn 2000, 705–735. Ronald R. Krebs.

"Perverse Institutionalism: NATO and the Greco-Turkish Conflict." *International Organization*, vol. 53, no. 2, spring 1999, 343–377. John S. Duffield. *Power Rules: The Evolution of NATO's Conventional Force Posture*. Stanford, CA: Stanford University Press, 1995; John S. Duffield. "What Are International Institutions?" *International Studies Review*, vol. 9, no. 1, spring 2007, 1–2; John S. Duffield. "Transatlantic Relations After the Cold War: Theory, Evidence, and the Future." *International Studies Perspectives*, vol. 2, no. 1, February 2001, 93–115; John S. Duffield. "NATO's Functions After the Cold War." *Political Science Quarterly*, vol. 109, no. 5, winter 1994–9595, 763–787; John S. Duffield. "Explaining the Long Peace in Europe: The Contributions of Regional Security Regimes." *Review of International Studies*, vol. 20, no. 4, October 1994, 369–388; John S. Duffield. "International Regimes and Alliance Behavior: Explaining NATO Conventional Force Levels." *International Organization*, vol. 46, no. 4, autumn 1992, 819–855. Thomas Risse-Kappen. "A Liberal Interpretation of the Transatlantic Security Community." Peter J. Katzenstein, ed. *The Culture of National Security: Norms and Identity in World Politics*. New York: Columbia University Press, 1996, 357–399; Karl W. Deutsch, Sidney A. Burrell, Robert A. Kann, Maurice Lee Jr., Martin Lichterman, Raymond E. Lindgren, Francis L. Loewenheim, and Richard W. Van Wagenen. *Political Community and the North Atlantic Area*. Princeton, NJ: Princeton University Press, 1957. Wallace J. Thies. *Why NATO Endures*. Cambridge: Cambridge University Press, 2009.

7. Mark J. C. Crescenzi, Jacob D. Kathman, Katja B. Kleinberg, and Reed M. Wood. "Reliability, Reputation, and Alliance Formation." *International Studies Quarterly*, vol. 56, no. 2, June 2012, 259–274.

8. Sarah Kreps. *Coalitions of Convenience*. New York: Oxford University Press, 2011; Daniel F. Baltrusaitis. *Coalition Politics and the Iraq War*. Boulder, CO: Lynne Rienner, 2009; Dominic Tierney. *How We Fight: Crusades, Quagmires, and the American Way of War*. New York: Little, Brown, 2010; Dominic Tierney. "Does Chain-Ganging Cause the Outbreak of War?" *International Studies Quarterly*, vol. 55, no. 2, June 2011, 285–304; Jason Davidson. *America's Allies and War: Kosovo, Afghanistan, and Iraq*. New York: Palgrave Macmillan, 2011.

9. Wallace J. Thies. *Friendly Rivals: Bargaining and Burden-Shifting in NATO*. Armonk, NY: M. E. Sharpe, 2003.

10. Alexander Thompson. *Channels of Power: The UN Security Council and U.S. Statecraft in Iraq*. Ithaca, NY: Cornell University Press, 2009; Alexander Thompson. "Coercion Through International Organizations: The Security Council and Logic of Information Transmission." *International Organization*, vol. 60, no. 3, January 2006, 1–34.

11. Alexander Thompson. "Coercion Through International Organizations: The Security Council and Logic of Information Transmission." *International Organization*, vol. 60, no. 3, January 2006, 9.

12. Ibid., 10.

13. Ibid., 11.

14. See David A. Baldwin. "Power and International Relations." Walter Carlsnaes, Beth A. Simmons, Thomas Risse, eds. *Handbook of International Relations.* 2nd ed. Thousand Oaks, CA: Sage Publications, 2013, 273–297.

15. Harold Sprout. "In Defense of Diplomacy. Politics Among Nations: The Struggle for Power and Peace." *World Politics,* vol. 1, no. 3, April 1949, 410. My thanks to David Baldwin for suggesting that I look at this piece.

16. Pew Global Attitudes Project. "47-Nation Pew Global Attitudes Survey." Accessed 7/14/2012. http://pewglobal.org/reports/pdf/256.pdf.

17. See Barry Buzan. *The United States and the Great Powers: World Politics in the Twenty-First Century.* Cambridge, UK: Polity Press, 2004; Ralph G. Carter. "Leadership at Risk: The Perils of Unilateralism." *PS: Political Science and Politics,* vol. 36, no. 1, January 2003, 17–22.

18. G. John Ikenberry. "Is American Multilateralism in Decline?" *Perspectives on Politics,* vol. 1, no. 3, September 2003, 533.

19. See Robert Jervis. *American Foreign Policy in a New Era.* New York: Routledge, 2005, especially chapter 4.

20. Sarah Kreps explores the question of why the United States opted for multilateral war-fighting mechanisms when it could have adopted unilateral ones. See Sarah Kreps. *Coalitions of Convenience.* New York: Oxford University Press, 2011.

21. G. John Ikenberry. "Is American Multilateralism in Decline?" *Perspectives on Politics,* vol. 1, no. 3, September 2003, 534.

22. On democratic states, domestic politics, and treaty abrogation, see Brett Ashley Leeds, Michaela Attes, and Jeremy S. Vogel. "Interests, Institutions, and the Reliability of International Commitments." *American Journal of Political Science,* vol. 53, no. 2, April 2009, 461–476; Brett Ashley Leeds. "Alliance Reliability in Times of War: Explaining State Decisions to Violate Treaties." *International Organization,* vol. 57, no. 4, September 2003, 801–827.

23. See the very interesting collection of articles in Dimitris Bourantouris, Kostas Ifantis, and Panayotis Tsakonas, eds. *Multilateralism and Security Institutions in an Era of Globalization.* New York: Routledge, 2008.

24. See G. John Ikenberry. *After Victory: Institutions, Strategic Restraint, and the Rebuilding of Order After Major Wars.* Princeton, NJ: Princeton University Press, 2001.

25. However, even North Korea does not generally act without the sanction of China and cannot make war decisions in the absence of cooperation from its great-power ally.

26. Canada and New Zealand, too. See Sarah Kreps. *Coalitions of Convenience.* New York: Oxford University Press, 2011, 17. Fearon makes this point as well. See James D. Fearon. "International Institutions and Collective Authorization of the Use of Force." Alan S. Alexandroff, ed. *Can the World Be Governed?* Waterloo, ON: Wilfrid Laurier University Press, 2008, 160–195.

27. See Patricia A. Weitsman. *Dangerous Alliances: Proponents of Peace, Weapons of War*. Stanford, CA: Stanford University Press, 2004, 27–29.

28. On the use of indigenous allies on the ground, see Stephen D. Biddle. "Allies, Airpower, and Modern Warfare: The Afghan Model in Afghanistan and Iraq." *International Security*, vol. 30, no. 3, winter 2005–2006, 161–176. See also the discussion of minilateralism versus multilateralism in Miles Kahler. "Multilateralism with Small and Large Numbers." John Gerard Ruggie, ed. *Multilateralism Matters: The Theory and Praxis of an Institutional Form*. New York: Columbia University Press, 1993, 295–326.

29. Renato Corbetta and William J. Dixon. "Multilateralism, Major Powers, and Militarized Disputes." *Political Research Quarterly*, vol. 57, no. 1, March 2004, 5–14.

30. See, for example, Robert O. Keohane and Joseph Nye. "Two Cheers for Multilateralism." *Foreign Policy*, no. 60, Autumn 1985, 148–167; Brian Urquhart. "The Limits of Unilateralism." *Foreign Policy*, vol. 65, winter 1986–1987, 39–42; Giulio M. Gallarotti. "The Limits of International Organization: Systematic Failure in the Management of International Relations." *International Organization*, vol. 45, no. 2, spring 1991, 183–220; David A. Lake. "Powerful Pacifists: Democratic States and War." *American Political Science Review*, vol. 86, no. 1, March 1992, 24–37; John Gerard Ruggie, ed. *Multilateralism Matters: The Theory and Praxis of an Institutional Form*. New York: Columbia University Press, 1993; Patrick Stewart and Shepard Forman. *Multilateralism and U.S. Foreign Policy: Ambivalent Engagement*. Boulder, CO: Lynne Rienner, 2002.

31. See, for example, Michael N. Barnett. "Bringing in the New World Order: Liberalism, Legitimacy, and the United Nations." *World Politics*, vol. 49, no. 4, July 1997, 526–551; Ian Hurd. "Legitimacy and Authority in International Politics." *International Organization*, vol. 53, no. 2, spring 1999, 379–408; Ian Hurd. *After Anarchy: Legitimacy and Power in the United Nations*. Princeton, NJ: Princeton University Press, 2008; Bruce Cronin. "The Paradox of Hegemony: America's Ambiguous Relationship with the United Nations." *European Journal of International Relations*, vol. 7, no. 1, March 2001, 103–130. Alastair Iain Johnston argues that international institutions do not merely legitimize but instead socialize participating states into the norms of the international system. Alastair Iain Johnston. "Treating International Institutions as Social Environments." *International Studies Quarterly*, vol. 45, vol. 4, December 2001, 487–515.

32. Sarah Kreps. *Coalitions of Convenience*. New York: Oxford University Press, 2011, 52.

33. Robert Kagan. "Power and Weakness." *Policy Review*. June–July 2002, 3–28; Fareed Zakaria. "Our Way." *New Yorker*. October 14–21, 2002, 72–81; Joseph S. Nye Jr. "U.S. Power and Strategy After Iraq." *Foreign Affairs*. July–August 2003, 60–73; Joseph S. Nye Jr. *The Paradox of American Power: Why the World's Only Superpower Can't Go It Alone*. London: Oxford University Press, 2002; Colin Powell. "A Strategy of Partnerships." *Foreign Affairs*. January–February 2004, 22–34; David M. Malone and Yuen Foong Khong. *Unilateralism and U.S. Foreign Policy: International Perspectives*. Boulder, CO: Lynne

Rienner, 2003; William Drozdiak. "The North Atlantic Drift." *Foreign Affairs.* January–February 2005, 88–98; G. John Ikenberry. "Is American Multilateralism in Decline?" *Perspectives on Politics,* vol. 1, no. 3, September 2003, 533–550; Stephen G. Brooks and William C. Wohlforth. "International Relations Theory and the Case Against Unilateralism." *Perspectives on Politics,* vol. 3, no. 3, September 2005, 509–524.

34. See, for example, Andrew Bennett, Joseph Lepgold, and Danny Unger. "Burden Sharing in the Persian Gulf War." *International Organization,* vol. 48, no. 1, winter 1994, 39–75; Andrew Bennett, Joseph Lepgold, and Danny Unger, eds. *Friends in Need: Burden Sharing in the Persian Gulf War.* New York: St. Martin's, 1997; Ivo Daalder and Michael E. O'Hanlon. *Winning Ugly: NATO's War to Save Kosovo.* Washington, DC: Brookings Institution, 2000; Pierre Martin and Michael Brawley, eds. *Alliance Politics, Kosovo, and NATO's War: Allied Force or Forced Allies?* New York: Palgrave Macmillan, 2001; Benjamin S. Lambeth. *NATO's Air War for Kosovo: A Strategic and Operational Assessment.* Project Air Force Series on Operation Allied Force. Santa Monica, CA: Rand, 2001; Patricia A. Weitsman. "Alliance Cohesion and Coalition Warfare: The Central Powers and the Triple Entente." *Security Studies,* vol. 12, no. 3, spring 2003, 79–113.

35. For a discussion of the ways in which NATO is being transformed into a coalition framework, see Sten Rynning. *NATO Renewed: The Power and Purpose of Transatlantic Cooperation.* New York: Palgrave Macmillan, 2005, 119–168.

36. John G. Ruggie, ed. *Multilateralism Matters: The Theory and Praxis of an Institutional Form.* New York: Columbia University Press, 1993, 11.

37. Ibid., 14 (emphasis added).

38. Colin Powell. "A Strategy of Partnerships." *Foreign Affairs,* January–February 2004, 22–34; George W. Bush. "National Security Strategy." March 2006. Accessed 6/5/13. http://georgewbush-whitehouse.archives.gov/nsc/nss/2006/index.html.

39. See, for example, David Skidmore. "Understanding the Unilateralist Turn in U.S. Foreign Policy." *Foreign Policy Analysis,* vol. 1, no. 2, July 2005, 207–228; Glyn Prins, ed. *Understanding Unilateralism in U.S. Foreign Relations.* London: Royal Institute of International Affairs, 2002; Pascal Boniface. "The Specter of Unilateralism." *Washington Quarterly,* vol. 24, no. 3, summer 2001, 155–163; Stanley Hoffmann. "The High and Mighty." *American Prospect,* January 13, 2003, 28–31; Stanley Hoffmann. "America Alone in the World." *American Prospect,* August 30, 2002. Accessed 6/5/13. http://prospect.org/article/america-alone-world; Clyde Prestowitz. *Rogue Nation: American Unilateralism and the Failure of Good Intentions.* New York: Basic Books, 2003.

40. Steven G. Brooks and William C. Wohlforth. "International Relations Theory and the Case Against Unilateralism." *Perspectives on Politics,* vol. 3, no. 3, September 2005, 509–519.

41. Ralph G. Carter. "Leadership at Risk: The Perils of Unilateralism." *PS: Political Science and Politics,* vol. 36, no. 1, January 2003, 17–21.

42. Barry Buzan. *The United States and the Great Powers: World Politics in the Twenty-First Century.* Cambridge, UK: Polity Press, 2004, 169.

43. Sarah Kreps. *Coalitions of Convenience.* New York: Oxford University Press, 2011.

44. Steven G. Brooks and William C. Wohlforth. "International Relations Theory and the Case Against Unilateralism." *Perspectives on Politics,* vol. 3, no. 3, September 2005, 509.

45. Ralph G. Carter. "Leadership at Risk: The Perils of Unilateralism." *PS: Political Science and Politics,* vol. 36, no. 1, January 2003, 17.

46. Barry Buzan. *The United States and the Great Powers: World Politics in the Twenty-First Century.* Cambridge, UK: Polity Press, 2004, 169.

47. Sarah Kreps. *Coalitions of Convenience.* New York: Oxford University Press, 2011, 15.

48. See Patricia A. Weitsman. "The High Price of Friendship." *New York Times.* August 31, 2006. The Pew Global Attitudes Project tracks international public opinion. It has tracked a pervasive unilateralist image of the United States abroad and a sense that the United States fails to take into account other states' interests as it formulates its foreign policy. See the reports at http://pewglobal.org/reports, especially "US Image up Slightly, but Still Negative" (June 23, 2005) and "Global Unease with Major World Powers" (June 27, 2007).

49. For an interesting and important argument that the emphasis on ends with multilateralism misses a central point that the means of using multilateralism brings benefits in and of itself, see Vincent Pouliot. "Multilateralism as an End in Itself." *International Studies Perspectives,* vol. 12, no. 1, February 2011, 18–26.

50. Steven G. Brooks and William C. Wohlforth. "International Relations Theory and the Case Against Unilateralism." *Perspectives on Politics,* vol. 3, no. 3, September 2005, 509.

51. In other words, there is a distinction here between ideological multilateralism that manifests a genuine commitment to multilateralism and instrumental ideological multilateralism that is undertaken to represent or yield international legitimacy. A fine point of difference but is significant nevertheless. It helps us understand the difference between George H. W. Bush's use of multilateralism and that of his son George W. Bush. Again, thanks to Sammy Barkin for pointing this out.

52. My thanks to Sammy Barkin for this point.

53. For a review, see Patricia A. Weitsman. *Dangerous Alliances: Proponents of Peace, Weapons of War.* Stanford, CA: Stanford University Press, 2004.

54. Recent work on multilateral war fighting is very promising. See, for example, Sarah Kreps. *Coalitions of Convenience.* New York: Oxford University Press, 2011; Daniel F. Baltrusaitis. *Coalition Politics and the Iraq War.* Boulder, CO: Lynne Rienner, 2009; Dominic Tierney. *How We Fight: Crusades, Quagmires, and the American Way of War.* New York: Little, Brown, 2010; Jason Davidson. *America's Allies and War: Kosovo,*

Afghanistan, and Iraq. New York: Palgrave Macmillan, 2011. See also James H. Lebovic. *The Limits of U.S. Military Capability.* Baltimore: Johns Hopkins University Press, 2010. Lebovic's work does not focus on coalition capability but nevertheless contains important insights regarding contemporary U.S. warfare.

55. [Under direction of the chairman of the Joint Chiefs of Staff]. "Multinational Operations." Joint Publication 3-16. Revision First Draft. February 1, 2006. See also Dominic Tierney. *How We Fight: Crusades, Quagmires, and the American Way of War.* New York: Little, Brown, 2010.

56. Major Dean S. Mills, U.S. Air Force. "Coalition Interoperability: An International Adventure." *Air and Space Power Journal—Chronicles Online Journal,* 1998, 2. Accessed 7/7/2009. http://www.airpower.maxwell.af.mil/airchronicles/cc/mills.html.

57. See "Multilateral Interoperability Programme." Accessed 6/5/13. https://mipsite .lsec.dnd.ca/Public%20Document%20Library/99_Archives/02-Baseline_2.0/MIPGlos-MIP_Glossary/MIPGlossary-IT-CCWG-Edition2.4.pdf. The Multilateral Interoperability Program grew out of two other initiatives, the Battlefield Interoperability Program and the Quadrilateral Interoperability Programme. See the Multilateral Interoperability Programme Glossary. Edition 2.4. May 26, 2006, 4.

58. Patricia Weitsman. "With a Little Help from our Friends? The Costs of Coalition Warfare." *Origins: Current Events in Historical Perspective,* vol. 2, no. 4, January 2009. Accessed 6/5/13. http://origins.osu.edu/article/little-help-our-friends-costs-coalition-warfare.

59. Ibid.

60. See also the fascinating work by Auerswald and Saideman on caveats. David P. Auerswald and Stephen M. Saideman. *NATO in Afghanistan: Fighting Together, Fighting Alone.* Princeton, NJ: Princeton University Press, 2014; Stephen M. Saideman and David P. Auerswald. "Comparing Caveats: Understanding the Sources of National Restrictions upon NATO's Mission in Afghanistan." *International Studies Quarterly,* vol. 56, no. 1, March 2012, 67–84.

61. Cf. Paul Lewis. "Swiss to Vote on Disarming their Fortress." *New York Times.* October 22, 1989. On the economic implications of Swiss defense spending, see Thomas Bernauer, Vally Koubi, and Fabio Ernst. "National and Regional Consequences of Swiss Defense Spending." *Journal of Peace Research,* vol. 46, no. 4, July 2009, 467–484.

62. On motivations for forming alliances, see Patricia A. Weitsman. *Dangerous Alliances: Proponents of Peace, Weapons of War.* Stanford, CA: Stanford University Press, 2004; Patricia A. Weitsman. "Wartime Alliances Versus Coalition Warfare: How Institutional Structure Matters in the Multilateral Prosecution of Wars." *Strategic Studies Quarterly,* vol. 4, no. 2, summer 2010, 113–136.

63. Kenneth Waltz. *Theory of International Politics.* Reading, MA: Addison-Wesley Publishing, 1979; Stephen M. Walt. *Origins of Alliances.* Ithaca, NY: Cornell University Press, 1987; Glenn H. Snyder. *Alliance Politics.* Ithaca, NY: Cornell University Press, 1997;

Randall Schweller. "Bandwagoning for Profit: Bringing the Revisionist State Back In." *International Security*, vol. 19, no. 1, Summer 1994, 72–107.

64. See T. V. Paul. "Soft Balancing in the Age of U.S. Primacy." *International Security*, vol. 30, no. 1, summer, 2005, 46–71; Steven G. Brooks and William C. Wohlforth. "International Relations Theory and the Case Against Unilateralism." *Perspectives on Politics*, vol. 3, no. 3, September 2005, 509–524.

65. Thomas Christensen and Jack Snyder. "Chain Gangs and Passed Bucks: Predicting Alliance Patterns in Multipolarity." *International Organization*, vol. 44, no. 2, spring 1990, 137–168; Thomas Christensen. "Perceptions and Alliances in Europe, 1865–1940." *International Organization*, vol. 51, no. 1, winter 1997, 65–97.

66. John J. Mearsheimer. *The Tragedy of Great Power Politics*. New York: Norton, 2001.

67. Thomas Christensen and Jack Snyder. "Chain Gangs and Passed Bucks: Predicting Alliance Patterns in Multipolarity." *International Organization*, vol. 44, no. 2, spring 1990, 137–168; Thomas Christensen. "Perceptions and Alliances in Europe, 1865–1940." *International Organization*, vol. 51, no. 1, winter 1997, 65–97.

68. See Dominic Tierney. "Does Chain-Ganging Cause the Outbreak of War?" *International Studies Quarterly*, vol. 55, no. 2, June 2011, 285–304. Inherent in the idea of balancing is signaling and deterring threats. For more on this, see James Fearon. "Signaling Versus the Balance of Power and Interests: An Empirical Test of a Crisis Bargaining Model." *Journal of Conflict Resolution*, vol. 38, no. 2, June 1994, 236–269; James D. Morrow. "Alliances, Credibility, and Peacetime Costs." *Journal of Conflict Resolution*, vol. 38, no. 2, June 1994, 270–297; Brett Ashley Leeds. "Do Alliances Deter Aggression? The Influence of Military Alliances on the Initiation of Militarized Interstate Disputes." *American Journal of Political Science*, vol. 47, no. 3, July 2003, 427–439.

69. Paul W. Schroeder. "Alliances, 1815–1945: Weapons of Power and Tools of Management." Klaus Knorr, ed. *Historical Dimensions of National Security Problems*. Lawrence: University Press of Kansas, 227–262.

70. Patricia A. Weitsman. "Intimate Enemies: The Politics of Peacetime Alliances." *Security Studies*, vol. 7, no. 1, autumn 1997, 156–192; Patricia A. Weitsman. *Dangerous Alliances: Proponents of Peace, Weapons of War*. Stanford, CA: Stanford University Press, 2004.

71. Andrew Long, Timothy Nordstrom, and Kyeonghi Baek. "Allying for Peace: Treaty Obligations and Conflict Among Allies." *Journal of Politics*, vol. 69, no. 4, November 2007, 1103–1117.

72. Patricia A. Weitsman. *Dangerous Alliances: Proponents of Peace, Weapons of War*. Stanford, CA: Stanford University Press, 2004, 2.

73. Patricia A. Weitsman. "Intimate Enemies: The Politics of Peacetime Alliances." *Security Studies*, vol. 7, no. 1, autumn 1997, 156–192; Patricia A. Weitsman. *Dangerous*

Alliances: Proponents of Peace, Weapons of War. Stanford, CA: Stanford University Press, 2004.

74. Jeremy Pressman. *Warring Friends: Alliance Restraint in International Politics.* Ithaca, NY: Cornell University Press, 2008.

75. Kenneth Waltz. *Theory of International Politics.* Reading, MA: Addison-Wesley Publishing, 1979; Stephen M. Walt. *Origins of Alliances.* Ithaca, NY: Cornell University Press, 1987; Glenn H. Snyder. *Alliance Politics.* Ithaca, NY: Cornell University Press, 1997; Randall Schweller. "Bandwagoning for Profit: Bringing the Revisionist State Back In." *International Security,* vol. 19, no. 1, summer 1994, 72–107.

76. Randall Schweller. "Bandwagoning for Profit: Bringing the Revisionist State Back In." *International Security,* vol. 19, no. 1, summer 1994, 72–107.

77. Ibid.; Kenneth Waltz. *Theory of International Politics.* Reading, MA: Addison-Wesley Publishing, 1979; Stephen M. Walt. *Origins of Alliances.* Ithaca, NY: Cornell University Press, 1987.

78. Patricia A. Weitsman. *Dangerous Alliances: Proponents of Peace, Weapons of War.* Stanford, CA: Stanford University Press, 2004.

79. Robert J. Art. "Europe Hedges Its Security Bets." *Balance of Power Revisited: Theory and Practice in the 21st Century.* T. V. Paul, James Wirtz, and Michael Fortmann, eds. Stanford, CA: Stanford University Press, 2004, 179–213.

80. On ideology, see, e.g., Mark L. Haas. "Ideology and Alliances: British and French External Balancing Decisions in the 1930s." *Security Studies,* vol. 12, no. 4, summer 2003, 34–79; John M. Owen IV. "When Do Ideologies Produce Alliances? The Holy Roman Empire, 1517–1555." *International Studies Quarterly,* vol. 49, no. 1, March 2005, 73–99. On regime type, see, e.g., Randolph M. Siverson and Juliann Emmons. "Birds of a Feather: Democratic Political Systems and Alliances Choices in the Twentieth Century." *Journal of Conflict Resolution,* vol. 35, no. 2, June 1991, 285–306. Randolph M. Siverson and Harvey Starr. "Regime Change and the Restructuring of Alliances." *American Journal of Political Science,* vol. 38, no. 1, February 1994, 145–161. Suzanne Werner and Douglas Lemke. "Opposites Do Not Attract: The Impact of Domestic Institutions, Power, and Prior Commitments on Alignment Choices." *International Studies Quarterly,* vol. 41, no. 3, September 1997, 529–546. Michael C. Williams. "The Institutions of Security: Elements of a Theory of Security Organizations." *Cooperation and Conflict,* vol. 32, no. 3, September 1997, 287–307. Mark Peceny and Caroline C. Beer, with Shannon Sanchez·Terry. "Dictatorial Peace?" *American Political Science Review,* vol. 96, no. 1, March 2002, 15–26. On identity, see, e.g., Peter J. Katzenstein, ed. *The Culture of National Security.* New York: Columbia University Press, 1996. Michael C. Williams. "The Institutions of Security: Elements of a Theory of Security Organizations." *Cooperation and Conflict,* vol. 32, no. 3, September 1997, 287–307; Michael C. Williams. "Identity and the Politics of Security." *European Journal of International Relations,* vol. 4, no. 2, June 1998, 204–25. On domestic politics, see Kevin Narizny. "The Political Economy of Alignment: Great Britain's Com-

mitment to Europe, 1905–39." *International Security*, vol. 27, no. 4, spring 2003, 184–219. Michael N. Barnett and Jack S. Levy. "Domestic Sources of Alliances and Alignments: The Case of Egypt, 1962–1973." *International Organization*, vol. 45, no. 3, summer 1991, 369–395. Steven R. David. *Choosing Sides: Alignment and Realignment in the Third World.* Baltimore: Johns Hopkins University Press, 1991. Steven R. David. "Explaining Third World Alignment." *World Politics*, vol. 43, no. 2, January 1991, 233–256.

81. Ole Holsti, P. Terrence Hopmann, and John Sullivan. *Unity and Disintegration in International Alliances.* New York: John Wiley and Sons, 1973, 16; Patricia A. Weitsman. "Intimate Enemies: The Politics of Peacetime Alliances." *Security Studies*, vol. 7, no. 1, autumn 1997, 156–192; Patricia A. Weitsman. *Dangerous Alliances: Proponents of Peace, Weapons of War.* Stanford, CA: Stanford University Press, 2004.

82. See Patricia A. Weitsman. "Intimate Enemies: The Politics of Peacetime Alliances." *Security Studies*, vol. 7, no. 1, autumn 1997, 156–192; Patricia A. Weitsman. *Dangerous Alliances: Proponents of Peace, Weapons of War.* Stanford, CA: Stanford University Press, 2004.

83. See Patricia A. Weitsman. "Alliance Cohesion and Coalition Warfare: The Central Powers and the Triple Entente." *Security Studies*, vol. 12, no. 3, spring 2003, 79–113; Patricia A. Weitsman. *Dangerous Alliances: Proponents of Peace, Weapons of War.* Stanford, CA: Stanford University Press, 2004.

84. On alliance reliability in wartime, see especially Brett Ashley Leeds. "Alliance Reliability in Times of War: Explaining States Decisions to Violate Treaties." *International Organization*, vol. 57, no. 4, September 2003, 801–827; Brett Ashley Leeds, Andrew Long, and Sara McLaughlin Mitchell. "Reevaluating Alliance Reliability: Specific Threats, Specific Promises." *Journal of Conflict Resolution*, vol. 44, no. 5, October 2000, 686–699.

85. Cf. G. John Ikenberry, who writes: "Security alliances involve relatively well-defined, specific, and limited commitments, an attractive feature for both the leading military power and its partners. States know what they are getting into and what the limits are on their obligations and liabilities." G. John Ikenberry. "America and the Reform of Global Institutions." Alan S. Alexandroff, ed. *Can the World Be Governed?* Waterloo, ON: Wilfrid Laurier University Press, 2008, 129.

86. Patricia A. Weitsman. "Alliance Cohesion and Coalition Warfare: The Central Powers and the Triple Entente." *Security Studies*, vol.12, no. 3, Spring 2003, 79–113.

87. This is an important caveat: because NATO is a distinctive alliance in regard to the degree of institutionalization, examining other alliances in wartime may culminate in different observations. Cf. ibid.

88. Nora Bensahel. *The Counterterror Coalitions: Cooperation with Europe, NATO, and the European Union.* Santa Monica, CA: Rand, 2003, p. 16.

89. The definition of cohesion comes from Ole Holsti, P. Terrence Hopmann, and John Sullivan. *Unity and Disintegration in International Alliances.* New York: John

Wiley and Sons, 1973; see Patricia A. Weitsman. *Dangerous Alliances: Proponents of Peace, Weapons of War.* Stanford, CA: Stanford University Press, 2004.

90. Patricia A. Weitsman. "Intimate Enemies: The Politics of Peacetime Alliances." *Security Studies,* vol. 7, no. 1, autumn 1997, 156–192; Patricia A. Weitsman. *Dangerous Alliances: Proponents of Peace, Weapons of War.* Stanford, CA: Stanford University Press, 2004.

91. Patricia A. Weitsman. "Alliance Cohesion and Coalition Warfare: The Central Powers and the Triple Entente." *Security Studies,* vol. 12, no. 3, spring 2003, 79–113.

92. Cohesion derives from internal threats as well. Here I am looking exclusively at external threats. Another caveat: I am examining alliances under conditions of threat. I do not mean to imply that alliances are not interesting under conditions of low or nonexistent internal or external threats, but that is not my focus here.

93. See, e.g., Richard Norton-Taylor and Ian Colbain. "Eight British Soldiers Killed in the Bloodiest Day in the Afghan Mission." *The Guardian.* July 10, 2009. Accessed 7/15/2012. http://www.guardian.co.uk/uk/2009/jul/10/afghanistan-british-soldiers-eight-casualties.

94. "Afghan Strategy Right Says PM." *BBC News.* July 11, 2009. Accessed 7/15/2012. http://news.bbc.co.uk/2/hi/uk_news/8146082.stm.

95. Patricia A. Weitsman. "Alliance Cohesion and Coalition Warfare: The Central Powers and the Triple Entente." *Security Studies,* vol. 12, no. 3, spring 2003, 79–113. See Jason Davidson's excellent book on burden sharing in contemporary coalition warfare. Jason Davidson. *America's Allies and War.* New York: Palgrave Macmillan, 2011; Daniel Baltrusaitis. *Coalition Politics and the Iraq War: Determinants of Choice.* Boulder, CO: Lynne Rienner, 2009.

96. Cf. Sarah Anderson, Phyllis Bennis, and John Cavanagh. "Coalition of the Willing or Coalition of the Coerced? How the Bush Administration Influences Allies in Its War on Iraq." Monograph. February 26, 2003. Washington, DC: Institute for Policy Studies; Paul Gilfeather. "Coalition of the Bribed, Bullied, and Blind." *London Mirror.* March 22, 2003.

97. Nora Bensahel. *The Counterterror Coalitions: Cooperation with Europe, NATO, and the European Union.* Santa Monica, CA: Rand, 2003.

98. Glenn H. Snyder. "The Security Dilemma in Alliance Politics." vol. 36, no. 4, July 1984, 461–495; Glenn H. Snyder. *Alliance Politics.* Ithaca, NY: Cornell University Press, 1997. Patricia A. Weitsman. *Dangerous Alliances: Proponents of Peace, Weapons of War.* Stanford, CA: Stanford University Press, 2004.

99. Peacetime alliances are just formal or informal agreements between two or more states intended to further (militarily) the national security of the participating states, operating when the signatories are not at war. If war begins and the alliance does not dissolve, it transitions to a wartime alliance. If the alliance endures beyond the war, it reverts to a peacetime alliance.

100. Patricia A. Weitsman. *Dangerous Alliances: Proponents of Peace, Weapons of War.* Stanford, CA: Stanford University Press, 2004, 35. Cf. Alliance Treaty Obligations and Provisions data, in Brett Ashley Leeds, Jeffrey M. Ritter, Sara McLaughlin Mitchell, and Andrew G. Long. "Alliance Treaty Obligations and Provisions, 1815–1944." *International Interactions,* vol. 28, no. 3, 2002, 237–260.

101. Or out of a desire to craft a response to an international crisis in a way that strengthens global institutions such as the United Nations so that it might become more effective in other issue areas as well. I am grateful to Nora Bensahel for this point.

102. Frank Walker. "Our Pilots Refused to Bomb 40 Times." *Sydney Morning Herald.* March 14, 2004.

103. Nora Bensahel. *The Counterterror Coalitions: Cooperation with Europe, NATO, and the European Union.* Santa Monica, CA: Rand, 2003.

104. This is a strategy that is not without costs—an unsuccessful or conflict-fraught wartime mission may undermine those alliances.

105. Richard A. Cody and Robert L. Maginnis. "Coalition Interoperability: ABCA's New Focus." *Military Review.* November–December 2006. Reprinted in *Canadian Army Journal,* vol. 10, no. 1, spring 2007. Accessed 6/4/13. http://www.army.forces.gc.ca/caj/documents/vol_10/iss_1/CAJ_vol10.1_11_e.pdf.

106. Russell E. Bryant and David A. Breslin. "Toward Improved Coalition Interoperability—A Coalition Environmental Approach in the International Strategic Arena." *Naval Sea Systems Command.* June 2002, 2. Accessed 8/1/2009. http://www.dtic.mil/cgi-bin/GetTRDoc?AD=ADA467717&Location=U2&doc=GetTRDoc.pdf.

107. Richard A. Cody and Robert L. Maginnis. "Coalition Interoperability: ABCA's New Focus." *Military Review.* November–December 2006, 1. Accessed 8/1/2009. http://findarticles.com/p/articles/mi_m0PBZ/is_6_86/ai_n17093422/?tag=content;col1.

108. Ibid., 1–2.

109. Patricia A. Weitsman. "The High Price of Friendship." *New York Times.* August 31, 2006.

110. My thanks to Asher Balkin for his work on this section. See Patricia A. Weitsman and Asher E. Balkin. "(W)hither Unilateralism? Coalition Warfare in the New Millennium." Paper presented at the annual meeting of the American Political Science Association. Philadelphia, PA. September 2006.

111. [Under direction of the chairman of the Joint Chiefs of Staff]. "Multinational Operations." Joint Publication 3-16. Revision First Draft. February 1, 2006, appendix B.

112. Ibid. An important point that Nora Bensahel makes in *The Counterterror Coalitions* is that the United States has forged its counterterror coalitions bilaterally rather than multilaterally. In other words, during Operation Enduring Freedom in Afghanistan, the United States used capabilities and resources offered to it by its allies bilaterally rather than availing itself of collective NATO capabilities. The Kosovo experience revealed the problems associated with a joint command structure during wartime and

the painstaking process of collective decision making and military planning. As a consequence, the United States sought to work with countries bilaterally rather than multilaterally in the wars in Afghanistan and Iraq. See Nora Bensahel. *Counterterror Coalitions.* Santa Monica, CA: Rand, 2003, 6–8, 15–16.

113. For an analysis of alliance termination, see Brett Ashley Leeds, Michaela Mattes, and Jeremy S. Vogel. "Interests, Institutions, and the Reliability of International Commitments." *American Journal of Political Science,* vol. 53, no. 2, April 2009, 461–476; Brett Ashley Leeds and Burcu Savun. "Terminating Alliances: Why Do States Abrogate Agreements? *Journal of Politics,* vol. 69, no. 4, November 2007, 1118–1132.

114. Mlada Bukovansky. *Legitimacy and Power Politics.* Princeton, NJ: Princeton University Press, 2002.

115. For an excellent overview, see Ian Clark. *Legitimacy in International Society.* Oxford: Oxford University Press, 2005. See also Shane P. Mulligan. "The Uses of Legitimacy in International Relations." *Millennium,* vol. 34, no. 2, February 2006, 349–375; Hideaki Shinoda. "The Politics of Legitimacy in International Relations: A Critical Examination of NATO's Intervention in Kosovo." *Alternatives: Global, Local, Political,* vol. 25, no. 4, October–December 2000, 515–536; Ian Hurd. "Legitimacy and Authority in International Politics." *International Organization,* vol. 53, no. 2, spring 1999, 379–408; Hideaki Shinoda. *After Anarchy: Legitimacy and Power in the United Nations.* Princeton, NJ: Princeton University Press, 2008.

116. The most thorough analysis of this process, foundational to the ideas of realist institutionalism, may be found in Alexander Thompson. *Channels of Power: The UN Security Council and U.S. Statecraft in Iraq.* Ithaca, NY: Cornell University Press, 2009; Alexander Thompson. "Coercion Through International Organizations: The Security Council and Logic of Information Transmission." *International Organization,* vol. 60, no. 3, January 2006, 1–34.

Chapter 3

1. Alexander Thompson. "Coercion Through International Organizations: The Security Council and Logic of Information Transmission." *International Organization,* vol. 60, no. 3, January 2006, 1–34; Alexander Thompson. *Channels of Power: The UN Security Council and U.S. Statecraft in Iraq.* Ithaca, NY: Cornell University Press, 2009.

2. There are a number of exceptional books and articles on the Gulf War. See, for example, Thomas A. Keaney and Eliot A. Cohen. *Gulf War Air Power Survey Summary Report.* Washington, DC: U.S. Government Printing Office, 1993; Michael R. Gordon and Bernard E. Trainor. *The Generals' War: The Inside Story of the Conflict in the Gulf.* New York: Little, Brown, 1995; Rick Atkinson. *Crusade: The Untold Story of the Persian Gulf War.* New York: Houghton Mifflin Harcourt, 1994; Lawrence Freedman and Efraim Karsh. *The Gulf Conflict, 1990-1991: Diplomacy and War in the New World Order.*

Princeton, NJ: Princeton University Press, 1995; Anthony H. Cordesman. *The Iraq War: Strategy, Tactics, and Military Lessons.* Westport, CT: Praeger, 2003; Richard N. Haas. *War of Necessity, War of Choice: A Memoir of Two Iraq Wars.* New York: Simon and Schuster, 2009; Keith L. Shimko. *The Iraq Wars and America's Military Revolution.* New York: Cambridge University Press, 2010. This is just a tiny sampling; there are many other excellent chronologies, memoirs, and analyses, as will be apparent as this chapter unfolds.

3. On the crafting of these operations from the American perspective, see Richard N. Haass. *War of Necessity, War of Choice: A Memoir of Two Iraq Wars.* New York: Simon and Schuster, 2009, especially 17–153.

4. Thomas A. Keaney and Eliot A. Cohen. *Gulf War Air Power Survey Summary Report.* Washington, DC: U.S. Government Printing Office, 1993, 166.

5. The work on power by David A. Baldwin is seminal in understanding the difference between power capabilities and the exercise of power. For a review, see David Baldwin. "Power and International Relations"; Walter Carlsnaes, Beth A. Simmons, and Thomas Risse, eds. *Handbook of International Relations.* 2nd ed. Thousand Oaks, CA: Sage Publications, 2013, 273–297.

6. CENTCOM. Accessed 2/17/2012. http://www.centcom.mil/en/about-centcom/our-history.

7. U.S. Department of Defense. *Final Report to Congress: Conduct of the Persian Gulf War.* Washington, DC: U.S. Department of Defense, 1992, 60.

8. Clyde H. Farnsworth. "Egypt's 'Reward': Forgiven Debt." *New York Times.* April 10, 1991; Steven Greenhouse. "Half of Egypt's $20.2 Billion Debt Being Forgiven by U.S. and Allies." *New York Times.* May 27, 1991; "Egypt's Economy: Sinkhole No More." *Economist.* March 13, 1997; Alexander Thompson. *Channels of Power: The UN Security Council and U.S. Statecraft in Iraq.* Ithaca, NY: Cornell University Press, 2009, 61.

9. U.S. Department of Defense. *Final Report to Congress: Conduct of the Persian Gulf War.* Washington, DC, 1992, 62–64.

10. Peter de la Billière. *Storm Command: A Personal Account of the Gulf War.* New York: HarperCollins, 1992, 303. Khaled bin Sultan reports, "Working in parallel, Schwarzkopf and I were often in close and instant agreement. Sometimes, however, we disagreed significantly, and at other times we were obliged to negotiate with each other to reach a compromise. He was not an easy man to deal with, but neither was I." *Desert Warrior.* New York: HarperCollins, 1995, 191; see also 200–204.

11. Public Broadcasting Service. Accessed 2/13/2012. http://www.pbs.org/wgbh/pages/frontline/gulf/oral/billiere/2.html.

12. CENTCOM. "Operation Desert Shield/Desert Storm, Executive Summary." Declassified, 1991, 7. These were parallel, though not equivalent, since the United States' force commitment was so much larger than anyone else's. See Khaled bin Sultan. *Desert Warrior.* New York: HarperCollins, 1995, 193–197.

13. Mark David Mandeles, Thomas Hone, and Sanford S. Terry. *Managing "Command and Control" in the Persian Gulf War*. Westport, CT: Praeger, 1996, 35.

14. CENTCOM. "Operation Desert Shield/Desert Storm, Executive Summary." Declassified, 1991, 7–9.

15. Nora Bensahel. *The Coalition Paradox: The Politics of Military Cooperation*. Ph.D. diss., Stanford University, 1999, 50n67.

16. Thomas A. Keaney and Eliot A. Cohen. *Gulf War Air Power Survey Summary Report*. Washington, DC: U.S. Government Printing Office, 1993, 159.

17. See U.S. Department of Defense, Unified Command Plan. 2011. Accessed 7/12/2012. http://www.defense.gov/home/features/2009/0109_unifiedcommand/.

18. Thomas A. Keaney and Eliot A. Cohen. *Gulf War Air Power Survey Summary Report*. Washington, DC: U.S. Government Printing Office, 1993, 52. There were challenges within the U.S. military in planning this first stage of the operation as well; see 129–130.

19. Nora Bensahel. *The Coalition Paradox: The Politics of Military Cooperation*. Ph.D. diss., Stanford University, 1999, 50; Major Barry A. Maxwell. "Establishing Theater Command and Control in a Coalition of Nations: Requirements for U.S. Doctrine." School of Advanced Military Studies, U.S. Army Command and General Staff College. Fort Leavenworth, KS, 1992.

20. CENTCOM. "Operation Desert Shield/Desert Storm, Executive Summary." Declassified, 1991, 6. For a flow chart explaining these relationships, see Major Barry A. Maxwell, "Establishing Theater Command and Control in a Coalition of Nations: Requirements for U.S. Doctrine." School of Advanced Military Studies, U.S. Army Command and General Staff College, Fort Leavenworth, KS, 1992, 22; Khaled bin Sultan. *Desert Warrior*. New York: HarperCollins, 1995, 244–247.

21. CENTCOM. "Operation Desert Shield/Desert Storm, Executive Summary." Declassified, 1991, 11.

22. Major Jeffrey W. Yaeger. "Coalition Warfare: Surrendering Sovereignty." *Military Review*, vol. 72, no. 11, November 1992, 61.

23. Nora Bensahel. *The Coalition Paradox: The Politics of Military Cooperation*. Ph.D. diss., Stanford University, 1999, 73.

24. Public Broadcasting Service. Accessed 2/12/2012. http://www.pbs.org/wgbh/pages/frontline/gulf/oral/billiere/2.html.

25. For Schwarzkopf's account of the doctrinal and actual disputes among the U.S. Air Force, Navy, and Marines over the use of airpower in theater, see for example, the PBS *Frontline* interview with General Schwarzkopf, both accessed 2/12/2012: http://www.pbs.org/wgbh/pages/frontline/gulf/oral/schwarzkopf/4.htmlhttp://www.pbs.org/wgbh/pages/frontline/gulf/oral/schwarzkopf/5.html; see also Thomas A. Keaney and Eliot A. Cohen. *Gulf War Air Power Survey Summary Report*. Washington, DC: U.S. Government Printing Office, 1993, 153, 215–216. There was also tension between civilian and military

personnel in decision making. See Richard N. Haass, *War of Necessity, War of Choice: A Memoir of Two Iraq Wars,* New York: Simon and Schuster, 2009, 124.

26. For a more detailed description of Black Hole and its origins, see Mark David Mandeles, Thomas Hone, and Sanford S. Terry. *Managing "Command and Control" in the Persian Gulf War.* Westport, CT: Praeger, 1996, 10–42

27. For more on the British perspective regarding the intelligence shortcomings, see also the following, accessed 2/12/2012: http://www.pbs.org/wgbh/pages/frontline/gulf/oral/billiere/3.html for more on the British perspective regarding the intelligence short-comings. See also Mark David Mandeles, Thomas Hone, and Sanford S. Terry. *Managing "Command and Control" in the Persian Gulf War.* Westport, CT: Praeger, 1996, 35, 94–97, 114–115.

28. Mark David Mandeles, Thomas Hone, and Sanford S. Terry. *Managing "Command and Control" in the Persian Gulf War.* Westport, CT: Praeger, 1996, 80.

29. Ibid., 150.

30. Thomas A. Keaney and Eliot A. Cohen. *Gulf War Air Power Survey Summary Report.* Washington, DC: U.S. Government Printing Office, 1993, 5.

31. Mark David Mandeles, Thomas Hone, and Sanford S. Terry. *Managing "Command and Control" in the Persian Gulf War.* Westport, CT: Praeger, 1996, 3. The authors have an excellent discussion of CENTAF structure and the reorganization of December 1990 at 23–27.

32. Ibid., 123.

33. See Patricia Weitsman. "With a Little Help from our Friends? The Costs of Coalition Warfare." *Origins: Current Events in Historical Perspective,* vol. 2, no. 4, January 2009. Accessed 5/25/13. http://origins.osu.edu/article/little-help-our-friends-costs-coalition-warfare.

34. De la Billière said that he and Schwarzkopf made a conscious effort not to let this stand in the way of effective cooperation. In the aftermath of the nine British soldiers being killed by U.S. forces, de la Billière said to Schwarzkopf, "I want to make it quite clear this is not going to stand between the British and the Americans in terms of the effective prosecution of the war." Accessed 2/12/2012. http://www.pbs.org/wgbh/pages/frontline/gulf/oral/billiere/3.html.

35. Thomas A. Keaney and Eliot A. Cohen. *Gulf War Air Power Survey Summary Report.* Washington, DC: U.S. Government Printing Office, 1993, 60.

36. Public Broadcasting Service. Accessed 2/12/2012. http://www.pbs.org/wgbh/pages/frontline/gulf/oral/billiere/3.html.

37. Public Broadcasting Service. Accessed 2/14/2012. http://www.pbs.org/wgbh/pages/frontline/gulf/oral/horner/5.html.

38. Thomas A. Keaney and Eliot A. Cohen. *Gulf War Air Power Survey Summary Report.* Washington, DC: U.S. Government Printing Office, 1993, 131–132, 135, 156–157.

See also the following, accessed 2/12/2012: http://www.pbs.org/wgbh/pages/frontline/gulf/oral/schwarzkopf/5.html.

39. Thomas A. Keaney and Eliot A. Cohen. *Gulf War Air Power Survey Summary Report*. Washington, DC: U.S. Government Printing Office, 1993, 148–150. The reason for the decision to transmit these reports electronically was the use of the computer-assisted force management system. See John Paul Hyde, Johann W. Pfeiffer, and Toby C. Logan. "CAFMS Goes to War." Alan D. Campen, ed. *The First Information War*. Fairfax, VA: Armed Forces Communications and Electronic Association International Press, 1992. See also Mark David Mandeles, Thomas Hone, and Sanford S. Terry. *Managing "Command and Control" in the Persian Gulf War*. Westport, CT: Praeger, 1996, 27–33, 45–58.

40. For a summary of the changes, see Mark David Mandeles, Thomas Hone, and Sanford S. Terry. *Managing "Command and Control" in the Persian Gulf War*. Westport, CT: Praeger, 1996, Table 3-3, 50–51.

41. Thomas A. Keaney and Eliot A. Cohen. *Gulf War Air Power Survey Summary Report*. Washington, DC: U.S. Government Printing Office, 1993, 159. Interestingly, the British then were losing a disproportionate share of aircraft and lives and sought to fly higher, even if doing so meant less accuracy in hitting targets. In addition, it turned out that an older plane, nearing the end of its life cycle, wound up being more effective for prosecuting the war than the newer JBG233. See the following, accessed 2/12/2012: http://www.pbs.org/wgbh/pages/frontline/gulf/oral/billiere/2.html. For a slightly different version of events that suggests that the United States asked the RAF to take on this task, see the following, accessed 2/14/2012: http://www.pbs.org/wgbh/pages/frontline/gulf/oral/glosson/1.html.

42. My thanks to Daniel Baltrusaitis for pointing this out.

43. See Mark David Mandeles, Thomas Hone, and Sanford S. Terry. *Managing "Command and Control" in the Persian Gulf War*. Westport, CT: Praeger, 1996, 15.

44. Thomas A. Keaney and Eliot A. Cohen. *Gulf War Air Power Survey Summary Report*. Washington, DC: U.S. Government Printing Office, 1993, 220.

45. Public Broadcasting Service. Accessed 2/13/2012. http://www.pbs.org/wgbh/pages/frontline/gulf/oral/schwarzkopf/5.html.

46. Major Dean S. Mills. "Coalition Interoperability: An International Adventure." *Air and Space Power Journal*. 1995–1998. Accessed 2/23/2012. http://www.airpower.au.af.mil/airchronicles/cc/mills.html.

47. This is not to say that asymmetries were not felt or perceived by coalition partners. See Khaled bin Sultan. *Desert Warrior*. New York: HarperCollins, 1995. In this text, Khaled bin Sultan wrote that he saw one of his key roles as "making sure our all-powerful American allies did not swallow us up" (32) and that he wanted to resist a situation in which an "American was the all-powerful supreme commander who could do what he liked" (37). To this end, Khaled bin Sultan insisted that every meeting he had with Schwarzkopf take place in Khaled bin Sultan's office (192–193). See chapter 18 for his

discussion of being the "junior" partner in the war. For initial U.S. concerns over burden sharing and the constraints of multilateralism, see Richard N. Haass. *War of Necessity, War of Choice: A Memoir of Two Iraq War*. New York: Simon and Schuster, 2009, 89.

48. CENTCOM. "Operation Desert Shield/Desert Storm, Executive Summary." Declassified 1991, 1.

49. Thomas A. Keaney and Eliot A. Cohen. *Gulf War Air Power Survey Summary Report*. Washington, DC: U.S. Government Printing Office, 1993, 181–182.

50. Ibid., 197, 210.

51. Department of Defense. *Final Report to Congress: Conduct of the Persian Gulf War*. Washington, DC, 1992, 59–60. Appendix P of this report (723–731) provides detailed information about the financial and in-kind assistance contributed by coalition partners.

52. U.S. General Accounting Office. "Operation Desert Shield/Desert Storm: Update on Costs and Funding Requirements," GAO/NSIAD-92-194. May 1992, 2. Incremental rather than total costs are a better estimate of costs incurred by the United States. Total costs include those things the United States would be paying for even if Operations Desert Shield and Desert Storm had not been undertaken (e.g., regular pay of active-duty military personnel). Incremental costs are those costs that are incurred specifically because of the operations (e.g., imminent-danger pay to reservists, less normal drill pay). See ibid. For a discussion of the unique contributions of Saudi Arabia, Khaled bin Sultan. *Desert Warrior*. New York: HarperCollins, 1995, chapter 17; in contrast, see H. Norman Schwarzkopf. *It Doesn't Take a Hero*. New York: Bantam, 1992, chapters 19–20.

53. CENTCOM. "Operation Desert Shield/Desert Storm, Executive Summary." Declassified, 1991, 1. For troop deployments by country, see Katsuaki L. Terasawa and William. R. Gates. "Burden-Sharing in the Persian Gulf: Lessons Learned and Implications for the Future." *Defense Analysis*, vol. 2, no. 9, August 1993, 171–195.

54. See ibid.

55. See ibid..

56. See ibid.

57. Patricia A. Weitsman. "The High Price of Friendship." *New York Times*. August 31, 2006. This happened to some extent in the Persian Gulf War as well, but not nearly to the same degree.

58. Alexander Thompson. *Channels of Power: The UN Security Council and U.S. Statecraft in Iraq*. Ithaca, NY: Cornell University Press, 2009, 61.

59. Ibid., 61–62, 81–82.

60. Katsuaki L. Terasawa and William. R. Gates. "Burden-Sharing in the Persian Gulf: Lessons Learned and Implications for the Future." *Defense Analysis*, vol. 2, no. 9, August 1993, 171–195.

61. Andrew Bennett, Joseph Lepgold, and Danny Unger. "Burden Sharing in the Persian Gulf War." *International Organization*, vol. 48, no. 1, January 1994, 39–75.

62. Richard N. Haass. *War of Necessity, War of Choice: A Memoir of Two Iraq Wars.* New York: Simon and Schuster, 2009, 130.

63. See Michael N. Barnett's extremely interesting discussion of Arab identity and sovereignty following the Gulf War. "Regional Security after the Gulf War." *Political Science Quarterly*, vol. 111, no. 4, Winter 1996–1997, 597–618.

64. Alexander Thompson. *Channels of Power: The UN Security Council and U.S. Statecraft in Iraq.* Ithaca, NY: Cornell University Press, 2009, 80.

65. For the specific question of airpower effectiveness, see Thomas A. Keaney and Eliot A. Cohen. *Gulf War Air Power Survey Summary Report.* Washington, DC: U.S. Government Printing Office, 1993, 55–120. For an excellent review of whether the Gulf War represented a revolution in American military affairs, see Keith L. Shimko. *The Iraq Wars and America's Military Revolution.* New York: Cambridge University Press, 2010. See also Stephen Biddle. *Military Power: Explaining Victory and Defeat in Modern Battle.* Princeton, NJ: Princeton University Press, 2006; Daryl Press, "The Myth of Air Power in the Gulf War." *International Security*, vol. 26, no. 2, fall 2001, 5–44; John Mueller. "The Perfect Enemy: Assessing the Gulf War." *Security Studies*, vol. 5, no. 1, August 1995, 77–117.

66. Thomas A. Keaney and Eliot A. Cohen. *Gulf War Air Power Survey Summary Report.* Washington, DC: U.S. Government Printing Office, 1993, 47–48.

67. Ibid., 52.

68. Ibid., 158.

69. John Mueller. "The Perfect Enemy: Assessing the Gulf War." *Security Studies*, vol. 5, no. 1, August 1995, 77–117. See also John Mueller. *Policy and Opinion in the Gulf War.* Chicago: University of Chicago Press, 1994.

70. See, e.g., Thomas A. Keaney and Eliot A. Cohen. *Gulf War Air Power Survey Summary Report.* Washington, DC: U.S. Government Printing Office, 1993.

71. John Mueller. "The Perfect Enemy: Assessing the Gulf War." *Security Studies*, vol. 5, no. 1, August 1995, 77–117.

72. On the principal U.S. war aims, see Presidential Directive 54. January 15, 1991. Accessed 2/16/2012, http://bushlibrary.tamu.edu/research/pdfs/nsd/nsd54.pdf. See also Richard N. Haass. *War of Necessity, War of Choice: A Memoir of Two Iraq Wars.* New York: Simon and Schuster, 2009, 73, 115. For the initial Saudi position, see Haass, *War of Necessity*, 79–80.

73. See Public Broadcasting Service, accessed 2/13/2012: http://www.pbs.org/wgbh/pages/frontline/gulf/oral/billiere/1.html.

74. See ibid.

75. Ibid. There is also interesting discussion here of de la Billière, Paddy Hine, and Andy Massey prevailing on Schwarzkopf to use British Special Forces despite his reservations.

76. Public Broadcasting Service. Accessed 2/29/2012. http://www.pbs.org/wgbh/pages/frontline/gulf/script_b.html.

77. Public Broadcasting Service. Accessed 2/14/2012. http://www.pbs.org/wgbh/pages/frontline/gulf/oral/glosson/1.html.

78. Public Broadcasting Service. Accessed 2/13/2012. http://www.pbs.org/wgbh/pages/frontline/gulf/oral/schwarzkopf/1.html. See also Keith L. Shimko. *The Iraq Wars and America's Military Revolution*. New York: Cambridge University Press, 2010, 53.

79. Public Broadcasting Service. Accessed 2/13/2012. http://www.pbs.org/wgbh/pages/frontline/gulf/oral/schwarzkopf/1.html. See also Richard N. Haass. *War of Necessity, War of Choice: A Memoir of Two Iraq Wars*. New York: Simon and Schuster, 2009, 70. Cf. Alexander Thompson. "Coercion Through International Organizations: The Security Council and Logic of Information Transmission." *International Organization*, vol. 60, no. 3, January 2006, 1–34. See also Alexander Thompson. *Channels of Power: The UN Security Council and U.S. Statecraft in Iraq*. Ithaca, NY: Cornell University Press, 2009. In the former work, Thompson argues that King Fahd "strenuously resisted U.S. assistance" and that the Gulf states had deep reservations about a strong American presence in the region (17–18).

80. Department of Defense. *Final Report to Congress: Conduct of the Persian Gulf War*. Washington, DC: Department of Defense, 1992, 570. On cultural diversity in military teams, see Antoon J. van Vliet and Danielle van Amelsfoort. "Multinational Military Teams." Angela R. Febbraro, Brian McKee, and Sharon L. Riedel, eds. *Multinational Military Operations and Intercultural Factor*. Doc. No. RTO-TR-HFM-120. NATO Research and Technology Organisation. Findings of Research Task Group 120. November 2008, 4-1–4-16.

81. See, for example, Richard N. Haass. *War of Necessity, War of Choice: A Memoir of Two Iraq Wars*. New York: Simon and Schuster, 2009, 117–120.

82. Nora Bensahel. *The Coalition Paradox: The Politics of Military Cooperation*. Ph.D. diss., Stanford University, 1999, 60–61; U.S. Department of Defense. *Final Report to Congress: Conduct of the Persian Gulf War*. Washington, DC, 1992, 494, 559. Bensahel compellingly argues that one of the most important reasons the coalition worked was because of the ineffectiveness of Iraqi troops on the ground.

83. Mark David Mandeles, Thomas Hone, and Sanford S. Terry. *Managing "Command and Control" in the Persian Gulf War*. Westport, CT: Praeger, 1996, 15, 19.

84. Ibid., 22–23. For more on Glosson's account of the war, see the following: accessed 2/14/2012. http://www.pbs.org/wgbh/pages/frontline/gulf/oral/glosson/1.html.

85. Nora Bensahel. *The Coalition Paradox: The Politics of Military Cooperation*. Ph.D. diss., Stanford University, 1999, 90; George Bush, with Brent Scowcroft. *A World Transformed*. New York: Alfred A. Knopf, 1998, 342.

86. Khaled bin Sultan. *Desert Warrior*. New York: HarperCollins, 1995, 32, 265. Cf. Khaled bin Sultan's account of his "duels" with French Minister of Defense Chevènement (*Desert Warrior*. New York: HarperCollins, 1995, chapter 26).

87. For Schwarzkopf's account of the differences between U.S. and Saudi wishes regarding the retaking of Khafji, see, e.g., the following: accessed 2/13/2012. http://www .pbs.org/wgbh/pages/frontline/gulf/oral/schwarzkopf/4.html.

88. Richard N. Haass. *War of Necessity, War of Choice: A Memoir of Two Iraq Wars*. New York: Simon and Schuster, 2009, 130.

89. William Rosenau. *Special Operations Forces and Elusive Enemy Ground Targets: Lessons from Vietnam and the Persian Gulf War*. Santa Monica, CA: Rand, 2001, 29–44. See also Storer H. Rowley. "Frustrated Pilots Step Up Scud Hunt." *Chicago Tribune*. February 26, 1991. Accessed 12/14/2012. http://articles.chicagotribune.com/1991-02-26/ news/9101180561_1_scud-hunt-saudi-arabia-launch. My thanks to Stephen Saideman for underscoring the importance of the Scud hunt for coalition cohesion.

90. Mark Thompson. "Iraq: The Great Scud Hunt." *Time Magazine*. December 23, 2002. Accessed 12/14/2012. http://www.time.com/time/magazine/article/0,9171,1003916- 1,00.html.

91. R. W. Apple Jr. "War in the Gulf: Scud Attack; Scud Missile Hits a U.S. Barracks, Killing 27." *New York Times*. February 26, 1991. Accessed 12/14/2012. http://www.nytimes .com/1991/02/26/world/war-in-the-gulf-scud-attack-scud-missile-hits-a-us-barracks- killing-27.html.

92. Public Broadcasting Service. Accessed 2/13/2012. http://www.pbs.org/wgbh/ pages/frontline/gulf/oral/billiere/4.html.

93. Richard N. Haass. *War of Necessity, War of Choice: A Memoir of Two Iraq Wars*. New York: Simon and Schuster, 2009, 71–72. See also his discussion of the "international community" and near unanimity in world opinion that military force should not be used to alter borders or undermine sovereignty (132–133).

94. George Bush, with Brent Scowcroft. *A World Transformed*. New York: Alfred A. Knopf, 1998, chapter 17.

95. For details of the complexities of Arab public opinion toward Iraq, Saddam Hussein, and the Gulf War, see, e.g., Shibley Telhami. "Arab Public Opinion and the Gulf War." *Political Studies Quarterly*, vol. 108, no. 3, fall 1993, 437–452. For the complexities of polling in the United States before the Gulf War, see John Mueller. "American Public Opinion and the Gulf War: Some Polling Issues." *Public Opinion Quarterly*, vol. 57, no. 1, spring 1993, 80–91.

96. Alexander Thompson. "Coercion Through International Organizations: The Security Council and the Logic of Information Transmission." *International Organization*, vol. 60, no. 1, January 2006, 1–34; Alexander Thompson. *Channels of Power: The UN Security Council and U.S. Statecraft in Iraq*. Ithaca, NY: Cornell University Press, 2009. Thompson does an exceptional job detailing the mechanisms that underpin the relationship between the use of international organizations and legitimacy. His work is foundational to the ideas here.

97. Alexander Thompson. "Coercion Through International Organizations: The Security Council and the Logic of Information Transmission." *International Organization*, vol. 60, no. 1, January 2006, 1–34; Alexander Thompson. *Channels of Power: The UN Security Council and U.S. Statecraft in Iraq*. Ithaca, NY: Cornell University Press, 2009.

98. Gallup Poll Organization. "Gallup Poll Finds Public Highly Supportive of War." January 20, 1991. *Baltimore Sun*. Accessed 2/17/2012. http://articles.baltimoresun. com/1991-01-20/news/1991020034_1_war-job-approval-americans. The poll was conducted by "telephone interviews with a randomly selected national sample of 766 adults, 18 and older, conducted between Jan. 17 and 18, 1991. For results based on samples of this size, one can say with 95 percent confidence that the error attributable to sampling and other random effects could be plus or minus 4 percentage points."

99. Pew Research Center for the People and the Press. "Public Confidence in War Effort Falters: But Support for War Holds Steady." March 25, 2003. Accessed 2/17/2012. http://www.people-press.org/2003/03/25/public-confidence-in-war-effort-falters/#rally-effect-less-than-in-gulf-war.

100. Alexander Thompson. "Coercion Through International Organizations: The Security Council and the Logic of Information Transmission." *International Organization*, vol. 60, no. 1, January 2006, 25.

101. Ibid., 25–26.

102. John Mueller. *Policy and Opinion in the Gulf War*. Chicago: University of Chicago Press, 1994, 32, especially See also Tables 57 and 58, 219.

103. Alexander Thompson. *Channels of Power: The UN Security Council and U.S. Statecraft in Iraq*. Ithaca, NY: Cornell University Press, 2009, 82–83.

104. Alexander Thompson. "Coercion Through International Organizations: The Security Council and the Logic of Information Transmission." *International Organization*, vol. 60, no. 1, January 2006, 1–34; Alexander Thompson. *Channels of Power: The UN Security Council and U.S. Statecraft in Iraq*. Ithaca, NY: Cornell University Press, 2009.

105. John Mueller. *Policy and Opinion in the Gulf War*. Chicago: University of Chicago Press, 1994, 217–222.

106. Ibid., 8; George Bush, with Brent Scowcroft. *A World Transformed*. New York: Alfred A. Knopf, 1998, chapter 15.

107. George Bush, with Brent Scowcroft. *A World Transformed*. New York: Alfred A. Knopf, 1998, chapter 15.

108. John Mueller. *Policy and Opinion in the Gulf War*. Chicago: University of Chicago Press, 1994, 8.

Chapter 4

1. Tim Youngs, Mark Oakes, and Paul Bowers. *Kosovo: NATO and Military Action*. Research Paper No. 99/34. March 24, 1999. London: House of Commons Library, 8.

2. Ibid., 8–19.

3. Belgium, Canada, Czech Republic, Denmark, France, Germany, Greece, Hungary, Iceland, Italy, Luxembourg, the Netherlands, Norway, Poland, Portugal, Spain, Turkey, the United Kingdom, and the United States. The three newest member states, Czech Republic, Hungary, and Poland, became full members of NATO less than two weeks before Operation Allied Force began. See Benjamin S. Lambeth. *NATO's Air War for Kosovo: A Strategic and Operational Assessment.* Santa Monica, CA: Rand, 2001, 10.

4. Ibid., 12. See also William M. Arkin. "Operation Allied Force: The Most Precise Application of Air Power in History." Andrew J. Bacevich and Eliot A. Cohen, eds. "Introduction: Strange Little War." *War over Kosovo: Politics and Strategy in a Global Age.* New York: Columbia University Press, 2001, 1–37.

5. W. K. Clark. *Waging Modern War: Bosnia, Kosovo, and the Future of Combat.* New York: Public Affairs, 2002, 168–169. The decision to fight an air war was highly consequential and resulted in exacerbated conflict on the ground. On Clark's failure to anticipate this response, see Michael Ignatieff. *Virtual War: Kosovo and Beyond.* New York: Macmillan, 2001, 96.

6. Daily reports on developments during the campaign. Accessed 3/1/2012. http://www.nato.int/kosovo/all-frce.htm.

7. See Patricia A. Weitsman. *Dangerous Alliances: Proponents of Peace, Weapons of War.* Stanford, CA: Stanford University Press, 2004.

8. Secretary of Defense William S. Cohen and Joint Chiefs of Staff General Henry H. Shelton. "Joint Statement on Kosovo After Action Review." To Senate Armed Services Committee. October 14, 1999. Accessed 3/1/2012. http://www.au.af.mil/au/awc/awcgate/kosovoaa/jointstmt.htm.

9. Ibid.

10. For details on this, as well as how the consensus mechanism works, see Paul Gallis. "NATO's Decision-Making Process." Congressional Research Service Report for Congress. Order Code RS21510. Updated May 5, 2003.

11. NATO. "The Military Committee." Accessed 3/13/2012. http://www.nato.int/cps/en/natolive/topics_49633.htm.

12. In 2003, SHAPE and SACLANT were transformed into Atlantic Command Operations (ACO) and Atlantic Command Transformation (ACT). See NATO. "Atlantic Command Transformation." Accessed 8/31/12. http://www.nato.int/cps/en/natolive/topics_52092.htm?selectedLocale=en.

13. Benjamin S. Lambeth. *NATO's Air War for Kosovo: A Strategic and Operational Assessment.* Santa Monica, CA: Rand, 2001, 207.

14. Secretary of Defense William S. Cohen and Joint Chiefs of Staff General Henry H. Shelton. "Joint Statement on Kosovo After Action Review." To Senate Armed Services Committee. October 14, 1999. Accessed 3/1/2012. http://www.au.af.mil/au/awc/awcgate/kosovoaa/jointstmt.htm.

15. Benjamin S. Lambeth. *NATO's Air War for Kosovo: A Strategic and Operational Assessment.* Santa Monica, CA: Rand, 2001, 185.

16. John Peters, Stuart Johnson, Nora Bensahel, Timothy Liston, and Traci Williams. *European Contributions to Operation Allied Force.* Santa Monica, CA: Rand, 2001, 25–26.

17. Ibid., 28.

18. Paul C. Strickland. "USAF Aerospace—Power Doctrine: Decisive or Coercive? NATO's War over Kosovo, Yugoslavia: The Role of Air Power." *Aerospace Power Journal,* vol. 14, no. 3, fall 2000, 13–25.

19. John Peters, Stuart Johnson, Nora Bensahel, Timothy Liston, and Traci Williams. *European Contributions to Operation Allied Force.* Santa Monica, CA: Rand, 2001, 26. Cf. Secretary of Defense William S. Cohen and Joint Chiefs of Staff General Henry H. Shelton. "Joint Statement on Kosovo After Action Review." To Senate Armed Services Committee. October 14, 1999. Accessed 3/1/2012. http://www.au.af.mil/au/awc/awcgate/kosovoaa/jointstmt.htm. Cohen and Shelton asserted that during the campaign, mechanisms were developed to delegate target approval authority to military commanders, although political authorities retained control of targets that had the risk of high collateral damage. According to Cohen and Shelton, this was a "flexible mechanism for meeting the military requirements of the campaign while preserving the necessary level of political oversight."

20. Public Broadcasting Service. PBS *Frontline* interview with Lieutenant General Short. Accessed 3/6/2012. http://www.pbs.org/wgbh/pages/frontline/shows/kosovo/interviews/short.html.

21. Ibid.

22. Within countries there was dissension, of course, as well. For a discussion of civil-military relations in the United States during the Kosovo operation, see Andrew J. Bacevich. "Neglected Trinity: Kosovo and the Crisis in U.S. Civil-Military Relations." Andrew J. Bacevich and Eliot A. Cohen, eds. *War over Kosovo: Politics and Strategy in a Global Age.* New York: Columbia University Press, 2001, 155–188.

23. Benjamin S. Lambeth. *NATO's Air War for Kosovo: A Strategic and Operational Assessment.* Santa Monica, CA: Rand, 2001. 185.

24. John Peters, Stuart Johnson, Nora Bensahel, Timothy Liston, and Traci Williams. *European Contributions to Operation Allied Force.* Santa Monica, CA: Rand, 2001, 40.

25. Ibid.

26. Nora Bensahel. *The Counterterror Coalitions: Cooperation with Europe, NATO, and the European Union.* Santa Monica, CA: Rand, 2003; Benjamin S. Lambeth. *NATO's Air War for Kosovo: A Strategic and Operational Assessment.* Santa Monica, CA: Rand, 2001, 204–208.

27. Wesley K. Clark. *Waging Modern War: Bosnia, Kosovo, and the Future of Combat.* New York: Public Affairs, 2002, 175–176.

28. Ibid., 385.

29. Joseph Fitchett. "Top U.S. General Calls Command Standoff in Kosovo 'Troubling': Disobeying Orders: NATO Veil Lifted." *International Herald Tribune.* September 11, 1999.

30. Wesley Clark. *Waging Modern War: Bosnia, Kosovo, and the Future of Combat.* New York: Public Affairs, 2002, 396.

31. Ibid.

32. Ibid., 396–399.

33. Michael W. Lamb Sr. *Operation Allied Force: Golden Nuggets for Future Campaigns.* Air War College. Maxwell Paper No. 27. August. Maxwell Air Force Base: Air Force University Press, 2002, 20.

34. My thanks to Daniel Baltrusaitis for making this point about the comparability of friendly-fire incidents case to case; when no ground troops are involved, clearly friendly-fire episodes are not comparable to cases in which ground troops are committed.

35. Secretary of Defense William S. Cohen and Joint Chiefs of Staff General Henry H. Shelton. "Joint Statement on Kosovo After Action Review." To Senate Armed Services Committee. October 14, 1999. Accessed 3/1/2012. http://www.au.af.mil/au/awc/awcgate/kosovoaa/jointstmt.htm.

36. U.S. Department of Defense. "Report to Congress: Kosovo/Operation Allied Force After-Action Report." January 31, 2000. 25.

37. A normal day during Operation Allied Force saw perhaps five hundred aircraft taking off from forty-seven bases across Europe, refueling midair, undertaking bombing missions, refueling again, returning, and taking off for another bombing mission, for a total of some thirty-five thousand sorties. James A. Kitfield. "Another Look at the Air War That Was." *Air Force Magazine,* vol. 82, no. 10, October 1999, 39–43.

38. John A. Tirpak. "The NATO Way of War." *Air Force Magazine,* vol. 82, no. 12, December 1999, 24–27.

39. John Peters, Stuart Johnson, Nora Bensahel, Timothy Liston, and Traci Williams. *European Contributions to Operation Allied Force.* Santa Monica, CA: Rand, 2001, 18–24.

40. Michael W. Lamb Sr. *Operation Allied Force: Golden Nuggets for Future Campaigns.* Air War College. Maxwell Paper No. 27. August. Maxwell Air Force Base: Air Force University Press, 2002, 2.

41. Prepared Statement of the Honorable William S. Cohen, Secretary of Defense, to the Senate Armed Services Committee Hearing on Operation Allied Force. April 15, 1999, 2.

42. U.S. General Accountability Office. "Military Operations: Some Funds for Fiscal Year 1999. Contingency Operations Will Be Available for Future Needs." GAO/NSIAD-99-244BR. Washington, DC, September 1999, 2.

43. U.S. General Accountability Office. "Kosovo Air Operations: Need to Maintain Alliance Cohesion Resulted in Doctrinal Departures." GAO-01-784. Washington, DC, July 2001, 3.

44. U.S. General Accountability Office. "European Security: U.S. and European Contributions to Foster Stability and Security in Europe." GAO-02-174. Washington, DC, November 2001, 1.

45. Ibid., 51.

46. U.S. Department of Defense. *Allied Contributions to the Common Defense: A Report to the United States Congress by the Secretary of Defense.* Washington, DC. March 2001, chapter 2.

47. Elinor Sloan. "DCI: Responding to the U.S.-Led Revolution in Military Affairs." *NATO Review*, vol. 48, no. 1, spring–summer 2000, 4.

48. Ibid., 4–7; John Peters, Stuart Johnson, Nora Bensahel, Timothy Liston, and Traci Williams. *European Contributions to Operation Allied Force.* Santa Monica, CA: Rand, 2001, 56–57.

49. U.S. Department of Defense. "Report to Congress: Kosovo/Operation Allied Force After-Action Report." January 31, 2000, 2.

50. Ibid., 24–25.

51. For example, the French. See Pierre Martin and Mark R. Brawley, eds. *Alliance Politics, Kosovo, and NATO's War: Allied Force or Forced Allies?* New York: Palgrave Macmillan, 2000, 5.

52. Public Broadcasting Service. *Frontline* interview with Secretary of State Madeleine Albright. Accessed 3/13/2012. http://www.pbs.org/wgbh/pages/frontline/shows/kosovo/interviews/albright.html; Madeleine Albright. *Madam Secretary: A Memoir.* New York: Hyperion Press, 2003, 281.

53. On the implications of Kosovo for American grand strategy and as a departure from the traditional way of war, see Eliot S. Cohen's "Kosovo and the New American Way of War" and James Kurth's "First War of the Global Era: Kosovo and U.S. Grand Strategy," in Andrew J. Bacevich and Eliot A. Cohen, eds. *War over Kosovo: Politics and Strategy in a Global Age.* New York: Columbia University Press, 2001, 38–96. For a discussion of the United States' moral commitment to in Kosovo, see in the same volume Alberto R. Coll. "Kosovo and the Moral Burdens of Power," 124–154.

54. Charles A. Kupchan. "Kosovo and the Future of U.S. Engagement in Europe." Pierre Martin and Mark R. Brawley, eds. *Alliance Politics, Kosovo, and NATO's War: Allied Force or Forced Allies?* New York: Palgrave Macmillan, 2000, 76–77.

55. Louise Richardson. "A Force for Good in the World? Britain's Role in the Kosovo Crisis." Pierre Martin and Mark R. Brawley, eds. *Alliance Politics, Kosovo, and NATO's War: Allied Force or Forced Allies?* New York: Palgrave Macmillan, 2000, 145–164.

56. Pierre Martin and Mark R. Brawley, eds. *Alliance Politics, Kosovo, and NATO's War: Allied Force or Forced Allies?* New York: Palgrave MacMillan, 2000, 3–5, especially 229 for a chart of allied reactions. See also in the same volume Alex Macleod. "France: Kosovo and the Emergence of a New European Security," 113–130; David G. Haglund. "Allied Force or Forced Allies? The Allies' Perspective," 91–92. In the same volume, Kim

Richard Nossal and Stéphane Roussel. "Canada and the Kosovo War: The Happy Follower," argue that most U.S. allies were entrapped by U.S. decision making rather than motivated by fears of abandonment (see 182, 186–189), though in this case the United States did not pressure Canada in that regard.

57. Milada Anna Vachudová. "The Atlantic Alliance and the Kosovo Crisis: The Impact of Expansion and the Behavior of New Allies." Pierre Martin and Mark R. Brawley, eds. *Alliance Politics, Kosovo, and NATO's War: Allied Force or Forced Allies?* New York: Palgrave Macmillan, 2000, 204–205.

58. Charles A. Kupchan. "Kosovo and the Future of U.S. Engagement in Europe." Pierre Martin and Mark R. Brawley, eds. *Alliance Politics, Kosovo, and NATO's War: Allied Force or Forced Allies?* New York: Palgrave Macmillan, 2000, 84.

59. See Peter Rudolf. "Germany and the Kosovo Conflict." Pierre Martin and Mark R. Brawley, eds. *Alliance Politics, Kosovo, and NATO's War: Allied Force or Forced Allies?* New York: Palgrave Macmillan, 2000, 132.

60. U.S. Department of Defense. "Report to Congress: Kosovo/Operation Allied Force After-Action Report." January 31, 2000. xiv.

61. Michael W. Lamb Sr. *Operation Allied Force: Golden Nuggets for Future Campaigns.* Air War College. Maxwell Paper No. 27. August. Maxwell Air Force Base: Air Force University Press, 2002, 1.

62. Secretary of Defense Cohen and Chairman of the Joint Chiefs of Staff Shelton. "Joint Statement on Kosovo After-Action Review." To Senate Armed Services Committee. October 14, 1999, 1. See the rest of that report for more details on which aspects of the campaign were most successful. Accessed 3/1/2012. http://www.au.af.mil/au/awc/awcgate/kosovoaa/jointstmt.htm.

63. John Mueller makes this argument in the context of the Gulf War, in "The Perfect Enemy: Assessing the Gulf War." *Security Studies*, vol. 5, no. 1, August 1995, 77–117. See also Andrew J. Bacevich and Eliot A. Cohen. "Introduction: Strange Little War." Andrew J. Bacevich and Eliot A. Cohen, eds. *War over Kosovo: Politics and Strategy in a Global Age.* New York: Columbia University Press, 2001, ix.

64. U.S. General Accountability Office. "Kosovo Air Operations: Need to Maintain Alliance Cohesion Resulted in Doctrinal Departures." GAO-01-784. Washington, DC, July 2001, 6.

65. Ibid., 4. See also Secretary of Defense William Cohen's interview with PBS's *Frontline.* Accessed 3/6/2012. http://www.pbs.org/wgbh/pages/frontline/shows/kosovo/interviews/cohen.html.

66. Peter Rudolf. "Germany and the Kosovo Conflict." Pierre Martin and Mark R. Brawley, eds. *Alliance Politics, Kosovo, and NATO's War: Allied Force or Forced Allies?* New York: Palgrave Macmillan, 2000, 137.

67. Public Broadcasting Service. PBS *Frontline* interview with General Wesley Clark. Accessed 3/6/2012. http://www.pbs.org/wgbh/pages/frontline/shows/kosovo/

interviews/clark.html. See also NATO's Military Committee Chairman General Klaus Naumann's interview. Accessed 3/6/2012. http://www.pbs.org/wgbh/pages/frontline/ shows/kosovo/interviews/naumann.html; Philip Everts. "War Without Bloodshed? Public Opinion and the Conflict over Kosovo." Philip Everts and Pierangelo Isernia, eds. *Public Opinion and the International Use of Force*. London: Routledge, 2001, 234–238.

68. Public Broadcasting Service. PBS *Frontline* interview with UK Prime Minister Tony Blair. Accessed 3/6/2012. http://www.pbs.org/wgbh/pages/frontline/shows/kosovo/ interviews/blair.html.

69. See Louise Richardson. "A Force for Good in the World? Britain's Role in the Kosovo Crisis." Pierre Martin and Mark R. Brawley, eds. *Alliance Politics, Kosovo, and NATO's War: Allied Force or Forced Allies?* New York: Palgrave Macmillan, 2000, 148.

70. Public Broadcasting Service. PBS *Frontline* interview with General Wesley Clark. Accessed 3/6/2012. http://www.pbs.org/wgbh/pages/frontline/shows/kosovo/interviews/ clark.html.

71. Public Broadcasting Service. PBS *Frontline* interview with NATO's Military Committee chairman, Klaus Naumann. Accessed 3/6/2012. http://www.pbs.org/wgbh/ pages/frontline/shows/kosovo/interviews/naumann.html.

72. U.S. Department of Defense. "Report to Congress: Kosovo/Operation Allied Force After-Action Report." January 31, 2000.

73. Ibid., xvii.

74. Public Broadcasting Service. PBS *Frontline* interview with General Wesley Clark. Accessed 3/6/2012. http://www.pbs.org/wgbh/pages/frontline/shows/kosovo/interviews/ clark.html.

75. Michael W. Lamb Sr. *Operation Allied Force: Golden Nuggets for Future Campaigns*. Air War College. Maxwell Paper No. 27. August. Maxwell Air Force Base: Air Force University Press, 2002, 4.

76. Prepared Statement of the Honorable William S. Cohen, Secretary of Defense, to the Senate Armed Services Committee Hearing on Operation Allied Force. April 15, 1999, 1. On this view that Milošević's strategy would be to "wait out" NATO or divide it, see Andrew Bacevich and Eliot A. Cohen, eds. *War over Kosovo: Politics and Strategy in a Global Age*. New York: Columbia University Press, 2001, 10.

77. For details on the planning, see William M. Arkin. "Operation Allied Force: The Most Precise Application of Air Power in History." Andrew J. Bacevich and Eliot A. Cohen, eds. *War over Kosovo: Politics and Strategy in a Global Age*. New York: Columbia University Press, 2001, 1–37.

78. Public Broadcasting Service. Interview with Secretary of Defense William Cohen. Accessed 3/20/2012. http://www.pbs.org/wgbh/pages/frontline/shows/kosovo/inter views/cohen.html.

79. Thanks to Nora Bensahel for pointing this out.

80. See, for example, U.S. Department of Defense. "Report to Congress: Kosovo/ Operation Allied Force After-Action Report." January 31, 2000; as well as Secretary of Defense William Cohen's interview with PBS *Frontline.* Accessed 3/6/2012. http://www .pbs.org/wgbh/pages/frontline/shows/kosovo/interviews/cohen.html.

81. The action took place on the eve of NATO's fiftieth anniversary—the symbolism here certainly underscores the fact that there was an ideological component to this mission, even if strategic concerns prevailed.

82. For an excellent analysis about the degree to which states value their alliances and the consequences, see Jason Davidson. *America's Allies and War: Kosovo, Afghanistan, and Iraq.* New York: Palgrave Macmillan, 2011.

83. U.S. General Accountability Office. "Kosovo Air Operations: Need to Maintain Alliance Cohesion Resulted in Doctrinal Departures." GAO-01-784. Washington, DC, July 2001.

84. Public Broadcasting Service. PBS *Frontline* interview with Secretary of Defense William Cohen. Accessed 3/8/2012. http://www.pbs.org/wgbh/pages/frontline/shows/ kosovo/interviews/cohen.html.

85. See Thomas George Weiss. *Humanitarian Intervention: Ideas in Action.* Cambridge, UK: Polity, 2007.

86. See, e.g., Alberto R. Coll. "Kosovo and the Moral Burdens of Power." Andrew J. Bacevich and Eliot A. Cohen, eds. *War over Kosovo: Politics and Strategy in a Global Age.* New York: Columbia University Press, 2001, 124–154.

87. Louis Henkin. "Kosovo and the Law of 'Humanitarian Intervention.'" *American Journal of International Law,* vol. 93, no. 4, October 1999, 825. See also Alan K. Henrikson. "The Constraint of Legitimacy: The Legal and Institutional Framework of Euro-Atlantic Security." Pierre Martin and Mark R. Brawley, eds. *Alliance Politics, Kosovo, and NATO's War: Allied Force or Forced Allies?* New York: Palgrave Macmillan, 2000, 41–55. Henrikson writes that the argument that the previous UN resolutions implicitly authorized force is weak because the language of the resolutions, "additional measures" was understood to indicate that the UN Security Council would have to authorize any further action (48).

88. United Nations. "Security Council Demands All Parties End Hostilities and Maintain a Ceasefire in Kosovo." Accessed 3/9/2012. http://www.un.org/News/Press/ docs/1998/19980923.sc6577.html; United Nations. "Security Council Imposes Arms Embargo on Federal Republic of Yugoslavia, Pending Action to Resolve Kosovo Crisis." Accessed 3/9/2012. http://www.un.org/News/Press/docs/1998/19980331.SC6496.html.

89. United Nations. "UN Resolution 1203 (1998)." Accessed 3/19/2012. http://www .un.org/peace/kosovo/98sc1203.htm.

90. Louis Henkin. "Kosovo and the Law of 'Humanitarian Intervention.'" *American Journal of International Law,* vol. 93, no. 4, October 1999, 825.

91. Ibid.

92. Pierre Martin and Mark R. Brawley, eds. *Alliance Politics, Kosovo, and NATO's War: Allied Force or Forced Allies?* New York: Palgrave Macmillan, 2000, 3.

93. Alan K. Henrikson. "The Constraint of Legitimacy: The Legal and Institutional Framework of Euro-Atlantic Security." Pierre Martin and Mark R. Brawley, eds. *Alliance Politics, Kosovo, and NATO's War: Allied Force or Forced Allies?* New York: Palgrave Macmillan, 2000, 42.

94. Ibid., 50.

95. See, e.g., Alex Macleod. "France: Kosovo and the Emergence of a New European Security." Pierre Martin and Mark R. Brawley, eds. *Alliance Politics, Kosovo, and NATO's War: Allied Force or Forced Allies?* New York: Palgrave Macmillan, 2000, 118.

96. Public Broadcasting Service. "Rising Concern." Accessed 3/9/2012. http://www.pbs.org/newshour/bb/europe/jan-june99/regional_5-18.html.

97. Mark Gillespie. "Crisis in Kosovo: Questions and Answers About American Public Opinion." *Gallup News Service.* April 16, 1999. Accessed 3/12/2012. http://www.gallup.com/poll/3925/Crisis-Kosovo-Questions-Answers-About-American-Public-Opinion.aspx.

98. Kim Richard Nossal and Stéphane Roussel. "Canada and the Kosovo War: The Happy Follower." Pierre Martin and Mark R. Brawley, eds. *Alliance Politics, Kosovo, and NATO's War: Allied Force or Forced Allies?* New York: Palgrave Macmillan, 2000, 191.

99. Philip Everts. "War Without Bloodshed? Public Opinion and the Conflict over Kosovo." Philip Everts and Pierangelo Isernia, eds. *Public Opinion and the International Use of Force.* London: Routledge 2001, 234.

100. Mark Gillespie. "Crisis in Kosovo: Questions and Answers About American Public Opinion." *Gallup News Service.* April 16, 1999. Accessed 3/12/2012. http://www.gallup.com/poll/3925/Crisis-Kosovo-Questions-Answers-About-American-Public-Opinion.aspx.

101. Philip Everts. "War Without Bloodshed? Public Opinion and the Conflict over Kosovo." Philip Everts and Pierangelo Isernia, eds. *Public Opinion and the International Use of Force.* London: Routledge, 2001, 224.

102. Polish citizens favored NATO intervention 54 percent to 31 percent; Hungarians were split 48 percent to 41 percent in favor of military action. Philip Everts. "War Without Bloodshed? Public Opinion and the Conflict over Kosovo." Philip Everts and Pierangelo Isernia, eds. *Public Opinion and the International Use of Force.* London: Routledge 2001, 232.

103. Philip Everts. "War Without Bloodshed? Public Opinion and the Conflict over Kosovo." Philip Everts and Pierangelo Isernia, eds. *Public Opinion and the International Use of Force.* London: Routledge 2001, 234.

104. Ibid., 232.

105. Ibid., 241.

106. See, e.g., Alberto R. Coll. "Kosovo and the Moral Burdens of Power." Andrew J. Bacevich and Eliot A. Cohen, eds. *War over Kosovo: Politics and Strategy in a Global Age.* New York: Columbia University Press, 2001, 141–147.

107. Philip Everts. "War Without Bloodshed? Public Opinion and the Conflict over Kosovo." Philip Everts and Pierangelo Isernia, eds. *Public Opinion and the International Use of Force.* London: Routledge 2001, 242, 249–250.

108. Alexander Thompson. *Channels of Power: The UN Security Council and U.S. Statecraft in Iraq.* Ithaca, NY: Cornell University Press, 2009.

109. Pierre Martin and Mark R. Brawley, eds. *Alliance Politics, Kosovo, and NATO's War: Allied Force or Forced Allies?* New York: Palgrave Macmillan, 2000, 2.

110. Philip Everts. "War Without Bloodshed? Public Opinion and the Conflict over Kosovo." Philip Everts and Pierangelo Isernia, eds. *Public Opinion and the International Use of Force.* London: Routledge 2001, 233, 241.

111. Ibid., 251.

Chapter 5

1. Sarah Kreps. *Coalitions of Convenience: United States Military Interventions After the Cold War.* New York: Oxford University Press, 2011; David Malone. "Uncle Sam's Coalition of One." *Globe and Mail* (Toronto). December 11, 2001.

2. Benjamin S. Lambeth. *Air Power Against Terror: America's Conduct of Operation Enduring Freedom.* Santa Monica, CA: Rand, 2005, 24–25.

3. Bob Woodward. *Bush at War.* New York: Simon and Shuster, 2002, 45.

4. Quoted in Bob Woodward. *Bush at War.* New York: Simon and Shuster, 2002, 45.

5. See, e.g., Sarah Kreps. *Coalitions of Convenience: United States Military Interventions After the Cold War.* New York: Oxford University Press, 2011; David Malone. "Uncle Sam's Coalition of One." *Globe and Mail* (Toronto). December 11, 2001; Pew Research Center Poll. "Bush's Ratings Improve, But He's Still Seen as Unilateralist: Americans and Europeans Differ Widely on Foreign Policy Issues." April 17, 2002. Accessed 8/26/10. http://pewglobal .org/2002/04/17/americans-and-europeans-differ-widely-on-foreign-policy-issues.

6. Benjamin S. Lambeth. *Air Power Against Terror: America's Conduct of Operation Enduring Freedom.* Santa Monica, CA: Rand, 2005, 55.

7. UK Parliament. "Operation Enduring Freedom and the Conflict in Afghanistan: An Update." Research Paper No. 01/81. October 31, 2001. House of Commons Library, 10, 26–27.

8. Ibid., 27; House of Commons Debate. Armed Forces Deployment. October 26, 2001, col. 550.

9. House of Commons Debate. September 14, 2001. "International Terrorism and the Attacks in the USA," col. 607; UK Parliament. "11 September 2001: The Response." Research Paper No. 01/72. October 3, 2001, 23.

10. Julian Borger and Richard Norton-Taylor. "US Special Forces Cross the Border into Afghanistan: Small Units Behind the Lines Search for al-Qaida Targets." *The Guardian.* October 19, 2001. Accessed 1/10/2013. http://www.guardian.co.uk/world/2001/oct/20/afghanistan.terrorism6; UK Parliament. "11 September 2001: The Response." Research Paper No. 01/72. October 3, 2001, 97. As early as September 23, there were reports of British Special Air Service troops clashing with Taliban forces in Afghanistan. BBC News. "SAS Clash with Taliban." September 23, 2001. See also Macer Hall, Philip Sherwell, and Christina Lamb. "SAS to join American Special Forces." *Telegraph.* September 16, 2001. Lambeth raises the possibility that this was British disinformation. Benjamin S. Lambeth. *Air Power Against Terror: America's Conduct of Operation Enduring Freedom.* Santa Monica, CA: Rand, 2005, 70. The CIA and Special Forces were on the ground in the territory controlled by the Northern Alliance to help the Northern Alliance organize against the Taliban. My thanks to Roshan Noorzai for pointing this out.

11. More specifically, these countries and organizations were Afghanistan, Albania, Armenia, Australia, Austria, Azerbaijan, Bahrain, Bangladesh, Belgium, Bosnia, Brazil, Bulgaria, Canada, Chile, Cyprus, Czech Republic, Denmark, Egypt, the European Union, Finland, France, Georgia, Germany, Ghana, Greece, the Gulf Cooperation Council, Hungary, Iceland, India, Indonesia, Ireland, Israel, Iran, Italy, Japan, Jordan, Kazakhstan, Kuwait, Kyrgyzstan, Latvia, Luxembourg, Mexico, Moldova, NATO, the Netherlands, New Zealand, Nicaragua, Norway, Oman, the Organization of American States, Pakistan, the Palestinian Authority, the People's Republic of China, the Philippines, Poland, Portugal, Qatar, Republic of the Congo, Romania, Russia, Saudi Arabia, Slovakia, South Korea, Spain, Sudan, Sweden, Tajikistan, Thailand, Turkey, Turkmenistan, Ukraine, the United Kingdom, the United Nations, Uzbekistan, Venezuela, and Yemen. For details regarding each country's and organization's offer of assistance, see David J. Gerleman, Jennifer E. Stevens, and Steven A. Hildreth. "Operation Enduring Freedom: Foreign Pledges of Military and Intelligence Support." CRS Report for Congress. Library of Congress. Order Code RL31152. October 17, 2001.

12. David J. Gerleman, Jennifer E. Stevens, and Steven A. Hildreth. "Operation Enduring Freedom: Foreign Pledges of Military and Intelligence Support." CRS Report for Congress. Library of Congress. Order Code RL31152. October 17, 2001, 2.

13. David J. Gerleman, Jennifer E. Stevens, and Steven A. Hildreth. "Operation Enduring Freedom: Foreign Pledges of Military and Intelligence Support." CRS Report for Congress. Library of Congress. Order Code RL31152. October 17, 2001, 3.

14. Ibid., 4. France had close relationships with some groups in Afghanistan fighting the Taliban, particularly Ahmad Shah Masood, the central resistance leader against the Taliban, who was killed just before the 9/11 attacks. My thanks to Roshan Noorzai for pointing this out.

15. See ibid.; see also UK Parliament. "11 September 2001: The Response." Research Paper No. 01/72. October 3, 2001.

16. White House. Office of the Press Secretary. October 7, 2001. Statement by the President. Accessed 6/1/13. http://georgewbush-whitehouse.archives.gov/news/releases/2001/10/20011007-8.html.

17. For a detailed outline of country-by-country contributions as of June 2002, see Anthony Cordesman. *The Lessons of Afghanistan: Warfighting, Intelligence, and Force Transformation.* Washington, DC: Center for Strategic and International Studies, 2002, 82–100.

18. UK Ministry of Defense. "Defeating International Terrorism: Campaign Objectives." December 3, 2001. Accessed 7/6/2010. http://webarchive.nationalarchives.gov.uk/+/http://www.operations.mod.uk/veritas/faq/objectives.htm. This case is an important and interesting one of alliance restraint in regard to the relationship between the United States and the Northern Alliance. For excellent work and analytical discussion of alliance restraint, see Jeremy Pressman. *Warring Friends: Alliance Restraint in International Politics.* Ithaca, NY: Cornell University Press, 2008.

19. Benjamin S. Lambeth. *Air Power Against Terror: America's Conduct of Operation Enduring Freedom.* Santa Monica, CA: Rand, 2005, 61. See Patricia A. Weitsman. "Wartime Alliances Versus Coalition Warfare: How Institutional Structure Matters in the Multilateral Prosecution of Wars." *Strategic Studies Quarterly,* vol. 4, no. 2, summer 2010, 113–136. On the extensive support necessary from coalition partners to get Operation Enduring Freedom going, see Benjamin S. Lambeth. *Air Power Against Terror: America's Conduct of Operation Enduring Freedom.* Santa Monica, CA: Rand, 2005, 66–69.

U.S. Army. "The United States Army in Afghanistan: Operation Enduring Freedom, October 2001–March 2002." U.S. Army Center for Military History Pub. No. 70-83-1; Rand National Defense Research Institute. "Operation Enduring Freedom: An Assessment." Research brief, RB-9148-CENTAF (2005) Santa Monica, CA: Rand, 2005.

20. U.S. Army. "The United States Army in Afghanistan: Operation Enduring Freedom, October 2001–March 2002." U.S. Army Center for Military History Pub. No. 70-83-1; Rand National Defense Research Institute. "Operation Enduring Freedom: An Assessment." Research brief, RB-9148-CENTAF (2005). Santa Monica, CA: Rand, 2005.

21. Max Boot. "The New American Way of War." *Foreign Affairs,* vol. 82, no. 4, July–August 2003, 52.

22. Benjamin S. Lambeth. *Air Power Against Terror: America's Conduct of Operation Enduring Freedom.* Santa Monica, CA: Rand, 2005, 109.

23. My thanks to Roshan Noorzai for this point.

24. Bob Woodward. *Bush at War.* New York: Simon and Shuster, 2002, 51.

25. Benjamin S. Lambeth. *Air Power Against Terror: America's Conduct of Operation Enduring Freedom.* Santa Monica, CA: Rand, 2005, 153–160.

26. Nora Bensahel. *The Counterterror Coalitions: Cooperation with Europe, NATO, and the European Union.* Santa Monica, CA: Rand, 2003, 55–63.

27. Tommy Franks. *American Soldier.* New York: HarperCollins, 2004, 270–271.

28. My thanks to Roshan Noorzai for underscoring this point.

29. Raynell Andreychuk. "219 PC 10 E BIS-Alliance Cohesion." NATO Parliamentary Assembly, Annual Session in Warsaw: Committee Reports, 2010. Accessed 8/12/2010. http://www.nato-pa.int/Default.asp?SHORTCUT=2078.

30. Lolita C. Baldor. "Pentagon Pays to Train, Equip Afghan Partners." Associated Press. April 1, 2010. Accessed 5/8/2012. http://www.airforcetimes.com/news/2010/04/ap_afghanistan_partners_040110. This article details the congressional caps on spending on allies in Afghanistan and how the money was allocated. In addition to the six countries mentioned, Yemen was a major recipient.

31. Patricia Weitsman. "The High Price of Friendship." *New York Times.* August 31, 2006. Accessed 5/8/2012. http://www.nytimes.com/2006/08/31/opinion/31iht-edweit.2653587.html.

32. Michael J. McNerney. "Stabilization and Reconstruction in Afghanistan: Are PRTs a Model or a Muddle?" *Parameters*, vol. 35, no. 4, winter 2005–2006, 32.

33. NATO. "ISAF in Afghanistan, History." Accessed 8/13/2010. http://www.isaf.nato.int/history.html. See also David P. Auerswald and Stephen M. Saideman. *NATO in Afghanistan: Fighting Together, Fighting Alone.* Princeton, NJ: Princeton University Press, 2014; Stephen M. Saideman and David P. Auerswald. "Comparing Caveats: Understanding the Sources of National Restrictions upon NATO's Mission in Afghanistan." *International Studies Quarterly*, vol. 56, no. 1, March 2012, 67–84.

34. Vincent Morelli and Paul Belkin. "NATO in Afghanistan: A Test of the Transatlantic Alliance." Congressional Research Service Report No. 7-5700. December 3, 2009.

35. Media Operations Centre. NATO HQ. "NATO in Afghanistan: Master Narrative as of 6 October 2008," 13. Accessed 8/13/2010. http://file.wikileaks.org/file/nato-master-narrative-2008.pdf.

36. Ali Jalali. "The Future of Afghanistan." *Parameters*, vol. 36, no. 1, spring 2006, 10.

37. See Raynell Andreychuk. "219 PC 10 E BIS-Alliance Cohesion." NATO Parliamentary Assembly 055 PC 10 E. 2010 Spring Session. Accessed 8/12/2010. http://www.nato-pa.int/Default.asp?SHORTCUT=2078. David P. Auerswald and Stephen M. Saideman. *NATO in Afghanistan: Fighting Together, Fighting Alone.* Princeton, NJ: Princeton University Press, 2014. These authors do an exceptional job detailing the national versus multilateral objectives and assessing each country by state type. See also Stephen M. Saideman and David P. Auerswald. "Comparing Caveats: Understanding the Sources of National Restrictions upon NATO's Mission in Afghanistan." *International Studies Quarterly*, vol. 56, no. 1, March 2012, 67–84; Vincent Morelli and Paul Belkin. "NATO in Afghanistan: A Test of the Transatlantic Alliance." Congressional Research Service No. 7-5700. December 3, 2009, 10–12.

38. Ralf Beste, Konstantin von Hammerstein, and Alexander Szandar. "Shrinking Solidarity in Afghanistan? Debate Flares Anew About German Military Mission."

Der Spiegel. May 28, 2007. Accessed 8/17/10. http://www.spiegel.de/international/germany/0,1518,485289,00.html. For an exceptional discussion of the chain of command, see David P. Auerswald and Stephen M. Saideman. *NATO in Afghanistan: Fighting Together, Fighting Alone.* Princeton, NJ: Princeton University Press, 2014, chapter 2.

39. NATO and ISAF. "International Security Assistance Force (ISAF): Key Facts and Figures." Accessed 4/28/2012. http://www.isaf.nato.int/images/stories/File/2012-01-23%20ISAF%20Placemat-final.pdf.

40. The German Marshall Fund of the United States, "Transatlantic Trends 2009 Partners." Accessed 6/1/13. http://trends.gmfus.org/files/archived/doc/2009_English_Key.pdf.

41. CIA Red Cell. Red Cell Special Memorandum. "Afghanistan: Sustaining West European Support for the NATO-Led Mission—Why Counting on Apathy Might Not Be Enough." March 11, 2010. Accessed 8/16/10. http://file.wikileaks.org/file/cia-afghanistan.pdf.

42. Raynell Andreychuk. "219 PC 10 E BIS-Alliance Cohesion." NATO Parliamentary Assembly 2010 Spring Session. Accessed 8/12/2010. http://www.nato-pa.int/Default.asp?SHORTCUT=2078.

43. Paul Reynolds. "Aims of the London Conference on Afghanistan." BBC News. January 28, 2010. Accessed 8/17/10. http://news.bbc.co.uk/2/hi/south_asia/8480368.stm.

44. Raynell Andreychuk. "219 PC 10 E BIS-Alliance Cohesion." NATO Parliamentary Assembly 2010 Spring Session. Accessed 8/12/2010. http://www.nato-pa.int/Default.asp?SHORTCUT=2078.

45. UN Office on Drugs and Crime. Extract from Conference Communiqué. January 28, 2010. Accessed 8/17/10. http://www.unodc.org/afghanistan/en/Events/london-conference-january-2010.html. For the full communiqué, see the following: accessed 8/17/10. http://centralcontent.fco.gov.uk/central-content/afghanistan-hmg/resources/pdf/conference/Communique-final.

46. UK National Archives. "Kabul Conference." Accessed 8/17/10. http://afghanistan.hmg.gov.uk/en/conference.

47. Vincent Morelli and Paul Belkin. "NATO in Afghanistan: A Test of the Transatlantic Alliance." Congressional Research Service No. 7-5700. December 3, 2009, 17. See also Judy Dempsey and David S. Cloud. "Europeans Balking at New Afghan Role." *New York Times.* September 14, 2005.

48. Michael J. McNerney. "Stabilization and Reconstruction in Afghanistan: Are PRTs a Model or a Muddle?" *Parameters,* vol. 35, no. 4, winter 2005–2006, 32. See also the ISAF PRT Handbook, 4th ed. Accessed 8/18/2010. https://www.cimicweb.org/Documents/PRT%20CONFERENCE%202010/PRT%20Handbook%20Edition%204.pdf.

49. Vincent Morelli and Paul Belkin. "NATO in Afghanistan: A Test of the Transatlantic Alliance." Congressional Research Service No. 7-5700. December 3, 2009, 17–18. This is just one example of many.

50. Richard A. Oppel and Rod Nordland. "U.S. Is Reining in Special Operations Forces in Afghanistan." *New York Times.* March 15, 2010. See also Michael Innes. "A New Command Structure in Afghanistan." *Foreign Policy.* March 18, 2010. Accessed 8/18/2010. http://afpak.foreignpolicy.com/posts/2010/03/18/a_new_command_structure_in_afghanistan. Stephen Castle. "U.S. Gains More Control as It Fights Afghan War." *New York Times.* June 11, 2009. See also Carlotta Gall and David E. Sanger. "Civilian Deaths Undermine Allies' War on Taliban." *New York Times.* May 13, 2007.

51. Ian Hope. "Unity of Command in Afghanistan: A Forsaken Principle of War." March 15. Carlisle, PA: U.S. Army War College, 2008, 14.

52. Norman Friedman. *Terrorism, Afghanistan, and America's New Way of War.* Annapolis, MD: Naval Institute Press, 2003, 164; Anthony H. Cordesman. *The Lessons of Afghanistan: War Fighting, Intelligence, and Force Transformation.* Washington, DC: Center for Strategic and International Studies, 2002, 74.

53. Ian Hope. "Unity of Command in Afghanistan: A Forsaken Principle of War." March 15. Carlisle, PA: U.S. Army War College, 2008, 22.

54. See Michael Innes. "A New Command Structure in Afghanistan." *Foreign Policy.* March 18, 2010. Accessed 8/24/2010. http://afpak.foreignpolicy.com/posts/2010/03/18/a_new_command_structure_in_afghanistan. Christopher Lamb and Martin Cinnamond. "Unity of Effort: Key to Success in Afghanistan." *Strategic Forum,* no. 248, October 2009. Washington, DC, Institute for National Strategic Studies, National Defense University, 1–12; Steven Erlanger. "NATO Reorganizes Afghan Command Structure." *New York Times.* August 4, 2009.

55. Michael Hastings. "The Runaway General." *Rolling Stone Magazine.* June 22, 2010.

56. WikiLeaks. "Afghan War Diary." Accessed 8/24/10. http://wikileaks.org/wiki/Afghan_War_Diary,_2004-2010. See also Nick Davies. "Afghanistan War Logs: Task Force 373—Special Forces Hunting Top Taliban: Previously Hidden Details of US-Led Unit Sent to Kill Top Insurgent Targets are Revealed for the First Time." *The Guardian.* July 25, 2010. Accessed 8/24/10. http://www.guardian.co.uk/world/2010/jul/25/task-force-373-secret-afghanistan-taliban.

57. ISAF, "ISAF Command Structure." Accessed 6/7/13. http://www.isaf.nato.int/isaf-command-structure.html.

58. By my own count. For a record of the number and circumstances of coalition fatalities of Operation Enduring Freedom, see http://www.cnn.com/SPECIALS/2004/oef.casualties/.

59. James Sturcke. "Decorated British Soldier was 'Killed by Nato Bullet.'" *The Guardian.* November 29, 2009. Accessed 6/21/2012. http://www.guardian.co.uk/afghanistan/story/0,,2219061,00.html.

60. The friction even comes out in the graffiti on bathroom walls in Afghanistan. See Graeme Smith. "The War on the Walls." *Globe and Mail* (Toronto). November 29, 2007.

61. David Leigh. "Afghan War Logs: Friendly Fire Deaths Plagued Invasion from the Start: British Soldiers Both Perpetrators and Victims in Repeated Cases of Deadly Confusion Among Allies." *The Guardian*. July 25, 2010. Accessed 8/26/10. http://www .guardian.co.uk/world/2010/jul/25/friendly-fire-deaths-toll-afghanistan. For more on the British in Helmand Province, see Theo Farrell. "Improving in War: Military Adaptation and the British in Helmand Province, Afghanistan, 2006–2009." *Journal of Strategic Studies*, vol. 33, no. 4, August 2010, 567–594; Theo Farrell. "Appraising Moshtarak: The Campaign in Nad-e-Ali District, Helmand." London, Royal United Service Institute (RUSI) Briefing Note. June 2010.

62. Data from WikiLeaks. Image developed by Alastair Dant and David Leigh. "Afghanistan War Logs." *The Guardian*. July 25, 2010. Accessed 8/26/10. http://www.guardian .co.uk/world/datablog/interactive/2010/jul/25/afghanistan-war-logs-events. See also the following, accessed 8/26/10: http://wardiary.wikileaks.org/afg/sort/type/friendly_fire_0 .html. For all cables on friendly fire in Afghanistan, see the following, accessed 4/27/2012: http://wikileaks.org/afg/sort/category/blue_blue_0.html and http://wikileaks.org/afg/ sort/type/friendly_fire_0.html. See also Joanna Chiu. "Canada, Wikileaks, and 'Friendly Fire,'" *Seaword Magazine*. December 8, 2010. Accessed 12/19/2012. http://seawordmag .com/2010/12/08/canada-wikileaks-and-friendly-fire.

63. See David P. Auerswald and Stephen M. Saideman. *NATO in Afghanistan: Fighting Together, Fighting Alone*. Princeton, NJ: Princeton University Press, 2014; Stephen M. Saideman and David P. Auerswald. "Comparing Caveats: Understanding the Sources of National Restrictions upon NATO's Mission in Afghanistan." *International Studies Quarterly*, vol. 56, no. 1, March 2012, 67–84.

64. "The Afghanistan Mission Network (AMN): Reaping the Rewards of Network-Enabled Operations." 2011. Accessed 4/27/2012. http://www.nc3a.nato.int/SiteCollection Documents/GM's%20Koblenz%20IT%20Speech%202011%20reviewed%20GM.pdf. See also Anthony H. Cordesman. *The Lessons of Afghanistan: War Fighting, Intelligence, and Force Transformation*. Washington, DC: Center for Strategic and International Studies, 2002, 81.

65. "The Afghanistan Mission Network (AMN): Reaping the Rewards of Network-Enabled Operations." 2011. Accessed 4/27/2012. http://www.nc3a.nato.int/SiteCollec tionDocuments/GM's%20Koblenz%20IT%20Speech%202011%20reviewed%20GM .pdf. See also NATO. "Interoperability for Joint Operations." Accessed 4/27/2012. http:// www.nato.int/docu/interoperability/interoperability.pdf. NATO Parliamentary Assembly. 177 STC 06 E. "Interoperability: The Need for Transatlantic Harmonisation." http:// www.nato-pa.int/default.asp?SHORTCUT=1004. See also Barry Rosenberg. "Battlefield Network Connects Allied Forces in Afghanistan: Commanders Can Access Dozens of Critical Warfighting Applications." September 14, 2010. Accessed 4/29/2012. http:// defensesystems.com/articles/2010/09/02/c4isr-2-afghan-mission-network-connects-allies.aspx.

66. David P. Auerswald and Stephen M. Saideman. *NATO in Afghanistan: Fighting Together, Fighting Alone.* Princeton, NJ: Princeton University Press, 2014.; Stephen M. Saideman and David P. Auerswald. "Comparing Caveats: Understanding the Sources of National Restrictions upon NATO's Mission in Afghanistan." *International Studies Quarterly*, vol. 56, no. 1, March 2012, 67–84.

67. Anthony H. Cordesman. *The Lessons of Afghanistan: War Fighting, Intelligence, and Force Transformation.* Washington, DC: Center for Strategic and International Studies, 2002, 82.

68. For details, see ibid., 82–100.

69. United Press International. "Obama, NATO's Rasmussen Discuss End of Combat in Afghanistan." May 31, 2013. Accessed 6/2/13. http://www.upi.com/Top_News/US/2013/05/31/Obama-NATOs-Rasmussen-discuss-end-of-combat-in-Afghanistan/UPI-13701369987200/. See also Matthew Rosenberg. "Karzai Says U.S. Bases Can Stay, Raising Some Eyebrows in West." *New York Times.* May 9, 2013. Accessed 6/2/13. http://www.nytimes.com/2013/05/10/world/asia/karzai-says-us-can-keep-afghan-bases-after-2014.html. Devin Dwyer, Jonathan Karl, and Luis Martinez. "Obama, Karzai Say U.S. Will Transition to Support Role in Afghanistan." ABC World News. January 11, 2013. Accessed 6/1/13. http://abcnews.go.com/Politics/OTUS/president-obama-hamid-karzai-us-combat-operations-afghanistan/story?id=18190529; Michael R. Gordon and Mark Landler. "Decision on Afghan Troop Levels Calculates Political and Military Interests." *New York Times.* February 12, 2013. Accessed 6/1/13. http://www.nytimes.com/2013/02/13/us/politics/obama-to-announce-troops-return.html?_r=0. Associated Press. "NATO to Discuss Post-2014 Afghan War Commitments, but Not Release Final Troop Numbers." *Washington Post.* June 4, 2013. Accessed 6/8/13

70. NATO and ISAF. "International Security Assistance Force (ISAF): Key Facts and Figures." Accessed 4/30/2012. http://www.nato.int/isaf/docu/epub/pdf/placemat.pdf. This is a larger proportion than in the earlier days of ISAF. In February 2008, 15,000 of the total 43,250 ISAF troops were U.S. troops. NATO. "International Security Assistance Force." Accessed 8/27/10. http://www.nato.int/isaf/docu/epub/pdf/placemat_archive/isaf_placemat_080206.pdf. There are and have been troops deployed outside of Afghanistan for OEF. See Amy Belasco. "Troop Levels in the Afghan and Iraq Wars, FY2011–FY2012: Cost and Other Potential Issues." July 2, 2009. Congressional Research Service. CRS Report for Congress No. R40682. Accessed 4/28/2012. http://www.fas.org/sgp/crs/natsec/R40682.pdf.

71. Bob Woodward. *Bush at War.* New York: Simon and Schuster, 2002, 172–173. On the critical importance of the cooperation of Uzbekistan at the outset of OEF, see also Tommy Franks. *American Soldier.* New York: HarperCollins, 2004, 255–256.

72. Todd Harrison. "Analysis of the FY 2012 Defense Budget." Center for Strategic and Budgetary Assessments, vi. Accessed 4/29/2012. http://www.csbaonline.org/wp-content/uploads/2011/07/2011.07.16-FY-2012-Defense-Budget.pdf.

73. Amy Belasco. "The Cost of Iraq, Afghanistan, and Other Global War on Terror Operations Since 9/11." Congressional Research Service. CRS Report for Congress No. 7-5700. March 29, 2011, ii. Accessed 4/29/2012. http://www.fas.org/sgp/crs/natsec/RL33110.pdf.

74. "Afghan War 'Has Cost the UK £17 Bn.'" *Defence Management Journal*. April 25, 2012. Accessed 4/29/2012. http://www.defencemanagement.com/news_story.asp?id=19568.

75. Ian McPhedran. "Each Soldier in Afghanistan Costs Taxpayers a Million Dollars." *Daily Telegraph*. January 18, 2012. Accessed 4/29/2012. http://www.dailytelegraph .com.au/news/each-soldier-in-afghanistan-costs-taxpayers-a-million-dollars/story-e6freuy9-1226246792609.

76. Tilman Brück, Olaf J. de Groot, and Friedrich Schneider. "The Economic Costs of the German Participation in the Afghanistan War." *Journal of Peace Research*, vol. 48, no. 6, November 2011, 3. The number in the text is the official German government estimate of spending up to 2012, though unofficial estimates place the number as high as 47 billion (or US$62.28 billion).

77. John Irish. "France Won't Cut Force in Afghanistan Despite 500 Million Euro Cost." Reuters. August 3, 2010. Accessed 11/28/2012. http://www.reuters.com/article/2010/08/03/idUSLDE6720DA. This number is based on official estimates of $500 million for fiscal 2010 provided by the French defense minister and reports of similar levels of spending for fiscal 2009–2012.

78. See David P. Auerswald and Stephen M. Saideman. *NATO in Afghanistan: Fighting Together, Fighting Alone*. Princeton, NJ: Princeton University Press, 2014; Stephen M. Saideman and David P. Auerswald. "Comparing Caveats: Understanding the Sources of National Restrictions upon NATO's Mission in Afghanistan." *International Studies Quarterly*, vol. 56, no. 1, March 2012, 67–84.

79. George W. Bush. *Decision Points*. New York: Crown Publishers, 2010, 212.

80. Ibid., 211.

81. My thanks to Daniel Baltrusaitis for making this point.

82. Laura Roselle. "Strategic Narratives of War: Fear of Entrapment and Abandonment During Protracted Conflict." 7th Pan-European International Relations Conference. Stockholm. September 2010, especially 19.

83. George W. Bush. *Decision Points*. New York: Crown Publishers, 2010, 192.

84. Mark Magnier and Kim Willsher. "France's Doubts on Afghanistan a Boon for Taliban." *Los Angeles Times*. January 20, 2012. Accessed 4/30/2012. http://articles.latimes .com/2012/jan/20/world/la-fg-afghan-deaths-20120121.

85. On the ways in which this withdrawal could be handled, see David Cortright. *Ending Obama's War: Responsible Military Withdrawal from Afghanistan*. Boulder, CO: Paradigm Publishers, 2011.

86. Laura Roselle. "Strategic Narratives of War: Fear of Entrapment and Abandonment During Protracted Conflict." 7th Pan-European International Relations Conference. Stockholm. September 2010.

87. Ibid. On this analogy, see Thomas H. Johnson and M. Chris Mason. "Refighting the Last War: Afghanistan and the Vietnam Template." *Military Review.* November–December 2009, 2–14.

88. See the preponderance of evidence in Laura Roselle. "Strategic Narratives of War: Fear of Entrapment and Abandonment During Protracted Conflict." 7th Pan-European International Relations Conference. Stockholm. September 2010.

89. "U.S. Delivers 'Powerful Commitment' to Afghanistan." *USA Today.* July 8, 2012. Accessed 7/13/2012. http://www.usatoday.com/news/washington/story/2012-07-06/clinton-afghanistan-karzai/56074534/1.

90. Matthew Rosenberg, "Karzai Says U.S. Bases Can Stay, Raising Some Eyebrows in West." *New York Times.* May 9, 2013. Accessed 6/2/13. http://www.nytimes.com/2013/05/10/world/asia/karzai-says-us-can-keep-afghan-bases-after-2014.html.

91. Ole Holsti, P. Terrence Hopmann, and John Sullivan. *Unity and Disintegration in International Alliances.* New York: John Wiley and Sons, 1973, 16; Patricia A. Weitsman. *Dangerous Alliances: Proponents of Peace, Weapons of War.* Stanford, CA: Stanford University Press, 2004, 35–36.

92. See UK Ministry of Defense. "Defeating International Terrorism: Campaign Objectives." House of Commons Library Deposited Paper. 01/1460. December 3, 2001; White House. Office of the Press Secretary. October 7, 2001. Statement by the president announcing military strikes in Afghanistan.

93. Richard B. Andres, Craig Willis, and Thomas E. Griffith Jr. "Winning with Allies: The Strategic Value of the Afghan Model." *International Security*, vol. 30, no. 3, winter 2005–2006, 124–160; Stephen D. Biddle. "Allies, Airpower, and Modern Warfare: The Afghan Model in Afghanistan and Iraq." *International Security*, vol. 30, no. 3, winter 2005–2006, 161–176.

94. My thanks to Roshan Noorzai for pointing this out. See Seth G. Jones. *Counterinsurgency in Afghanistan.* Santa Monica, CA: Rand, 2008.

95. Benjamin S. Lambeth. *Air Power Against Terror: America's Conduct of Operation Enduring Freedom.* Santa Monica, CA: Rand, 2005, 110–111.

96. My thanks to Roshan Noorzai for underscoring this point.

97. Benjamin S. Lambeth. *Air Power Against Terror: America's Conduct of Operation Enduring Freedom.* Santa Monica, CA: Rand, 2005, 112. As Roshan Noorzai pointed out to me, the United States was able to rescue Karzai, though not Haq. For an account of the mission of protecting Karzai in 2001, see Eric Blehm. *The Only Thing Worth Dying For.* New York: HarperCollins, 2010.

98. Benjamin S. Lambeth. *Air Power Against Terror: America's Conduct of Operation Enduring Freedom.* Santa Monica, CA: Rand, 2005, 147.

99. David Rohde. "A Nation Challenged: Kabul; British in Accord with Afghans on Force to Keep Order in Kabul." *New York Times.* December 19, 2001.

100. Michael R. Gordon. "A Nation Challenged: War Goals; One War, Differing Aims." *New York Times.* December 18, 2001.

101. Benjamin S. Lambeth. *Air Power Against Terror: America's Conduct of Operation Enduring Freedom.* Santa Monica, CA: Rand, 2005, 146. See also Norman Friedman. *Terrorism, Afghanistan, and America's New Way of War.* Annapolis, MD: Naval Institute Press, 2003, 200.

102. Raynell Andreychuk. "219 PC 10 E BIS-Alliance Cohesion." NATO Parliamentary Assembly Spring Session 2010.

103. Vincent Morelli and Paul Belkin. "NATO in Afghanistan: A Test of the Transatlantic Alliance." Congressional Research Service No. 7-5700. December 3, 2009, 18–30. See David P. Auerswald and Stephen M. Saideman *NATO in Afghanistan: Fighting Together, Fighting Alone.* Princeton, NJ: Princeton University Press, 2014; Stephen M. Saideman and David P. Auerswald. "Comparing Caveats: Understanding the Sources of National Restrictions upon NATO's Mission in Afghanistan." *International Studies Quarterly,* vol. 56, no. 1, March 2012, 67–84. It is notable that NATO has adapted and transformed according to changing missions. For an exceptional look at this dynamic in the context of Afghanistan, see Theo Farrell and Sten Rynning. "NATO's Transformation Gaps: Transatlantic Differences and the War in Afghanistan." *Journal of Strategic Studies,* vol. 33, no. 5, October 2010, 675–701.

104. Vincent Morelli and Paul Belkin. "NATO in Afghanistan: A Test of the Transatlantic Alliance." Congressional Research Service No. 7-5700. December 3, 2009, 26.

105. I am very grateful to Stephen Saideman for making this point.

106. President Bush's speech of October 7, 2001. Accessed 4/23/2012. http://www.pbs.org/newshour/terrorism/combating/bush_10-7.html.

107. Benjamin E. Goldsmith, Yusaku Horiuchi, and Takashi Inoguchi. "American Foreign Policy and Global Public Opinion: Who Supported the War in Afghanistan?" *Journal of Conflict Resolution,* vol. 49, no. 3, June 2005, 408–429. The authors indicate that people from sixty-three countries and regions were polled, but only sixty-two appear in the table with the data.

108. Ibid., 412. More specifically, only twenty-five of the sixty-two countries had 50 percent or more respondents answering in the affirmative to the question, "Do you personally agree or disagree with the United States military action in Afghanistan?" The single-choice answers available were the following: "agree with the U.S. military action," "disagree with the U.S. military action," and "don't know." There are additional limitations to inferences made on the basis of these data (see 412). For the misrepresentation of British support for the war in Afghanistan, see David Miller. "Opinion Polls and the Misrepresentation of Public Opinion on the War with Afghanistan." *Television and New Media,* vol. 3, no. 2, May 2002, 153–161.

109. Alexander Thompson. *Channels of Power: The UN Security Council and U.S. Statecraft in Iraq.* Ithaca, NY: Cornell University Press, 2009.

110. Pew Research Center. Pew Global Attitudes Project. "Support for War in Afghanistan," data from 2007, 2008, 2009, 2010, and 2011. The question posed was the fol-

lowing: "Do you think the U.S. and NATO should keep military troops in Afghanistan until the situation has stabilized, or do you think the U.S. and NATO should remove their troops as soon as possible?" Accessed 4/24/2012. http://www.pewglobal.org/database/?in dicator=9&survey=8&response=Keep%20troops%20in%20Afghanistan&mode=table.

111. USA Today/Gallup Poll Survey. "In U.S., Half Say U.S. Should Speed Up Afghanistan Withdrawal." March 15, 2012. Accessed 4/27/2012. http://www.gallup.com/ poll/153260/Half-Say-Speed-Afghanistan-Withdrawal.aspx. For troop levels, see Amy Belasco. "Troop Levels in the Afghan and Iraq Wars, FY2011–FY2012: Cost and Other Potential Issues." Congressional Research Service. CRS Report for Congress. July 2, 2009. Accessed 4/27/2012. http://www.fas.org/sgp/crs/natsec/R40682.pdf.

112. General Accountability Office. "Provincial Reconstruction Teams." October 1, 2008. GAO-09-86R, Accessed 4/24/2012. http://www.gao.gov/new.items/d0986r.pdf.

113. Joshua S. Fouts. "Public Diplomacy: Practitioners, Policy Makers, and Public Opinion." Report of the Diplomacy and World Public Opinion Forum. April 2006. Washington, DC, 27.

114. For the text of these resolutions, see the following: accessed 4/30/2012. http:// www.un.org/Docs/scres/2001/sc2001.htm.

115. See the following text: accessed 4/30/2012. http://www.un.org/News/dh/latest/ afghan/afghan-agree.htm.

116. George W. Bush. *Decision Points.* New York: Crown Publishers, 2010, 191, 207.

117. Ibid., 220.

118. Ibid., 192.

119. Ibid., 207.

120. Ibid., 212. See David P. Auerswald and Stephen M. Saideman. *NATO in Afghanistan: Fighting Together, Fighting Alone.* Princeton, NJ: Princeton University Press, 2014; Stephen M. Saideman and David P. Auerswald. "Comparing Caveats: Understanding the Sources of National Restrictions upon NATO's Mission in Afghanistan." *International Studies Quarterly,* vol. 56, no. 1, March 2012, 67–84. According to Brigadier General Yossi Kuperwasser of the Israel Defense Forces, Bush's second election was a validation of the legitimacy of action of previous four years. See "Battle for Hearts and Minds." Cable No. 04TELAVIV6505, from U.S. embassy in Tel Aviv. December 22, 2004. Accessed 4/27/2012. http://wikileaks.org/cable/2004/12/04TELAVIV6505.html.

121. Mark Moyar. "The L-Word in Afghanistan: Can the United States Provide What Kabul Needs?" *Foreign Affairs.* November 15, 2009; Jon Boone. "US-Afghan Relations Sink Further as Hamid Karzai Accused of Drug Abuse." *The Guardian.* April 7, 2010; "Afghan Elections: Negative Public Perception Overshadows Fraud Safeguards." Cable No. 09KABUL2295, from U.S. embassy in Kabul. August 10, 2009. Accessed 4/27/2012. http://cablegatesearch.net/cable.php?id=09KABUL2295&q=afghanistan%20legiti macy. "Afghans Divided over Presidential Election as Results Are Announced." Cable No. 09KABUL2765, from U.S. embassy in Kabul. September 10, 2009. Accessed 4/26/2012.

http://wikileaks.org/cable/2009/09/09KABUL2765.html. "Media Reaction: Afghanistan, NATO Mideast, U.S.-Climate, Western Hemisphere, Turkey, EU-Greece, Northern Ireland; Berlin." Cable No. 10BERLIN209, from U.S. embassy in Berlin. February 24, 2010. Accessed 4/27/2012. http://wikileaks.org/cable/2010/02/10BERLIN209.html. Judy Dempsey. "Karzai Seeks End to NATO Reconstruction Teams." *New York Times*. February 6, 2011; "National Front: Referendum on Karzai?" Cable No. 07KABUL919, from U.S. embassy in Kabul. March 20, 2007. Accessed 4/27/2012. http://wikileaks.org/cable/2007/03/07KABUL919.html. See also Thomas H. Johnson and M. Chris Mason. "Refighting the Last War: Afghanistan and the Vietnam Template." *Military Review*. November–December 2009, 4.

122. NATO. "NATO's Operational Mentor and Liaison Teams (OMLTs)." Accessed 4/27/2012. http://www.aco.nato.int/page26571951.aspx. For an overview, see NATO, Public Diplomacy Division, Press and Media Section, Media Operations Centre, NATO HQ Brussels. "Fact Sheet: NATO's Operational Mentor and Liaison Teams (OMLTs) October 2009." Accessed 6/2/13. http://www.nato.int/isaf/topics/factsheets/omlt-factsheet.pdf. See also David P. Auerswald and Stephen M. Saideman. *NATO in Afghanistan: Fighting Together, Fighting Alone*. Princeton, NJ: Princeton University Press, 2014; Stephen M. Saideman and David P. Auerswald. "Comparing Caveats: Understanding the Sources of National Restrictions upon NATO's Mission in Afghanistan." *International Studies Quarterly*, vol. 56, no. 1, March 2012, 67–84.

123. For an excellent description of the efforts to rebuild the Afghan National Army and Afghan National Police, see Terrence K. Kelly, Nora Bensahel, and Olga Oliker. *Security Force Assistance in Afghanistan: Identifying Lessons for Future Efforts*. Santa Monica, CA: Rand, 2011.

124. "Spain Raises OEF-ISAF Coordination with NATO." Cable No. 07USNATO302. May 14, 2007, released August 30, 2011. Accessed 4/26/2012. http://dazzlepod.com/cable/07USNATO302.

125. "Allies Receptive to Frank Presentation by Petraeus." Cable No. 09USNATO73, from U.S. NATO Mission. February 20, 2009. Accessed 4/27/2012. http://wikileaks.org/cable/2009/02/09USNATO73.html.

126. USA Today/Gallup Poll Survey. "In U.S., Half Say U.S. Should Speed Up Afghanistan Withdrawal." March 15, 2012. Accessed 4/27/2012. http://www.gallup.com/poll/153260/Half-Say-Speed-Afghanistan-Withdrawal.aspx.

127. See the following: all accessed 4/27/2012. "Hundreds of Slaughtered Civilians Isn't a 'Huge' Number for Obama." January 31, 2012. http://rt.com/usa/news/drones-civilian-death-obama-187. "Predator Drones and Unmanned Aerial Vehicles." *New York Times*. March 20, 2012. http://topics.nytimes.com/top/reference/timestopics/subjects/u/unmanned_aerial_vehicles/index.html. Dexter Filkins. "Operators of Drones Are Faulted in Afghan Deaths." *New York Times*. May 29, 2010. http://www.nytimes.com/2010/05/30/world/asia/30drone.html.

128. My thanks to Stephen Saideman and Daniel Baltrusaitis for pointing this out.

129. Anthony Cordesman. *The Lessons of Afghanistan: Warfighting, Intelligence, and Force Transformation.* Washington, DC: Center for Strategic and International Studies, 2002, 81.

Chapter 6

1. On the evolution of the Bush administration's thinking in this regard, see "Transcript of Private Hearing of Sir Anthony Brenton, KCMG, Minister, Washington DC (including Periods as Charge d'Affaires) January 2001–March 2004." Accessed 5/28/2012. http://www.iraqinquiry.org.uk/news/20110714-documentsreleased.aspx. See also Todd S. Purdum and Staff of the *New York Times. A Time of Our Choosing: America's War in Iraq.* New York: Times Books, Henry Holt and Company, 2003, especially 9–77.

2. For the text of the full speech, see the following: accessed 5/18/2012. http://articles.cnn.com/2001-09-20/us/gen.bush.transcript_1_joint-session-national-anthem-citizens?_s=PM:US.

3. For the text of this speech, see "Text of President Bush's 2002 State of the Union Address." Accessed 5/18/2012. http://www.washingtonpost.com/wp-srv/onpolitics/transcripts/sou012902.htm.

4. For the full text of this speech, see "Text of Bush's Speech at West Point." Accessed 5/18/2012. http://www.nytimes.com/2002/06/01/international/02PTEX-WEB.html?pagewanted=all.

5. *National Security Strategy September 2002* is available at the following: accessed 5/18/2012. http://georgewbush-whitehouse.archives.gov/nsc/nss/2002.

6. See "United Nations Security Council Resolution 1441 (2002)." Accessed 5/30/2013. http://www.un.org/depts/unmovic/documents/1441.pdf.

7. See "Authorization for Use of Military Force Against Iraq Resolution of 2002." Accessed 5/18/12. http://www.gpo.gov/fdsys/pkg/PLAW-107publ243/html/PLAW-107publ243.htm.

8. President Bush's State of the Union Address. January 28, 2003. Accessed 5/18/2012. http://www.washingtonpost.com/wp-srv/onpolitics/transcripts/bushtext_012803.html.

9. Project for a New American Century. "Statement of Principles." June 3, 1997. Accessed 7/13/2012. http://www.newamericancentury.org/statementofprinciples.htm.

10. Robert Kagan. "Multilateralism, American Style." *Washington Post.* September 3, 2002.

11. David P. Auerswald and Stephen M. Saideman. *NATO in Afghanistan: Fighting Together, Fighting Alone.* Princeton, NJ: Princeton University Press, 2014, chapter 1.

12. Bulgaria, Estonia, Latvia, Lithuania, Romania, Slovakia, and Slovenia. These countries formally acceded to the alliance on March 29, 2004. NATO. Accessed 5/21/2012. http://www.nato.int/docu/update/2004/03-march/e0329a.htm.

13. CNN. "Bush: Join 'Coalition of Willing.'" November 20, 2002. Accessed 5/21/2012. http://edition.cnn.com/2002/WORLD/europe/11/20/prague.bush.nato.

14. CNN. "Bush Declares War." March 19, 2003. Accessed 5/21/2012. http://articles.cnn.com/2003-03-19/us/sprj.irq.int.bush.transcript_1_coalition-forces-equipment-in-civilian-areas-iraqi-troops-and-equipment?_s=PM:US.

15. See Jason W. Davidson. *America's Allies and War: Kosovo, Afghanistan, and Iraq.* New York: Palgrave MacMillan, 2011, 157–167. See also Thomas E. Ricks. *Fiasco: The American Military Adventure in Iraq.* New York: Penguin, 2006, 346–348. One exceptionally important component of this war was (and is) the use of private military firms, a silent, less visible component of the "coalition." See Thomas E. Ricks. *The Gamble: General David Petraeus and the American Military Adventure in Iraq, 2006–2008.* New York: Penguin Press, 2009, 268–270.

16. Thomas E. Ricks. *Fiasco: The American Military Adventure in Iraq.* New York: Penguin, 2006, 346.

17. Al Goodman. "Spain: No Combat Role in Iraq War." CNN World. March 18, 2003. Accessed 12/17/2012. http://articles.cnn.com/2003-03-18/world/sprj.irq.spain_1_spanish-troops-minister-jose-maria-aznar-combat-troops?_s=PM:WORLD.

18. See Jason W. Davidson. *America's Allies and War: Kosovo, Afghanistan, and Iraq.* New York: Palgrave MacMillan, 2011, 133–147.

19. Stephen A. Carney. *Allied Participation in Operation Iraqi Freedom.* Washington, DC: Center of Military History, U.S. Army, 2011, 6.

20. George W. Bush. *Decision Points.* New York: Crown Publishers, 2010, 223. See also Tommy Franks. *American Soldier.* New York: Harper Collins, 2004, especially chapters 10–12.

21. Stephen A. Carney. *Allied Participation in Operation Iraqi Freedom.* Washington, DC: Center of Military History, U.S. Army, 2011, 6–9.

22. See NATO. "NATO's Assistance to Iraq." Accessed 5/21/2012. http://www.nato.int/cps/en/natolive/topics_51978.htm.

23. Squadron Leader Sophy Gardner, RAF. "Operation Iraqi Freedom: Coalition Operations." *Air and Space Power Journal.* December 1, 2004. Accessed 5/23/2012. http://www.airpower.au.af.mil/airchronicles/apj/apj04/win04/gardner.html. See Gardner's chart on the command structure. Sir Anthony Brenton asserted that the UK-U.S. relationship was very good, with the exception of links to the U.S. Department of Defense and with Cheney's office. See "Transcript of Private Hearing of Sir Anthony Brenton, KCMG, Minister, Washington DC (including Periods as Charge d'Affaires) January 2001–March 2004," 56. Accessed 5/28/2012. http://www.iraqinquiry.org.uk/news/20110714-documentsreleased.aspx.

24. Squadron Leader Sophy Gardner, RAF. "Operation Iraqi Freedom: Coalition Operations." *Air and Space Power Journal.* December 1, 2004. Accessed 5/23/2012. http://www.airpower.au.af.mil/airchronicles/apj/apj04/win04/gardner.html.

25. Ibid.

26. Frank Walker. "Our Pilots Refused to Bomb 40 Times." *Sydney Morning Herald.* March 14, 2004. This is typical—all pilots have authority to not drop bombs—but it illustrates the challenges of operating with multiple rules of engagement. Thanks to Stephen Saideman for making this point.

27. For the cockpit footage, see http://www.youtube.com/watch?v=4I6-2NJhnf4.

28. See Robert Mendick. "WikiLeaks: Pentagon Logs Show How British Repeatedly Came Under 'Friendly Fire.'" *The Telegraph.* October 23, 2010. Accessed 12/19/2012. http://www.telegraph.co.uk/news/worldnews/middleeast/iraq/8082525/Wikileaks-Pentagon-logs-show-how-British-troops-repeatedly-came-under-friendly-fire.html.

29. Public Broadcasting Service. *Frontline* interview with Lieutenant General Conway. "The Invasion of Iraq." Accessed 5/28/2012. http://www.pbs.org/wgbh/pages/front line/shows/invasion/interviews/conway.html. See also the hundred-page U.S. Central Command Memo of March 6, 2004. "Investigation of Suspected Friendly Fire Incident Near Nasiriya, Iraq, 23 March, 2003."

30. Squadron Leader Sophy Gardner, RAF. "Operation Iraqi Freedom: Coalition Operations." *Air and Space Power Journal.* December 1, 2004. Accessed 5/23/2012. http://www.airpower.au.af.mil/airchronicles/apj/apj04/win04/gardner.html.

31. Thomas E. Ricks. *Fiasco: The American Military Adventure in Iraq.* New York: Penguin, 2006, 240. See also CNN transcripts. "Iraqi Police Killed in Confusing Firefight." Aired September 12, 2003. Accessed 12/21/2012. http://transcripts.cnn.com/TRAN SCRIPTS/0309/12/nfcnn.01.html.

32. Claire Heiniger Schwerin. "Army Fields Next-Generation Blue Force Tracking System." U.S. Army. July 14, 2011. Accessed 5/30/2012. http://www.army.mil/article/61624. See also Giles Ebbutt. "Blue-Force Tracking Evolves for the Modern Battlefield." *Jane's Defense and Security Intelligence and Analysis.* June 11, 2008. Accessed 5/30/2012. http://www.janes.com/products/janes/defence-security-report.aspx?id=106592 6194.

33. Rod Nordland and Timothy Williams. "Iraq Force Soon to Be a Coalition of One." *New York Times.* July 28, 2009.

34. Squadron Leader Sophy Gardner, RAF. "Operation Iraqi Freedom: Coalition Operations." *Air and Space Power Journal.* December 1, 2004. Accessed 5/23/2012. http://www.airpower.au.af.mil/airchronicles/apj/apj04/win04/gardner.html.

35. Keith L. Shimko. *The Iraq Wars and America's Military Revolution.* New York: Cambridge University Press, 2010, 167–168.

36. See Patricia A. Weitsman. "The High Price of Friendship." *New York Times.* August 31, 2006. On the issue of burden sharing, see the excellent work by Daniel F. Baltrusaitis. *Coalition Politics and the Iraq War: Determinants of Choice.* Boulder, CO: Lynne Rienner, 2009; and by Jason W. Davidson. *America's Allies and War: Kosovo, Afghanistan, and Iraq.* New York: Palgrave Macmillan, 2011.

37. See George Wright. "Bush Pledges $3bn Aid to Pakistan." *The Guardian.* June 25, 2003. Accessed 1/9/2013. http://www.guardian.co.uk/pakistan/Story/0,2763,984792,00. html. See also Jane Perlez. "Aid to Pakistan for Tribal Areas Raises Concerns." *New York Times,* July 16, 2007.

38. Charlie LeDuff and David Rohde. "Turkey Won't Send More Troops to Iraq Military Leader Says It's Not Our War." *New York Times,* March 27, 2003; Sharon Otterman. "Iraq: US-Turkey Relations." Council on Foreign Relations. March 31 2003. Accessed 1/90/2013. http://www.cfr.org/publication/7795/iraq.html. See also Stephen J. Hedges and Catherine Collins. "US Woos War Allies with Cash, Weapons." *Chicago Tribune.* February 2, 2003; Brian Knowlton. "U.S. Aid Prods Turkey on Troops for Iraq." *International Herald Tribune.* September 10, 2003.

39. Eric Schmitt. "Rumsfeld Says Russia Should Move Out of Moldova." *New York Times.* June 27, 2004.

40. Thom Shanker and Nicholas Kulish. "Russia Lashes Out on Missile Deal." *New York Times.* August 15, 2008. President Obama canceled plans for the deployment of the antimissile interceptors in Poland and radar in the Czech Republic in 2009.

41. Patricia A. Weitsman. "The High Price of Friendship." *New York Times.* August 31, 2006.

42. Ibid. It is very difficult to calculate total costs of the war. See Joseph E. Stiglitz and Linda J. Bilmes. *The Three Trillion Dollar War: The True Cost of the Iraq Conflict.* New York: W. W. Norton, 2008. Stephen Biddle puts it nicely when he writes, "Low-cost regime change has shifted into higher-cost counter-insurgency." "Speed Kills? Reassessing the Role of Speed, Precision, and Situation Awareness in the Fall of Saddam." *Journal of Strategic Studies,* vol. 30, no. 1, February 2007, 4.

43. Joseph A. Christoff. "Stabilizing and Rebuilding Iraq: Coalition Support and International Donor Commitments." General Accountability Office. GAO-07-827T. May 9, 2007, i.

44. See Rod Nordland and Timothy Williams. "Iraq Force Soon to Be a Coalition of One." *New York Times.* July 28, 2009.

45. Ibid. For data on military contributions to stability operations from March 2003 to 2007, see Daniel F. Baltrusaitis. *Coalition Politics and the Iraq War: Determinants of Choice.* Boulder, CO: Lynne Rienner, 2009, 9. The data can be updated from their original source, the Brookings Institution's Iraq Index website. Accessed 5/28/2012. http://www.brookings.edu/about/centers/saban/iraq-index. See also Joseph A. Christoff. "Stabilizing and Rebuilding Iraq: Coalition Support and International Donor Commitments." General Accountability Office. GAO-07-827T. May 9, 2007, 5.

46. "Q&A: What Is the Coalition of the Willing?" *New York Times* (from Council on Foreign Relations). March 28, 2003. Accessed 5/16/2012. http://work.colum.edu/~amiller/coalition.htm.

47. Joseph A. Christoff. "Stabilizing and Rebuilding Iraq: Coalition Support and International Donor Commitments." General Accountability Office. GAO-07-827T. May 9, 2007, 2–3. For a list of the donor countries, see pages 12–14 of the report.

48. On this topic, see again the excellent work by Daniel F. Baltrusaitis. *Coalition Politics and the Iraq War: Determinants of Choice.* Boulder, CO: Lynne Rienner, 2009; Jason W. Davidson, *America's Allies and War: Kosovo, Afghanistan, and Iraq.* New York: Palgrave Macmillan.

49. See Rod Nordland and Timothy Williams. "Iraq Force Soon to Be a Coalition of One." *New York Times.* July 28, 2009. For extensive data on which countries withdrew their troops and when, Wikipedia is surprisingly accurate and informative. Accessed 5/16/2012. http://en.wikipedia.org/wiki/Multi-National_Force_-_Iraq.

50. For an exceptional review of the idea that Iraq posed a crisis to NATO, see Wallace J. Thies. "Was the Invasion of Iraq NATO's Worst Crisis Ever? How Would We Know? Why Should We Care?" *European Security,* vol. 16, no. 1, March 2007, 29–50. See also his more elaborate argument in *Why NATO Endures.* New York: Cambridge University Press, 2009.

51. George W. Bush. Presidential Radio Address. March 22, 2003. Accessed 5/24/2012. http://georgewbush-whitehouse.archives.gov/news/releases/2003/03/20030322.html.

52. James H. Lebovic. *The Limits of U.S. Military Capability: Lessons from Vietnam and Iraq.* Baltimore: Johns Hopkins University Press, 2010, 203.

53. Keith L. Shimko. *The Iraq Wars and America's Military Revolution.* New York: Cambridge University Press, 2010, 161.

54. Ibid., 143.

55. "Report: Leaked British Papers Dispute Iraq War Claims." *USA Today.* November 22, 2009. Accessed 5/28/12. http://www.usatoday.com/news/world/2009-11-22-leaked-uk-documents_N.htm.

56. Keith L. Shimko. *The Iraq Wars and America's Military Revolution.* New York: Cambridge University Press, 2010, 152.

57. Tel. No. 294. Brenton Telegram, Iraq: UN Endgame, March 6, 2003. See this and other documents at the Iraq Inquiry website. Accessed 5/28/2012. http://www.iraqinquiry.org.uk/news/20110714-documentsreleased.aspx.

58. "Transcript of Private Hearing of Sir Anthony Brenton, KCMG, Minister, Washington D.C. (including Periods as Charge d'Affaires) January 2001–March 2004," 28. Accessed 5/28/2012. http://www.iraqinquiry.org.uk/news/20110714-documentsreleased.aspx.

59. Public Broadcasting Service. *Frontline* interview with Lieutenant General Conway. "The Invasion of Iraq." Accessed 5/28/2012. http://www.pbs.org/wgbh/pages/frontline/shows/invasion/interviews/conway.html. Lieutenant General David D. McKiernan, commander of combined allied land forces in the 2003 invasion of Iraq, also expressed

approval of the speed of the advance of the British on Basra. See his interview at the following: accessed 5/28/2012. http://www.pbs.org/wgbh/pages/frontline/shows/invasion/interviews/mckiernan.html. See also Todd S. Purdum and Staff of the *New York Times. A Time of Our Choosing: America's War in Iraq.* New York: Times Books, Henry Holt and Company, 2003, especially chapter 11.

60. "Transcript of Private Hearing of Sir Anthony Brenton, KCMG, Minister, Washington D.C. (including Periods as Charge d'Affaires) January 2001–March 2004," 28. Accessed 5/28/2012. http://www.iraqinquiry.org.uk/news/20110714-documentsreleased .aspx.

61. John F. Burns. "Britain's Iraq Pullout Timeline Reported." *New York Times.* December 10, 2008. Accessed 12/17/2012. http://www.nytimes.com/2008/12/11/world/europe/11britain.html.

62. BBC News. "Poland Was 'Misled' over Iraq WMD." March 18, 2004. Accessed 5/28/2012. http://news.bbc.co.uk/2/hi/europe/3525356.stm.

63. Mike Nizza. "Australia Looks Back on Iraq War." *New York Times.* June 2, 2008. Accessed 5/28/2012. http://thelede.blogs.nytimes.com/2008/06/02/australia-looks-back-on-iraq-war.

64. Sabra Lane. "Australia Warned of Handling Prisoners over to Iraq." ABC News, World Today. March 27, 2012. Accessed 5/28/12. http://www.abc.net.au/news/2012-03-27/intelligence-warned-of-handing-prisoners-to-iraq/3915722.

65. BBC News. "Iraq War Dominates Italy-US Talks." October 31, 2005. Accessed 5/28/12. http://news.bbc.co.uk/2/hi/europe/4394402.stm.

66. Keith L. Shimko. *The Iraq Wars and America's Military Revolution.* New York: Cambridge University Press, 2010, 183. See also Thomas E. Ricks. *The Gamble: General David Petraeus and the American Military Adventure in Iraq, 2006–2008.* New York: Penguin Press, 2009. Ricks discusses the particularly difficult period from late 2005 to 2006 during which the United States reassessed and revamped its strategy. He has a very interesting and insightful analysis of Petraeus and his role in the redesigning of Iraq strategy in the war's later years. See also his book, *The Generals: American Military Command from WWII to Today.* New York: Penguin Press, 2012.

67. Reuters. "Leaked Iraq War Report Details Lack of Cohesion." November 22, 2009. Accessed 5/28/2012. http://uk.reuters.com/article/2009/11/22/uk-britain-iraq-idUKTRE5AL10E20091122. "Report: Leaked British Papers Dispute Iraq War Claims." *USA Today.* November 22, 2009. Accessed 5/28/2012. http://www.usatoday.com/news/world/2009-11-22-leaked-uk-documents_N.htm. See also Keith L. Shimko. *The Iraq Wars and America's Military Revolution.* New York: Cambridge University Press, 2010, 148–150, 158.

68. According to Lieutenant General Raad Al-Hamdani, who was in charge of Iraq's Republican Guard south of Baghdad to Najaf, the central strategic mistakes on the Iraqi side were dividing the country into four separate commands; problematic command

and coordination among the different commands, with no unified armed forces; a lack of strategic vision; the absence of political-military discussion; the absence of authority on the part of the military to act without orders; corruption and the absence of military spirit; and a low percentage of actual forces fighting. See his interview with PBS *Frontline*. Accessed 5/28/2012. http://www.pbs.org/wgbh/pages/frontline/shows/invasion/interviews/raad.html.

69. Stephen Biddle. "Speed Kills? Reassessing the Role of Speed, Precision, and Situation Awareness in the Fall of Saddam." *Journal of Strategic Studies*, vol. 30, no 1, February 2007, 6.

70. Public Broadcasting Service. *Frontline* interview with Lieutenant General William Scott Wallace. "The Invasion of Iraq." Accessed 5/28/2012. http://www.pbs.org/wgbh/pages/frontline/shows/invasion/interviews/wallace.html.

71. This is reminiscent of the findings by Samuel A. Stouffer, Arthur A. Lumsdaine, Marion Harper Lumsdaine, Robin M. Williams Jr., M. Brewster Smith, Irving L. Janis, Shirley A. Star, and Leonard S. Cottrell Jr. *Studies in Social Psychology in World War II: The American Soldier.* Princeton, NJ: Princeton University Press, 1949. This is the largest study of combat motivation, which looks at the experiences of more than five hundred thousand soldiers in World War II, exploring, among other things, why soldiers fought and what motivated them. Most answered, "Just to get through."

72. Thomas E. Ricks. *The Gamble: General Petraeus and the American Military Adventure in Iraq, 2006–2008.* New York: Penguin Press, 2009, 10; see also Thomas E. Ricks. *Fiasco: The American Military Adventure in Iraq.* New York: Penguin, 2006 as well as his compelling work, *The Generals: American Military Command from World War II to Today.* New York: Penguin Press, 2012.

73. Ian Fisher. "Italy Planning to Start Pullout of Iraq Troops." *New York Times.* March 16, 2005. Accessed 5/26/2012. http://www.nytimes.com/2005/03/16/international/europe/16italy.html?_r=1.

74. Natsuyo Ishibashi. "The Dispatch of Japan's Self-Defense Forces to Iraq: Public Opinion, Elections, and Foreign Policy." *Asian Survey*, vol. 47, no. 5, September–October 2007, 766–789; see Natsuyo Ishibashi. *Alliance Security Dilemmas in the Iraq War: German and Japanese Responses.* New York: Palgrave Macmillan, 2012.

75. "Transcript of Private Hearing of Sir Anthony Brenton, KCMG, Minister, Washington D.C. (including Periods as Charge d'Affaires) January 2001–March 2004," 33. Accessed 5/28/2012. http://www.iraqinquiry.org.uk/news/20110714-documentsreleased.aspx.

76. On the alliance security dilemma in relation to Germany and Japan, see Natsuyo Ishibashi. *Alliance Security Dilemmas in the Iraq War: German and Japanese Responses.* New York: Palgrave Macmillan, 2012.

77. "Anti-War Protesters Hold Global Rallies." *USA Today.* February 15, 2003. Accessed 5/18/12. http://www.usatoday.com/news/world/iraq/2003-02-15-protests_x.htm.

See also David S. Meyer and Catherine Corrigall-Brown. "Coalitions and Political Context: U.S. Movements Against Wars in Iraq." *Mobilization: An International Journal*, vol. 10, no. 3, October 2005, 327–346.

78. "Millions Join Global Anti-War Protests." BBC World Edition. February 17, 2003. Accessed 5/18/2012. http://news.bbc.co.uk/2/hi/europe/2765215.stm.

79. William Horsely. "Polls Find Europeans Oppose Iraq War." BBC News. February 11, 2003. Accessed 5/24/2012. http://news.bbc.co.uk/2/hi/europe/2747175.stm.

80. Julie Kim. "Iraq Coalition: Public Opinion Indicators in Selected European Countries." CRS Report for Congress, 2004. Accessed 5/24/2012. http://congressional research.com/RS21794/document.php?study=Iraq+Coalition+Public+Opinion+Indi cators+in+Selected+European+Countries; BBC World Opinion Poll. "World View of US Role Goes From Bad to Worse." January 23, 2007. Accessed 5/24/2012. http://news .bbc.co.uk/2/shared/bsp/hi/pdfs/23_01_07_us_poll.pdf; Christopher Marquis. "After the War: Opinion; World View of U.S. Sours After Iraq War." *New York Times*. June 4, 2003.

81. World Public Opinion. Accessed 5/24/2012. http://www.worldpublicopinion.org/ pipa/articles/international_security_bt/394.php?lb=btis&pnt=394&nid=&id.

82. Ibid.

83. Patricia A. Weitsman. "With a Little Help from Our Friends? The Costs of Coalition Warfare." *Origins: Current Events in Historical Perspective*, vol. 2, no. 4, January 2009. Accessed 5/30/13. http://origins.osu.edu/article/little-help-our-friends-costs-coalition-warfare.

84. Susan Page. "Vote May Have Big Impact on Views of Iraq War." *USA Today*. December 14, 2005. Accessed 5/28/2012. http://www.usatoday.com/news/washington/2005-12-14-bush-polls_x.htm.

85. Rod Nordland and Timothy Williams. "Iraq Force Soon to Be a Coalition of One." *New York Times*. July 28, 2009. A post exchange is an on-base store.

86. Julie Kim. "Iraq Coalition: Public Opinion Indicators in Selected European Countries." CRS Report for Congress, 2004. Accessed 5/24/2012. http://congressional research.com/RS21794/document.php?study=Iraq+Coalition+Public+Opinion+Indica tors+in+Selected+European+Countries.

87. Nicholas Kulish. "War Crimes Case Weighs on Poland." *International Herald Tribune*. November 28, 2007; Vanessa Gera. "Polish Troops Leave Iraq with Drop in Violence." Associated Press. October 8, 2008. Accessed 7/13/2012. http://www.ohio .com/news/nation/polish-troops-leave-iraq-with-drop-in-violence-1.128350; Associated Press. "Opposition Party Wins Polish Election." October 21, 2007. Accessed 7/13/2012. http://www.msnbc.msn.com/id/21411682/ns/world_news-europe/t/opposition-party-wins-poland-election/#.UACNlHCD6_A.

88. Patricia A. Weitsman. "The High Price of Friendship." *New York Times*. August 31, 2006; Patricia A. Weitsman. "With a Little Help from Our Friends? The Costs of Coalition Warfare." *Origins: Current Events in Historical Perspective*, vol. 2,

no. 4, January 2009. Accessed 5/30/13. http://origins.osu.edu/article/little-help-our-friends-costs-coalition-warfare.

89. There is comprehensive public opinion poll data here from before the start of the war to its conclusion. "PollingReport.com: Iraq." Accessed 5/24/2012. http://www.pollingreport.com/iraq.htm.

90. Alexander Thompson. *Channels of Power: The UN Security Council and U.S. Statecraft in Iraq.* Ithaca, NY: Cornell University Press, 137–143.

91. Ibid., 160–161.

92. Alexander Thompson. *Channels of Power: The UN Security Council and U.S. Statecraft in Iraq.* Ithaca, NY: Cornell University Press, 180–203.

93. PollingReport.com. Accessed 5/24/2012. http://www.pollingreport.com/iraq18.htm; see also World Public Opinion. Accessed 5/24/2012. http://www.worldpublicopinion.org/pipa/articles/international_security_bt/107.php?lb=btun&pnt=107&nid=&id=; http://www.worldpublicopinion.org/pipa/articles/international_security_bt/106.php?lb=btun&pnt=106&nid=&id=.

94. The data can be found at the following link: accessed 5/24/2012. http://www.usatoday.com/news/world/2003-02-14-eu-survey.htm. This was true of Japan as well. See Natsuyo Ishibashi. "The Dispatch of Japan's Self-Defense Forces to Iraq: Public Opinion, Elections, and Foreign Policy." *Asian Survey,* vol. 47, no. 5, September–October 2007, 4. Cf. Alexander Thompson. *Channels of Power: The UN Security Council and U.S. Statecraft in Iraq.* Ithaca, NY: Cornell University Press, 187–193.

95. See excerpts from the interview with UN Secretary-General Kofi Annan. September 16, 2004. Accessed 5/24/2012. http://news.bbc.co.uk/2/hi/middle_east/3661640.stm.

96. See Alexander Thompson's exceptional work on this in his *Channels of Power: The UN Security Council and U.S. Statecraft in Iraq.* Ithaca, NY: Cornell University Press, 2009, chapter 6.

97. "Transcript of Private Hearing of Sir Anthony Brenton, KCMG, Minister, Washington DC (including Periods as Charge d'Affaires) January 2001–March 2004," 24. Accessed 5/28/2012. http://www.iraqinquiry.org.uk/news/20110714-documentsreleased.aspx.

98. Daniel F. Baltrusaitis. *Coalition Politics and the Iraq War: Determinants of Choice.* Boulder, CO: Lynne Rienner, 2009, 7.

99. UN Security Council Resolution 1511. Accessed 5/29/12. http://www.un.org/Docs/sc/unsc_resolutions03.html.

100. Daniel F. Baltrusaitis. *Coalition Politics and the Iraq War: Determinants of Choice.* Boulder, CO: Lynne Rienner, 2009, 7–8.

101. February 2012 report (mismarked February 2011) from the Brookings Institution's Iraq Index. Accessed 5/29/12. http://www.brookings.edu/about/centers/saban/iraq-index.

102. Pew Global Attitudes Project. "From Hyperpower to Declining Power: Changing Global Perceptions of the U.S. in the Post–September 11 Era." September 7, 2011. Accessed 5/29/12. http://www.pewglobal.org/2011/09/07/from-hyperpower-to-declining-power.

Chapter 7

1. Agence-France Presse. "Libyan Minister Recalls Arrest that Sparked Uprising." *Al Arabiya*, February 16, 2012. Accessed 6/15/2012. http://english.alarabiya.net/articles/2012/02/16/195107.html.

2. Ian Black. "Libya's Day of Rage Met by Bullets and Loyalists." *The Guardian.* February 17, 2011. Accessed 6/15/2012. http://www.guardian.co.uk/world/2011/feb/17/libya-day-of-rage-unrest.

3. Reuters. "Defiant Gaddafi Vows to Die as Martyr, Fight Revolt." February 22, 2011. Accessed 6/15/2012. http://www.reuters.com/article/2011/02/22/us-libya-protests-idUSTRE71G0A620110222.

4. For country-by-country details, see BBC News Middle East. "Libya Protests: Evacuation of Foreigners Continues." February 25, 2011. Accessed 6/15/2012. http://www.bbc.co.uk/news/world-middle-east-12552374.

5. For the texts of the resolutions, see the following: accessed 6/15/2012. http://www.un.org/Docs/sc/unsc_resolutions11.htm. For an excellent analysis of the British and French decisions to intervene, see Jason W. Davidson. "France, Britain and the Intervention in Libya: An Integrated Analysis." *Cambridge Review of International Affairs*, vol. 26, no. 2, 310–329.

6. Jeremiah Gertler. "Operation Odyssey Dawn (Libya): Background and Issues for Congress." Congressional Research Service. March 28, 2011, 16.

7. Joe Quartararo Sr., Michael Rovenolt, and Randy White. "Libya's Operation Odyssey Dawn: Command and Control." *Prism*, vol. 3, no. 2, March 2012. Accessed 6/15/2012. http://www.ndu.edu/press/libyas-operation-odyssey-dawn.html. See also "Libya: Revolution and Aftermath." *New York Times.* June 11, 2012. Accessed 6/15/2012. http://topics.nytimes.com/top/news/international/countriesandterritories/libya/index.html. For the text of UN Security Council Resolution 1970, see the following: accessed 6/15/2012. http://www.un.org/News.

8. UN Security Council Resolution 1973 (2011). Adopted March 17, 2011. For the text of this resolution, see the following: accessed 6/15/2012. http://www.un.org/Docs/sc/unsc_resolutions11.htm.

9. The initial assault on Libya actually began with French aircraft strikes that occurred even before the end of the emergency meeting of allied decision makers in Paris on Saturday, March 19, 2011. See David D. Kirkpatrick, Steven Erlanger, and Elisabeth Bumiller. "Allies Open Air Assault on Qaddafi's Forces in Libya." *New York Times*, March 19, 2011. Accessed 6/26/2012. http://www.nytimes.com/2011/03/20/world/africa/20libya.html?_r=2&hp.

10. See Tony Karon. "Is Libya a New Model of U.S. Intervention, or an Afghanistan Do-Over?" *Time World*. August 31, 2011. Accessed 7/17/2012. http://world.time .com/2011/08/31/is-libya-a-new-model-of-u-s-intervention-or-an-afghanistan-do-over. Cf. Fareed Zakaria. "How the Lessons of Iraq Paid Off in Libya." *Time Magazine*, September 5, 2011. Accessed 7/17/2012. http://www.time.com/time/magazine/article/0,9171,2090374,00.html.

11. Jeremiah Gertler. "Operation Odyssey Dawn (Libya): Background and Issues for Congress." Congressional Research Service. March 28, 2011, 14–15.

12. Adrian Johnson and Saqeb Mueen, eds. "Short War, Long Shadow: The Political and Military Legacies of the 2011 Libya Campaign." *Whitehall Report, RUSI.* January 2012, ix–xii; Romania's Permanent Delegation to NATO. "Romania's Participation to Operation Unified Protector." Accessed 6/16/2012. http://nato.mae.ro/en/node/464; U.S. Mission to NATO. "Libya: A Success Story." Ambassador's Speeches and Statements. Atlantic Council Remarks. Accessed 6/16/2012. http://nato.mae.ro/en/node/464. See also Tony Karon. "Is Libya a New Model of U.S. Intervention, or an Afghanistan Do-Over." *Time Magazine.* August 31, 2011. Accessed 6/25/2012. http://world.time.com/2011/08/31/ is-libya-a-new-model-of-u-s-intervention-or-an-afghanistan-do-over. The Croatian government sent just two officers to participate in OUP. They were deployed to the Combined Air Operations Center in Poggio Renatico, Italy. See NATO. "Croatia in NATO." Accessed 12/18/2012. http://nato.mfa.hr/?mh=56&mv=617&id=12639.

13. Joe Quartararo Sr., Michael Rovenolt, and Randy White. "Libya's Operation Odyssey Dawn: Command and Control." *Prism*, vol. 3, no. 2, March 2012. Accessed 6/16/2012. http://www.ndu.edu/press/libyas-operation-odyssey-dawn.html.

14. Ibid.

15. Jeremiah Gertler. "Operation Odyssey Dawn (Libya): Background and Issues for Congress." Congressional Research Service. March 28, 2011, 14–15.

16. Ibid., 15.

17. U.S. Africa Command. "Transcript: Update by Admiral Locklear, III, on Operation Odyssey Dawn." Accessed 6/7/2012. http://www.africom.mil/getArticle.asp? art=6259.

18. Gregory K. James, Larry Holcomb, and Chad T. Manske. "Joint Task Force Odyssey Dawn: A Model for Joint Experience, Training, and Education." *Joint Force Quarterly*, no. 64, first quarter 2012, 25.

19. NATO. "NATO and Libya." Accessed 6/7/2012. http://www.nato.int/cps/en/nato live/topics_71652.htm.

20. U.S. Africa Command. "Transcript: Update by Admiral Locklear, III, on Operation Odyssey Dawn." Accessed 6/7/2012. http://www.africom.mil/getArticle.asp?art=6259.

21. Ibid.

22. NATO. "NATO and Libya." Accessed 6/7/2012. http://www.nato.int/cps/en/nato live/topics_71652.htm.

23. Ibid.

24. My thanks to Daniel Baltrusaitis for pointing this out. See Joe Quartararo Sr., Michael Rovenolt, and Randy White. "Libya's Operation Odyssey Dawn: Command and Control." *Prism*, vol. 3, no. 2, March 2012. Accessed 6/15/2012. http://www.ndu.edu/press/libyas-operation-odyssey-dawn.html.

25. John A. Tirpak. "Lessons from Libya." *Air Force Magazine*. December 2011. Accessed 6/13/2012. http://www.airforcemagazine.com/MagazineArchive/Pages/2011/December%202011/1211libya.aspx.

26. My thanks to Daniel Baltruisaitis for making this point.

27. Clara M. O'Donnell and Justin Vaïsse. "Is Libya NATO's Final Bow?" Opinion. December 2, 2011. Brookings Institution. Accessed 12/20/12. http://www.brookings.edu/research/opinions/2011/12/02-libya-odonnell-vaisse.

28. CNN Wire Staff. "NATO Refuses to Apologize for Libyan 'Friendly Fire' Attack." *CNN World*. April 8, 2011. Accessed 6/25/2012. http://articles.cnn.com/2011-04-08/world/libya.war_1_nato-forces-nato-operation-civilians/2?_s=PM:WORLD.

29. MSNBC.com News Service. "How to Avoid Friendly Fire? Libya Rebels Try Pink: Vehicles Painted After NATO Mistakenly Hit Two Convoys, Killing 18." MSNBC. com. April 28, 2011. Accessed 6/25/2012. http://www.msnbc.msn.com/id/42496271/ns/world_news-mideast_n_africa/t/how-avoid-friendly-fire-libya-rebels-try-pink/#.T-h4OPFrq_A.

30. Xan Rice. "Libya: Rebels in Misrata 'Killed by NATO Friendly Fire.'" *The Guardian*. April 28, 2011. Accessed 6/25/2012.
http://www.guardian.co.uk/world/2011/apr/28/libya-rebels-misrata-killed-nato; MSNBC.com News Service. "How to Avoid Friendly Fire? Libya Rebels Try Pink: Vehicles Painted After NATO Mistakenly Hit Two Convoys, Killing 18." MSNBC.com. April 28, 2011. Accessed 6/25/2012. http://www.msnbc.msn.com/id/42496271/ns/world_news-mideast_n_africa/t/how-avoid-friendly-fire-libya-rebels-try-pink/#.T-h4OPFrq_A.

31. "NATO 'Friendly Fire' Kills Libyan Rebels." Middle East Online. August 14, 2011. Accessed 6/25/2012. http://www.middle-east-online.com/english/?id=47614.

32. For example, there were numerous episodes of Gadhafi's forces firing on other loyalists. See "Friendly Fire Creating Problems for NTC Fighters Besieging Sirte." *Tripoli Post*. October 15, 2011. Accessed 6/25/2012. http://www.tripolipost.com/articledetail.asp?c=1&i=7098.

33. For example, a Libyan rebel fighter told the *New York Times* that the fighters were not advancing beyond the western rebel positions twenty-five miles west of Ajdabiya, to lessen the chance that NATO would mistakenly attack them. See Alan Colwell and Rod Nordland. "NATO Split Widens over Scope of Libya Military Action." *New York Times*. April 12, 2011. Accessed 6/25/2012. http://www.nytimes.com/2011/04/12/world/africa/13libya.html?pagewanted=all.

34. Karen DeYoung and Greg Jaffe. "NATO Runs Short on Some Munitions in Libya." *Washington Post.* April 15, 2011. Accessed 6/13/2012. http://www.washingtonpost.com/world/nato-runs-short-on-some-munitions-in-libya/2011/04/15/AF3O7ElD_story.html.

35. Joe Quartararo Sr., Michael Rovenolt, and Randy White. "Libya's Operation Odyssey Dawn: Command and Control." *Prism,* vol. 3, no. 2, March 2012. Accessed 6/15/2012. http://www.ndu.edu/press/libyas-operation-odyssey-dawn.html.

36. Cmdr. Bruce Black and Cmdr. M. Barry Tanner. "Responding at the Speed of Change: NCTS Sicily Supports Operation Odyssey Dawn and Operation Unified Protector." *CHIPS: The Department of the Navy's Information Technology Magazine.* October–December 2011. Accessed 12/20/2012. http://www.doncio.navy.mil/CHIPS/ArticleDetails.aspx?id=3024.

37. Ian Brzezinski. "Lesson from Libya: NATO Alliance Remains Relevant." *National Defense.* November 2011. Accessed 6/25/2012. http://www.nationaldefensemagazine.org/archive/2011/November/Pages/LessonFromLibyaNATOAllianceRemainsRelevant.aspx.

38. Geoff Ziezulewicz. "Libya Mission Ends, but NATO's Direction Still Up in the Air." *Stars and Stripes.* October 28, 2011. Accessed 6/13/2012. http://www.stripes.com/news/libya-mission-ends-but-nato-s-direction-still-up-in-the-air-1.159043.

39. Adrian Johnson and Saqeb Mueen, eds. "Short War, Long Shadow: The Political and Military Legacies of the 2011 Libya Campaign." *Whitehall Report, RUSI.* January 2012, ix–xii. Cf. "NATO Operations in Libya: Data Journalism Breaks Down Which Country Does What." *The Guardian.* Accessed 6/13/2012. http://www.guardian.co.uk/news/datablog/2011/may/22/nato-libya-data-journalism-operations-country#data.

40. Jessica Rettig. "End of NATO's Libya Intervention Means Financial Relief for Allies: The Pentagon Alone Spent $1.1 Billion on the Libya Mission." *U.S. News and World Report.* October 31, 2011. Accessed 6/15/2012. http://www.usnews.com/news/articles/2011/10/31/end-of-natos-libya-intervention-means-financial-relief-for-allies.

41. Gerard O'Dwyer. "$110 Million Bill for Danish Libya Mission." *Defense News.* January 12, 2012. Accessed 7/19/2012. http://www.defensenews.com/apps/pbcs.dll/article?AID=2012301120006.

42. Jessica Rettig. "End of NATO's Libya Intervention Means Financial Relief for Allies: The Pentagon Alone Spent $1.1 Billion on the Libya Mission." *U.S. News and World Report.* October 31, 2011. Accessed 6/15/2012. http://www.usnews.com/news/articles/2011/10/31/end-of-natos-libya-intervention-means-financial-relief-for-allies.

43. Ibid.

44. U.S. Senate Armed Services Committee. "Testimony of Admiral James G. Stavridis, United States Navy Commander, United States European Commander Before the 112th Congress." March 1, 2012, 4. Accessed 6/15/2012. http://www.google.com/url?sa=t&rct=j&q=&esrc=s&source=web&cd=5&ved=0CFoQFjAE&url=http%3A%2F%

2Farmed-services.senate.gov%2Fstatemnt%2F2012%2F03%2520March%2FStavri
dis%252003-01-12.pdf&ei=v5PbT6voE6rY2gXZl6n_BQ&usg=AFQjCNHGgnjnRn6J
_bxb4f2lJ6t-M9IT3A.

45. Ivo H. Daadler and James G. Savridis. "NATO's Success in Libya." *New York Times*. October 30, 2011. See also the authors' *Foreign Affairs* article, "NATO's Victory in Libya." March–April 2012; see also Ambassador Ivo Daalder, U.S. Permanent Representative to NATO. "Remarks to the Press and Operation Unified Protector." September 8, 2011. Accessed 6/15/2012. http://nato.usmission.gov/libya-oup-90811.html.

46. Jorge Benitez. "What Percent of NATO Strikes in Libya Were Carried Out by the US?" August 22, 2011. Accessed 2/18/2012. http://globalpublicsquare.blogs.cnn
.com/2011/08/22/what-percent-of-nato-strikes-in-libya-were-carried-out-by-the-u-s.
"Cameron-Britain Should be Proud of Role in Libya." September 2, 2011. Accessed 12/18/2012. https://www.gov.uk/government/news/cameron-britain-should-be-proud-of-role-in-libya; Tom Blackwell. "Canada Contributed a Disproportionate Amount to Libya Air Strike." *National Post* (Don Mills, ON). August 25, 2011. Accessed 12/18/2012.
http://news.nationalpost.com/2011/08/25/canada-contributed-a-disproportionate-amount-to-libya-air-strikes-sources. Sources suggest that the United Arab Emirates and Qatar joined in flying strike sorties, but information regarding the number of sorties and targets is scarce. See "NATO After Libya." *Economist*. September 3, 2011. Accessed 12/20/2012. http://www.economist.com/node/21528248.

47. Ivo H. Daadler and James G. Savridis. "NATO's Success in Libya." *New York Times*. October 30, 2011.

48. Robert M. Gates. "The Security and Defense Agenda (Future of NATO)." Speech delivered in Brussels, Belgium. June 20, 2011. Accessed 6/13/2012. http://www.defense
.gov/speeches/speech.aspx?speechid=1581.

49. Ambassador Ivo Daalder, U.S. Permanent Representative to NATO. "Remarks to the Press and Operation Unified Protector." September 8, 2011. Accessed 6/15/2012. http://nato.usmission.gov/libya-oup-90811.html.

50. Ian Brzezinski. "Lesson from Libya: NATO Alliance Remains Relevant." *National Defense*. November 2011. Accessed 6/25/2012. http://www.nationaldefensemagazine
.org/archive/2011/November/Pages/LessonFromLibyaNATOAllianceRemainsRelevant
.aspx.

51. Spencer Ackerman. "Libya: The *Real* U.S. Drone War." *Wired*. October 20, 2011. Accessed 6/26/2012. http://www.wired.com/dangerroom/2011/10/predator-libya. See also Thom Shanker. "Obama Sends Armed Drones to Help NATO in Libya War." *New York Times*. April 21, 2011. Accessed 6/26/2012. http://www.nytimes.com/2011/04/22/
world/africa/22military.html.

52. David S. Cloud. "Pentagon Mulls NATO Request for More U.S. Drones in Libya Campaign." *Los Angeles Times*. July 21, 2011. Accessed 6/26/2012. http://articles.latimes
.com/2011/jul/21/world/la-fg-drones-libya-20110722.

53. See "Predator Drones and Unmanned Aerial Vehicles." *New York Times.* March 20, 2012. Accessed 6/26/2012. http://topics.nytimes.com/top/reference/timestop ics/subjects/u/unmanned_aerial_vehicles/index.html.

54. See Jamie M. Fly. "What Is Obama's Goal in Libya." *National Review Online.* March 21, 2011. Accessed 6/25/2012. http://www.nationalreview.com/corner/262604/ what-obama-s-goal-libya-jamie-m-fly#.

55. Mark Landler. "For Obama, Some Vindication of Approach to War." *New York Times.* October 20, 2011. Accessed 6/25/2012. http://www.nytimes.com/2011/10/21/world/ africa/qaddafis-death-is-latest-victory-for-new-us-approach-to-war.html. See also Eric Schmitt. "U.S. Gives Its Air Power Expansive Role in Libya." *New York Times.* March 28, 2011. Accessed 6/25/2012. http://www.nytimes.com/2011/03/29/us/29military.html.

56. Daily Mail Reporter. "Who's in Charge? Germans Pull Forces out as Coalition Falls Apart." *Daily Mail.* March 22, 2011. Accessed 6/25/2012. http://www.dailymail.co.uk/ news/article-1368693/Libya-war-Germans-pull-forces-NATO-Libyan-coalition-falls-apart.html.

57. See James Kitfield. "Obama: The Reluctant Warrior on Libya." *The Atlantic.* March 18, 2011. Accessed 6/25/2012. http://www.theatlantic.com/politics/archive/2011/03/ obama-the-reluctant-warrior-on-libya/72678.

58. "Sarkozy's Pro-NATO Policy Is Much More Than Symbolism: View." *Bloomberg.* September 4, 2011. Accessed 6/25/2012. http://www.bloomberg.com/news/2011-09-05/ sarkozy-s-pro-nato-policy-on-libya-is-much-more-than-just-symbolism-view.html.

59. Jeremiah Gertler. "Operation Odyssey Dawn (Libya): Background and Issues for Congress." Congressional Research Service. March 28, 2011, 17.

60. Con Coughlin. "Libya: Can Britain and France Really Run this Conflict?" *Telegraph.* March 22, 2011. Accessed 6/25/2012. http://www.telegraph.co.uk/comment/ columnists/concoughlin/8399184/Libya-Can-Britain-and-France-really-run-this-conflict.html.

61. Damien McElroy and James Kirkup. "Libya: Italy Rejects Calls to Join Ground Attack Operations." *Telegraph.* April 15, 2011. Accessed 6/25/2012. http://www.telegraph .co.uk/news/worldnews/africaandindianocean/libya/8454507/Libya-Italy-rejects-calls-to-join-ground-attack-operations.html.

62. James Blitz and Anna Fifield. "NATO's Internal Strains Worsen Over Libya." *Financial Times: Middle East and North Africa.* June 15, 2011. Accessed 6/25/2012. http:// www.ft.com/intl/cms/s/0/d9e40adc-9772-11e0-af13-00144feab49a.html#axzz1yqourg2a.

63. Jim Garamone. "Leaders Describe Path to Peace in Libya." American Air Forces Press Service, U.S. Department of Defense. April 15, 2011. Accessed 7/19/2012. http:// www.defense.gov/news/newsarticle.aspx?id=63580. See also Jim Garamone. "Coalition Launches 'Operation Odyssey Dawn.'" American Air Forces Press Service, U.S. Department of Defense. March 19, 2011. Accessed 7/19/2012. http://www.defense.gov/news/ newsarticle.aspx?id=63225.

64. Ibid.

65. Jeremiah Gertler. "Operation Odyssey Dawn (Libya): Background and Issues for Congress." Congressional Research Service. March 28, 2011, 17.

66. Nicole Ameline, Rapporteur. "177 DSCTC 11 E rev. 1 final: NATO Operations Under a New Strategic Concept and the EU as an Operational Partner." NATO Parliamentary Assembly, 2011 Annual Session. Accessed 6/1/2012. http://www.nato-pa.int/default.asp?SHORTCUT=2592.

67. Eric Schmitt. "NATO Sees Flaws in Air Campaign Against Qaddafi." *New York Times.* April 14, 2012. Accessed 12/20/2012. http://www.nytimes.com/2012/04/15/world/africa/nato-sees-flaws-in-air-campaign-against-qaddafi.html?pagewanted=all&_r=1&.

68. Associated Press. "Clinton Seeks to Restore NATO Consensus on Libya." *USA Today.* April 14, 2011. Accessed 6/16/2012. http://www.usatoday.com/news/world/2011-04-12-koussa-gadhafi-libya-britain.htm; Tristana Moore. "Behind a United Front, NATO Meeting Deepens Cracks in the Alliances." *Time Magazine.* April 16, 2011. Accessed 6/16/2012. http://www.time.com/time/world/article/0,8599,2065749,00.html; cf. NATO. "In Berlin, NATO Allies and Partners Show Unity and Resolve on All Fronts." April 14–15, 2011. Accessed 6/16/2012. http://www.nato.int/cps/en/natolive/news_72775.htm?.

69. Jackie Northam. "Not Your Cold War NATO: Alliance to Examine Itself." National Public Radio. May 17, 2012. Hear or read the story at the following link: accessed 6/25/2012. http://www.npr.org/2012/05/17/152873919/not-your-cold-war-nato-alliance-to-examine-itself.

70. "Who's In Charge? Germans Pull Forces out as Coalition Falls Apart." *Daily Mail.* March 22, 2011. Accessed 6/25/2012. http://www.dailymail.co.uk/news/article-1368693/Libya-war-Germans-pull-forces-NATO-Libyan-coalition-falls-apart.html. See also Steven Erlanger. "Confusion over Who Leads Libya Strikes and for How Long." *New York Times.* March 21, 2011. Accessed 6/25/2012. http://www.nytimes.com/2011/03/22/world/africa/22nato.html.

71. Jorge Benitez. "Denmark Criticizes NATO's Libya Operation." NATO Source, Atlantic Council. October 11, 2012. Accessed 12/20/2012. http://www.acus.org/natosource/denmark-criticizes-natos-libya-operation.

72. Gregory K. James, Larry Holcomb, and Chad T. Manske. "Joint Task Force Odyssey Dawn: A Model for Joint Experience, Training, and Education." *Joint Force Quarterly,* no. 64, first quarter 2012, 26–27. See also U.S. Senate Armed Services Committee. "Testimony of Admiral James G. Stavridis, United States Navy Commander, United States European Commander Before the 112th Congress." March 1, 2012, 11–12. Accessed 6/15/2012. http://www.google.com/url?sa=t&rct=j&q=&esrc=s&source=web&cd=5&ved=0CF0QFjAE&url=http%3A%2F%2Farmed-services.senate.gov%2Fstatemnt%2F2012%2F03%2520March%2FStavridis%252003-01-12.pdf&ei=v5PbT6voE6rY2gXZl6n_BQ&usg=AFQjCNHGgnjnRn6J_bxb4f2lJ6t-M9IT3A.

73. U.S. Navy. "USS Mount Whitney: History." Accessed 6/16/2012. http://www .mtwhitney.navy.mil.

74. Gregory K. James, Larry Holcomb, and Chad T. Manske. "Joint Task Force Odyssey Dawn: A Model for Joint Experience, Training, and Education." *Joint Force Quarterly*, no. 64, first quarter 2012, 28.

75. John A. Tirpak. "Lessons from Libya." *Air Force Magazine*. December 2011. Accessed 6/13/2012. http://www.airforce-magazine.com/MagazineArchive/Pages/2011/ December%202011/1211libya.aspx.

76. Robert Densmore. "French Pilots over Libya Decline US Intel; Clearance Just Too Slow." AOL Defense. September 21, 2011. Accessed 12/20/2012. http://defense.aol .com/2011/09/21/french-pilots-over-libya-decline-us-intel-clearance-just-too-sl.

77. "NATO to Hold Talks on Libya, Afghanistan Wars." *Al Arabiya*. October 5, 2011. Accessed 6/13/2012. http://www.alarabiya.net/articles/2011/10/05/170293.html.

78. Karen DeYoung and Greg Jaffe. "NATO Runs Short on Some Munitions in Libya." *Washington Post*. April 15, 2011. Accessed 6/13/2012. http://www.washingtonpost .com/world/nato-runs-short-on-some-munitions-in-libya/2011/04/15/AF3O7ElD_ story.html; John A. Tirpak. "Lessons from Libya." *Air Force Magazine*. December 2011. Accessed 6/13/2012. http://www.airforce-magazine.com/MagazineArchive/Pages/2011/ December%202011/1211libya.aspx.

79. Alan Colwell and Rod Nordland. "NATO Split Widens over Scope of Libya Military Action." *New York Times*. April 12, 2011. Accessed 6/25/2012. http://www.nytimes .com/2011/04/12/world/africa/13libya.html?pagewanted=all.

80. Ian Brzezinski. "Lesson from Libya: NATO Alliance Remains Relevant." *National Defense*. November 2011. Accessed 6/25/2012. http://www.nationaldefensemagazine. org/archive/2011/November/Pages/LessonFromLibyaNATOAllianceRemainsRelevant .aspx.

81. Amar C. Bakshi. "Roundup: Global Opinion of Libyan Intervention." *CNN World*. March 21, 2011. Accessed 6/19/2012. http://globalpublicsquare.blogs.cnn.com/ 2011/03/21/1784.

82. "The 2011 Arab Public Opinion Poll." Brookings Institution. November 21, 2011. Accessed 6/19/2012. http://www.brookings.edu/research/reports/2011/11/21-arab-public-opinion-telhami.

83. Pew Center Publications. "Public Wary of Military Intervention in Libya." Pew Research Center for the People and the Press. March 14, 2011. Accessed 6/19/2012. http://pewresearch.org/pubs/1927/strong-opposition-us-involvement-libya-military-overcommitted.

84. Pew Center Publications. "Modest Support for Libya Airstrikes, No Clear Goal Seen." Pew Research Center for the People and the Press. March 28, 2011. Accessed 6/19/2012. http://pewresearch.org/pubs/1941/poll-airstrikes-libya-right-wrong-decision-lengthy-involvement-moammar-gadhafi-remove.

85. Pew Center Publications. "Fewer See Clear Goal in Libya; Opposition to Arming Rebels Rating Middle East Foreign Policy Goals." Pew Research Center for the People and the Press. April 5, 2011. Accessed 6/19/2012. http://pewresearch.org/pubs/1950/poll-fewer-see-goal-libya-policy-goals-middle-east-terrorism-oil-democracy-israel; Pew Center Publications. "Libya: Steady Views, Declining Interest." Pew Research Center for the People and the Press. September 8, 2011. Accessed 6/19/2012. http://pewresearch.org/pubs/2098/libya-gadhafi-air-strikes. See also the Rasmussen reports, Gallup survey, and CBS polls that show more support for the intervention. Adam B. Schaeffer and Sabrina L. Schaeffer. "Libya and Public Opinion." National Review Online. March 25, 2011. Accessed 6/19/2012. http://www.nationalreview.com/articles/262992/libya-and-public-opinion-adam-b-schaeffer#.

86. Jerry Latter. "The Politics Wire." Ipsos MORI. April 13, 2011. Accessed 6/19/2012. http://www.ipsos-mori.com/newsevents/blogs/thepoliticswire/697/Intervention-in-Libya-and-public-opinion-around-our-involvement.aspx.

87. Julio Godoy. "Libya: Broad German Consensus Against a 'Risky War.'" Global Geopolitics and Political Economy. March 20, 2011. Accessed 6/19/2012. http://globalgeopolitics.net/wordpress/2011/03/20/libya-broad-german-consensus-against-a-risky-war.

88. Kareem Shaheen. "GCC Wants No-Fly Zone Over Libya." The National (Abu Dhabi). March 8, 2011. Accessed 6/21/2012. http://www.thenational.ae/news/uae-news/politics/gcc-wants-no-fly-zone-over-libya.

89. UN Security Council, Update Report No. 1, "Libya." March 14, 2011. Accessed 6/21/2012. http://www.securitycouncilreport.org/site/c.glKWLeMTIsG/b.6621881/k.63C4/Update_Report_No_1brLibyabr14_March_2011.htm.

90. Vivienne Walt. "The Coalition's Arab Allies: Firm Support or Window Dressing." Time Magazine. March 21, 2011. Accessed 6/21/2012. http://www.time.com/time/world/article/0,8599,2060551,00.html.

91. UN Office of the Special Adviser on the Prevention of Genocide. "Responsibility to Protect." Accessed 6/21/2012. http://www.un.org/en/preventgenocide/adviser/responsibility.shtml.

92. Simon Adams. "R2P and the Libya Mission." Los Angeles Times. September 28, 2011. Accessed 6/21/2012. http://articles.latimes.com/2011/sep/28/opinion/la-oe-adams-r2p-20110928.

93. Michael W. Doyle. "The Folly of Protection: Is Intervention Against Qaddafi's Regime Legal and Legitimate?" Foreign Affairs. March 20, 2011.

94. David Rieff. "R2P, R.I.P." New York Times, November 7, 2011.

95. Alexander Thompson. Channels of Power: The U.N. Security Council and US Statecraft in Iraq. Ithaca, NY: Cornell University Press, 2009.

96. Fareed Zakaria. "How the Lessons of Iraq Paid Off in Libya." Time Magazine. September 5, 2011. Accessed 6/25/2012. http://www.time.com/time/magazine/

article/0,9171,2090374,00.html; Tony Karon. "Is Libya a New Model of U.S. Intervention, or an Afghanistan Do-Over?" *Time Magazine.* August 31, 2011. Accessed 6/25/2012. http://world.time.com/2011/08/31/is-libya-a-new-model-of-u-s-intervention-or-an-afghanistan-do-over.

97. Alexander Thompson. *Channels of Power: The U.N. Security Council and US Statecraft in Iraq.* Ithaca, NY: Cornell University Press, 2009.

98. Jorge Benitez. "National Contributions to NATO's Smart Defense Initiative." Atlantic Council. May 23, 2012. Accessed 6/25/2012. http://www.acus.org/natosource/national-contributions-natos-smart-defense-initiative; NATO. "Smart Defence." Accessed 6/25/2012. http://www.nato.int/cps/en/natolive/topics_84268.htm; Stéphane Abrial. "NATO in a Time of Austerity." *New York Times.* May 17, 2012. Accessed 6/25/2012. http://www.nytimes.com/2012/05/18/opinion/nato-in-a-time-of-austerity.html; European Defence Agency. "Political Resolution Drives Pooling & Sharing." April 18, 2012. Accessed 6/25/2012. http://www.eda.europa.eu/News/12-04-18/Political_resolution_drives_pooling_sharing; European Defence Agency. "EDA's Pooling & Sharing." European Defense Agency fact sheet. November 30, 2011. Accessed 6/25/2012. http://www.eda.europa.eu.

99. Stéphane Abrial. "NATO in a Time of Austerity." *New York Times.* May 17, 2012. Accessed 6/25/2012. http://www.nytimes.com/2012/05/18/opinion/nato-in-a-time-of-austerity.html; NATO. "Smart Defence and Interoperability." NATO Multimedia Library. June 13, 2012. Accessed 6/25/2012. http://natolibguides.info/smartdefence.

Chapter 8

1. Russell F. Weigley. *The American Way of War: A History of U.S. Military History and Policy.* Bloomington: Indiana University Press, 1973.

2. Max Boot. "The New American Way of War." *Foreign Affairs,* vol. 82, no. 4, July–August 2003.

3. Norman Friedman. *Terrorism, Afghanistan, and America's New Way of War.* Annapolis, MD: Naval Institute Press, 2003, 166–171.

4. Dominic Tierney. *How We Fight: Crusades, Quagmires, and the American Way of War.* New York: Little, Brown, 2010.

5. On the similarity or difference between the Libyan operation and its predecessors in Afghanistan and Iraq, see Tony Karon. "Is Libya a New Model of U.S. Intervention, or an Afghanistan Do-Over?" *Time World.* August 31, 2011. Accessed 7/17/2012. http://world.time.com/2011/08/31/is-libya-a-new-model-of-u-s-intervention-or-an-afghanistan-do-over.

6. See Stephen M. Walt. *Origins of Alliances.* Ithaca, NY: Cornell University Press, 1987.

7. For an excellent discussion of authority and hegemony, see David A. Lake. "American Hegemony and the Future of East-West Relations." *International Studies Perspectives,* vol. 7, no. 1, February 2006, 23–30.

8. John J. Mearsheimer. "The False Promise of International Institutions." *International Security*, vol. 19, no. 3, winter 1994–1995, 5–49.

9. Micah Zenko and Emma Welch. "Where the Drones Are: Mapping the Launch Pads for Obama's Secret Wars." *Foreign Policy*. May 29, 2012. Accessed 12/18/2012. http://www.foreignpolicy.com/articles/2012/05/29/where_the_drones_are. However, a new unmanned aerial vehicle, the X-47B, has been developed to launch from aircraft carriers at sea, with a first successful trial of its catapult from the USS *George H. W. Bush* in May 2013. While this drone is not yet operational, it has made the viability of sea-based drones more likely in the near term. Extensive at-sea tests are expected in the coming years, since the Pentagon would like to be engaging in robotic missions off carriers by 2019. In addition to meaning that the United States would be less dependent on friends to base its drones worldwide, it also means that U.S. military reach will be expanded, particularly vis-à-vis China. In comparison to today's navy fighter jet, these sea-based drones will increase the unrefueled combat radius threefold and will increase the number of hours airborne by five to ten times what is currently possible. See David Axe. "The Case for Sea-based Drones." *Reuters*. May 14, 2013. Accessed 5/29/13. http://blogs.reuters.com/great-debate/2013/05/14/the-case-for-sea-based-drones/; Associated Press. "US' Next Big Weapon: Sea-Based Drones." May 16, 2011. Accessed 5/29/13. http://www.newser.com/story/118663/us-navy-unmanned-drones-to-counter-chinas-military-rise.html.

10. John Duffield. "What Are International Institutions?" *International Studies Review*, vol. 9, no. 1, spring 2007, 1–22.

11. Joseph M. Grieco. "The Maastricht Treaty, Economic and Monetary Union and the Neo-Realist Research Programme." *Review of International Studies*, vol. 21, no.1, January 1995, 21–40.

12. See Kenneth Oye, ed. *Cooperation Under Anarchy*. Princeton, NJ: Princeton University Press, 1986.

13. Wallace J. Thies develops this theme of NATO members advancing one another's interests and encouraging their allies to grow stronger in this extremely interesting book. Wallace J. Thies. *Why NATO Endures*. Cambridge: Cambridge University Press, 2009.

14. Department of Defense. "Quadrennial Defense Review Report." February 2010, 26–30, 57–69.

15. Ibid., 28–30.

16. Ibid., 63–64.

INDEX

Page numbers with "t" or "f" indicate material in tables or figures.